Financial Statement Fraud

Prevention and Detection

Zabihollah Rezaee

Foreword by Joseph T. Wells

John Wiley & Sons, Inc.

New York • Chichester • Weinheim • Brisbane • Singapore • Toronto

ISBN 0-471-09216-9

Printed in the United States of America.

10 9 8 7 6 5 4 3 2 1

About the Author

Zabihollah Rezaee is the Thompson-Hill Chair of Excellence and Professor of Accountancy at The University of Memphis. He received his B. S. degree from the Iranian Institute of Advanced Accounting, his M. B. A from Taleton State University in Texas, and his Ph. D. from the University of Mississippi. Professor Rezaee holds several certifications, including Certified Public Accountant (CPA), Certified Fraud Examiner (CFE), Certified Management Accountant (CMA), Certified Internal Auditor (CIA), and Certified Government Financial Manager (CGFM).

Professor Rezaee has published over 135 articles in a variety of accounting and business journals, such as the *Journal of Accounting and Economics, Journal of Business, Finance and Accounting, Journal of Accountancy, Journal of Accounting, Auditing and Finance, Management Accountants, Internal Auditor, Advances in Accounting, Advances in Public Interest and Accounting, Auditing: Journal of Theory and Practice, and Forensic Accounting.* Professor Rezaee has published several articles on forensic accounting and financial statement fraud.

Active within the accounting profession and the academic and business communities, Professor Rezaee has made over 120 presentations at conferences and workshops throughout the world. He teaches financial, management, and international accounting and auditing, and has also been involved in financial and management consulting with national and international organizations, such as the United Nations. Professor Rezaee is the author of *Financial Institutions, Valuations, Mergers and Acquisitions,* John Wiley & Sons, 2001, and has served on the editorial boards of several journals, including the *Forensic Accounting Journal.* He received the 1998 Distinguished Research Award at Middle Tennessee State University and the Lybrand Bronze Medal for Outstanding Article in 1999, which is awarded by the Institute of Management Accountants.

To my son, Nick.

Acknowledgments

I acknowledge the American Institute of Certified Public Accountants, the Institute of Internal Auditors, the Institute of Management Accountants, the Association of Certified Fraud Examiners, the Securities and Exchange Commission, the American Accounting Association, the Committee of Sponsoring Organizations of the Treasury Commission, the National Association of Corporate Directors, and the Big Five Professional Services Firms for permission to quote and reference their professional standards and other publications.

The encouragement and support of my colleagues at The University of Memphis are also acknowledged. Special thanks go to Professor John J. Pepin, Dean of the Fogelman College of Business and Economics, and Professor Ken Lambert, Director of the School of Accountancy at The University of Memphis for their valuable inputs, encouragement, and continuous support. I thank the members of the John Wiley & Sons, Inc., team for their hard work and dedication, including Michael Lisk for managing the book through the production process, Colleen Scollans for marketing efforts, and Tim Burgard and John DeRemigis for their editorial guidance.

I express my appreciation to the following individuals for their comprehensive review of this book: Larry Crumbley, Editor of the *Journal of Forensic Accounting*; Steve Albrecht, Associate Dean Marriott School at Brigham Young University; Joseph T. Wells, Founder and Chairman of the Association of Certified Fraud Examiners; and Lynn Turner Director of the Center for Quality Financial Reporting at Colorado State University and the former Chief Accountant of the SEC.

My sincere thanks are due to my family—my sisters, Mansoureh and Zahra, my wife, Soheila, my father, Fazlollah, and my son, Nick. Without their love, enthusiasm, and support, this book would not have come to fruition when it did.

Zabihollah Rezaee

Foreword

At the start of a new century, financial statement fraud has increasingly become a serious problem for business, government, and investors. Indeed, the issue threatens to undermine the confidence of capital markets, corporate leaders, and even the venerable audit profession.

Auditors in particular have been hit hard for their seeming inability to find fraud on a massive scale. Monetary judgments in the hundreds of millions of dollars against CPA firms have become commonplace.

Many who should know say the audit process—as we have known it for the last 75 years—is doomed. But that may not be all bad. For if an audit fails to find these huge crimes, engineered at the very top of our public enterprises, what good is it?

The Supreme Court of the United States agreed with that premise in 1984 when it affirmed that the independent auditor was indeed the "public watchdog." But in the two decades since that pronouncement, we've continued to see too many situations where the watchdog was asleep, toothless, or too old to chase its quarry.

Moreover, in the last three decades, the largest CPA firms have undergone a paradigm shift; no longer do they make most of their money from traditional audits, but from services and products they sell to the very clients they are scrutinizing. In short, critics say the watchdog is too close to the flock to be able to see.

To learn history's valuable lessons, we need to look at where we've been to know where we should be going. From recorded history until the beginning of the last century, the auditor's primary role was to detect and deter fraud. It was much easier to do back then: businesses were small, financial transactions were few, and transnational corporations and financial conglomerates were unheard of.

But as commerce picked up speed, the auditor had to do more with less; scrutinizing each and every transaction for fraud became a physical impossibility. From the time of the stock market crash of 1929—due in no small part to rampant fraud—until the 1980s, the focus of the audit became different. During that period, the auditor spent most of his effort on reporting issues.

It didn't take financial scoundrels long to notice that the watchdog wasn't barking any more. In the 1970s, an enterprising insurance salesman named Stanley Goldblum made a mockery of the audit as it had been traditionally conducted. Right under the nose of his independent CPA firm, Goldblum's company, Equity Funding, easily managed to add 65,000 phony policyholders to its rolls, along with $800 million in fake assets.

Goldblum's scam was only the beginning of a cascade of spectacular audit failures from the savings and loan debacle to Enron. And the refrain has only grown louder: "Where were the auditors?"

The answer, strangely enough, is that the auditors were too busy auditing to find fraud. But don't blame them, for they were doing only what they were taught. Or more correctly, not taught.

As any accounting graduate in the last 30 years will tell you, the amount of anti-fraud training in college is not just inadequate; it's practically non-existent. In a recent study by Peterson and Reider, they could only locate 14 colleges and universities in the United States that offered a fraud examination course. Part of the reason has been the lack of authoritative texts in the field.

Zabihollah Rezaee's book, *Financial Statement Fraud: Prevention and Detection,* is bound to make a real difference. Exceptionally well researched and chocked with up-to-date case examples, *Financial Statement Fraud* not only explains in understandable language how these schemes are committed, it offers valuable advice on how to prevent and detect them.

But Dr. Rezaee's work goes much beyond helping educate accounting students and auditors. It is a valuable reference guide for fraud examiners, audit committees, management and regulators; and one other important cog in this wheel: the investors who stand to lose everything.

Education is the sword needed to strike a blow against white-collar crime. And in this war, *Financial Statement Fraud* is a powerful weapon.

Joseph T. Wells
Founder and Chairman of the Board
Association of Certified Fraud Examiners

Preface

For the capital markets to function efficiently and effectively, market participants, including investors and creditors, must have confidence in financial information disseminated to the market. Market participants must trust the quality, integrity, and reliability of published audited financial statements. Financial statement fraud is a serious threat to market participants' confidence in financial information. Fraud is estimated to cost U.S. organizations more than $400 billion annually, with average organization fraud loses of around 6 percent of the reported total revenue, from which about 80 percent is caused by top executives, according the Association of Certified Fraud Examiners. Financial statement fraud has cost investors more than $100 billion during the past several years according to Lynn E. Turner, the former chief accountant of the Securities Exchange Commission. Financial statement fraud committed by Enron Corporation is estimated to have caused a loss of about $80 billion in market capitalization to investors, including sophisticated financial institutions, and employees who held the company's stock in their retirement accounts. These figures are conservative and definitely underestimated primarily because most frauds are either undetected and/or unreported.

The primary focus of this book is on financial statement fraud prevention and detection. Financial statement fraud, for purposes of this book, is defined as deliberate and material misstatement of financial statements issued by publicly traded companies to mislead users of financial statements, particularly investors and creditors. The public, financial community, accounting profession, Securities and Exchange Commission (SEC), and Congress are all significantly concerned about the frequency and magnitude of financial statement frauds occurring in corporate America. Several reports (e.g., COSO report, 1999; The Blue Ribbon Committee, 1999) have addressed the role of responsible and effective corporate governance in preventing and detecting financial statement fraud. These reports have made numerous suggestions to promote more responsible corporate governance and to enhance the quality, integrity, and reliability of the financial reporting process.

The study of financial statement fraud and a book such as this are valuable primarily because the efficiency and health of the capital markets largely depend on the quality, integrity, usefulness, and reliability of the financial information received by the market. Financial statement fraud can significantly contribute to unhealthy and inefficient capital markets. Therefore, the prevention and detection of financial statement fraud is crucial to the economic growth and prosperity of the nation. This book assesses the consequences of financial statement fraud and its impact on the integrity and quality of the financial reporting process and suggests ways to improve prevention and detection. The focus is on the importance of corporate governance in preventing, detecting, and correcting financial statement fraud.

Although this book examines the incidences of financial statement fraud and suggests many ways to prevent and detect its occurrences, it is by no means all-inclusive. The intent is not to give the impression that the numerous incidents of fraudulent financial reporting activities and the engagement of some publicly traded companies in financial statement fraud are normal activities of corporations. It is trusted that publicly traded companies in the United States have a responsible corporate governance, use a reliable financial reporting process, and conduct their business in an ethical and legal manner; however, the entire society, business community, accounting profession, and government have a vested interest in preventing and detecting of financial statement fraud because it undermines the confidence in corporate America. The importance of a book on financial statement fraud can be further understood by citing comments made by the former chairperson of the SEC, Arthur Levitt. In describing the current financial reporting environment, Levitt (1998, 14) states: "We are witnessing the erosion in the quality of earnings and therefore the quality of financial reporting." This trend should be reversed by holding publicly traded companies more accountable for producing high-quality financial reports free of material misstatements caused by errors and fraud. The collapse of Enron, the biggest corporate failure of recent times, has caused lawmakers (e.g., Congress), and regulators (e.g., SEC) to address the integrity and quality of the financial reporting process as well as adequacy and revelance of financial disclosures. By focusing on the role of corporate governance, this book provides better understanding of why financial statement fraud may occur and how it can be prevented and detected.

PURPOSE OF THE BOOK

Financial statement frauds committed recently by large companies such as Enron Corp., Waste Management, Sunbeam, Lucent, Xerox, MicroStrategy, Knowledge-Ware, Raytheon, Cendant, and Rite Aid, to name just a few, have received considerable attention from investors, the public, and the SEC. Financial statement fraud is a serious threat to the confidence in the financial reporting system and capital markets. For example, Enron filed the largest bankruptcy in U.S. history in December 2001 after disclosing that it had overstated earnings by more than half a billion dollars for four consecutive years and established private partnerships that kept billions of dollars of debt off its books. Enron used sophisticated financing vehicles known as Special Purpose Entities (SPEs) and other derivative instruments to increase leverage without having to report debt on the balance sheet. The commission of financial statement fraud has forced Enron, the seventh biggest Fortune 500 company, with a market capitalization of $80 billion to file Chapter 11 bankruptcy protection. These high-profile cases of financial statement frauds have raised serious concerns regarding a lack of adequate and responsible corporate governance and accountability. It is the top management team's responsibility to prevent financial statement frauds before they occur and to design adequate and effective internal control structures to detect and correct fraudulent financial activities. The "tone at the top" set by the board of directors and its representative audit committees to disallow any unusual business practices, aggressive accounting methods, earnings management, or violations of the company's applicable laws and regulations as well as code of business conduct plays an important role in preventing and detecting financial statement fraud.

This book focuses on only publicly traded companies experiencing financial statement fraud. The SEC Accounting and Auditing Enforcement Releases (AAERs) reports publicly traded companies that are accused by the SEC of violating Rule 10(b)-5 of the 1934 Act. The Treadway Commission report indicates that 87 percent of the SEC enforcement actions from 1982 to 1986 dealt with financial statement fraud, whereas the other 13 percent related to misappropriation of assets. Fraud literature typically classifies management fraud into misappropriation of assets and fraudulent financial reporting. Financial statement fraud and management fraud have also been used interchangeably. This book underscores the significance of financial statement fraud and provides theoretical and practical guidance to the board of directors, audit committees, management, internal auditors, and external auditors to recognize, prevent, detect, and correct financial statement frauds. The contents of this book, including a brief synopsis of each chapter, are summarized to provide the reader an overview of the theme of the book.

Management should provide relevant, useful, and reliable information to investors and creditors beyond what is required under the existing generally accepted accounting principles (GAAP), which heavily rely on historical costs and arbitrary writeoffs of intangible assets. Quality financial reports increase value relevance of financial information presented by management and, if the information is submitted to attestation by an independent auditor, its credibility would improve. The credible and relevant information would reduce the information risk of financial reports which, in turn, would make the capital markets more efficient. More efficient capital markets would result in a lower cost of capital for the company and likely higher security prices. Thus, high-quality financial information free of material errors, irregularities, and fraud has positive effects for all market participants. Publicly traded corporations and their top executives benefit by having access to cheaper capital, which would result in creating shareholder value and, thus, more stock options and other compensation incentives for top executives. Investors and creditors benefit by receiving reliable, useful, and relevant information in assessing their investment opportunities and less concern about the lack of quality and integrity of financial reports. The economy operates more effectively and productively because the capital markets are more efficient in establishing fair security prices.

Recent high-profile alleged financial statement frauds have raised serious concerns about (1) the role of corporate governance including the board of directors and audit committees; (2) the integrity and ethical values of top management teams, especially when the CEOs and CFOs are being convicted of cooking the books; (3) the inadequacy and ineffectiveness of internal controls; (4) the ineffectiveness of audit functions in detecting financial statement fraud; and (5) the substantial declines in the market capitalization of alleged fraudulent companies. Corporate governance participants, including the board of directors, the audit committee, top management teams, internal auditors, external auditors, and governing bodies (e.g., SEC, AICPA, NYSE, NASD, POB) are all responsible for the quality, integrity, and reliability of the financial reporting process and the assurance that published financial statements are free of material misstatements caused by errors and fraud. Prevention of financial statement fraud is commonly management's responsibility whereas for while its detection has been traditionally assumed by external auditors.

The Enron debacle, caused by the commission of financial statement fraud, is expected to lead to (1) the establishment of new regulations to improve corporate financial disclosures and; (2) the requirement of a more effective oversight of public accounting firms; and (3) the creation of a new accounting industry self-regulating organization that will operate under SEC supervision. Both management and external auditors are currently facing increasing scrutiny by the SEC and severe penalties for engaging in the commission of financial statement fraud, which often starts with a small misstatement or earnings management of quarterly financial reports that are presumed not to be material. The fraud eventually grows into full-blown "cooking the books", which is subject to harsh penalties by the SEC and lawsuits by damaged investors. The SEC's Director of Enforcement, Richard H. Walker, stated: "Cooking the books and you will go directly to jail without passing Go". This book is intended to provide useful reference and suggestions for corporate governance participants to (1) effectively prevent, detect, and correct financial fraud; (2) attempt to refrain from alleged engagements in cooking the books; and (3) avoid suffering the potential severe penalties for the commission of financial statement fraud. Nevertheless, financial statement fraud cannot be completely eliminated despite the existence of responsible corporate governance and the increased scrutiny by the SEC. Thus, users of published audited financial statements, particularly investors and creditors, should be skeptical when reading, assessing, and using financial information.

ORGANIZATION OF THE BOOK

The focus of this book is on the importance of corporate governance in preventing and detecting financial statement fraud. The organization of the book provides the maximum flexibility in choosing the amount and order of materials on financial statement fraud. This book is organized into four parts, as follows:

Part	Subject	Chapters
1	Financial Reporting and Financial Statement Fraud	1 & 2
2	Financial Statement Fraud Profile, Taxonomy, and Schemes	3–5
3	Corporate Governance and Its Role in Preventing and Detecting Financial Statement Fraud	6–12
4	Computer Fraud and Forensic Accounting	13 & 14

The fourteen chapters of this book are organized into four parts. The first part contains two chapters, which describe the magnitude and extent of financial statement fraud that threatens the integrity and quality of the financial reporting process. These chapters examine financial statement fraud, its definition, costs, the nature and significance as well as the financial reporting process of publicly traded companies.

Part 2, containing Chapters 3 through 5, discusses financial statement fraud profiles, taxonomies, and schemes. Chapter 3 presents profiles of several companies alleged by the SEC for engaging in financial statement fraud, reviews their alleged financial statements fraud cases, and demonstrates that "cooking the books" causes financial statement fraud, which results in a crime. Chapter 4 presents a model consisting of conditions, corporate structure, and choices (3 Cs) in explaining and analyzing motivations, opportunities, and rationalizations for the commission of financial statement frauds. Chapter 5 identifies and discusses taxonomies and schemes of financial statement fraud in an attempt to provide better understanding of symptoms (red flags) of financial statement fraud and management motivations to engage in financial statement fraud.

Part 3 consists of Chapters 6 through 12, which constitute the foundation of the book. Chapter 6 defines corporate governance, its participants and roles in preventing and detecting financial statement fraud. Chapter 7 discusses the role of the board of directors in ensuring responsible corporate governance and a reliable financial reporting process. Chapter 8 examines the audit committee's role in overseeing the effectiveness of corporate governance, integrity and quality of financial reports, adequacy and effectiveness of internal control structure, and quality of audit function. Chapter 9 discusses the role of management in corporate governance and the financial reporting process. Management is primarily responsible for the quality, integrity, and reliability of the financial reporting process. Chapter 10 examines internal auditors' responsibility for prevention and detection of financial statement fraud. Chapter 11 discusses the responsibility of independent auditors in discovering financial statement fraud and providing reasonable assurance regarding the quality, integrity, and reliability of published financial statements. Chapter 12 discusses the role of several governing bodies (e.g., SEC, FASB, AICPA, POB, ISB, NYSE, NASD) that directly or indirectly influence corporate governance and the financial reporting process of publicly traded companies.

Part 4 includes two chapters. Chapter 13, entitled "Fraud in a Digital Environment", examines electronic commerce strategies, changes in business environment, electronic financial reporting, including extensible business reporting language (XBRL), and computer fraud. Chapter 14 presents forensic accounting practices including fraud investigation, litigation consulting engagements, and expert witnessing services. This chapter also discusses forensic accounting education and methods of integrating forensic accounting topics into the accounting curriculum.

INTENDED AUDIENCE

This book is designed for anyone wishing to obtain an understanding and knowledge of the financial reporting process; how to improve the quality, integrity, and reliability of financial reports; and the role of corporate governance including the board of directors, the audit committee, internal auditors, external auditors, and governing bodies (i.e., SEC, AICPA, NYSE, NASD, POB) in preventing, detecting, and correcting financial statement fraud. This book should be beneficial to the following groups:

1. Corporations and their executives (i.e., presidents, CEOs, CFOs, accountants).

   Corporations should have responsible corporate governance and a reliable financial reporting process. Corporate governance guidelines and financial reporting standards and principles presented in this book should help publicly traded companies and their executives to appreciate the importance of high quality and reliable financial reports free of material misstatements caused by errors, irregularities, and frauds.

2. The boards of directors and their representative audit committees.

   Boards of directors and audit committees oversee corporate governance, the financial reporting process, and audit functions. A vigilant and effective board of directors and audit committees can play an important role in preventing, detecting, and reducing financial statement fraud. This book, by discussing the authoritative reports (i.e., Treadway Commission, the Blue Ribbon Committee, SEC) on the role of the board of directors and audit committees underscores their importance as part of corporate governance mechanism.

3. Auditors, both internal and external.

   Although management is primarily responsible for the quality, integrity, and reliability of the financial reporting process and fair presentation of financial statements, auditors provide assurance on financial information and lend more credibility to published financial statements. The role of external auditors (CPAs) in corporate governance is to detect financial statement fraud and to provide reasonable assurance that audited financial statements are free of material misstatements due to errors and frauds. Internal auditors' association with corporate governance and the financial reporting process is through assisting management to effectively discharge its managerial and reporting responsibilities. This book discusses professional standards for both internal and external auditors to assist them in preventing and detecting financial statement fraud.

4. Governing Organizations.

   Governing organizations, such as the SEC, AICPA, POB, NYSE, and the NASD, influence public companies' financial reporting process and their corporate governance. The frequency and magnitude of financial statement fraud has encouraged these organizations to continue their scrutiny of corporations' financial practices and processes. This book presents applicable rules and regulations pertaining to these practices and policies.

5. Users of financial statements, particularly investors and creditors.

   For the capital markets to function efficiently and effectively, market participants, including investors and creditors, must have confidence in the financial reporting process and financial information disseminated to the market. Financial statement fraud can be a serious threat to market participants' confidence in financial information. This book suggests that market participants be skeptical when assessing financial reports.

6. Business schools and accounting programs.

   This book, by presenting forensic accounting practices (i.e., fraud investigation, litigation consulting, and expert witnessing) and education can be very useful as an educational and reference source for business and accounting students at both graduate and undergraduate levels. This book can be utilized as a basic or supplementary text by business schools and accounting departments in teaching corporate governance, the financial reporting process, audit functions, and forensic accounting.

7. Other professionals.

   Professionals, such as attorneys, financial analysts, accountants, and law enforcement officials, who provide legal and financial services to corporations should find this book helpful in addressing the significance of financial statement fraud and ways to prevent, detect, and correct fraud.

Contents

Chapter 1

Financial Statement Fraud Defined

INTRODUCTION

We all remember the "irrational exuberance" that Federal Reserve Board Chairman Alan Greenspan said characterized the stock market in the mid-1990s; however, since then, the Dow Jones average has gained more than 4,000 points. Until recently, corporate America dismissed financial statement fraud as "irrational irregularities." Now, virtually any organization is affected by fraud in general, and financial statement fraud in particular. Not a day goes by without more news about fraud, especially financial statement fraud that undermines the quality, reliability, and integrity of the financial reporting process. The Enron debacle, caused by fraudulent financial activities, has raised serious concerns regarding the integrity and reliability of financial reports, as well as the quality and effectiveness of financial audits. Daily and online information about financial statement fraud can be obtained from a variety of sources. This chapter (1) addresses financial statement fraud, its definition, nature, and significance; (2) discusses the financial reporting process of corporations; and (3) examines the role of corporate governance in preventing and detecting financial statement fraud.

DEFINITION OF FINANCIAL STATEMENT FRAUD

A complete understanding of the nature, significance, and consequences of fraudulent financial reporting activities requires a proper definition of financial statement fraud. *Fraud,* in general, is defined in Webster's New World Dictionary as "the intentional deception to cause a person to give up property or some lawful right." The legal definition of *fraud* can also be found in court cases. One example of such a definition is: "A generic term, embracing all multifarious means which human ingenuity can devise, and which are resorted to by one individual to get advantage over another by false suggestions by suppression of truth and includes all surprise, trick, cunning, dissembling, and any unfair way by which another is cheated."[1]

The definition of *financial statement fraud* can be found in several authoritative reports and textbooks. Financial statement fraud has been defined differently in the academic literature by academicians, in the professional literature by practitioners, and in official pronouncements by authoritative bodies. Financial statement fraud is defined by the Association of Certified Fraud Examiners as:

> The intentional, deliberate, misstatement or omission of material facts, or accounting data which is misleading and, when considered with all the information made available, would cause the reader to change or alter his or her judgment or decision.[2]

The Treadway Commission report defines financial statement fraud as "International or reckless conduct, whether [by] act or omission, that results in material misleading financial statements."[3]

Previous books provided the following definitions of financial statement fraud:

- "Fraud committed to falsify financial statements, usually committed by management and normally involving overstating income or assets."[4]
- "The involvement of upper level executives in misrepresentations or misappropriations which are either perpetrated or covered up through fraudulent (misleading) financial reporting.[5]

Clear definitions of financial statement fraud are difficult to discern from pronouncement and/or authoritative statements primarily because, until recently, the accounting profession did not use the word *fraud* in its professional pronouncements. Instead, the terms *intentional mistakes* or *irregularities* were used. Recently, the American Institute of Certified Public Accountants (AICPA), in its Statement of Auditing Standards (SAS) No. 82, refers to financial statement fraud as intentional misstatements or omissions in financial statements.

The common thread among these definitions is that fraud in general, and financial statement fraud in particular, is deliberate deception with the intent to cause harm, injury, or damage. The word *fraud* is a generic term used to describe any deliberate act to deceive or mislead another person, causing harm or injury. This intentional, wrongful act can be differentiated and defined in many ways, depending on the classes of perpetrators. For example, frauds committed by individuals (e.g., embezzlement) are distinguished from frauds perpetrated by corporations (financial statement fraud) in terms of the classes of perpetrators. The terms *financial statement fraud* and *management fraud* have been used interchangeably primarily because (1) management is responsible for producing reliable financial reports; and (2) the fair presentation, integrity, and quality of the financial reporting process is the responsibility of management. Exhibit 1.1 classifies fraud into management fraud and employee fraud and provides further classification of these two types of fraud.

Textbook writers (e.g., Elliott and Willingham, 1980; Robertson, 2000),[6,7] have viewed the terms *management fraud* and *financial statement fraud* as synonymous because financial statement fraud typically occurs with the consent or knowledge of management. The report to the nation (ACFE, 1996) classified fraud into the three categories of asset misappropriation, financial statement fraud, and corruption.[8] These three types of fraud schemes are interrelated. For example, any asset misappropriations of embezzling assets can also cause financial statement fraud. Elliot and Willingham (1980) define financial statement fraud as "the de-

Exhibit 1.1. Types of Fraud

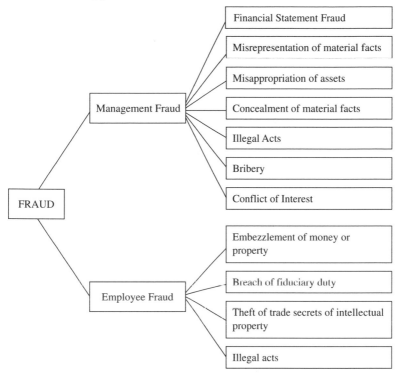

liberate fraud committed by management that injures investors and creditors through materially misleading financial statements."[9]

This definition focus is on only one group of victims of financial statement fraud, namely outsiders, including investors and creditors. Victims of financial statement fraud can be foreseen or foreseeable person(s) affected adversely by using fraudulent financial reporting in making financial decisions. These victims can be insiders, including employees, internal auditors, audit committees, executives, the board of directors, and managers, who may suffer a financial loss (e.g., loss of position) and/or reputation loss (e.g., loss of integrity and standing) as a result of the commission of financial statement fraud. Victims can be outsiders, including investors, creditors, suppliers, customers, partners, governmental agencies, external auditors, legal counsels, underwriters, depositors, and any persons that may be affected adversely by using published financial statement fraud.

The focus of this book is on all victims of financial statement fraud, particularly investors and creditors. Thus, the definition of *financial statement fraud* adopted in this book is comprehensive, including both inside and outside victims. It is defined as deliberate misstatements or omissions of amounts or disclosures of financial statements to deceive financial statement users, particularly investors and creditors. Financial statement fraud may involve the following schemes:

- Falsification, alteration, or manipulation of material financial records, supporting documents, or business transactions.
- Material intentional omissions or misrepresentations of events, transactions, accounts, or other significant information from which financial statements are prepared.
- Deliberate misapplication of accounting principles, policies, and procedures used to measure, recognize, report, and disclose economic events and business transactions.
- Intentional omissions of disclosures or presentation of inadequate disclosures regarding accounting principles and policies and related financial amounts.

Financial statement fraud is committed with the intent to deceive, mislead, or injure investors and creditors. Financial statement fraud as used in this book is defined as a deliberate, wrongful act committed by publicly traded companies, through the use of materially misleading financial statements, that causes harm and injury to investors and creditors. In this definition, the class of perpetrators is publicly traded companies; the type of victims is investors and creditors; and the means of perpetration is misleading published financial statements. This definition of financial statement fraud is similar to the one described by Elliott and Willingham (1980) in their book *Management Fraud: Detection and Deterrence.*[10] This definition focuses on the deliberate wrongful act committed by publicly traded companies that harms users through materially misleading financial statements. The responsibility for preventing and detecting financial statement fraud should be assumed by the financial information supply chain consisting of the board of directors, the audit committee, the top management team (e.g., CEO, CFO, controllers, treasurers), internal auditors, and external auditors. The responsibility for detecting financial statement fraud has been traditionally assumed by external auditors.

Financial statement frauds are an inherent choice of dishonesty in corporate America. Their rewards are much better than other white-collar crimes; physical dangers are minimal; the probability of detection is not great; and their punishments are often not very severe in terms of fines and jail time. Financial statement frauds are deliberate criminal and/or unethical actions by publicly traded companies to falsify financial information for the purpose of deceiving parties (e.g., investors, creditors, regulators) outside the company. Fraudulent financial statements can be used to unjustifiably sell stock, obtain loans or trades credit, and/or improve managerial compensation and bonuses. The important issues addressed in this book are how to effectively and efficiently prevent and detect financial statement fraud.

The pervasiveness of fraudulent activities during the past two decades encouraged the establishment in 1992 of the National White Collar Crime Center (NWCC) through funding from the Bureau of Justice Assistance (BJA) of the U.S. Department of Justice.[11] The NWCC was established to maintain a formally structured national support system for states and local law enforcements and regulatory agencies to prevent, investigate, and prosecute white-collar and economic crimes, including investment fraud, telemarketing fraud, commodities fraud, securities fraud, advanced-fee loan schemes, and boiler room operations. The NWCC provides a broad range of no-cost services to its members, including information sharing, case funding, and training and research. To address the significance of financial statement fraud, several organizations and authoritative bodies have provided online web sites with fraud information. Exhibit 1.2 lists a sample of these web sites and related descriptions.

NATURE OF FINANCIAL STATEMENT FRAUD

Financial statement fraud has become known through daily press reports challenging the corporate responsibility and integrity of major companies such as Lucent, Xerox, Rite Aid, Waste Management, MicroStrategy, KnowledgeWare, Raytheon, Enron, and Sunbeam, which were recently alleged by the Securities and Exchange Commission (SEC) for committing fraud. Top management teams, including chief executive officers (CEOs) and chief financial officers (CFOs) of these companies, are being convicted of cooking the books and often sentenced to jail terms. Occurrences of financial statement fraud by aforementioned high-profile companies, just naming a few, have raised concerns about the integrity and reliability of the financial reporting process and have challenged the role of corporate governance in preventing and detecting financial statement fraud.

Former SEC chairperson Arthur Levitt, in a speech addressed at New York University regarding the present state of financial reporting, expressed a great concern that "we are witnessing a gradual, but noticeable erosion in the quality of financial reporting." He further noted the existence of a "grey area . . . where accounting practices are perverted; where managers cut corners; where earnings reports reflect the desires of management rather than underlying financial performance of the company."[12] This perceived emergent distrust in the quality of financial information can adversely affect the efficiency of the capital market and the confidence of its participants, including investors and creditors, in the financial reporting process. This distrust and lack of confidence have emerged as a result of recent high-profile financial statement fraud committed by major corporations such as Enron Corp., Waste Management, Sunbeam, Rite Aid, Xerox, KnowledgeWare, MicroStrategy, and Lucent. These incidents have raised serious concerns about (1) the role of corporate governance including the board of directors and audit committees; (2) the integrity and ethical values of these companies' top management teams, especially when CEOs and CFOs are indicted for cooking the books and, in many cases, are convicted; (3) the ineffectiveness of audit functions in detecting these financial statement frauds; (4) the substantial declines in the market capitalization of the alleged fraud companies and the likelihood of filing for bankruptcy protection; and (5) considerable lawsuits by injured investors, creditors and employees. This emerging trend of distrust in the quality of

Exhibit 1.2.   Sample of Fraud Web Sites

Web Site	Short Discussion
http://getzoff.com/business_fraud/20questions.htm	Lists 20 different symptoms of various fraudulent financial activities and their possible sources, including abnormal inventory shortages, out-of-balanced general ledgers.
www.sec.gov	Offers the SEC Accounting and Auditing Enforcement Actions brought against publicly traded companies alleging the commission of financial statement fraud.
www.fraudnews.com	Provides useful information on fraud awareness, news, reports, alerts, events, and tools.
www.yake.com/methodology/body.html	Provides investigative services for the accounting profession and develops methodology to identify financially distressed companies.
www.herring.com/mag/issue22/crime.html	Provides profiles of the perpetrators of white-collar crime and fraud deterrence and detection methodologies.
www.bus.lsu.edu/accounting/faculty/lcrumbley/forensic.htm	Provides useful information on forensic accounting and fraud detection.
www.acct.tamu.edu/kratchman/holmes.htm	Offers forensic accounting information.
www.ustreas.gov/org/fl.tcfinfraudinst.htm	Financial Fraud Institute establishes and presents formal training courses and practical exercise applications pertaining to the investigation of white-collar crime violations, computer fraud, and financial statement fraud.
www.securities.standford.edu/about/cavent.html	Offers investors, policy makers, the judiciary, and the media research tools that provide a thorough and careful look into the workings of class action litigation.
www.fraudness.com/ItemView.cfm	Provides services of the fraud defense network.

financial information should be reversed, and the capital market and its participants should regain their confidence through quality financial information and their trust through vigilant, active, effective, and responsible corporate governance.

Financial statement fraud often starts with a small misstatement or earnings management of quarterly financial reports that presumes not to be material but eventually grows into full-blown fraud and producing materially misleading annual financial statements. Financial statement fraud is harmful in many ways. It creates the following problems:

- Undermines the quality and integrity of the financial reporting process.
- Jeopardizes the integrity and objectivity of the auditing profession, especially auditors and auditing firms.
- Diminishes the confidence of the capital markets, as well as market participants, in the reliability of financial information.
- Makes the capital market less efficient.
- Adversely affects the nation's economic growth and prosperity.
- May result in huge litigation costs.
- Destroys the careers of individuals involved in financial statement fraud, such as top executives banned from serving on the board of directors of any public companies or auditors being barred from practice of public accounting.
- Causes bankruptcy or substantial economic losses by the company engaged in financial statement fraud.
- Encourages excessive regulatory intervention.
- Causes destructions in the normal operations and performance of alleged companies.

COST OF FINANCIAL STATEMENT FRAUD

A day may not go by without a front-page headline story in the popular financial press on financial statement fraud. The frequency and magnitude of economic loss by investors and creditors caused by financial statement fraud have drawn the attention of the financial press, regulators, and standard setters. Financial statement fraud has been one of the dominating corporate news stories during recent years. Considerable publicity and substantiated evidence have been generated regarding the number and magnitude of fraudulent financial activities, which have undermined the integrity of the financial reporting process and have contributed to substantial economic losses by investors and creditors. Fraud has eroded the public's confidence in the usefulness and reliability of published financial statements.

The actual cost of fraud is difficult, if not impossible, to quantitatively measure for many reasons. First, empirical studies show that only a small portion of all frauds, including financial statement fraud, is discovered. Second, even if the fraud is discovered, not all cases are reported because companies attempt to preserve their images by firing the fraudsters and pretending that the incident never happened. Third, fraud surveys in reporting the extent and magnitude of fraud are not always accurate, and they are subject to the limitation of any typical survey study in the sense that the respondents often report their perception rather than the reality. Finally, companies typically do not pursue civil or criminal actions; by firing the fraudsters, many companies believe that they have prevented further occurrences of fraud.

Published statistics on the possible cost of financial statement fraud are only educated estimates, primarily because it is impossible to determine actual total costs since not all fraud is detected, not all detected fraud is reported, and not all reported fraud is legally pursued. The reported statistics, however, are astonishing. The Association of Certified Fraud Examiners (1996) indicated that fraud costs U.S. organizations more than $400 billion annually or at least 6 percent of their gross revenue, with the average organization losing more than $9 a day per employee to fraud and abuse.[13] The report also states that (1) losses from fraud caused by managers and executives (mostly financial statement frauds) were 16 times greater than those caused by nonmanagerial employees (mostly embezzlements, thefts); (2) nearly 58 percent of the reported fraud and abuse cases were committed by nonmanagerial employees, 30 percent by managers, and the other 12 percent by owners/executives; and (3) occupational fraud and abuses consist of three types of asset misappropriation: fraudulent statements, bribery, and corruption. Albrecht, Wernez, and Williams (1995) reported that 30 percent of all business failures are caused by white-collar crime.[14] Albrecht and Searcy (2001) state that more than 50 percent of U.S. corporations in 2000 were victims of frauds, with the loss of more than $500,000, on average, for each company.[15] Financial statement fraud has cost investors more than $100 billion during the past several years according to Lynn E. Turner, the former chief accountant of the Securities Exchange Commission. Financial statement fraud committed by Enron Corporation is estimated to have caused a loss of about $80 billion in market capitalization to investors, including sophisticated financial institutions, and employees who held the company's stock in their retirement accounts.[16]

These studies and their related statistics provide only underestimated direct economic losses resulted from financial statement fraud. Other fraud costs are legal costs, increased insurance costs, loss of productivity, monthly costs, and adverse impacts on employees' morale, customers' goodwill, suppliers' trust, and negative stock market reactions. An important indirect cost of financial statement fraud is the loss of productivity caused by dismissal of the fraudsters and their replacements. The top management team is typically involved in financial statement fraud, which forces companies to fire well-experienced top executives and replace them with perhaps less-informed executives. Although these indirect costs cannot possibly be estimated, they should be considered when assessing the consequences of financial statement fraud. Farrell and Healy (2000, p. 18) stated, "the overall cost of fraud is over double the amount of missing money and assets."[17]

Financial statement fraud directly damages investors and creditors of committed fraud companies in the sense that they are bound to lose all or part of their investments if such fraud results in a bankruptcy, near failure, substantial reduction in the stock prices or delisting by organized stock exchanges. Financial statement fraud can also have a significant adverse impact on the confidence and trust of investors, other market participants, and the public in the quality and integrity of the financial reporting process. The collapse of Enron has caused about $80 billion lost in market capitalization which is devastating for significant numbers of investors, employees, and pensioners. This has raised the question of whether corporate financial statements can be trusted. Decreased confidence in the reliability of financial statements, resulting from fraudulent financial activities, affects all users and issuers of financial statements. Users of fraudulent financial statements will lose because their financial decisions (e.g., investment in the case of investors; transactions for suppliers; employment of employees) are made based on unreliable, misleading financial information. Issuers and perpetrators of financial statement fraud are adversely affected because investors and creditors will demand higher rates of return when there is unreasonable uncertainty about the quality of financial reports.

Unfortunately, no accurate, empirical method to assess and estimate the incidence and cost of financial statement fraud has been developed. The conventional measurement of financial statement fraud is based on the analysis of instances of fraudulent financial reporting alleged by the SEC in its Accounting and Auditing Enforcement Releases (AAER).[18] The AAERs report summaries of enforcement actions by the SEC against publicly traded companies, primarily involving alleged violations of Rule 10(b)-5 of the SEC 1934 Act of Section 17(a) of the 1933 Act concerning antifraud provisions as related to financial statement fraud. An example of this conventional method is the report commissioned by the Committee of Sponsoring Organizations of the Treadway Commission (COSO) in 1999.[19] This COSO-sponsored report identifies about 300 public companies that were alleged by the SEC for financial statement fraud during the 11-year period from January 1987 to December 1997; however, the SEC has also recently (1999 and 2000) filed about 200 allegations for financial statement fraud against high-profile companies such as Sunbeam, Enron Corp., Rite Aid, Lucent, Xerox, Waste Management, KnowledgeWare, Raytheon, and MicroStrategy. These alleged instances, however, provide only imprecise measurements and estimates of the actual occurrence of financial statement fraud. These measurements, by definition, are underestimated and exclusive, primarily because they do not include the undiscovered, nonprosecuted, and unalleged instances of financial statement fraud.

Even a small and infrequent financial statement fraud can affect investors and creditors, as well as the public's confidence in the quality of the financial reporting process. Public confidence depends on both the reported actual incidence of financial statement fraud and the perception of the extent that financial statements are threatened by fraudulent activities. Thus, even if the actual level of financial statement fraud may be low, investors and creditors may perceive that the problem exists. This requires that corporate governance take proper action to improve investor confidence in the financial reporting process.

Financial statement frauds can be classified into two categories—detected and undetected. It has been argued that only a small portion of financial statement fraud is detected, and most cases continue until they are discovered. Currently, there is no comprehensive source of all companies that were engaged in financial statement fraud. Alternatively, two sources gather data about firms committing financial statement fraud. The SEC's Accounting and Auditing Enforcement Releases (AAER) provide a list of firms that were subject to an SEC investigation for violating the SEC rules by engaging in fraudulent financial reporting activities. The second source is the financial press, including the *Wall Street Journal,* Wall Street Index, *New York Times,* and other popular press reporting of firms that have been convicted of fraudulent financial reporting activities or that have made an out-of-court settlement to end a class-action lawsuit. Companies that are investigated and/or convicted by the SEC of fraudulent financial reporting activities receive an AAER, which is often reported in the financial press. The financial press often reports on companies that have been convicted of financial statement fraud in the courts and those that made out-of-court class-action settlements and often deny any wrongdoing. Indeed, many AAERs reveal that investigated companies have paid a substantial fine and penalty for violating the SEC rules by issuing financial statement fraud while not admitting that they are guilty of a wrongdoing. These two sources are often not identical because not all companies that were subject to the SEC investigation result in a shareholder lawsuit and not all companies convicted in the courts are reported in AAERs.

FRAUD STUDIES

Four recent fraud studies conducted by the Committee of Sponsoring Organizations of the Treadway Commission (COSO), 1999; Institute of Management and Administration (IOMA) and The Institute of Internal Auditors, 1999; KPMG, 1998; and Ernst & Young, 2000, provide insights into a better understanding of fraud incidents, causes and effects of frauds, and ways to prevent and detect their occurrences. The results of these studies are summarized in Exhibit 1.3 in an attempt to (1) provide a better understanding of the pervasiveness of financial statement fraud threatening the integrity and quality of the financial reporting process; and (2) establish a set of recommendations for corporate governance in preventing and detecting financial statement fraud.

Lessons Learned from Fraud Studies

A vigilant and effective corporate governance can substantially reduce the instances of both employee and management frauds and considerably prevent and detect occurrences of financial statement fraud. A careful review of fraud studies presented in Exhibit 1.3 provides the following lessons and implications for corporate governance to prevent and detect financial statement fraud:

- Financial statement fraud is typically perpetrated by top management teams, including presidents, CEOs, CFOs, controllers, and other top executives. Thus, vigilant oversight function of the board of directors and its representative audit

Exhibit 1.3. Summary of Four Recent Financial Statement Fraud Studies

The 1999 COSO Report[1]	*The 1999 Business Fraud Survey*[2]

1. Most alleged financial statement frauds were committed by small companies (less than $100 million in total assets) that were not listed on the organized national stock exchanges (e.g., NYSE, Amex).
2. Financial pressures were important contributory factors for the occurrence of financial statement fraud.
3. Top management team including chief executive officers (CEOs) and chief financial officers (CFOs) were often involved in financial statement fraud.
4. The audit committees and boards of directors of the fraud companies were weak and ineffective in the sense that they rarely met and were composed of either insiders or others with significant ties to the company.
5. Financial statement frauds created severe consequences for committed companies, including bankruptcy, significant changes in ownership, and delisting by organizational national stock exchanges.
6. Cumulative amounts of financial statement frauds were relatively significant and large, with the average of $25 million and the median of $4.1 million for financial statement misstatement or misappropriation of assets.
7. More than half of the alleged financial statement frauds involved overstatement of revenues by recording revenues prematurely or fictitiously.
8. Most financial statement frauds were not isolated to a single fiscal period.
9. Fifty-five percent of the audit reports issued in the last year of the fraud period contained unqualified opinions.
10. Most sample fraud companies (56 percent) were audited by a Big Eight/Big Five auditing firm during the fraud period and the rest (44 percent) were audited by a non-Big Eight/Five auditor.

1. Half of the respondents (300 internal auditors across all industrial sectors including manufacturing, financial services, wholesalers, governmental agencies) believed employee fraud poses a greater threat to their organizations than management or financial statement fraud.
2. Nearly 15 percent reported management misappropriation as the greatest fraud risk to their organization.
3. Most (58 percent) believed that the greatest improvement in fraud detection efforts can be accomplished by holding management accountable to the same standards for misconduct as nonmanagerial employees.
4. Sixty percent of the respondents reported their department's fraud risk analysis process as being reactive in nature, and they suggested a more proactive stance on fraud prevention with the board of directors' awareness of known frauds and their related costs.
5. Most respondents (72 percent) reported that their organizations did not have fraud detection and deterrence software in place and suggested the use of computer software in a proactive and comprehensive program of fraud prevention and detection.
6. Communication of the organization's ethics and fraud program to all personnel can improve the effectiveness of fraud detection and prevention programs.
7. Most respondents (68 percent) reported that they never felt pressured to compromise the adherence to their organization's standards of ethical conduct.
8. Most respondents reported their organization's external auditors as being ineffective in preventing and detecting fraud by characterizing them as either "cavalier" or "arrogant and dangerous" in this respect.
9. Most respondents believed that more budget should be devoted to fraud-related activities and training in their internal audit department.

(continues)

Exhibit 1.3. *(Continued)*

The 1999 KPMG Survey[3]	*The 2000 Ernst & Young Survey*[4]
1. Determines the extent and magnitude of organizational frauds, including financial statement fraud, check fraud, inventory theft, and medical insurance claims fraud by surveying 5,000 leading U.S. publicly held companies, not-for-profit organizations.	1. Most (82 percent) of the surveyed senior executives from nearly 10,000 organizations across 30 different industries and in 15 countries indicated that all known frauds were perpetrated by employees and about 28 percent were committed by management.
2. Medical insurance claims fraud had the greatest average cost per incident followed by financial statement fraud.	2. Organizations that had not performed fraud vulnerability reviews were almost two-thirds more likely to have suffered a fraud within the previous 12 months.
3. Financial statement frauds resulted in an average loss of $1.24 million per incident.	3. Most respondents (80 percent) expressed serious concerns regarding the possibility of significant fraud within their organizations.
4. Poor internal controls and management override of controls were reported by most respondents as the two most common conditions for occurrence of fraud.	4. Nearly 33 percent of the respondents reported that a fraud vulnerability review had been recently performed in their organizations.
5. Various types of collusion between employees and external parties, as well as between employees and management, were cited as important causes of fraud.	5. More than 40 percent of respondents indicated lack of a specific policy regarding reporting fraud in their organizations.
6. Personal financial pressure, followed by substance abuse and gambling, were considered as important red flags signaling the possibility of fraud occurrence.	6. Most (80 percent) organizations that utilize the work of forensic accountants expressed their satisfaction with the performance of forensic accountants, investigating in preventing and detecting fraud.
7. Other frequently cited red flags are real or imagined grievances against the organization, ongoing transactions with related parties, increased stress, internal pressure, short vacations, and unusual hours.	
8. Suggested fraud prevention and detection strategies are review and improvement of internal controls, increasing the focus of top management teams by setting a tone at the top, providing training courses in fraud prevention and detection, establishing a corporate code of conduct, performing reference checks on new employees, and providing ethics training to employees.	

Sources in the order of presentation in the table, from left to right, are:

[1] Committee of Sponsoring Organizations of the Treadway Commission (COSO). 1999. *Fraudulent Financial Reporting: 1987–1997, An Analysis of U.S. Public Companies.*

[2] The Institute of Management and Administration (IOMA) and The Institute of Internal Auditors (IIA). 1999. "Business Fraud Survey."

[3] KPMG. 1999. "1998 Fraud Survey."

[4] Ernst & Young. 2000. "The Unmanaged Risk: An International Survey of the Effect of Fraud on Business."

committee in (1) setting "a tone at the top" demonstrating commitment to high-quality financial reports; (2) discouraging and punishing fraudulent financial activity; and (3) monitoring managerial decisions and actions as related to the financial reporting process can substantially reduce instances of financial statement fraud.

- Financial pressures, including substantial declines in both the quality and quantity of earnings, high earnings growth expectations, and an inability to meet analysts' earnings estimates, are often cited in these studies as motivations for management engagement in financial statement fraud. The board of directors and audit committee should closely monitor the pressures faced by senior executives; be aware of the gamesmanship practices between management analysts and auditors; and attempt to control and monitor such practices.

- Ineffective boards of directors and audit committees are cited as important contributing factors that increase the likelihood of occurrence of financial statement fraud. Publicly traded companies should focus considerably on director independence and expertise and qualifications. Companies should comply with the new SEC, NYSE, and NASD rules on audit committees and should establish vigilant and effective audit committees to oversee the quality, integrity, and reliability of financial reports. These audit committees should be independent, financially literate, well trained and experienced, and actively involved in corporate governance and the financial reporting process to be able to influence the prevention and detection of financial statement fraud.

- Lack of adequate and effective internal control structure has been cited as providing opportunities for the commission of financial statement fraud. The internal control structure can play an important role in preventing and detecting financial statement fraud by reducing the opportunities for perpetration of financial statement fraud and by red flagging the indicators of financial statement fraud.

- Quality financial audits performed by external auditors are expressed as an effective way to reduce the likelihood of fraud occurrence and increase the possibility of fraud detection and prevention. The new O'Malley Panel on Audit Effectiveness suggests the use of forensic-type field work audit procedures on every audit to improve the prospects of detecting material financial statement fraud by external auditors.[20] Forensic-type audit field work requires auditors to modify their neutral concept of professional skepticism and presume the possibility of dishonesty at various levels of management, including collusion, gamesmanship, earnings management, override of internal controls, and falsification of financial records and documents. Forensic-type audit procedures are further discussed in Chapter 11.

- These fraud studies reveal that multiperiod financial statement fraud typically starts with the misstatement of interim financial statements. This suggests that quarterly financial statements should be thoroughly reviewed by external auditors and, whenever possible, continuous auditing should be performed throughout the year.

- Fraud studies underscore the need for involvement of all corporate governance constituencies, including the board of directors, the audit committee, management, internal auditors, external auditors, and governing bodies as part of a broad effort to prevent and detect financial statement fraud and, thus, improve the quality, integrity, and reliability of financial statements.

- The Enron debacle, caused by the commission of financial statement fraud, is expected to lead to (1) the establishment of new regulations to improve corporate financial disclosures and; (2) the requirement of a more effective oversight of public accounting firms; and (3) the creation of a new accounting industry self-regulating organization that will operate under SEC supervision.[21]

SANCTIONS FOR PERPETRATIONS OF FINANCIAL STATEMENT FRAUD

The recent COSO-sponsored research on fraudulent financial reporting (Beasley et al. 1999)[22] reveals that relatively few individuals (i.e., senior executives) who perpetrated or engaged in alleged financial statement fraud explicitly admitted guilt or eventually served prison sentences, even though a significant number of alleged perpetrators were terminated or forced to resign from their executive positions. It can be argued that if these fraudsters do not receive severe sanctions and are given executive positions in other corporations, they may continue to engage in financial statement fraud; however, if perpetrators were sanctioned sufficiently and severely, they would not be available to obtain executive positions or, if they do, they would behave more ethically and conscientiously. Thus, imposing more severe sanctions on the perpetrators of financial statement fraud might help reduce instances of such fraud. Richard Walker, the SEC's Director of Enforcement, in discussing the SEC's concern regarding the commission of financial statement fraud by large publicly traded companies, warned fraudsters that "cooking the books and you will go to jail without passing Go."[23]

The Treadway Commission report (1987) recommended that those found to "cause, aid and abet, or participate in financial statement fraud be barred from corporate office."[24] The Treadway Commission (1987) also supported more criminal prosecutions and longer sentences for perpetrators of financial statement fraud. Public accountants are often barred from practice before the SEC for violations of the securities laws and pursuant to SEC Rule 2(e) antifraud provisions of the SEC Act of 1934. Thus, corporate executives engaged in financial statement fraud should also be barred from corporate office. Barring the perpetrators of financial statement fraud from corporate office should discourage top executives from engaging in fraudulent activities and, thus, reduce the probability of occurrence of financial statement fraud. In addition, perpetrators of financial statement fraud should be fined, and the amount of fines should be set at high levels to be effective as a deterrent for financial statement fraud. One possible danger of adopting such a severe penalty is the likelihood that innocent alleged executives may be penalized inappropriately or become more risk averse, resulting from fear of being wrongfully suspected of engaging in financial statement fraud. Former SEC chairperson Arthur Levitt initiated a policy of no tolerance for financial statement fraud by publicly traded companies and the agency's strategies to be aggressive in prosecuting fraudulent financial activities to improve the quality of financial reports. It is expected that the agency will continue its policy of aggressive financial statement fraud prevention and detection to ensure investors' rights.

In 1999, the SEC initiated a total of 525 enforcement cases consisting of 227 civil actions and 298 administration proceedings against registrants.[25] From the total of 525 enforcement cases, 94 cases (about 18 percent) were related to financial statement fraud. The alleged 1999 financial statement fraud cases are associated with a broad range of schemes, including (1) more than 34 percent involved improper revenue recognition; (2) about 18 percent were related to fraudulent asset valuations; (3) nearly 13 percent involved improper capitalization of expenses; (4) about 20 percent featured unacceptable earnings management; (5) nearly 10 percent involved large options or equity interest; and (6) another 5 percent involved miscellaneous cookie jar reserves. In addition, the SEC has increased its sanctions against individuals who commit fraud on behalf of publicly traded companies. In 1999, more than 120 corporate officers and employees were charged with engagement in financial statement fraud. The sanctioned individuals range from senior officers (e.g., CEO) to lower-level managers (e.g., district sales managers).

The SEC has recently taken financial statement fraud seriously as part of its number one priority by working closely with criminal prosecutors to attack financial statement fraud. About 100 of the SEC's enforcement cases filed in year 2000 involved financial statement fraud. Charges were filed against 29 publicly traded companies, 19 chief executive officers (CEOs), 19 chief financial officers (CFOs), 16 inside directors, and 1 outside director. The SEC civil financial statement fraud charges have resulted in fines against public companies and their top executives and, in some cases, have barred top executives from serving as officials for public companies. Furthermore, the SEC's criminal charges have led to convictions and jail time.

In a June 2000 speech, SEC Commissioner Isaac Hunt stated that "financial fraud constituted almost one-fifth of the case brought by the derision of enforcement in the last year . . . the commission is increasing its sanctions against individuals who commit fraud on behalf of the corporation."[26] The SEC sanctions are not only limited to top executives but are also applied to others within the corporate chain of command and external auditors who knowingly or recklessly are involved in financial statement fraud. Richard Walker, the SEC's Director of Enforcement, states that the agency continues "to see an unacceptably higher number of busted audits."[27] The SEC plans to bring more enforcement actions against companies, auditors, and those responsible for cooking the books.

OCCURRENCE, PREVENTION, AND DETECTION

Recently, there has been substantial publicity about the extent and magnitude of alleged financial statement fraud threatening the quality, integrity, and reliability of the financial reporting process, which have contributed to considerable economic losses by investors and creditors. These financial statement frauds have eroded the public's

Exhibit 1.4.   Financial Statement Fraud Prevention and Detection Process

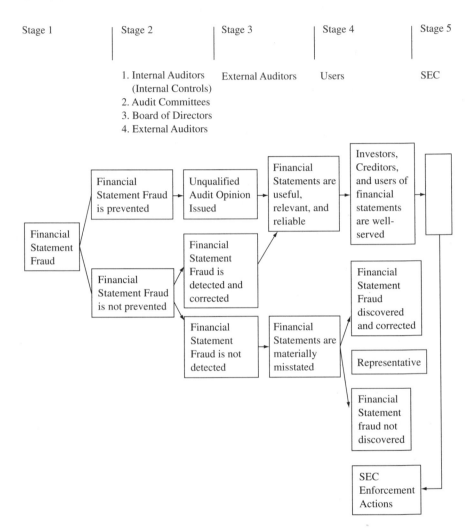

confidence in the financial reporting process and the audit function. This section describes the processes of financial statement fraud occurrence, prevention, and detection.

Exhibit 1.4 illustrates the five-stage process of financial statement fraud occurrence, prevention, and detection. At Stage 1, financial statement fraud occurs because management is motivated to mislead financial statement users, particularly investors and creditors. The opportunity for management deceptive actions exists, and management rationalizes its actions to engage in financial statement fraud. This first stage is thoroughly described and examined in Chapters 2 through 5.

At Stage 2, the existence of a responsible and effective corporate governance, consisting of a vigilant and active board of directors, an effective audit committee, and an adequate and effective internal audit function, discovers the intended financial statement fraud and prevents its occurrence. When financial statement fraud is prevented at this stage, the financial information is misleading; however, an ineffective and irresponsible corporate governance, along with the gamesmanship attitude of corporate governance, would fail to prevent the deliberate financial statement fraud perpetrated by management. This stage of the process is described and examined in Chapters 7 through 10.

At Stage 3, financial statements that may or may not contain material misstatements are audited by independent auditors. Independent auditors perform tests of controls and substantial tests in gathering sufficient and competent evidence to provide reasonable assurance that financial statements are free from material misstatements including fraudulent activities. When financial statement fraud is detected by independent auditors, the auditors are required to ask management to make corrections. If financial statement fraud is detected by the independent auditor and corrected by the company, then financial statements are fairly presented in conformity with generally accepted accounting principles (GAAP) and portray the company's true financial position, cash flows, and results of operations. Fairly presented financial statements accompanied by an unqualified audit report are considered useful, reliable, and relevant for decision making by investors, creditors, and other users of financial statements. These high-quality financial statements facilitate rational investment decisions contributing to efficient capital markets. This stage of the process is discussed in Chapter 11.

Financial statement fraud that is not initially prevented and not subsequently detected by independent auditors, accompanied by an unqualified audit report, and disseminated to investors, creditors, and the public, will be misleading. At this stage, whether or not financial statement fraud is discovered, it is considered harmful and detrimental to the integrity and quality of the financial reporting process. This will cause inefficiency in the capital markets, which may result in misallocation of the nation's economic resources.

At the last stage, if financial statement fraud is discovered, either by design or accidentally, the company will be subject to SEC enforcement actions and will be required to correct and restate misstated financial statements. This final stage is discussed in Chapter 12. The alleged company, its official, and its auditors then are subject to both civil and criminal lawsuit actions or administrative proceedings by the SEC. Any enforcement action by the SEC will have negative effects on:

- The reputation, prestige, and status of the alleged company.
- The top management team and other perpetrators of financial statement fraud. The company's officials will be subject to civil penalty, barred from serving on the board of directors or top management team of any publicly traded companies, and subject to criminal prosecutions, including jail time.
- The prestige, reputation, integrity, objectivity, and independence of auditors and auditing firms. Auditing firms may have to pay substantial fines to settle the

alleged audit fraud. The partners involved may be subject to fines or be barred permanently or temporarily from auditing public companies.

- The investing public, especially investors and creditors. Investors and creditors may lose their investment substantially if the alleged company goes bankrupt or if stock prices are adversely affected by the alleged financial statement fraud.
- The efficiency of the capital markets through reflection of high financial risk and low-quality financial reports.

CONCLUSION

Incidents of financial statement fraud have increased substantially over the past two decades, and affected individuals, especially investors and creditors, have lost millions of dollars. Financial statement fraud involves deliberate and material misrepresentation of a company's financial information with the intent to mislead users of financial statements, especially investors and creditors. Financial statement fraud is typically committed by the top management team with an opportunity and motive to distort the financial statements and a managerial style or attitude that promotes illicit behavior. High-profile financial statement fraud perpetrated by major corporations such as ZZZZBest, PharMor, Regina, MiniScribe, Waste Management, Rite Aid, Sunbeam, Xerox, MicroStrategy, Lucent, KnowledgeWare, Enron, and Raytheon, among others, has raised concern regarding the reliability and effectiveness of corporate governance and the quality and integrity of published audited financial statements.

The extent of financial statement fraud is unknown primarily because (1) reliable statistics are not available; (2) financial statement fraud continues until it is detected and revealed; and (3) the nature of financial statement fraud is changing in the light of technological advances (e.g., the Internet, electronic financial reporting) and globalization. The significance of financial statement fraud has also received the attention of both regulators and standard setters during the past two decades. The National Commission on Fraudulent Financial Reporting, better known as the Treadway Commission, was established in 1985 with the objective of (1) determining the extent to which the integrity of financial statements are threatened by the occurrence of fraud; (2) identifying causal factors that can lead to fraudulent financial reporting; and (3) making recommendations to public companies, regulators, and standard setters to reduce the incidents of financial statement fraud. Recommendations of the Treadway Commission and responses to these recommendations by the SEC, public companies, and the accounting profession are thoroughly discussed throughout the book.

ENDNOTES

1. Johnson v. McDonald, 170 Okl. 117; 39 P.2d 150.
2. Association of Certified Fraud Examiners. 1993. *Cooking the Books: What Every Accountant Should Know About Fraud.* No. 92-5401. Self-study Workbook: 12, Austin, TX.

3. National Commission on Fraudulent Financial Reporting (NCFFR). 1987. "Report of the National Commission on Fraudulent Financial Reporting" (October), New York.

4. Thornhill, W.T. and J.T. Wells. 1993. *Fraud Terminology Reference Guide.* Association of Certified Fraud Examiners, Austin, TX.

5. The Institute of Internal Auditors. 1986. The Institute of Internal Auditors Reports on Fraud. Altamonte Springs, FL.

6. Elliott, R.K. and J.J. Willingham. 1980. *Management Fraud: Detection and Deterrence.* New York: Petrocelli Books.

7. Robertson, J.C. 2000. *Fraud Examination for Managers and Auditors.* Austin, TX: Viesca Books.

8. Association of Certified Fraud Examiners (ACFE). 1996. Report to the Nation on Occupational Fraud and Abuse (The Walls Report). ACFE, Austin, TX.

9. Elliott, R.K. and J.J. Willingham. 1980. *Management Fraud: Detection and Deterrence.* New York: Petrocelli Books.

10. Ibid.

11. To learn more about the NWCC, contact the National White Collar Crime Center, Suite 450, 1001 Boulders Parkway, Richmond, VA; 23225-5513; 800/221-4424 or 804/323-3563.

12. Levitt, A. 1998 SEC chair from the speech, "The Numbers Game". NYU Center for Law and Business (September 28).

13. Association of Certified Fraud Examiners. 1996. Report to the Nation of Occupational Fraud and Abuse. Austin, TX.

14. Albrecht, W.S., G.A. Wernez, and T.L. Williams. 1995. *Fraud: Bringing Light to the Dark Side of Business.* Burr Ridge, IL: Irwin Publishing Co.

15. Albrecht, W.S. and D.J. Searcy. 2001. "Top 10 Reasons Why Fraud is Increasing in the U.S". *Strategic Finance.* (May): 58–61.

16. Hilzenrath, D. S. 2001. After Enron, New Doubts about Auditors. *Washington Post* (December 5): A01.

17. Farrel, R.B., and P. Healy. 2000. "White Collar Crime: A Profile of the Perpetrator and an Evaluation of the Responsibilities for Its Prevention and Detection". *Journal of Forensic Accounting* (January/June, Vol. 1, No.1): 17–34.

18. SEC's Accounting and Auditing Enforcement Release (AAER). Available: www.sec.gov.

19. Beasley, M.S., J.V. Carcello, and D.R. Hermanson. 1999. Fraudulent Financial Reporting: 1987–1997, An Analysis of U.S. Public Companies. Research Report Commissioned by the Committee of Sponsoring Organizations of Treadway Commission (COSO). Jersey City, NJ: AICPA.

20. O'Malley, S.F. 2000. The Panel on Audit Effectiveness: Report and Recommendations. Stamford, Ct: Public Oversight Board (August).

21. Schroeder, M. 2001. Enron Debacle Spurs Calls for Controls. *The Wall Street Journal* (December 14): A4.

22. Beasley, M.S., J.V. Carcello, and D.R. Hermanson. 1999. Fraudulent Financial Reporting: 1987–1997, An Analysis of U.S. Public Companies. Research Report Commissioned by the Committee of Sponsoring Organizations of Treadway Commission (COSO). Jersey City, NJ: AICPA.

23. Walker, R. H. 1999. Speech to the AICPA in Washington. SEC Director of Enforcement (December 7). Available: www.sec.gov.

24. National Commission on Fraudulent Financial Reporting (NCFFR). 1987. "Report of the National Commission on Fraudulent Financial Reporting" (October), New York, NY.

25. SEC. 1999. "Enforcement Cases Initiated by the Commission." Available: www.sec.gov.

26. Hunt, Isaac. C., Jr. "Current SEC Developments." Remarks of Commissioner Isaac C. Hunt, Jr., at the American Society of Corporate Secretaries, San Francisco, CA. June 30, 2000.

27. Walker, R. H. 1999. Speech to the AICPA in Washington. SEC Director of Enforcement (December 7). Available: www.sec.gov.

Chapter 2

Financial Reporting
of Public Companies

INTRODUCTION

This chapter discusses the financial reporting process of publicly traded companies, their reporting requirements, and characteristics of high-quality financial reports. This chapter also examines contract views of corporations and interactions between corporations and their contracting parties, expectations gaps between preparers of financial statements and their users, perceived problems of current financial reporting, and the ways financial reports can be improved in providing financial information free of misstatements caused by errors and fraud.

FINANCIAL REPORTING SYSTEM

The financial reporting system is a complex process that is influenced by a variety of factors, including technological, political, cultural, economic, and business environments. The National Commission on Fraudulent Financial Reporting, better known as the Treadway Commission, has broken down the financial reporting system into three fundamental elements: (1) companies; (2) independent public accountants; and (3) oversight bodies, as presented in Exhibit 2.1.[1]

Exhibit 2.1 describes the relationships of the three fundamental elements of the financial reporting system and their interactions with the users of such a system. A company and its management play an important role in the financial reporting system and process. They are primarily responsible for fair presentation of financial reports conforming with established criteria known as reporting standards. The integrity and quality of financial reports reflect management commitment and intent in preparing and disseminating reliable, relevant, and useful information about the company's financial position, results of operations, and cash flows. The board of directors and its representative audit committee oversee the financial reporting process even though the accounting department actually prepares the financial statements.

Independent public accountants, by virtue of being independent and knowledgeable, are engaged to render an opinion regarding the fair presentation of financial reports on the company's financial position and the results of operations in conformity with generally accepted accounting principles (GAAP). Independent public accountants lend more credibility and objectivity to published financial

Exhibit 2.1. Financial Reporting System
Source: Adapted from the Treadway Commission Report, Available: http://www.coso.org

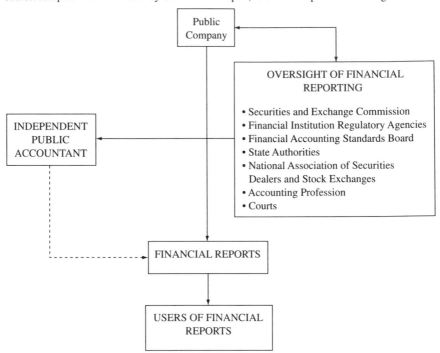

statements by reducing the information risk. Information risk is the probability that published financial statements may be inaccurate, biased, false, incomplete, and/or misleading.

Several oversight bodies influence a set of financial reporting standards for public companies, and they also monitor and enforce compliance with those standards. These oversight bodies consist of the Securities and Exchange Commission (SEC), Financial Accounting Standards Board (FASB), state authorities, courts, accounting profession, National Association of Securities Dealers (NASD), New York Stock Exchange (NYSE), and financial institution regulatory agencies. The SEC, in fulfilling its responsibility for administering the federal securities laws, establishes disclosure requirements for public companies. The SEC has traditionally maintained its oversight responsibility over financial reporting of publicly traded companies while, in most cases, has delegated its authority for establishing accounting standards to private sectors such as the FASB.

ANNUAL FINANCIAL REPORTING REQUIREMENTS

A company's annual report is typically the primary means of communication with current and potential investors and creditors. Thus, management attempts to use this vehicle to portray the company in a favorable manner by adding "gloss" to the annual report while complying with the reporting requirements set forth by the SEC.

Rule 14a-3 of the SEC Act of 1934 requires that annual reports provided to shareholders in connection with the annual meetings of shareholders include (1) audited financial statements consisting of balance sheets as of the two most recent fiscal years; (2) statements of income; and (3) cash flows for each of the three most recent years. In addition, Rule 14a-3 requires that the following information, as stated in Regulation S-K, be included in the annual report to shareholders:

- Selected quarterly financial data
- Summary of selected financial data for last five years
- Segment information
- Management's discussion and analysis of financial condition and results of operations
- Quantitative and qualitative disclosures about market risk
- Market price of company's common stock for each quarterly period within the two most recent fiscal years
- Description of business activities
- Disagreements with accountants on accounting and financial disclosure

The new SEC audit committee disclosure rule (2000) also requires an audit committee report to be published annually in the proxy statements for annual meetings of shareholders occurring after December 15, 2000. This report should state whether the audit committee has completed the following activities:

- Reviewed and discussed the audited financial statements with management.
- Received from the auditor a letter disclosing matters that, in the auditor's judgment, may reasonably be thought to bear on the auditor's independence from the company and discussed with them their independence.
- Recommended to the board of directors that the company's audited financial statements be included in the Annual Report on Form 10-K or Form 10-KSB.

HIGH-QUALITY FINANCIAL REPORTS

The SEC, since its inception nearly 70 years ago, has continued to protect investors through the fair and orderly operation of the capital markets. High-quality and transparent financial reports prepared based on full and fair disclosures promote efficient capital markets. Certain qualitative aspects of financial information are important in producing high-quality and transparent audited financial statements prepared in conformity with generally accepted accounting principles (GAAP) and audited in accordance with generally accepted auditing standards (GAAS).

The Statement of Financial Accounting Concept (SFAC) No. 1 entitled "Objectives of Financial Reporting by Business Enterprises" promulgated by the FASB in 1978 states that:

> Financial reporting should provide information that is useful to present and potential investors and creditors and other users in making rational investment, credit, and similar decisions. The information should be comprehensible to those who have a reasonable understanding of business and economic activities and are willing to study the information with reasonable diligence.[2]

HIGH-QUALITY FINANCIAL REPORTING

The financial reporting model that has been established through the continued efforts of both the public and private sectors is designed to provide users, particularly investors and creditors, with useful, reliable, relevant, comparable, consistent, and transparent information necessary to make informed and educated financial decisions.

Management, specifically the chief financial officer (CFO), is primarily responsible for fair presentation of financial statements in conformity with GAAP that portray the company's performance, cash flows, and financial position to investors, creditors, and other users of financial statements. Management should produce high-quality and transparent financial reports to (1) meet the needs of investors and creditors; (2) portray a true and clear picture of the company; and (3) present objective, consistent, and comparable financial results and conditions. The Statement of Financial Accounting Concepts (SFAC) No. 2 describes nine qualities and characteristics that make financial information useful for decision making by investors, creditors, and other users of financial statements.[3] The additional characteristic of transparency has been added to this list of nine characteristics discussed as follows:

1. *Relevance.* The financial information is viewed to be relevant if it makes a difference to decisions by decision makers (e.g., investors, creditors) and helps users to (1) assess past performance; (2) predict future performance; (3) confirm or correct expectations; and (4) provide feedback on earlier expectations. Relevance, which encompasses the concepts of predictive value, feedback value, and timeliness, indicates that information is relevant when it is capable of making a difference in a decision.
2. *Timeliness.* Timeliness means providing financial information to decision makers when they need such information and before the information loses its capacity and capability to influence decisions. It has been argued that historical financial statements do not provide timely, relevant information for investors and creditors to make investment decisions. Thus, online, real-time

electronic financial reports have been suggested to improve the timeliness of financial information. Extensible business reporting language (XBRL) and Internet-based financial reports, which are discussed in depth in Chapter 12, also enhance the timeliness of business reports.

3. *Reliability.* Financial information is reliable when investors and creditors consider the information to reflect economic conditions or events that it purports to represent. Reliability, which encompasses the notions of verifiability, neutrality, and representational faithfulness, is a measure of the integrity and objectivity of financial reports. Reliability provides assurance for users that the information is accurate and useful.

4. *Verifiability.* Verifiability is the extent to which different individuals using the same measurement material arrive at the same amount or conclusion. For example, cash is considered a verifiable financial item because different individuals can count the reported cash and reach the same conclusion about the ending balance of cash.

5. *Representational faithfulness.* Representational faithfulness means the degree of correspondence between the reported accounting numbers and the resources or events those numbers purport to represent. Representational faithfulness of published audited financial statements means the extent to which they reflect the economic reality and economic resources and obligations of the company as well as the transactions and events that change those resources and obligations.

6. *Neutrality.* High-quality financial information should be neutral in the sense that it is free from bias toward a predetermined result. Neutrality implies that management, in using its discretion to choose among a set of acceptable accounting methods, should select the method that reports the economic reality of the transactions or events.

7. *Comparability and Consistency.* High-quality financial statements require the use of standardized and uniform accounting standards and practices for measuring, recognizing, and disclosing similar financial transactions or economic events. The reported financial information of a particular company can be considered useful for decision making if the decision maker (e.g., investor, creditor) can compare it with similar information about other companies and with similar information about the same company for some other time period. Comparability and consistency suggest that comparability of information among companies and consistency in the application of methods over time enhances the information value and value relevance of financial reports.

8. *Materiality.* An amount or a disclosure is considered to be material if it influences or makes a difference to a decision maker. Materiality affects the quality, integrity, and reliability of financial statements because management uses its judgment to decide what may be material to users of financial statements.

Auditors use materiality judgment in determining the type of audit report when there is a departure from GAAP. Materiality threshold used by management in presenting financial information is recently being challenged by the SEC in many of the alleged financial statement fraud cases filed against publicly traded companies.

9. *Feasibility or Costs and Benefits.* High-quality financial information or disclosure must be feasibly practical and cost effective. Management, in deciding about a particular disclosure or implementation of a particular control activity, considers whether the perceived benefits to be derived from the decision exceed the perceived costs associated with it.

10. *Transparency.* High-quality financial information must be transparent in the sense that it provides the complete reporting and disclosure of transactions, which portray the financial conditions and operational results of the company in conformity with GAAP. Transparency enables financial statement users, including investors and creditors, to obtain the right information and ensure that financial information is factual and objective. The more transparent the financial reporting process, the easier it is to obtain and assess the nature of transactions and the quality of the related financial statements.

SIX-LEGGED STOOL OF THE FINANCIAL REPORTING PROCESS

High-quality financial reports, including reliable financial statements free of material misstatements caused by errors and fraud, can be achieved when there is a well-balanced functioning system of corporate governance, as depicted in Exhibit 2.2. This system comprises six groups: the board of directors, the audit committee, the top management team, internal auditors, external auditors, and governing bodies including the SEC, AICPA, NYSE, and NASD. These groups develop a "six-legged stool" that supports responsible corporate governance and reliable financial reports. Although the responsibility of these groups varies regarding preparation and dissemination of financial statements, a well-defined cooperative working relationship among these groups should reduce the probability of financial statement fraud. The responsibility of these groups in ensuring corporate governance and reliable financial statements is thoroughly examined in Chapters 6 through 12; however, a brief description of these groups' responsibility regarding the quality, reliability, and integrity of the financial reporting process is explained in the following section.

Fair presentation of financial statements, the representational faithfulness, verifiability, soundness, and neutrality of the financial information is the primary responsibility of the top management team. The board of directors and its representative and extension, the audit committee, have the ultimate monitoring re-

Exhibit 2.2. A Six-legged Stool of the Financial Reporting Process

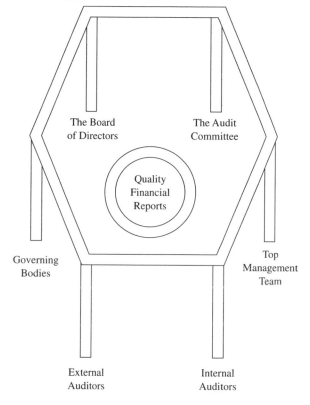

sponsibility of the financial reporting process. The Blue Ribbon Committee (1999) recommends that the audit committee (1) discusses with the external auditors the quality, not just the acceptability, of the company's accounting principles and practices applied in its financial reporting process; (2) communicates with external auditors the quality of financial reports in connection with the review of interim financial information; and (3) includes a "belief statement" about the fair presentation of the audited financial statements in accordance with GAAP[4]; however, the final rules adopted by the governing organizations of publicly traded companies require the audit committee to disclose in its report that it has recommended to the board of directors that the audited financial statements be included in the company's Annual Report on Form 10-K or Form 10-KSB. The new rules, which substantially incorporated all of the Blue Ribbon Committee recommendations, did not adopt one recommendation suggesting inclusion of a "belief statement in the audit committee report regarding the fairness of presentation of the audited financial statements."

High-quality financial reports require continuous improvements in the financial reporting process. The steps involved in producing high-quality and credible financial reports as stated in the Public Oversight Board (POB) report known as the Kirk Panel are as follows:

1. "The board of directors must recognize the primacy of its accountability to shareholders.
2. The auditor must look to the board of directors as the client.
3. The board and its audit committee must expect, and the auditor must deliver, candid communications about the quality of the company's financial reporting."[5]

The "six-legged stool" illustrated in Exhibit 2.2, which is based on the active participation of the board of directors, the audit committee, the top management team, internal auditors, external auditors, and governing bodies, fosters continuous improvements in the financial reporting process in producing high-quality financial reports. The Blue Ribbon Committee's Report on Improving the Effectiveness of Audit Committees suggested the "three-legged stool" involving participation of the CFO, the independent auditor, and the audit committee in improving the quality and integrity of financial reports.

CORPORATE FINANCIAL REPORTS

Companies listed on stock exchanges are required to publish annual and quarterly financial reports, including the three fundamental financial statements: (1) statement of financial position, which is better known as the balance sheet; (2) income statement; and (3) statement of cash flows. Company financial reports typically consist of the three fundamental financial statements, a statement of changes in owner's equity, notes to the financial statements, the auditor's report, a five-year comparative summary of key financial items, management's discussion and analysis of operations, high and low stock prices, and other financial and nonfinancial information. Financial reports are expected to provide useful, relevant, and reliable financial information to users of those reports for financial decision making.

Financial statements are used by organizations to communicate their social— and mostly, economic—reality to demonstrate the legitimacy of their actions to obtain resources necessary for their survival. Financial statements of publicly traded companies in the United States are expected to be prepared in conformity with GAAP and accompanied by an audit report issued by an independent and certified public accountant (CPA). GAAP are a set of standards and guidelines established to provide uniformity in the preparation of financial statements and to ensure their fair presentation in conveying reliable, relevant, and useful financial information. Thus, companies attempt to publish financial statements supported by a clean audit opinion, providing reasonable assurance regarding their fair presentation in conformity with GAAP in order to secure access to financial resources necessary for their survival.

Financial reports can be obtained in a hard copy, either directly from the issuing company or from the Securities and Exchange Commission (SEC), or electronically through the Internet and/or through the SEC's Electronic Data Gathering, Analysis, and Retrieval System (EDGAR). EDGAR is an online filing system for the collection, validation, indexing, acceptance, and submission of financial information primarily by corporations and others required by law to file forms with the SEC. The primary purpose of EDGAR is to enhance the efficiency and fairness of the capital market for the benefit of investors and corporations in particular, as well as the society and economy in general. EDGAR accelerates the process of filing requirements with the agency for the receipt, acceptance, dissemination, and analysis of time-sensitive corporate required financial information. As of May 6, 1996, all public domestic companies have been required to make their filings on EDGAR, except for filings made in paper because of a hardship exemption. The SEC has not yet allowed all documents to be filed electronically and, therefore, they are not available on EDGAR.

The actual annual reports submitted to the shareholders by corporations (except in the case of investment companies) are not required to be filed on EDGAR; however, the annual reports on Form 10-K or 10-KSB, containing much of the same information submitted to shareholders, are required to be filed on EDGAR. Documents submitted on the EDGAR system in either plain text or hypertext markup language (HTML) are official filings, whereas portable document format (PDF) documents are unofficial copies of filings in an Adobe Acrobat reader and may contain graphics.[6]

Financial reports, especially financial statements, should provide useful, relevant, and reliable information regarding the financial position of a company, the results and successes of its operations, its ability to exist and meet its obligations, the effectiveness of material policies and strategies, its future performance and prospects, and its growth and risk. Users of these reports have traditionally relied on management to provide relevant financial information. The integrity and quality of corporate governance determines the quality and reliability of the financial reporting process that generates financial reports. The integrity and quality of the financial reporting process have recently been scrutinized. Arthur Levitt, the former SEC chair, addressed this concern by stating, "we are witnessing an erosion in the quality of earnings, and therefore, the quality of financial reporting. Managing may be giving way to manipulations; integrity may be losing out to illusion."[7]

To obtain necessary financial resources, companies attempt to report favorable financial results on their financial statements prepared in accordance with GAAP and accompanied with a clean standard audit opinion. When financial results are favorable and meet investors' expectations conveyed through analysts' forecasts, companies have incentives to be more legitimate and ethical and less motivated to engage in fraudulent financial reporting; however, when financial results are less favorable or unfavorable, the firm may choose one of the following alternatives: (1) issue unfavorable financial results that are in compliance with GAPP; (2) violate GAAP to report more favorable financial results; and (3) engage in fraudulent financial activities to report more favorable financial results. Adoption of any of these aforementioned alternatives has a cost to the company and its executives and management.

First, reporting unfavorable financial results, even though accompanied by a clean audit opinion, may not be in the firm's best interests. Poor financial performance and results can be viewed as a reflection of lack of earnings growth and prosperity, which challenges the financial and economic legitimacy of the firm and may result in less favorable access to financial resources.

The selection of the second alternative forces the firm to compromise its financial reporting strategy to depart from GAAP in order to report more favorable financial results. The consequence of selecting this alternative is that the firm may receive a modified audit opinion (e.g., qualified, adverse), which may curtail the firm's access to financial resources, at reasonable cost, necessary for its survival. A large volume of empirical research demonstrates that firms that receive a modified audit opinion other than unqualified (1) obtain higher cost of capital; (2) receive a high-risk assessment; (3) are charged an interest rate premium; (4) have less favorable access to reasonable financial resources; and (5) receive unfavorable capital market reactions (e.g., Bamber and Stratton, 1997).[8]

The third alternative is when the firm engages in fraudulent financial activities to report more favorable financial results. In this case, the firm deliberately commits illegal actions to mislead users of financial statements about the company's poor or less favorable financial performance. If this deception is hidden from the auditor and/or the auditor is unable to detect the committed financial statement fraud, a fraudulent and misleading financial statement accompanied with a clean audit opinion will be issued. The lack of a responsible corporate governance may be viewed as a contributing factor for a firm to engage in financial statement fraud in response to pressures to report favorable financial results. Furthermore, the firm is more apt to issue financial statement fraud when the option is within the set of available and acceptable accounting alternatives. This chronological decision process is depicted in Exhibit 2.3.

CONTRACT VIEW OF CORPORATIONS

Sunder (1977) views an organization, in general, as a set of contracts among various participants.[9] In a business sector, a corporation has a set of contractual relationships with a broad range of participants, including shareholders, creditors, vendors, customers, employees, governmental agencies, and auditors, as depicted in Exhibit 2.4. Sunder (1977) provides a similar analysis of a firm as a set of contracts without mentioning the importance of corporate governance. Contracting

Exhibit 2.3. Chronological Decision Process

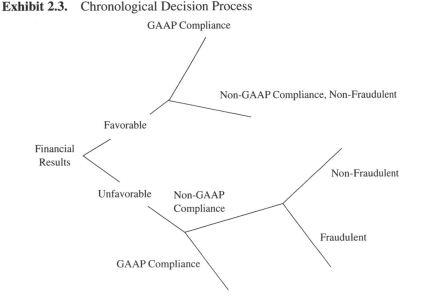

participants pursue their own goals and continue their contracting relationships with the firm as long as there is a goal congruence or mutual interest. For example, shareholders and creditors contribute capital to the firm and demand an expected rate of return on their investment. Vendors provide goods, services, machinery, and materials in return for payments. Customers pay cash for goods and services received. Employees provide labor, skills, and services and expect to be compensated for their efforts. Society in general, and government in particular, creates an environment that corporations fulfill their social responsibility and tax obligations. Contracting participants expect an inducement equal to the opportunity value of their contribution in order to continue their contract with the company. Corporations should make continuous improvements in their performance to satisfy contracting participants or, otherwise, the contractors may impose restrictions, sanctions, and eventually discontinue their contracts, which will be detrimental to the company's survival.

Corporate governance is responsible for assembling, implementing, managing, enforcing, modifying, monitoring, and maintaining the contract set of the company. Contracting participants have a variety of incentives and contributions. Corporate governance should develop a system of checks and balances that (1) accurately measures the contribution made by contracting participants (agents); (2) properly determines the amount of incentives due to them; (3) adequately manages the fair distribution of inducement to contracting agents; (4) effectively monitors the requirements and provisions of the contractual relationships with all agents for modifications, negotiations, continuations, renewals, and expirations; and (5) fairly discloses reliable, relevant, and useful financial information in order

Exhibit 2.4. Public Companies' Interactions with Their Stakeholders

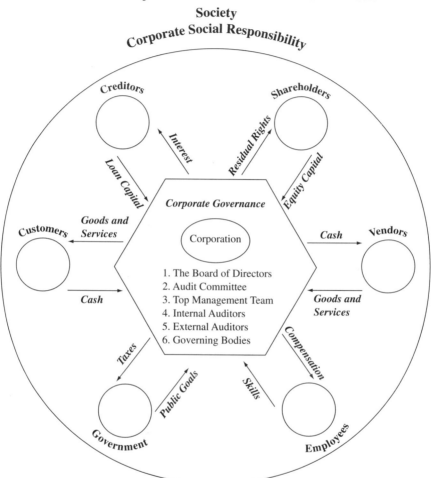

for contracting participants to make prudent economic decisions. Thus, one of the fundamental responsibilities of corporate governance is the accountability to contracting participants for fair presentation of financial statements to all agents, especially investors and creditors, who provide capital to the corporation. In the situations when a right combination of motivations, opportunities, and rationalization is present, corporations may benefit by misleading agents through engaging in financial statement fraud. This book primarily focuses on the financial reporting responsibility and accountability of corporate governance in preventing and detecting financial statement fraud.

Publicly traded corporations, by virtue of obtaining their capital from investors and creditors who are distant from their operations, place new demands on corporate governance. A set of financial standards is promulgated for corporations to ensure that corporate governance protects investors' and creditors' investment interests. The SEC is given authority by the U.S. Congress to issue accounting standards. The SEC has traditionally delegated this authority to the private sector standard-setting bodies (e.g., FASB). The accounting standards guide management and limit its discretion in measuring, recognizing, and disclosing the corporate economic events and transactions with contracting agents. In efficient and active capital markets, investors—both shareholders and bondholders—rely on the financial reporting process to provide them with useful, relevant, reliable information regarding financial conditions, results of operations, cash flows, and prospects of the company. The Internet-based technology mitigates both the asymmetry of information and the cost of obtaining information.

The U.S. capital market has fueled the longest economic growth and prosperity during the 1990s. More than one-third of the nation's wealth was invested in capital markets that had an aggregate value of $15 trillion, which was almost twice the gross national product.[10] More than 80 million investors nationwide have placed their trust and confidence in the capital markets, which are considered to be the most efficient, liquid, and resilient markets in the world. Lynn Turner, Chief Accountant at the SEC, stated that:

> The markets and their participants have gained investors' confidence through quality information and their trust through vigilant and active corporate governance. It is quality information that is the life-blood of markets: corporate governance that ensures the flow of that information is not severed.[11]

EXPECTATION GAP BETWEEN PREPARERS AND USERS OF FINANCIAL REPORTS

The American Institute of Certified Public Accountants (AICPA) Special Committee on Financial Reporting was established in 1991 to examine the needs of users of financial reports and to identify the types of financial information most useful and relevant for predicting future earnings and cash flows for financial decision making. The committee gathered a wide variety of documents and survey data regarding the relative priority users place on different kinds of financial information to determine potential improvements to the financial reporting process. The committee compiled its three years of findings in a comprehensive 1994 report entitled "Improving Business Reporting—A Customer Focus: Meeting the Information Needs of Investors and Creditors."[12] The committee made several recommendations for improving the usefulness and relevance of the types of information in business reporting and developed a comprehensive model of business reporting designed to be useful for decision making in assessing the risk of investments by users. The 10 fundamental elements of the committee's comprehensive model are as follows:

1. Four basic financial statements (e.g., balance sheet, income statement, statement of cash flows, statement of changes in owner's equity) and their related note disclosures
2. High-level operating data and performance measurements that management uses to manage the business
3. Management rationale and reasons for changes in financial, operating, and performance-related data, as well as the identity and past effect of key trends
4. A discussion of opportunities and risks, including those resulting from key trends
5. Management's plans, including critical success factors
6. Comparison of actual performance to previously disclosed opportunities, risks, and management plans
7. Information regarding directors, management, major shareholders, compensation, transactions, and relationships among related parties
8. Board objectives and strategies of the company
9. Scope and description of the business and properties
10. Effect of industry structure on the company

Anandarajan, Kleinman, and Palmon (2000) argue that there is an "expectations gap" between the needs of the users and the priorities of financial statement preparers.[13] Users of financial statements, particularly investors and creditors, do not receive the information they need to make prudent economic decisions. Anandarajan et al. (2000) discuss the following three factors that contribute to the perceived expectations gap: (1) deficiencies in the auditing and reporting standards; (2) lack of motivation to fully comply with these standards; and (3) lack of financial literacy, training, and cognitive limitations or preference of financial statement users.[14] These three factors, individually or collectively, can contribute to the perceived expectation gap between preparers and users of financial reports. For example, existing accounting and auditing standards have not addressed the degree of reliability of the Internet-based electronic financial statements and the extent of assurance provided by auditors regarding the fairness of electronic financial reports. Management may also be motivated to produce and disseminate inaccurate financial statements under pressure or in a needs environment.

PERCEIVED PROBLEMS OF CURRENT FINANCIAL REPORTING

In recent years, some concerns and criticisms have been expressed regarding the widening gap between the information needs of investors and creditors and information provided in the published financial statements. This gap has caused deteriorations in the quality of financial reports and a disconnect between financial information provided in these reports and the information needs of the capital market participants. In the emerging digital knowledge-based economy, financial statement users in general, and market participants in particular, need "(1) more disclosure of non-financial information; (2) more forward-looking information; and (3) more information about intangible assets."[15] The perceived problems in the existing financial reporting system that may provide both motivation and opportunity for financial statement fraud are discussed in the following pages (also see Anandarajan et al. 2000).[16]

Pressures to Manage Earnings

Publicly traded companies are pressured to report earnings that meet analysts' forecasts and expectations rather than focusing their efforts on continuously improving both quality and quantity of earnings, primarily because (1) missing the earnings expectations can cost a significant amount of dollars in the market capitalization, and (2) the top management team receives substantial bonuses based on earnings and stock prices. The high market capitalization and significant valuations of equity securities during the late 1990s have created pressures on management to achieve earnings estimates or other performance targets, typically determined by security analysts. The efficiency and competitiveness of the capital markets, in reflecting publicly available information into stock prices, have encouraged companies to achieve these targets by either continuously improving their performance and, thus, creating shareholder value or by attempting to make the numbers seem more positive and thus engaging in financial statement fraud. Nevertheless, missing those earnings forecasts or performance targets can cause considerable declines in market capitalization and, accordingly, reduced compensation for the top management team, whose incomes are typically tied into the earnings or stock price targets.

Schipper (1989) defines earnings management as "a purposeful intervention in the external financial reporting process with the intent of obtaining some private gain."[17] Top management teams may manipulate reported earnings using a broad range of both accounting and nonaccounting techniques (e.g., changing accounting methods, accounting estimates, timing, and method of revenue recognition). Healy (1985) concludes that earnings management using accruals is less costly with no disclosure requirement conforming to charges of accounting principles and estimates.[18]

Declining Quality of Corporate Earnings

High-quality annual financial statements start with reliable interim reporting. Thus, publicly traded companies should focus on the integrity, quality, and effectiveness of the interim financial reporting process. The 1999 Committee of Sponsoring Organizations (COSO) Report finds that financial statement fraud often begins with interim reporting because of the ineffectiveness of processes and internal controls surrounding the preparation of interim financial statements.[19] Earnings management practices have reduced the value relevance of reported earnings. Former chairperson of the SEC Arthur Levitt (1998) expressed concerns about the declining quality of corporate earnings, discussing financial issues such as earnings management, purchased research and development (R&D), writeoffs, and abuse of the materiality concept.[20]

Deficiencies in Reporting Certain Types of Information

A recent survey by the Association for Investment Management and Research (AIMR) indicates that most respondents (91 percent of buy-side and sell-side analysts) believed that published financial statements do not properly explain the implications of extraordinary, unusual, nonrecurring charges or disclose off-balance sheet assets or liabilities.[21] In the wake of Enron's collapse, financial regulators are considering new rules pertaining to accounting and reporting of financial instruments, derivatives and hedging activities, and comprehensive income. Lawmakers are considering new rules for energy derivatives accounting whereas the SEC is establishing new regulations to require more precise disclosures regarding publicly traded companies' accounting policies.[22] The additional disclosures are intended to provide relevant information regarding companies' condition and results.

Reporting Systems that Obfuscate Rather than Enlighten

Anandarajan et al. (2000) cited several studies that found that the current financial reporting process does more to obfuscate than enlighten, and the broader disclosure rules have not been adopted uniformly.[23] A survey conducted by Pricewaterhouse Coopers reveals that CEOs of technology companies believe that current financial reporting models do not serve their needs and result in lower stock prices for their companies.[24] The respondents (e.g., executives, analysts, investors) agreed that current reporting models do not properly measure and recognize the value of intangible assets. The emerging digital economy requires a value reporting model that properly measures the values of capital spending, R&D expenditures, brand value, market share, customer retention, intellectual capital, and other intangible assets not currently measured under the conventional financial reporting system.

Unsuitable Reporting Models

The global economy has transformed from an industry economy to a knowledge economy and now, with Internet-based technology, to a digital economy. Anandarajan et al. (2000) argue that the current financial models are more appropriate for a manufacturing economy than a knowledge or digital economy, primarily because they are based on historical cost.[25] Publicly traded corporations have become one of the most powerful forces shaping the global economy. Ownership of these companies has been depersonalized in the sense that they are not typically financed by only rich investors, but rather by average investors through their mutual and pension funds. Albrecht and Sack (2000) noted three fundamental drivers of change in the business environment.[26] First, Internet-based technological advances have made financial information preparation and dissemination inexpensive. These technologies have minimized many constraints to information, including time and space. Globalization is another major development that has significantly affected businesses worldwide, which has created an environment for global competition. The third fundamental change is the concentration of power in the large mutual and pension funds with unprecedented power over top executives of corporations.

Omission of Intangible Constructs

The current financial reporting problem is based on the historical cost that ignores intangible and nonfinancial measures. The globalization and technological advances have altered the ways corporations create shareholder value. Thus, accounting systems that are primarily based on tangible constructs are inadequate and ineffective in measuring, recognizing, and disclosing all business economic events that create shareholder value. The historical cost-based financial reporting process is out of date and unresponsive to the needs of users of financial reporting, especially investors and creditors. This historical model is oriented to tangible assets rather than the intangible assets that drive many of the values of today's digital economy and service and technology-based dot-com businesses. The Financial Accounting Standards Board (FASB) has recently (July 2000) issued two Statements of Financial Accounting Standards (SFAS) Nos. 141 and 142, "Business Combinations" and "Goodwill and Other Intangible Assets" respectively.[27, 28] The new SFAS require recognition of goodwill in business combination transactions and address financial and reporting for acquired goodwill and other intangible assets. The FASB issued these statements in response to the demand by investors, analysts, management, and users of financial statements for more relevant and reliable information about intangible assets. Intangible assets are no longer considered as "wasting assets." They are important economic resources for many organizations and are an increasing proportion of the assets acquired in many business transactions.

Predomination of Backward-Looking Information

Corporations have traditionally prepared and disseminated historical financial statements to investors and creditors for their prospective economic decision. The currently used historical financial reporting system by focusing on historical information and accrual earnings is not responsive to today's dynamic global business environment. The new financial reporting model should focus on presenting futuristic, relevant information on a continuous basis rather than historical information on a periodic basis. Thus, users of historical financial statements are forced to rely on other sources to learn about the company's prospects. Internet-based technologies enable the information systems to capture, analyze, and disseminate information in real-time and online. Investors and creditors can quickly and electronically access information. The discussion of the use of standardized electronic financial reporting under the extensible business reporting language (XBRL) format in improving the relevance, timeliness, and reliability of business and financial information is presented in Chapter 13.

Excessive and Improper Use of Financial Derivatives

Financial derivatives have grown rapidly during the past two decades primarily because of fundamental changes in global financial markets, advancements in computer technology, and fluctuations in interest and currency exchange rates. Derivatives have been used for a variety of purposes including risk management, financial schemes, tax planning, earnings, management, and speculation activities. However, the nature of risks associated with derivatives and how corporations use them are not well understood by many users of financial statements. The financial community and regulators are concerned with complexities, risks, lack of uniform accounting practices for derivatives and inadequate reporting of their fair values. The FASB, in its SFAS No. 133, addresses accounting and reporting standards for derivative instruments and hedging activities by requiring that entities recognize all derivatives as either assets or liabilities in their financial statements and measure them at fair value.[29] Nevertheless, the excessive and improper use of derivatives has lead to the creation of misleading and fraudulent financial statements. Derivatives are sophisticated financial instruments tied to the performance of underlying assets. Derivatives were excessively used by Enron Corporation which once was ranked as the nation's biggest trader of electricity and natural gas contracts and recently, in December 2001, filed for bankruptcy protection and caused a loss of about $80 billion in market capitalization. The collapse of Enron Corporation, the seventh biggest Fortune 500 company, demonstrates the need for proper regulations of the free-wheeling derivatives and over-the-counter tradings, as well as appropriate accounting and reporting of financial instruments, derivatives and hedging activities, and comprehensive income.

Generic Philosophy

To improve the relevance and usefulness of published financial statements, this assumption that a generic financial reporting format will satisfy all users should be changed. Thus, different formats should be produced to satisfy the needs of a wide variety of users. Because the primary purpose of corporations is to create shareholder value, the issue is whether the current financial reports reflect this shareholder value creation. Technological advances (e.g., the Internet) and globalization enable investors to capture, organize, and use information online and in real-time. Investors can quickly obtain both financial and nonfinancial information to make intelligent and prudent investment decisions. The emergence of an information knowledge economy undermines the relevance of the historical financial reporting process. It has been argued that the historical-cost financial reporting model is out of date and increasingly unresponsive to investors' needs for both financial and nonfinancial information. The current financial reporting model is better suited to a manufacturing economy than the emerging knowledge economy primarily because it is oriented to tangible assets rather than the intangible assets that drive many values of service- and technology-based businesses (e.g., dot-coms).

Perceived Lack of Proper Involvement of the Audit Process

Lack of audit effectiveness is perceived to be one of the fundamental reasons for auditors' inabilities to prevent financial statement fraud. The external auditors' role in preventing and detecting financial statement fraud has evolved during the past three decades in response to society's concern regarding high-profile incidents of fraudulent financial activities by publicly traded companies. Detection of fraud was the primary audit objective toward the beginning of the twentieth century. Since the middle of the twentieth century, determination of fairness of financial statements has gained prominence as an audit objective. The accounting profession position has been that an unqualified opinion should not be construed as a representation that financial statements are free of any errors or frauds. Users of financial statements, particularly investors and creditors, on the other hand, have typically assumed that detection of financial statement fraud has always been a primary objective of financial audits.

To narrow this perceived expectation gap, the AICPA has recently addressed auditors' responsibility for detecting fraud in its Statement on Auditing Standards (SAS) No. 82 entitled "Consideration of Fraud in a Financial Statement Audit."[30] SAS No. 82 and its implications in the financial reporting process are thoroughly examined in Chapter 11. The SEC has expressed concerns about auditors' ineffectiveness and failure to provide reasonable assurance that financial statements are not misleading. The 1999 COSO Report on fraudulent financial reporting made the following suggestions for auditors to improve their effectiveness in detecting financial statement fraud[31]:

- Challenge management to ensure that a baseline level of internal control is present.
- Monitor an organization's going-concern status, especially with new clients.
- Be aware of the possible complications arising from family relationships and from individuals holding significant power or incompatible job functions.
- Consider interim reviews of quarterly financial statements and the possible benefits of continuous auditing strategies.
- Consider and test internal controls related to transaction cutoff and asset valuation.
- Understand the risks unique to the client's industry and management's motivation toward aggressive reporting.

• Assess the substance and quality of client boards and be alert for boards dominated by insiders and others with strong ties to management of the company.

Types of Investors

Studies (Pava and Epstein, 1993; Anandarajan et al., 2000)[32, 33] argue that experienced investors rely more on financial statements than management discussion and analysis (MD&A), whereas unsophisticated investors rely highly on MD&A; however, selective information disclosed in the MD&A may not provide adequate and reliable information for investment decision making.

Technological advances and globalization have changed the way businesses operate. Thus, the financial reporting process should improve to ensure that global investors receive timely and relevant information about their investment in reflecting the true value of companies to their investors. To narrow this perceived gap between what the traditional financial reports can provide and the financial information needs of global investors in the emerging economy, Pricewaterhouse Coopers, one of the Big Five professional services firms, has developed the "Value Reporting" concept. Value Reporting is:

> A management framework that identifies, measures, and communicates the key business processes and assets, including intangibles, that underlie and derive corporate value and performance . . . [it presents] a comprehensive set of financial and other performance measures and processes, tailored to the company, that provides both historical and predictive indicators of shareholder value creation.[34]

Value Reporting provides a broad range of both financial and nonfinancial information, such as market share and growth, intellectual capital, recruitment and retention of essential personnel, and scope of directed knowledge management initiatives. By providing a broad range of performance data, both historical and projected, management is communicating to investors and other users of financial statements what the value drivers are and how they contribute to shareholder value creation. Value Reporting focuses on value creation and underlying business activities that are crucial to the company's ability to generate sustainable shareholder value.

Factors that are driving the attention toward Value Reporting are (1) changes in the global capital market (e.g., enhanced access to information, globalization, technological advances, growing interest in the concept of shareholder value, consolidation in the funds management industry); (2) changes in the internal focus of companies (e.g., greater focus on cash flow, the use of balanced scorecards for performance evaluation); and (3) recognition of inadequacies of the historical financial reporting system in providing timely and relevant information for decision making. Value Reporting, by focusing on providing relevant, transparent, timely, and credible financial and nonfinancial information, will continue to receive well-deserved attention from the business community and accounting profession as technologies and globalization continue to evolve.

CONCLUSION

This chapter presented the financial reporting process of publicly traded companies; examined the qualities and characteristics of useful, relevant, reliable, and transparent financial information; and suggested ways to improve the quality of financial reports. An effective corporate governance consisting of the board of directors, the audit committee, the top management team, internal auditors, external auditors, and governing bodies (e.g., SEC, AICPA) is responsible for producing and disseminating financial statements that are free of material misstatements caused by errors and fraud. Responsibilities and functions of each member of corporate governance in the context of financial information supply chain are thoroughly examined in Chapters 6 through 12.

ENDNOTES

1. National Commission on Fraudulent Financial Reporting. 1987. "Report of the National Commission on Financial Reporting (October). Available: www.coso.org/publications/NXFFR_Part_4.htm

2. Financial Accounting Standards Board. 1999. *Statements of Financial Accounting Concepts.* New York: John Wiley & Sons, Inc.

3. Financial Accounting Standards Board. 1990. *Statement of Financial Accounting Concepts No. 2: Qualitative Characteristics of Accounting Information.* New York: John Wiley & Sons.

4. Public Oversight Board. 1999. *Report and Recommendations of the Blue Ribbon Committee on Improving the Effectiveness of Corporate Audit Committees.* Stamford, CT: POB.

5. Public Oversight Board. 1994. *Strengthening the Professionalism of the Independent Auditors* (The Kirk Panel) Stamford, CT: POB.

6. Detailed and important information about EDGAR is available online at www.sec.gov/edaux/wedgar.htm

7. Levitt, A. 1998. SEC Chairperson from the speech given at New York University, "The Numbers Game". NYU Center for Law and Business. (September 28, 1998).

8. Bamber, E. M. and R. Stratton. 1997. "The Information Content of the Uncertainty-Modified Audit Report: Evidence from Bank Loan Officers". *Accounting Horizons* (June): 1–11.

9. Sunder, S. 1977. *Theory of Accounting and Control.* Cincinnati: Southwest College Publishing.

10. Turner, L. E. 2000. "Accounting Irregularities II: What's an Audit Committee to Do?" Speech by Chief Accountant of U.S. Securities and Exchange Commission, New York, NY. (October). Available: www.sec.org/news/speeches/spch414.htm

11. Ibid.

12. American Institute of Certified Public Accountants. 1994. "Improving the Business Reporting-A Customer Focus: Meeting the Information Needs of Investors and Creditors". AICPA Financial Reporting Special Committee. New York.

13. Anandarajan, A., G. Kleinman, and D. Palmon. 2000. "Investors' Expectations and the Corporate Information Disclosure Gap: A Perspective". *Research in Accounting Regulation* (Vol. 14): 246–260.

14. Ibid.

15. Upton, Wayne S., Jr. 2001. "Financial Accounting Series, Special Report: Business and Financial Reporting, Challenges from the New Economy". *Financial Accounting Standards Board* (No. 219-A, April).

16. Anandarajan, A., G. Kleinman, and D. Pulmon. 2000. "Investors' Expectations and the Corporate Information Disclosure Gap: A Perspective". *Research in Accounting Regulation* (Vol. 14): 246–260.

17. Schipper, K. 1989. "Commentary on Earnings Management". *Accounting Horizons* (3): 91–102.

18. Healy, P. 1985. "The Effect of Bonus Schemes on Accounting Decisions". *Journal of Accountancy and Economics* (Vol. 7): 85–107.

19. Beasley, M. S., J. V. Carcello, and D. R. Hermanson. 1999. Fraudulent Financial Reporting. 1987–1997: An Analysis of U.S. Public Companies. Research Report Commissioned by The Committee of Sponsoring Organizations of the Treadway Commission (COSO) Jersey City, NJ: AICPA.

20. Levitt, A. 1998. SEC Chairperson from the speech given at New York University, "The Numbers Game". NYU Center for Law and Business. (September 28, 1998).

21. Anonymous. 2000. "Corporate Reporting: IROs Criticized by Analysts". Investor Relations Business (February): 1, 8.

22. Schroeder, M and G Ip. 2001. The Enron Debacle Spotlights Huge Void in Financial Regulation. *The Wall Street Journal* (December 13): A1.

23. Anandarajan, A., G. Kleinman, and D. Pulmon. 2000. "Investors' Expectations and the Corporate Information Disclosure Gap: A Perspective". *Research in Accounting Regulation* (Vol. 14): 246–260.

24. Pricewaterhouse Coopers. 2000. "High Tech CEOs Say Current Financial Reports Undervalue Their Companies". Available: http://www.pwcglobal.com/extweb/nepressrelease

25. Anandarajan, A., G. Kleinman, and D. Pulmon. 2000. "Investors' Expectations and the Corporate Information Disclosure Gap: A Perspective". *Research in Accounting Regulation* (Vol. 14): 246–260.

26. Albrecht, Steve W., and Robert J. Sack. 2000. "Accounting Education: Charting the Course Through a Perilous Future". *Accounting Education Services* (August, No. 16).

27. Financial Accounting Standards Board (FASB). 2001. Statement of Financial Accounting Standards (SFAS) No. 141. *Business Combinations*. (FASB, Norwalk, Connecticut, July).

28. Financial Accounting Standards Board (FASB). 2001. Statement of Financial Accounting Standards (SFAS) No. 142. *Goodwill and Other Intangible Assets*. (FASB, Norwalk, Connecticut, July).

29. Financial Accounting Standards Board (FASB). 1998. Statement of Financial Accounting Standards (SFAS) No. 133. Accounting for Derivative Instruments and Hedging Activities. (FASB, Norwalk, Connecticut, June).

30. American Institute of Certified Public Accountants. 1997. Consideration of Fraud in a Financial Audit. SAS No. 82. New York: AICPA.

31. Beasley, M. S., J. V. Carcello, and D. R. Hermanson. 1999. Fraudulent Financial Reporting. 1987–1997: An Analysis of U.S. Public Companies. Research Report Commissioned by The Committee of Sponsoring Organizations of the Treadway Commission (COSO) Jersey City, NJ: AICPA.

32. Pava, M. C., and M. J. Epstein. 1993. "How Good is MD&A as an Investment Tool?" *Journal of Accountancy,* (175C3): 51–53.

33. Anandarajan, A., G. Kleinman, and D. Pulmon. 2000. "Investors' Expectations and the Corporate Information Disclosure Gap: A Perspective". *Research in Accounting Regulation* (Vol. 14): 246–260.

34. Pricewaterhouse Coopers, 2000. "Issues and Trends: Value Reporting." Available: www.pwcglobal.com.

Chapter 3

Cooking the Books Equals Fraud

INTRODUCTION

Market participants, including investors and creditors, expect vigilant and active corporate governance to ensure the integrity and quality of financial information. Financial statement fraud has received considerable attention from the public, press, investors, the financial community, and the Securities and Exchange Commission (SEC) because of high-profile, widespread fraud at big companies such as Lucent, Xerox, Rite Aid, Cendant, Sunbeam, Waste Management, and Enron Corp. Top management teams of these and other corporations were convicted of cooking the books and, in many cases, sentenced to jail terms. This chapter presents profiles of several companies alleged by the SEC of engaging in financial statement fraud; reviews these alleged financial statement fraud cases; and demonstrates that cooking the books causes financial statement fraud, which results in a crime.

FINANCIAL STATEMENT FRAUD

Financial statement fraud as defined in Chapter 1 is a deliberate attempt by corporations to deceive or mislead users of published financial statements, especially investors and creditors, by preparing and disseminating materially misstated financial statements. The focus is on intentional deception of users of financial reports through the preparation of unreliable financial statements. Motives and opportunities for producing fraudulent financial statements are contributing factors for the occurrence of financial statement fraud. The motivation for perpetration of financial statement fraud can be associated with the need to raise additional capital and ownership pressures. The opportunity to disseminate financial statement fraud can be related to ineffective and irresponsible corporate governance, sometimes caused by a large percentage of insiders on the board of directors and the audit committee.

Corporations may attempt to deceive users of financial reports when they are predisposed to fraudulent financial activities. A corporation is more apt to engage in fraudulent financial reporting when it has a strong motive to do so, because of economic and ownership pressures, and when its inadequate and ineffective corporate governance structure neither protects nor detects financial statement fraud.

Why Does Financial Statement Fraud Occur?

Financial statement fraud occurs for a wide variety of reasons, including when the existence of motives combines with the opportunity because of lack of responsible corporate governance and auditors' resistance toward requirements to perform fraud-detecting audit procedures as part of every financial statement audit.

The earnings numbers play an important role in efficiency of the capital markets by providing relevant and useful information regarding a firm's future prospects to investors. Empirical studies support the contention that reported earnings reflect value-relevant information. Corporations' strategies to meet or exceed analysts' earnings forecasts pressure management to achieve earnings targets. Management is motivated or, in most cases, rewarded when its bonus is tied into reported earnings to choose accounting principles that may result in misrepresentation of earnings.

Financial statement fraud may serve many purposes, including (1) obtaining credit, long-term financing, or additional capital investment based on misleading financial statements; (2) maintaining or creating favorable stock value; (3) concealing deficiencies in performance; (4) hiding improper business transactions (e.g., fictitious sales or misrepresented assets); and (5) resolving temporarily financial difficulties (e.g., insufficient cash flow, unfavorable business decisions, defense control in maintaining prestige). Management may also engage in financial statement fraud to obtain personal benefits of (1) increasing compensation through higher reported earnings; (2) enhancing value of personal holding of company stock such as stock-based compensation; (3) converting the company's assets for personal use; and (4) obtaining a promotion or maintaining the current position within the company.

Upper Echelons: A Corporation is a Reflection of Its Top Management Team

A fundamental question addressed in this book is, why do publicly traded companies engage in financial statement fraud? Ample anecdotal and empirical evidence indicates that corporate performance, including strategies, effectiveness, and ethical values, are reflections of values and cognitive bases of its top management team.[1] Top management team characteristics are classified into two broad categories of (1) *psychological cognitive base values* including ethical behavior, risk preference, and operating style; and (2) *observable characteristics* such as age, functional tracks, managerial experience, educational background, socioeconomic roots, group characteristics, and financial position.

Sensitivity of the stock market to earnings forecasts has encouraged management to avoid missing earnings expectations. Wall Street has traditionally hammered the stock when earnings expectations are not met; however, an efficient stock market should be affected in the longer term when corporations constantly dress up the current results using earnings management. The true earnings quality is driven by economic, value-added earnings performance. To improve the quality of earnings, some publicity traded companies employ managerial strategies and accounting standards choices that balance the short-term with the long-term prospects of their companies. Companies are more likely to engage in financial statement fraud when the selected accounting scheme is considered to be within a set of acceptable accounting alternatives; there is a strong motive to commit fraud; and the opportunity is available to actually issue fraudulent financial statements. The motive and opportunity may not play an important role if the fraud scheme is not viewed as an acceptable alternative.

PROFILE OF FINANCIAL STATEMENT FRAUD

Exhibit 3.1 summarizes a sample of the most recent high-profile financial statement fraud cases. The review of these cases underscores the importance of responsible corporate governance in preventing and detecting financial statement fraud. Review of these cases determines that five interactive factors explain these high-profile financial statement frauds. These interactive factors are cooks, recipes, incentives, monitoring, and end results, with the abbreviation of CRIME. The right combination of these factors is a prerequisite for engaging in financial statement fraud.

Cooks

The first letter in the word "Crime" is "C," which stands for "Cooks." Financial statement fraud cases presented in Exhibit 3.1 and the results of the 1999 COSO Report reveal that in most cases (more than 80 percent), the CEOs and/or CFO were associated with financial statement fraud.[2] Almost all financial statement frauds occur with participation, encouragement, approval, and knowledge of top management teams, including CEOs, CFOs, presidents, treasurers, and controllers. Other individuals typically involved with financial statement fraud are controllers, chief operation officers, board of director members, other senior vice presidents, and internal and external auditors.

Financial statement fraud has become the focus of public attention in recent years because of corporate wrongdoing in almost all industrial sectors. A consensus may be emerging that financial statement fraud is more often the result of actions or inactions, deliberate or inadvertent, by the top management team of publicly traded companies. This has been used as a basis and rationale for holding company officials personally responsible for occurrences of financial statement fraud, liable for resulting losses, and subject to fines as well as potential incarceration.

The 1999 COSO Report states that the top management team was involved in most of the studied cases. The CEO was involved in 72 percent of the cases, while the CFO was engaged in 63 percent, and the controller was named in more than

Exhibit 3.1. Sample of Financial Statement Fraud Cases

Company	Cooks	Recipe	Detection	Consequences
Cendant Corporation	Three former top executives	Earnings management by overstating revenue by $500 million between 1995 and 1997 through: 1. Fictitious revenues recorded for several years 2. Inappropriate recording of depreciation 3. Recognition of unrealized revenue	Current management after the integration of CUC International and Parsippany and dismissed external auditors	1. Possible prison time for top executives and fines. 2. More than $14 billion in market value disappeared. 3. $2.83 billion settlement of a shareholder lawsuit. 4. Ernst & Young accounting firm was sued by the new management. 5. Stock plummeted about 60 percent. 6. Cost more than $15 billion in market capitalization.
HBO & Company	Two former top executives, co-President and co-chief operating officers	Earnings management by inflating earnings by hundreds of millions of dollars from 1997 through March 1999.	Fraud was discovered by external auditors of combined McKesson HBO Company four months after McKesson Corporation merged with HBO & Company.	1. Share prices fell almost 50 percent in one day (from $65 to $32). 2. Possible 10 years of jail time and a $1 million fine for two former top executives. 3. Caused dozens of class action lawsuits against the company alleging securities fraud in the way sales were reported.

(continues)

Exhibit 3.1. (*Continued*)

Company	Cooks	Recipe	Detection	Consequences
Sunbeam Corporation	Chairman and Chief Executive Officer and four other former executives	Earnings management by creating recorded revenue on contingent sales; accelerating sales from later periods into the present quarter; and using improper bill-and-hold transactions.	Media reports questioned the company's performance and restructuring strategies.	1. Public investors who bought and held Sunbeam's stock in anticipation of a true turnaround lost billions of dollars. 2. Civil penalties and permanent bar of accused executives to become officers or directors of any public company. 3. Independent auditor Arthur Andersen paid $110 million to settle claims but did not admit fault or liability.
W.R. Grace & Company (chemical company)	Chief Financial Officer	Earnings Management: A reserve account was used to accumulate excess growing earnings to smooth declining earnings in subsequent years.	A whistle blower, the fired former in-house audit chief	The use of reserves account for earnings management was investigated by both internal and external auditors (PriceWaterhouse Coopers) without proper actions being taken.
Enron Corporation	Chairman, CEO, CFO	Overstating earnings, understating debt, and overstating equity through (1) creation of Special Purpose Entities (SPE); (2) issuance of common stock to those entities in exchange for notes receivable; and (3) inadequate disclosure of off-balance-sheet transactions (derivatives) and related financial activities	Media reports questioned the company's performance after departure of its chief executive officer and examination of its financial vehicles by federal regulators	1. Lawsuits by investors and employees 2. Filed Chapter 11 Bankruptcy Protection. 3. Loss of more than $80 billion in market capitalization. 4. Lawsuits against its auditor.

Company	Perpetrators	Accounting Issue	Discovery	Outcomes
Digital Lightwave, Inc.	Founder and majority stockholder former chief executive	Recognition of revenue based on fraudulent billings or transactions that were not completed or contained contingencies.	SEC enforcement officers	1. Resignation of the founder. 2. Restatement of previous years earnings. 3. Settlement of the case with shareholder by paying $4.24 million in cash and $1.8 million shares. 4. Stock fell by about 20 percent
MicroStrategy, Inc.	Three top executives including former chief financial officer	Overstatement of past revenues by capitalizing anticipated revenues from long-term software contracts.	Questioning the timing of MicroStrategy's revenue recognition by *Forbes* magazine	1. Restatement of past financial results. 2. MicroStrategy stock lost 92.4 percent of its value.
KnowledgeWare	Top management team including chief executives and six other executives	Materially inflated the reported earnings by engaging in a phony $356,500 software sale.	Shareholders' lawsuits and complaints	1. Chief executive paid $100,000 fine and disgorged $54,187 in incentive compensation. 2. The company was acquired at about one-half of its previously agreed share price.
Informix Corporation	Top management team and former auditors	Faking $2.95 million in revenue by backdating contracts, booking income, and unsold products.	An employee notified auditors and auditors recommended an investigation.	1. Auditors Ernst & Young settled dozens of securities fraud lawsuits for $142 million. 2. Agreed not to violate certain securities laws. 3. Cooperated with the SEC's investigation of former Informix officers.

(continues)

Exhibit 3.1. (*Continued*)

Company	Cooks	Recipe	Detection	Consequences
American Banknote Corporation (ABN)	Senior officers and directors, Chairman of the Board and CEO, director of ABN, executive vice president and general manager of ABNH, Corporate Controller	Systematic fraudulent scheme to inflate the revenues and net income of ABN Holographics, Inc. and its publicly held parent, ABN, to meet earnings forecasts and to condition the market for an initial public offering of stock by ABNH.	SEC enforcement actions	The SEC filed suit in the United States district court against current and former senior officers and directors of ABN and/or ABNH for violations of the antifraud, periodic reporting, record keeping, internal control, and lying to auditors provisions of the federal securities law. ABNH has consented to pay a $75,000 civil penalty for its violation.
Livent, Inc.	Nine former senior officers, directors, and members of the accounting staff Former Big-Five engagement partner	Engaged in a multifaceted and pervasive accounting fraud spanning eight years from 1990 through 1998. Improper revenue recognition, the failure to record, or the improper deferral and capitalization of expenses, overstating revenues by more than $59 million.	SEC enforcement actions	1. Livent, Inc. filed for Chapter 11 bankruptcy protection in U.S. bankruptcy court. 2. Barred directors and officers from serving as officers or directors of a public company.

			SEC enforcement actions	1. Violation of Rule 10-5(b) of the Securities Act of 1934

Company	Parties	Allegations		Actions
Aurora Foods, Inc.	Chief financial officer (CFO), Chief Executive Officer (CEO), other employees including senior financial analysts, manager of customer financial services	Overstating reported earnings and understating trade marketing expenses by more than $43 million by making inadequate or no accruals for already incurred trade marketing expenses.	SEC enforcement actions	1. Violation of Rule 10-5(b) of the Securities Act of 1934 2. Repayment of bonuses of the executives based on overstated earnings. 3. Barring the executives from serving as officers or directors of a public company. 4. Civil penalties for involved individuals ranging from $10,000 to $20,000. 5. Substantial reduction in price of stock from 4.4 per share to 2.50 per share.
Premier Laser Systems, Inc.	Executive Vice President, CFO	Overstating quarterly revenue by more than a third of its Form 10-Q by recognizing $2.4 million in revenue from purported sales of dental lasers to an entity that did not place an order.	SEC Enforcement Actions	1. Enforcement actions by the SEC. 2. Former CFO agreed to the entry of a permanent injunction and a $10,000 penalty. 3. Substantial reductions in share prices and eventually filed for Chapter 11 protection in March of 2000.

(continues)

Exhibit 3.1. (*Continued*)

Company	Cooks	Recipe	Detection	Consequences
Cyliok Corporation	Several executives in top management team including chief financial officer, vice president of sales	Improper revenue recognition of (1) transactions where the customer could cancel the order; (2) on orders from a distributor who was not credit worthy; and (3) contingent sales. More than 95 overstatements of revenue in 1998.	External auditors	1. A permanent injunction, disgorgement of each defendant's quarterly bonus and a civil penalty. 2. Substantial decline in stock price.
Computone Corporation	President and Chief Executive Officer, Controller and Chief Financial Officer, Vice President of Finance and Principal Accounting Officer, Vice President of International Sales, Vice President of Sales	Overstatement of revenue by recognizing revenue from orders that customers never placed, products that were not shipped to customers, shipments that were sent before customer's delivery date.	SEC enforcement actions	1. Executives barred from acting as an officer or director of a public company. 2. Pay penalties. 3. Stock prices plummeted from $7 per share to $2 per share.
Cylink	Chief Executive Officer (CEO), Chief Financial Officer (CFO), and other managerial employees	1. Recognition of revenues on orders where the customer had the right to return. 2. Shipment of orders to warehouse at the end of fiscal year and recognizing invoices as current assets. 3. Overstated revenue by 97 percent.	External auditors	1. Agreed to cease and desist orders. 2. Removal of involved individuals from their positions. 3. Stock price dropped from $23 per share to $1.56 per share.

Company	Positions	Description	Action Type	Consequences
Sirena Apparel Group, Inc.	Chief Executive Officer (CEO) and Chief Financial Officer (CFO)	Overstatement of the company's revenue through improper sales cutoffs for the quarter.	SEC enforcement actions	1. Consenting to a permanent injunction. 2. Paying a civil penalty of $30,000. 3. Barring from serving as an officer or director of a public company.
Craig Consumer Electronics	Chief Executive Officer (CEO) and Chief Financial Officer (CFO)	1. Inflate the accounts receivable by delaying the process of the sales returns. 2. Inflate inventory level used to secure a line of credit. 3. Overstatement of earnings.	SEC enforcement actions	1. Consenting to a permanent injunction. 2. Paying a civil penalty in the amount of $25,000. 3. Barring from serving as an officer or director for a period of five years.
First Merchants	President and CEO, Vice President of Strategic Planning, and CFO	1. Improperly accounted for delinquent and nonperforming loans to manipulate their allowance for credit losses. 2. Alteration of more than 7,000 customer accounts to make them appear current. 3. Overstatement of earnings and understatement of allowance for credit losses	SEC enforcement actions	1. A cease-and-desist order against top executives. 2. The company filed for Chapter 11 bankruptcy.
Raintree Healthcare Corporation	The President, CEO, CFO, and Controller	1. Overstatement of Medicare revenue to meet analysts' estimates. 2. Understating expenses.	External auditors	1. Stock fell more than 40 percent. 2. Filed Chapter 11 bankruptcy. 3. A permanent injunction. 4. A cease-and-desist order.

Exhibit 3.2.   Individuals Involved in Fraud Cases

Individuals	Studied Fraud Cases (%)
Chief Executive Officer (CEO)	72
Chief Financial Officer (CFO)	43
CEO and/or CFO	83
Controller	21
Chief Operating Officer	7
Other Vice President Positions	18
Board of Directors (Nonmanagement)	11
Lower-Level Personnel	10
Outsiders (e.g., Auditors, Customers)	38

Source: Beasley, M.S., J.V. Carcello, and D.R. Hermanson. 1999. *Fraudulent Financial Reporting: 1987–1997, An Analysis of U.S. Public Companies.* New York, NY: COSO.

21 percent. Exhibit 3.2 shows the list of individuals associated with the companies alleged for financial statement fraud. Cooks in these fraud cases, especially top executives (e.g., CEO, CFO), exerted excessive power resulting from weak and ineffective boards of directors and audit committee governance. Most of the studied fraud cases revealed that the company's board of directors was dominated by insiders and other directors with strong ties to management, and about 25 percent of companies did not even have an audit committee. Ineffective corporate governance creates an environment that increases the opportunity for the top management team to engage in manipulation activities and perpetrate financial statement fraud. Financial statement fraud is typically perpetrated by top executives and/or with their knowledge as shown in Exhibit 3.2.

Recipes

The second letter in the word "Crime" is "R," which stands for Recipes. Financial statement fraud can be committed in a variety of ways, ranging from most frequently occurring such as revenue frauds to least commonly occurring such as accounts payable frauds. Auditors would be expected to detect the most frequent methods of financial statement frauds in that they should know more about and be better at detecting common fraud schemes. Earnings management was the most common method of engaging in financial statement fraud. Financial statement fraud can also vary from direct falsification of transactions and events to intentional delay (early) recognition of transactions or events that eventually occur. An example of the former is intentional overstatement of sales by creating phony invoices, whereas the latter would be intentionally overstating sales using legitimate shipments that were recorded after the end of the reporting period. Fictitious transaction frauds are often considered more aggressive methods of fraud schemes that occur more frequently and draw more attention from auditors and regulators than intentional early (delayed) recognition of transactions. Premature recognition of transactions and events that eventually occur is considered less fraudulent than fictitious transaction schemes.

Certain types of financial statement fraud make it easier for a plaintiff's attorney to argue and convince judges and juries that the auditor should be held responsible for discovering the fraud. The frequently and commonly occurring frauds and fictitious transaction frauds typically result in a higher likelihood of auditor litigation, primarily because judges and juries expect the prudent and professional auditor to detect these types of frauds. Thus, an auditor who does not detect these frauds would be more likely to be charged for negligence and the resulting failure to detect the fraud. Several studies examine independent auditors' association with financial statement fraud. Bonner, Palmrose, and Young (1998) investigated whether certain types of financial reporting fraud result in a higher probability of litigation against independent auditors.[3] Bonner et al. (1998) concluded that auditors are more likely to be sued when the frauds are of a common variety or when the frauds stem from fictitious transactions.

The fraud cases presented in Exhibit 3.1 and the findings of the 1999 COSO Report on Fraudulent Financial Reporting indicate that most financial statement fraud (about 90 percent) involved the manipulation, alteration, and falsification of reported financial information, with a small percentage (almost 10 percent) involving misappropriation of assets. Fraud schemes are many and often involve more than one technique to misstate financial statements. Most misstatements or financial statement frauds are caused by overstating of revenues and assets, whereas about 20 percent involved understatements of liabilities and expenses. The 1999 COSO Report reveals that more than half of the alleged fraud cases were perpetrated through overstating revenues by recording revenues prematurely or fictitiously. Fraudulent revenue schemes often used by companies are (1) bill and hold sales transactions; (2) side agreements revenue transaction; (3) conditional sales; (4) improper recognition of consignment sales as completed sales; (5) unauthorized shipments; and (6) illegitimate cutoff of sales transactions at the end of the reporting period. These and other sham transactions are thoroughly examined in Chapter 5. Recipes of financial statement fraud can range from overstating revenues and assets to understating liabilities and expenses, which typically began with misstatement of interim financial statements and continued into annual financial statements.

Incentives

The third letter in the word "Crime" is "I," that stands for "INCENTIVES" and explains the most common motivations for companies and their cooks to perpetrate financial statement fraud. Economic incentives are typical in financial statement fraud cases, even though other motives such as psychotic, egocentric, or ideological motives can play a role in financial statement fraud. Economic pressure and the incentives to meet Wall Street forecasts are the fundamental motives for publicly traded companies to engage in financial statement fraud.

Financial statement frauds are typically committed for a broad variety of reasons and are motivated by many factors. Prior research (e.g., Robertson, 2000) has identified the following reasons as the primary motivations for financial statement fraud[4]:

- Meet company goals and objectives.
- Show compliance with financing covenants.
- Receive performance-related bonuses.
- Obtain new financing or more favorable terms on existing financing.
- Attract investment through the sale of stock.
- Disclose unrealistic increased earnings per share.
- Dispel negative market perception.

Psychotic motivation is viewed as the "habitual criminal" and is not common to financial statement fraud. Those in corporate governance positions are significantly scrutinized for their behaviors (e.g., management, top executives, auditors). Egocentric motivations are any pressures to fraudulently achieve more personal prestige. This type of motive can be seen in those people with aggressive behavior who desire to achieve higher functional authority in the corporation. Ideological motivations encourage individuals to think their behavior or cause is morally superior and can be seen in aggressive top executives who attempt to be market leaders or improve their market position in the industry. The economic motive of meeting analysts' forecasts and making Wall Street happy, coupled with egocentric and ideological motives, are the primary causes of financial statement fraud.

Incentives provide motivation to engage in financial statement fraud. Agency theory suggests that the presence of conflicts of interest between the top management team and shareholders as well as creditors adversely affects the quality and integrity of the financial reporting process and increases the probability of financial statement fraud. Empirical studies (e.g., Latham and Jacob, 2000; Carter and Stover, 1991)[5, 6] identify two fundamental variables of management stock ownership and proximity to debt covenant limits that affect management's propensity to engage in financial statement fraud. These studies suggest goal congruence between management and shareholders in the 0 to 5 percent and in the above 25 percent ranges of management stock ownership; however, in the range of 5 to 25 percent, the opportunistic behavior by management is anticipated, and thus the probability of financial statement fraud increases.

Empirical studies (Latham and Jacobs, 2000; Dechow et al., 1996)[7, 8] find a positive retention between closeness of debt covenant limits measured by a high debt/equity ratio and a management decision to manipulate earnings and thus, creating an environmental trait that increases the probability of financial statement fraud. Management will be pressured not to violate debt covenants. Thus, the closeness of debt covenant limits can create incentives for the top management team to cook the books. Prior studies (Lys and Watts, 1994; Carcello and Palmrose, 1994)[9, 10] also examined financial distress measured in terms of weak financial condition and poor financial performance as an incentive mechanism. These studies conclude that incentives to engage in financial statement fraud by providing misleading financial information increase when the firm is in financial distress. Thus, as the company's financial condition and performance deteriorate, the probability of financial statement fraud increases.

The most recent financial statement fraud cases summarized in Exhibit 3.1 and the results of the 1999 COSO Report on Fraudulent Financial Reporting show the following reasons for companies and their cooks (fraudsters) to engage in financial statement fraud: (1) avoid reporting a pretax loss and to exaggerate financial performance; (2) meet or exceed security analysts' expectations of earnings' growth; (3) increase the stock price and create demand for issuing new shares; (4) obtain national stock exchange listing status or meet minimum exchange listing requirements to prevent being delisted; and (5) cover up assets misappropriated for personal use.

Monitoring

The fourth letter in the word "Crime" is "M," which stands for Monitoring. Responsible corporate governance that sets the "tone at the top" by demanding high-quality financial reporting and not tolerating misstated financial statements is the most important proactive monitoring mechanism for preventing and detecting financial statement fraud. The second most important monitoring mechanism is the presence of inadequate and effective internal control structure. Although management is primarily responsible for designing and maintaining internal controls, the audit committee, internal auditors, and external auditors should ensure that internal controls are adequate and effective in preventing, detecting, and correcting financial statement fraud and leave no room for management to override control activities. This brings to the monitoring mechanism the important role that the audit committee can play in overseeing the integrity and quality of the financial reporting process and the effectiveness of the internal control structure. Companies should view the audit committee as a value-added oversight function and not merely a window dressing position to satisfy the new requirements of the SEC, NYSE, and NASD for audit committees.

The importance of effective internal and external audit functions in preventing and detecting financial statement fraud is supported in the literature and authoritative standards and reports. Internal auditors are viewed as the first defensive line against financial statement fraud. External auditors have traditionally been held accountable for detecting financial statement fraud. Companies should hire tough external auditors who help them prevent and detect financial statement fraud rather than those that rubber stamp management assertions to collect fees for audit and other consulting services. The financial reporting process of publicly traded companies includes a monitoring mechanism. The monitoring mechanism consists of direct oversight function of the board of directors, the audit committee, external auditors, and regulatory agencies; and indirect oversight function by those who follow the company in the role of owner/investor as an intermediary such as analysts, institutional investors, and investment bankers.

Monitoring can create an environment that reduces the likelihood of financial statement fraud. For example, an adequate and effective financial reporting process and related internal control structure or the existence of vigilant corporate governance can reduce the likelihood of financial statement fraud. Publicly traded companies are required to issue their financial statements in accordance with GAAP and have the financial statements audited by an independent auditor. The independent audit of financial statements lends more credibility, objectivity, and dependability to the published financial statements. Companies' primary goal is to create and increase shareholder value by meeting analysts' forecasts regarding earnings performance. Companies with strong financial statements and favorable earnings performance have less financial stress in achieving their goal of creating shareholder value; however, companies with financial stress and an aggressive strategy of exceeding analysts' and investors' expectations have more incentives to avoid complying with GAAP requirements when such compliance results in the issuance of less favorable financial position and performance. Thus, financial statement fraud is more likely to occur when a company has a strong motive and economic reason to report a more favorable financial performance and position than otherwise would be reported by complying with GAAP requirements. The company's decision to engage in fraudulent financial reporting activities is further motivated by the extent and magnitude of owner-managers' ownership arrangements.

Publicly traded companies are required by the SEC (Rule 1316 of the 1934 Act) to issue audited financial statements in conformity with GAAP. Companies are also required to establish responsible corporate governance to monitor the effectiveness of their operations and to ensure the issuance of reliable financial statements. Companies that engage in financial statement fraud can neutralize the effectiveness of their corporate governance by having unitary leadership for their board of directors; establishing ineffective audit committees consisting of inside and gray directors who do not meet often; and using ineffective audit functions.

The opportunity to engage in financial statement fraud increases when a company is not ethically and structurally determined to comply with GAAP requirements and when there is no responsible and effective corporate governance to prevent and detect fraudulent financial reporting activities. Opportunities to commit financial statement fraud typically arise from a lack of responsible corporate governance with no vigilant oversight functions. Examples of opportunities for financial statement fraud are as follows:

- Lack of vigilant oversight by the board of directors and/or audit committee
- Inadequate and ineffective internal control structure
- Nonexistence of internal audit function and/or ineffective internal audit function

- Lack of due diligence external audits
- Unusual or complex transactions
- Financial estimates requiring substantial discretion or subjective judgment by management

The extent of monitoring of the financial reporting process should be negatively correlated with the probability of occurrence of financial statement fraud. The board of directors and its representative audit committees are responsible for overseeing the integrity and quality of the financial reporting process in providing reliable, relevant, and useful financial statements. O'Brien and Bhushan (1990)[11] find a significant positive relationship between firm size, analyst following, and institutional ownership. The extent of monitoring—either direct (corporate governance) or indirect (analysts)—and greater numbers of individuals following a company and collecting information about a company can create an environment that permits no error, irregularities, and fraud (Latham and Jacobs, 2000). The greater institutional and analyst following could also be viewed as increasing the likelihood of detection of financial statement fraud.

Quality of monitoring by the board of directors, audit committees, auditors, institutional investors, and financial analysts can have a significant impact on the probability of prevention and detection of financial statement fraud. Prior research (e.g., Deis and Giroux, 1992; Latham, Jacobs, and Rough, 1998; Palmrose, 1987)[12–14] found a positive association between auditor brand name (Big Five versus non-Big Five) and the perception of audit quality and the probability of detecting financial statement fraud. The perception is that Big Five professional services firms are more likely to detect financial statement fraud than non-Big Five firms because they have (1) greater ability to withstand client pressure; (2) greater concern for their reputation; (3) better resources, both competent personnel and advanced technology; and (4) a more appropriate audit strategy and process. Thus, the presence of responsible corporate governance could create an environment that permits fewer errors, irregularities, and/or financial statement fraud.

End Results

The last letter in the word "Crime" is "E," which stands for "End Results." The summary of financial statement fraud cases presented in Exhibit 3.1 and findings of the 1999 COSO Report on Fraudulent Financial Reporting indicate that the consequences associated with financial statement fraud can be severe. Adversarial consequences typically range from filing for Chapter 11 bankruptcy (36 percent of alleged fraud) to changing owners (15 percent), delisting by the national stock exchange (21 percent), and substantial decline in stock value (58 percent). Top executives involved in "cooking the books" often suffer personal consequences of (1) losing the value of their stock-based compensation; (2) being forced to resign or being fired (about 30 percent of top executives); (3) being barred by the SEC from serving as officers or directors of another publicly traded company; and (4) being sanctioned for fines or jail terms. Independent auditors involved in financial statement fraud also often suffer personal and professional consequences. For example, in the alleged Waste Management financial statement fraud, four of the partners of Arthur Andersen associated with the audit of Waste Management were barred from practicing before the SEC for some time period ranging from one year to five years, and they paid $120,000 in civil fines. In addition, Arthur Andersen was fined $7 million for signing off on a financial statement for Waste Management that inflated its earnings by more than $1 billion over four years.

There must be a strong motivation for corporations to engage in financial statement fraud, primarily because the costs of corporate offenses can be significant. Baucus and Baucus (1997)[15] studied the consequences of firms convicted of a variety of illegal acts and found that the convicted firms have a reduced sales growth and lower returns on sales and net assets. The convicted firms suffered from immediate and prolonged reductions in revenues as customers exit the firms and increased long-term costs associated with acquiring capital. The seriousness of violations is typically associated with the significance of the long-term consequences paid by the convicted firms.

Davidson, Worrell, and Lee (1994)[16] find that the capital markets did not view all corporate offenses as equally severe and thus, the market reacted differently to the seriousness of violations by corporations. They found no evidence of stock market effect for firms indicted for tax evasion, theft of trade secrets, kickbacks, and overcharging customers, whereas they detected significant negative stock market effect for firms indicted on charges of bribery, price fixing, or fraudulent financial reporting. Dechow, Sloan, and Sweeney (1996) find that the cost of capital for firms convicted of financial statement fraud significantly increased.[17] Feroz, Park, and Pastena (1991)[18] studied 188 firms that were sanctioned by the SEC and found that penalties paid by firms for even unsuccessful financial statement fraud are also significant. They discovered that more than 72 percent of the enforcement targets fired or forced the resignation of top executives and about 81 percent were sued by their shareholders.

These studies found evidence indicating that firms engaged in and/or convicted of financial statement fraud typically pay high consequences for their illegal actions because their legitimacy is challenged and their financing activities in obtaining resources are more difficult and costly. Given the high cost associated with financial statement fraud and even unsuccessful fraudulent financial reporting activities, the decision by corporations to engage in such activities must be justified by strong motives that compel firms to behave illegally.

Financial statement frauds may be prosecuted in a civil action and/or a criminal action. Civil action can be brought by investors alleging fraudulent financial activities committed by corporations. Criminal cases, however, are brought by the government and are often investigated by law enforcement agents with the assistance of a prosecutor's office and a grand jury. Corporations can be held criminally liable for financial statement fraud or other offenses committed by their agents if conducted in the scope of the agent's duty and with the intended purpose of benefiting the company. Despite all the possible negative consequences of financial statement fraud (e.g., substantial reduction in stock prices, losing the status of being listed on organized stock exchanges, lawsuits, fines, jail time, loss of position and employment), companies may engage in financial statement fraud when the right combination of motive, opportunity, and rationalization exists. For example, management with strong motivation and provided opportunity may justify its aggressive earnings management attitude by stating that meeting financial analysts' forecasts is in the best interest of investors in the sense that it creates shareholder value.

In summary, the impact and effectiveness of monitoring can be measured by the extent of institutional ownership and analyst following, auditor, and investment banker identity. The effect of incentives can be assessed by management stock ownership and debt-to-equity ratio as a proxy for debt covenants and the sum of accounts receivable and inventory to total assets and financial condition representing the risk of potential litigation.

Latham and Jacobs (2000)[19] find that fraud firms (1) have a greater management stock ownership; (2) have higher variability of returns; (3) are more closely followed as measured by larger institutional ownership and analyst following; (4) have a higher-quality investment banker; and (5) have lower insider (other than management) stock ownership. They did not find any evidence of significant differences between fraud firms and nonfraud firms in terms of auditor identity (e.g., Big Five versus non-Big Five) and proximity to debt covenant limits. Their results suggest that more monitoring is observed for fraud firms compared to nonfraud firms, which is consistent with the perception that fraud firms are more closely monitored, which results in discovery of financial statement fraud.

FINANCIAL STATEMENT FRAUD CASE ANALYSIS

In this section, a real financial statement fraud case is analyzed in light of the five interactive fraud factors: cooks, recipes, incentives, monitoring, and end results (CRIME), as depicted in Exhibit 3.3. Recently, Arthur Andersen, one of the "Big Five," agreed to pay a $7 million fine to settle allegations of audit fraud that it helped overstate a client's profit by nearly $1.4 billion. In this lawsuit, the SEC claimed that Andersen "knowingly and recklessly" issued false and misleading audit reports for Waste Management, Inc. for four years from 1992 to 1996. Although under the settlement Andersen neither admitted nor denied wrongdoing, it consented to an injunction for fraud. In addition to the settlement, three of Chicago-based Andersen's current and former partners, Robert E. Allgyer, Edward G. Maier, and Walter Cercavschi, were also fined a total of $120,000. A fourth partner, Robert K. Kutsenda, was also found to have engaged in improper professional audit conduct. All four Andersen partners were banned from practicing as accountants for a number of years, ranging from one to five years. This landmark fraud case is (1) the largest-ever civil penalty against a Big Five professional services firm; (2) the first

Exhibit 3.3. Financial Statement Fraud Interaction (Crime)

antifraud injunction in more than 20 years; and (3) the largest restatement of fraudulent earnings reported by a company in U.S. history. (See Exhibit 3.3)

Waste Management was formed in 1998, when Waste Services of Houston acquired Waste Management of Illinois. This case involving allegations of financial statement fraud originally drew analysts' attention in 1997 when the company's new chief executive officer (CEO) quit after three months. Analysts concluded that the departed CEO might have discovered accounting problems. The SEC began examining Waste Management's books in November 1997 when the company announced that a change in accounting methods would result in a $1.2 billion loss and reduce reported retained earnings over the previous five years of $1 billion.

Andersen has been auditing Waste Management Services since 1971, before the garbage removal company went public. A new team of accountants at Andersen now audits the company. Auditors at Andersen, in 1992, found that their client misstated taxes, insurance, and deferred costs by $93.5 million, but the client refused to restate financial statements to correct the mistake. In the subsequent year, the auditors documented another $128 million misstatement that would have reduced income from continuing operations by 12 percent. Nevertheless, the auditors determined that the misstatement was not material to require disclosure. In 1995, another $160 million misstatement was considered by auditors to be immaterial and, thus, not warranting disclosure on the financial statements. During 1992 to 1996, Waste Management continued to engage in $1.4 billion in financial statement fraud, and auditors did not stand up to management to perform thorough audits to prevent, detect, and correct fraudulent financial activities by knowingly and recklessly committing audit fraud.

The important lesson to be learned from this landmark accounting and auditing fraud case is financial statement fraud equals CRIME, where "C" stands for Cooks, "R" is Recipes, "I" is Incentives, "M" is Monitoring, or lack of it, and "E" is End Results. This fraud scheme is further discussed in Chapter 4. Nevertheless, the financial statement fraud equals CRIME scheme fits this case well as described in the following paragraph and depicted in Exhibit 3.4.

First, the financial statement fraud was committed by Waste Management in excess of $1.4 billion from 1992 to 1996 through overstatement of financial position. Second, cooks were the top management team, including the chief financial officer and chief accounting officer, at Waste Management and four partners of Andersen. Third, the recipe was overstatement of earnings and hidden expenses for five years, causing misstatements in the published audit financial statements. Fourth, there were several incentives for the client and auditors to engage in financial statement fraud. There were tremendous pressures on management to meet earnings' expectations and make Wall Street happy. Today, the pressures on management to beat analysts' forecasts are greater than ever in a capital market where information and stock prices move instantaneously and efficiently. Auditors were also under pressure to retain their clients at the expense of compromising their ethical conduct and professional responsibilities. Andersen considered Waste Management as a "crown jewel" client and failed to stand up to management pressure to disclose discovered misstatements in the financial statements for several years. In addition, there were apparent conflicts of interest between the top management team of Waste Management and auditors of Andersen in the sense that (1) every chief financial officer and chief accounting officer in Waste Management's history had previously worked as an auditor at Andersen; (2) over several years, Andersen billed Waste Management more fees for management advisory services than auditing services ($11.8 million for other services compared to $7.5 million for auditing); (3) an Andersen affiliate billed Waste Management an additional $6 million for consulting services; and (4) the compensation of Andersen's lead partner on the Waste Management audits was based in part on the amount of money Andersen billed Waste Management for nonaudit services.

Exhibit 3.4.   Financial Statement Fraud Formula

Cooks	+
Recipes	+
Incentives	+
Monitoring (lack of)	+
End Results	=
CRIME	

Monitoring in this fraud scheme formula refers to the lack of existence of a responsible corporate governance in monitoring management functions for fair presentation of financial statements in conformity with GAAP. Absence of oversight function by the audit committee of Waste Management, coupled with ineffective monitoring of the top management team by the board of directors and inadequacy and ineffectiveness of the internal control structure in preventing, detecting, and correcting financial statement fraud, might have been a significant contributing factor to the misstatements and audit failures. During the 1995 financial statement audit, the assigned auditors informed a managing partner at Andersen of about $67 million of misstatements and Waste Management's fraudulent accounting practice of using one-time gains to mask other misstatements; however, the managing partner, under the environment of no board of directors or audit committee oversight, considered the misstatements not to be material and insufficient to be disclosed and warrant a qualified disclaimer or adverse audit report.

The last letter in "Crime" is "E," which stands for end results or consequences. The financial statement fraud committed by Waste Management resulted in the following outcomes:

- The settlement of a shareholder class action in Chicago that cost the company and its auditor, Andersen, a combined total of $220 million, where Andersen paid $75 million.
- Waste Management to take a total of $3.54 billion in charges and writedowns in 1997 when the fraudulent accounting practices were initially uncovered.
- Stock prices of Waste Management fell down substantially upon discovery and announcement of financial statement fraud.
- The top management team at Waste Management, including the chief financial officer and the chief accounting officer, were forced to resign.
- A settlement agreement was filed in a lawsuit pending in a Boston federal court.
- The SEC initiative to levy restrictions on the consulting services that can be offered to audit clients.
- The auditors at Andersen were charged with "knowingly and recklessly" issuing false and misleading audit reports for several years.
- The auditors consented to an injunction of fraud that is the first antifraud injunction in more than 20 years against a "Big Five" accounting firm.
- One former and three current partners of Andersen were barred for several years from auditing a U.S. publicly traded company.
- Andersen paid a record $7 million fine, which is the largest ever civil penalty against a "Big Five" accounting firm.
- Three of Chicago-based Andersen's current and former partners were fined a total of $120,000 in a civil lawsuit.

Andersen has also recently agreed to pay to settle an accounting fraud lawsuit in connection with the audit of Sunbeam. The SEC also filed suit against four Sunbeam executives, including former CEO Al Dunlap, better known as "Chainsaw," for earnings management. Andersen, once viewed as the conscience of the accounting profession, is now facing a fusillade of litigation involving its audits of the collapsed Enron Corporation.

FRAUD PREVENTION AND DETECTION STRATEGIES

The pervasiveness of financial statement fraud by high-profile corporations such as Lucent, Xerox, Enron Corp., Sunbeam, Waste Management, Rite Aid, KnowledgeWare, W.R. Grace, MicroStrategy, Raytheon, and Livent Theater encourage publicly traded companies to take proactive roles by establishing strategies to prevent and detect financial statement fraud. The corporate fraud prevention and detection strategies should be developed to foster the quality, integrity, and reliability of the financial reporting process. These strategies should include:

1. *Fraud Vulnerability Reviews.* Fraud vulnerability reviews should be performed both periodically and continuously. Corporations should consider and implement fraud vulnerability reviews and fraud hotlines that can be used by insiders (e.g., employees, internal auditors) and outsiders (e.g., customers, suppliers) to report fraudulent activities. Furthermore, corporations should establish an appropriate whistle-blowing policy (discussed in Chapter 5) and usc forensic accounting techniques to combat financial statement fraud.

2. *Gamesmanship Review.* A gamesmanship review is a comprehensive assessment of a top management team's philosophies, attitudes, operating styles, decisions, actions, beliefs, and ethical values pertaining to the financial reporting process and continuous review of management's financial reporting relationships with security analysts, internal auditors, external auditors, the board of directors, and the audit committee. A periodic gamesmanship review can improve the quality of financial reporting by preventing and reducing the possibility of collusion between financial statement fraud perpetrators. Gamesmanship and its influence on the risk of financial statement fraud is thoroughly examined in Chapter 9.

3. *Fraud Prevention Program.* Corporations should develop fraud prevention programs, establish appropriate policies and procedures, communicate fraud policies and procedures to everyone within the corporation, enforce compliance with the policies and periodically assess their effectiveness in preventing and detecting financial statement fraud. Fraud prevention programs should be implemented and enforced by a group consisting of forensic accountants, internal auditors, investigators, attorneys, and human resource personnel. The program should clearly specify that fraud prevention policies and procedures apply to all employees, including management. This group should periodically report to the board of directors and its representative audit committee regarding the accuracy and effectiveness of the program.

4. *Enforcement Procedures.* The SEC has recently considered combating financial statement fraud by publicly traded companies as its first priority, as evidenced by several fraud allegations recently brought against corporations, their
executives, and auditors. In 1999, the SEC filed more than 90 financial statement and reporting actions, which was about a 15 percent increase over the
previous year. The SEC's Enforcement Division Director Richard H. Walker,
in the 1999 AICPA National Conference on SEC Developments, warned that:

> Combating fraud remains a No.1 priority. There are indicators that financial state-
> ment fraud is still all too common . . . the division is turning the number game of
> Monopoly . . . cook the books and go directly to jail without passing Go."[20]

In following the SEC's enforcement procedures, corporations should develop their
internal fraud enforcement procedures and create severe penalties for cooking the
books. Perpetrators of financial statement fraud, from top executives to employees, should understand that cooking the books is a crime that will be prosecuted.
Companies should adopt no tolerance policies for financial statement fraud. Thus,
any top executives or employees who engaged in financial statement fraud should
be dismissed or, alternatively, their stock options or bonuses should be adjusted or
canceled if the company has to restate its financial statements resulting from
fraudulent financial activities.

CONCLUSION

The opportunity to engage in financial statement fraud increases as the firm's
control structure weakens and as its corporate governance becomes less effective. According to Loebbecke et al. (1989), financial statement fraud is a function of three factors: conditions, motive, and attitude. First, the firm must be
predisposed to choose to depart from GAAP.[21] Then the firm is more apt to actually issue financial statement fraud if there is a strong motive and opportunity
to do so. Companies take the risk of having to suffer the adverse consequences
of issuing financial statement fraud as long as there is some uncertainty that their
deceptive and illegal actions may not be detected. Given this uncertainty, companies may engage in financial statement fraud if the firm is (1) predisposed toward violating GAAP requirements by issuing fraudulent financial statements as
acceptable accounting practices; (2) motivated to prepare fraudulent financial
statements in response to internal and external economic and ownership pressures; and (3) provided with the opportunity because of irresponsible and ineffective monitoring by corporate governance.

This chapter, by presenting discussion and related fraud cases, demonstrates
that financial statement fraud equals CRIME when "C" stands for Cooks, "R" is
Recipe, "I" is Incentives, "M" is Monitoring, or lack of it, and "E" is End Results.
The financial statement fraud equals crime scheme fits many enforcement actions

brought against publicly traded companies by the SEC. Successful financial statement fraud may lead to more fraudulent financial reporting activities. Several studies concluded that firms convicted of illegal actions have a history of prior violations (e.g., Baucus and Near, 1991; Davidson et al., 1994).[22, 23]

ENDNOTES

1. Hambrick, D. C., and P. A. Mason. 1984. "Upper Echelons: The Organization as a Reflection of Its Top Managers". *Academy of Management Review* (Vol. 9, No. 2): 193–206.

2. Beasley, M. S., J. V. Carcello, and D. R. Hermanson. 1999. Fraudulent Financial Reporting: 1987–1997, An Analysis of Public Companies. New York, NY: COSO.

3. Bonner, S. E., Z. V. Palmrose, and S. M. Young. 1998. "Fraud Type and Auditor Litigation: An Analysis of SEC Accounting and Auditing Enforcement Releases". *The Accounting Review* (October, Vol. 73, No. 4): 503–532.

4. Robertson, J. C. 2000. *Fraud Examination for Managers and Auditors.* Austin, TX: Viesca Books.

5. Latham, C. K., and F. A. Jacobs. 2000. "Monitoring and Incentive Factors Influencing Misleading Disclosures." *Journal of Managerial Issues* (Vol. XII, No. 2, Summer): 169–187.

6. Carter, R., and R. Stover. 1991. "Management Ownership and Firm Value Compensation Policy: Evidence from Converting Savings and Loan Associations." *Financial Management* (Winter): 80–90.

7. Latham, C., and F. Jacobs. 2000. "Monitoring and Incentives Factors Influencing Misleading Disclosures". *Journal of Managerial Issues* (Summer): 169–187.

8. Dechow, P. M., R. G. Sloan, and A. P. Sweeney. 1996. "Causes and Consequences of Earnings Manipulation: An Analysis of Firms Subject to Enforcement Actions by the SEC." *Contemporary Accounting Research* 13 (Spring): 1–36.

9. Lys, T., and R. Watts. 1994. "Lawsuits Against Auditors." *Journal of Accountancy Research* 32 (Supplement): 65–93.

10. Carcello, J. V. and Z. V. Palmrose. 1994. "Author Litigation and Modified Reporting on Bankrupt Clients." *Journal of Accountancy Research* 32 (Supplement): 1–30.

11. O'Brien, P. C., and R. Bhushan. 1990. Analyst Following and Institutional Ownership. *Journal of Accounting Research* (Supplement): 55–73.

12. Deis, D., and G. Giroux. 1992. "Determinants of Audit Quality in the Public Sector". *The Accounting Review* 67 (October): 462–479.

13. Latham, C., F. Jacobs, and P. Roush. 1998. "Does Auditor Tenure Matter?" *Research in Accounting Regulation* (Fall): 165–178.

14. Palmrose, Z. 1987. "Litigation and Independent Auditors: The Role of Business Failures and Management Fraud." *Auditing: A Journal of Practice and Theory* 6(2): 90–103.

15. Baucus, M., and D. Baucus. 1997. "Paying the Piper: An Empirical Examination of Long-term Financial Consequences of Illegal Corporate Behavior." *Academy of Management Journal* 40 (February): 129–151.

16. Davidson, W., D. Worrell, and C. Lee. 1994. "Stock Market Reactions to Announced Corporate Illegalities." *Journal of Business Ethics* (13): 583–613.

17. Dechow, P., R. Sloan, and A. Sweeney. 1996. "Causes and Consequences of Earnings Manipulation: An Analysis of Firms Subject to Enforcement Actions by the SEC." *Contemporary Accounting Research* 13(Spring): 1–36.

18. Feroz, E., K. Park, and V. Pastena. 1991. "The Financial and Market Effect of the SEC's Accounting and Auditing Enforcement Releases." *Journal of Accounting Research* 29 (Supplement): 107–142.

19. Latham, C., F. Jacobs, and P. Roush. 1998. "Does Auditor Tenure Matter?" *Research in Accounting Regulation* (Fall): 165–178.

20. American Institute of Certified Public Accountants (AICPA). "1999 AICPA National Conference on SEC Developments." *The CPA Journal* (March): 33–38.

21. Loebbecke, J. K., and M. M. Eining and J. J. Willingham. 1989. Auditors' Experience with Material Irregularities: Frequency, Nature, and Detectability. *Auditing: A Journal of Practice and Theory* (9): 1–28.

22. Baucus, M. S., and J. P. Near. 1991. "Can Illegal Corporate Behavior Be Predicted? An Event History Analysis." *Academy of Management Journal* (34): 9–36.

23. Davidson, W., D. Worrell, and C. Lee. 1994. "Stock Market Reactions to Announced Corporate Illegalities." *Journal of Business Ethics* (13): 583–613.

Chapter 4

Realization, Prevention, and Detection

INTRODUCTION

This chapter presents a model consisting of conditions, corporate structure, and choice (3Cs) to explain and analyze motivations, opportunities, and rationalizations for financial statement fraud. The right combination of these three factors increases the likelihood of financial statement fraud. This chapter also focuses on economic—external antecedent and internal antecedent—factors of financial statement fraud. Top management team characteristics, as well as financial statement fraud prevention, detection, and correction strategies are also examined.

REALIZATION

There is evidence that the general public is becoming increasingly aware of financial statement fraud committed by publicly traded companies. An extensive review of actual financial statement fraud cases and the related literature (see Exhibit 3.1, Chapter 3) suggests that financial statement fraud will occur if:

- Favorable conditions for financial statement fraud exist;
- The corporate structure provides opportunities and motivations for the top management team to commit financial statement fraud (e.g., economic gain); and
- The top management team has a choice to select among a set of accounting principles and practices the one that rationalizes its decision to engage in financial statement fraud.[1]

Three variables that may explain financial statement fraud are conditions (pressure, need), corporate structure, and choice (intent or proactive exploitation).[2] The right combination of these three variables creates sufficient incentives and motivation for any company to engage in financial statement fraud.

Loebbecke et al. (1989) suggest a model consisting of (1) conditions in which the company allows the perpetration of financial statement fraud (e.g., inadequate and ineffective internal control structure); (2) management's motivations for committing financial statement fraud (e.g., meeting analysts' earnings expectations);

and (3) management's ethical attitudes showing a possible willingness to engage in financial statement fraud.[3]

THE 3CS MODEL

This book uses a model consisting of **conditions, corporate structure,** and **choice** (3Cs) in explaining motivations, opportunities, and rationalizations for financial statement fraud. The perpetration of financial statement fraud can be made possible with the 3Cs presence. Financial statement fraud may be committed for several reasons. These reasons fall under the three categories to perpetrate financial statement fraud.

A fraud scheme focusing on the 3Cs of conditions, corporate structure, and choice is examined in this chapter to explain preexisting financial statement fraud causes and predict as well as discover the potential financial statement fraud. Although the presence of a single factor can signal the possibility of fraud, the combination of two or more factors at any one time increases the likelihood that fraud might have occurred. If any of the three factors is missing, then the probability of financial statement fraud is diminished. Using the three-factor model to predict and discover financial statement fraud is consistent with guidelines in existing auditing standards (SAS No. 82 and SIAS No. 3).

Conditions

Environmental variables provide justification and rationalization in terms of the tradeoff of costs against benefits of committing financial statement fraud. This variable of cost/benefit assessment is based on the utilitarian concept in ethics that suggests evaluation of consequences of actions or behavior should be considered before undertaking the action or decision. This concept works well in a free enterprise system, which suggests that financial statement fraud will occur if and when the benefits to the fraudster(s) outweigh the associated costs calculated using the probability and consequences of detection. Within this framework, financial statement fraud will occur especially in situations of economic pressure resulting from a continuous deterioration of earnings, a downturn in organizational performance, a continuous decline in industry performance, or a general economic recession. Economic motives are typically common in financial statement fraud, even though other types of motives such as psychotic, egocentric, or ideological motives discussed in Chapter 3 can also play a role.

Pressure on a corporation to meet analysts' earnings estimates can be a factor stimulating earnings management and resulting in financial statement fraud. Earnings management seems to be a tactical response to a perceived need to meet earnings expectations. Management evaluates the benefit of earnings management calculated in terms of positive effect on the company's stock price or the cost saving of preventing the negative impact on share prices for not meeting earnings forecasts against the possible cost of consequences of engaging in financial statement fraud and the probability of detection, prosecution, and sanction.

Financial statement fraud is likely to increase when the perpetrator has the opportunity and the motive to engage in fraudulent financial activities. Financial statement fraud may occur for various reasons. In most instances, these reasons fall under the existence of conditions to commit financial statement fraud. The following conditions help to explain some of the impetus behind financial statement fraud:

- Lack of responsible corporate governance
- Ineffective board of directors
- Nonexistent or ineffective audit committee
- Presence of a dominant top management team with little or no accountability
- No review of top executives' activities and no requirements for executive disclosures
- Existence of material related-party transactions
- Inadequate and ineffective internal audit functions
- Frequent changes in external auditors or selection of inexperienced external auditors
- Inability to obtain credit
- Unfavorable economic conditions
- Insufficient cash flows to support the reported earnings growth
- Restrictive loan agreements
- Excessive bad debt expenses resulting from inability in collecting receivables
- Excessive investment and/or losses
- Dependence on only a few customers

Corporate Structure

Because financial statement fraud is typically committed by the top management team level rather than lower management or employees, one would expect incidences to occur most often in an environment characterized by irresponsible and ineffective corporate governance. Management would be more reluctant to engage in financial statement fraud when an effective corporate governance mechanism increases the probability of prevention and detection. Monitoring and oversight functions of corporate governance, including the board of directors and the audit committee, are thoroughly examined in Chapter 6. Corporate governance refers to the way a corporation is governed through proper accountability for managerial and financial performance. The characteristics and attributes of corporate governance most likely to be associated with financial statement fraud are aggressiveness, cohesiveness, loyalty, opportunism, trust, and control effectiveness. Aggressiveness and opportunism can be signified by the company's attitude and motivations toward beating analysts' forecasts about quarterly earnings or annual earnings per share and the attempt to make Wall Street happy by reporting unjustifiable favorable financial performance. Cohesiveness and loyalty attributes create an environment that reduces the likelihood of whistle-blowing and increases the probability of coverup attempts. Trust and control ineffectiveness can cause those in an oversight function (e.g., board of directors, audit committee) as well as assurance function (e.g., internal auditors, external auditors) to be less effective in detecting fraud. The cohesiveness can cause a sharply defined group boundary of corporate governance that creates high cooperation among corporate governance members to conceal financial statement fraud and impose greater restriction of fraudulent financial information to leak to outsiders. This cohesiveness can encourage more collusion in the development of financial statement fraud, and if the fraud is discovered by internal or external auditors, push them for coverup. When the members of corporate governance establish trust, it creates less room for suspicion and skepticism, which in turn may reduce the likelihood of detection of fraud by auditors.

Choice

Management can use its discretion to choose between the shortcut alternative of engaging in illegal earnings management or ethical strategies of continuous improvements of both quality and quantity of earnings. Specifically, when neither environmental pressure nor corporate structure is a significant influence, financial statement fraud could occur simply as one of management's strategic tools or discretions motivated by aggressiveness, lack of moral principles, or misguided creativity or innovation. Under these circumstances, financial statement fraud is a matter of choice, regardless of environmental pressure or need or corporate structure.

Perpetrators of financial statement fraud may be motivated to commit the fraud regardless of consequences of their actions whether or not the sanctions exists. A company may, in good faith, view its regulations and requirements as too harsh and, to diminish their adverse impacts, may engage in financial statement fraud.

The three variables of conditions of pressure or need, corporate structure, and choices may each function separately, or perhaps more likely in combination in contributing to financial statement fraud. The right combination of these variables is a perfect recipe for financial statement fraud, as depicted in Exhibit 4.1

ECONOMIC FACTORS

Economists have studied crime and punishment from a rational calculation of expected costs and benefits based on a strictly utilitarian theory. Famous economist Gary Becker (1964) argued that crimes could be prevented by setting a penalty equal to the net social cost of the crime divided by the probability of detection.[4] Cohen (1992)[5] and Macey (1991)[6] employed Becker's basic model to examine

Exhibit 4.1. Interactions of 3Cs of Financial Statement Fraud

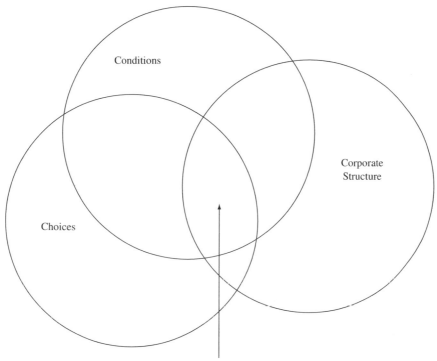

Conditions

Corporate
Structure

Choices

High Probability of the occurrence of
financial statement fraud

illegal corporate activities. This utilitarian model suggests that top executives of publicly traded companies are unlikely to engage in financial statement fraud primarily because accused managers may share a small fraction of the overall gains resulting from financial statement fraud, whereas they may bear a proportionately large share of possible costs of fines, prison terms, and potential loss to their reputations. This model and its justifications, however, contradict the overwhelming evidence regarding the occurrences of financial statement fraud by many publicly traded companies, primarily because of managers (1) overestimating the potential benefits of engaging in financial statement fraud; (2) underestimating the probability of detection; (3) underestimating or ignoring the potential costs; (4) being aggressive or risk takers; and (5) rationalizing their actions in light of other influential factors (e.g., peer pressure, compensation package, ownership structure).

Daboub, Rasheed, and Priem and Gray (1995) provide an alternative method of explaining illegal corporate behavior in general and why corporations may engage in financial statement fraud in particular.[7] Although the Daboub et al. (1995) model is designed to analyze illegal corporate activities, it is also applicable to financial statement fraud committed by corporations. Implications of the Daboub et al. (1995) model for financial statement fraud are discussed in the following sections.

EXTERNAL ANTECEDENT FACTORS

External antecedent factors that could contribute to financial statement fraud are industry culture and environmental characteristics.

Industry Culture

The industry in which a company operates is an important variable in explaining occurrences of financial statement fraud. Prior research finds evidence that firms in certain industries are more likely to commit illegal acts (e.g., Simpson, 1986; Baucus and Near, 1991).[8,9] The industry can impact on the probability of a firm's engagement in financial statement fraud in several ways. Baucus (1990)[10] found evidence indicating that industry culture (e.g., shared norms, values, beliefs) predisposes managers to engage in illegal acts. Examples are the price-fixing scandal in the heavy electronic equipment industry in the 1960s, fraudulent financial activities in the savings and loan industry in the 1980s, and violation of consumer privacy in high-tech industry during the 1990s. Another way that industry and especially leading firms in the industry can affect corporal illegality, including financial statement fraud, is through the concept known as *organizational isomorphism* (DiMaggio and Powell, 1983).[11] This concept suggests that corporations tend to pattern themselves after successful companies in their industry. Thus, firms within an industry learn to engage in illegal activities through observation of and introduction to other firms in that industry. Finally, the peer pressure defined by the environment in which the firm operates or the pressures that the firm experiences in that particular industry can motivate management to engage in financial statement fraud.

Environmental Characteristics

Environmental characteristics can play an important role in the way organizations operate and behave. For example, Staw and Szawagkowski (1975)[12] found that in less munificent environments, firms are more likely to engage in illegally questionable activities. Baucus and Near (1991)[13] argue that illegal behavior was likely when resources were scarce but was even more probable when the environment was munificent.

INTERNAL ANTECEDENT FACTORS

Internal antecedent factors that may explain illegal corporate behavior, including engagement in financial statement fraud, are size, history, and corporate governance.

Size

Empirical studies have produced contradictory and inconsistent results regarding the impact of organization size and criminality. Simpson (1986)[14] concludes that large firms are more likely to behave illegally. Baucus and Near (1991)[15] found evidence indicating that large firms were almost twice as likely as smaller firms to behave illegally, while moderate-sized firms were only 10 percent more likely to behave illegally than smaller firms. There are several plausible explanations regarding the positive relationship between size and illegal corporate behavior (Daboub et al., 1995).[16] First, size is considered as a proxy for complexity, which creates inefficiency in the internal control system through lack of proper communication and coordination. The second explanation is that large firms do not necessarily engage in more illegal behavior; however, because of their size and visibility, they are more likely to be investigated by regulators (e.g., SEC). The final explanation is that size facilitates illegal corporate behavior because it provides opportunities for fraudsters, especially in a decentralized organization.

Despite all these plausible explanations regarding the size and the extent of illegal corporate behavior, there is no clear and concrete evidence indicating that larger firms engage in more illegal acts, including financial statement fraud. Ironically, the 1999 COSO Report reveals that the 204 studied fraud companies were relatively small compared to public registrants.[17] The COSO Report finds that the typical size of most alleged fraud companies ranged well below $100 million in total assets, and most of them (about 78 percent) were not listed on the New York or American Stock Exchanges. The COSO Report suggests that the inability or unwillingness of small companies to design and maintain adequate and effective internal controls is a contributory factor influencing the likelihood of financial statement fraud.

Corporate Governance

Irresponsible corporate governance may cause a firm to behave illegally. Especially during periods of poor financial performance, corporations may attempt to cut costs, which may make the system of internal control less effective in preventing and detecting financial statement fraud. Several aspects of corporate governance (inadequate and ineffective system and control) have been suggested as predictors of corporate wrongdoing. Responsible and effective corporate governance and its role in preventing and detecting fraud is examined in detail in Chapter 6.

Corporate History

A corporate history of wrongdoing, including engagement in financial statement fraud, is in itself a predictor of future wrongdoing and fraud. Reported material offenses by a corporation suggest the existence of norms or culture within the company and its corporate governance that condones or even encourages such behavior (Baucus and Near, 1991).[18]

TOP MANAGEMENT TEAM CHARACTERISTICS

Top management team characteristics have been viewed both in authoritative reports (e.g., Treadway Commission, SAS No. 53, 78, and 82) and empirical research (Daboub, 1995) to affect the likelihood of financial statement fraud. The notion that top management should set a tone to influence ethical conduct and outcomes is a popular one often mentioned in the authoritative reports. The decision by top management to engage in financial statement fraud is not often an isolated incident, but rather a sequence of events that meander toward financial statement fraud; however, management is responsible for the quality of financial reports and deterrence of financial statement fraud. The consensus appears to be that financial statement fraud occurs with top management team involvement, initiative, and/or knowledge.

The potential conflict of interest between shareholders of a publicly traded corporation and its top management team (e.g., chief executive officer) is an example of a principal-agent problem. If shareholders had adequate information regarding operational, investment, and financing opportunities and related managerial strategies and actions, they could design a contract specifying, implementing, and enforcing managerial actions; however, separation of corporations from their owners and remoteness of shareholders prevent them from knowing what actions that CEO can take and whether the undertaken action(s) will increase shareholder value. *Agency theory* suggests that executives' compensation plans should be designed to give management incentives to select and implement actions that increase shareholder value. Shareholders want economic value added to all managerial actions and decisions, which can be achieved when the expected return on the action exceeds the expected costs. CEOs, however, consider their own welfare and personal gains and the costs of pursuing particular actions or decisions. There may be a potential conflict of interest when top executives' compensation plans are not tied to shareholders' value creation. Thus, it is appropriate and economically feasible to pay CEOs on the basis of shareholder wealth or value creation.

There are many mechanisms through which executives' compensation policy can be tied to shareholder value creation and provide incentives for shareholder value creation to improve executives' performance. Examples of these mechanisms are stock options, compensations, performance-based bonuses, salary adjustments, and performance-based dismissal decisions. These compensation strategies may provide incentives for CFOs to engage in earnings management by overstating earnings to receive higher compensations. Any excessive earnings management can deteriorate the quality of financial reports. The agency literature suggests links between shareholder value creation, financial investment and operational policy, compensation plans, ownership structure, and control.

A research report commissioned by the Committee of Sponsoring Organizations (COSO, 1999) studied more than 200 companies involved in alleged instances of financial statement fraud as identified by the SEC in Accounting

Auditing Enforcement Releases (AAERs) issued during the 11-year period from January 1987 to December 1997. The COSO Report examined several key company and management characteristics for a sample of those companies involved in financial statement fraud and made several recommendations to improve the quality of the financial reporting process. Findings of the 1999 COSO Report and their implications for reducing financial statement fraud are summarized in Exhibit 4.2.[19]

FINANCIAL STATEMENT FRAUD PREVENTION

Corporate governance is responsible for establishing and monitoring ongoing mechanisms that identify and eliminate the causes of financial statement fraud by mitigating the effects of motive, opportunity, rationalization, and lack of integrity. This continuous mechanism is the most effective way to prevent financial statement fraud. Elements of this continuous mechanism are (1) vigilant corporate governance; (2) a corporate code of conduct; (3) an adequate and effective internal control structure; (4) an internal audit function; and (5) external audit services. Exhibit 4.3 presents prevention, detection, and correction mechanisms to reduce the likelihood of financial statement fraud.

Corporations that are confined and operate within a set of acceptable laws and regulations, including accounting and ethical standards, have fewer options available to them for fraud than those that ignore their applicable laws and regulations. Corporations that operate within socially, ethically, and legally accepted parameters are perceived to be legitimate, with responsible corporate governance and reliable financial reporting. Corporations that choose to behave illegally typically have a broader range of available alternatives, primarily because they can choose from a set of legal options as well as from the set of illegal behavior.

Corporate governance is determined by organizational structure, which defines the decisions of authority, established decision-making policies, and standard operating procedures that conform to the acceptable patterns of behavior. Behaviors that are consistent with the defined set of norms and expectations are perceived to be legitimate. When these cognitive frameworks of corporate governance become firmly established, they begin to define the corporate culture of ways things are done. Corporate governance that is consistent with the structure and decision-making routines and patterns of behavior of one company may be different and inconsistent with the structures of another company. Companies that choose to act illegally select a behavior that many other companies would not consider to be normal or within their set of socially acceptable behaviors. Thus, companies that choose to engage in fraudulent financial activities choose an accounting alternative from a set of both generally accepted and unaccepted primarily illegal accounting methods to prepare their financial statements.

Lack of existence of responsible corporate governance does not necessarily mean that the company will engage in financial statement fraud. There must be a

Exhibit 4.2. Findings of the 1999 COSO Report

Category	Findings	Implications
1. Companies Involved	Publicly traded companies that committed financial statement fraud: (1) were relatively small with less than $100 million in total assets; (2) about 78 percent were not listed on the New York or American Stock Exchange; and (3) were experiencing net losses.	1. Pressures of financial strain or distress may have provided incentives for the commission of financial statement fraud. 2. Small companies' inability or unwillingness to implement adequate and effective internal controls might have been a contributing factor in the commission of financial statement fraud.
2. Nature of the Frauds	1. Cumulative amount of frauds were relatively large, with the average of $25 million. 2. Most frauds were not isolated to a single period. 3. Most commonly used financial statement fraud schemes involved overstatement of revenues and assets.	1. The quality and reliability of interim or quarterly financial statements are important because financial statement fraud often starts with the interim reports and carries on into annual reports. 2. Tests of controls and substantive test transactions cutoffs and asset valuation at the year-end are crucial.
3. Corporate Governance	1. Top executives (e.g., CEO, CFO) were commonly engaged in financial statement fraud. 2. Fraud companies had either no audit committee or their audit committee met about once a year. 3. Most boards of directors of fraud companies were dominated by insiders or "gray" directors with little work experience and considerable equity ownership. 4. Family relationships among directors and/or executives were fairly common.	1. A responsible corporate governance in monitoring the pressures faced by senior executives is crucial. 2. A vigilant audit committee overseeing the integrity, quality, and reliability of the financial reporting process is critical. 3. Adequate and effective internal controls can play an important role in preventing and detecting fraud. 4. Family relationships among directors can create significant power or incompatible functions.
4. Independent Auditors	1. Most companies that committed financial statement fraud were audited by Big Eight/Five financial services firms. 2. All types of audit reports were issued during the fraud period, with most containing unqualified opinions. 3. Independent auditors were not often engaged in the commission of financial statement fraud. 4. More than one-fourth of fraud companies changed auditors during the fraud period.	1. Independent auditors should be more skeptical in obtaining and understanding and assessing risks unique to their client's industry, management's motivation toward aggressive reporting, and the internal control structure. 2. Independent auditors should place a significant focus on red flags (weak board of directors and audit committee, ineffective internal controls) signaling the likelihood of the occurrence of financial statement fraud.

Source: Beasley, M.S., J.V. Carcello, and D.R. Hermanson. 1999. *Fraudulent Financial Reporting: 1987–1997, An Analysis of U.S. Public Companies.* Research Commissioned by the Committee of Sponsoring Organizations of the Treadway Commission (COSO).

Exhibit 4.3. Financial Statement Fraud: Prevention and Detection

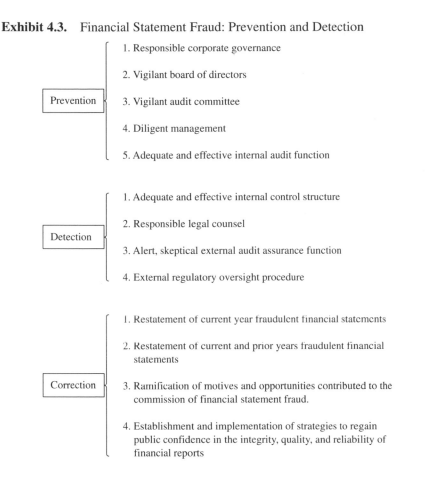

Prevention
1. Responsible corporate governance
2. Vigilant board of directors
3. Vigilant audit committee
4. Diligent management
5. Adequate and effective internal audit function

Detection
1. Adequate and effective internal control structure
2. Responsible legal counsel
3. Alert, skeptical external audit assurance function
4. External regulatory oversight procedure

Correction
1. Restatement of current year fraudulent financial statements
2. Restatement of current and prior years fraudulent financial statements
3. Ramification of motives and opportunities contributed to the commission of financial statement fraud.
4. Establishment and implementation of strategies to regain public confidence in the integrity, quality, and reliability of financial reports

reason for the company to act illegally and an opportunity for it to actually engage in the preparation and dissemination of fraudulent financial statements. A company may engage in issuing fraudulent financial statements if it finds a set of acceptable accounting alternatives to justify its actions and seizes the motive and opportunity to commit illegal action. The commission of financial statement fraud can be made possible when the 3Cs (i.e., conditions, corporate structure, and choices) discussed earlier in this chapter are present. Thus, the most effective mechanism for preventing financial statement fraud is to focus on the 3Cs and assess their effects on financial statement fraud.

FINANCIAL STATEMENT FRAUD DETECTION

Prevention of financial statement fraud is the best strategy to ensure the quality and integrity of financial reports; however, companies often cannot prevent occurrences of financial statement fraud. Thus, any unprevented financial statement fraud should be detected by internal and/or external auditors. Financial statement fraud can be detected by identifying signs and signals of fraud, so-called red flags. Several reports have provided lists of red flags indicating early warning signals of potential financial statement fraud. Using the red-flags approach to detect financial statement fraud is thoroughly examined in Chapter 5. Observation of an individual's lifestyle and habits and related changes may provide some indication of red flags that may indirectly affect financial statement fraud (e.g., spending more money than the salary justifies, drinking excessively, becoming irritable easily, not relaxing, taking drugs).

Because the focus of this book is on financial statement fraud perpetrated by management in an attempt to mislead users of financial statements, especially investors and creditors, special attention is placed on identifying "business red flags." Business red flags are those conditions and circumstances that arise from the perceived need to overcome "financial difficulties," such as an inability to meet analysts' forecasts, increased competition, and cash flow shortages. Management often views these financial difficulties as 'temporary,' attempting to overcome them by manipulating financial statements to make the company look better financially in order to obtain a new loan or issue stock. Examples of these conditions and circumstances are as follows:

- Lack of vigilant corporate governance
- Lack of vigilant oversight board and audit committee
- Inadequate and ineffective internal control structure
- Too much emphasis on meeting earnings forecast and expectations
- Domination of business decision by an individual or a small group
- Aggressive managerial attitude in meeting unrealistic corporate goals
- Company profit lays the industry average profit
- Existence of material and unusual related-party transactions
- Significant turnover in the accounting personnel
- Frequent disputes with independent auditors

CORRECTION PROCEDURES

Correction mechanisms for preexisting financial statement fraud are those reactive steps taken by fraud companies to eliminate the committed fraud and its impacts on the quality, reliability, and integrity of financial statements and to prevent further occurrence of fraud. Correction mechanisms are designed to accomplish the following:

- Restate the current year fraudulent financial statements.
- Restate the current year as well as prior years' fraudulent financial statements.

- Identify the 3Cs (conditions, corporate culture, choice) and assess their impact on further occurrences of financial statement fraud.
- Eliminate motives and opportunities that contributed to the financial statement fraud.
- Establish and implement strategies to regain public confidence in the integrity, quality, and reliability of the financial reporting process.
- Reassess the impact of the committed financial statement fraud on the established fraud prevention and detection strategies and continuously monitor the effectiveness of the process of implementing these strategies.

PREVENTION, DETECTION, AND CORRECTION STRATEGIES

Publicly traded companies should establish fraud prevention, detection, and correction strategies to effectively monitor the 3Cs (conditions, corporate structure, and choices) presented in this chapter. Examples of these strategies are (1) establishing a responsible corporate governance, vigilant board of directors and audit committee, diligent management, and adequate and effective internal audit functions; (2) using an alert, skeptical external audit function, responsible legal counsel, adequate and effective internal control structure, and external regulatory procedures; and (3) implementing appropriate corporate strategies for correction of the committed financial statement fraud, elimination of the probability of its future occurrences, and restatement of confidence in the financial statement process. Interactions of these three strategies of prevention, detection, and correction are depicted in Exhibit 4.4.

When the aforementioned strategies are properly and effectively performed, the opportunity for financial statement fraud is substantially reduced. Financial statement fraud occurs when one or a combination of these strategies are relaxed because of self-interest, lack of due diligence, pressure, overreliance, or lack of dedication. The opportunity of financial statement fraud is significantly increased when these strategies are inadequate and ineffective.

CONCLUSION

Opportunity to engage in financial statement fraud increases as the company's internal control structure weakens and as its corporate governance becomes less responsible and effective. The occurrence of financial statement fraud is a function of three factors of conditions, corporate structure, and choices (3Cs) presented in this chapter. The company is more apt to commit financial statement fraud if there is a strong motive and opportunity to do so. Companies may take the risk of having to suffer the adverse consequence of the commission of financial statement fraud as long as there is some uncertainty that their deception and illegal actions may not be detected. Successful hiding of financial statement fraud may lead to

Exhibit 4.4.   Interactive Fraud Prevention, Detection, and Corrective Strategies

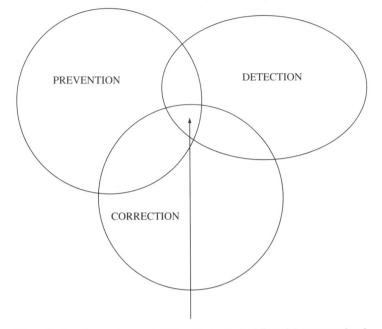

Most effective strategy, low probability of occurrence of financial statement fraud

more fraudulent financial reporting activities. This chapter describes financial statement fraud prevention, detection, and correction strategies that if implemented properly would improve the quality, integrity, and reliability of published audited financial statements.

ENDNOTES

1. Green, B.P., and T. G. Calderon. 1996. "Information Privity and the Internal Auditor's Assessment of Fraud Risk Factors." *Internal Auditing* (Spring): 4–15.

2. Szwajkowski, E. 1985. "Organizational Illegality: Theoretical Integration and Illustrative Application." *Academy of Management Review* (Vol. 10, No. 3): 558–567.

3. Loebbecke, J. K., and M. M. Eining and J. J. Willingham. 1989. Auditors' Experience with Material Irregularities: Frequency, Nature, and Detectability. *Auditing: A Journal of Practice and Theory* (9): 1–28.

4. Becker, G.S. 1964. "Crime and Punishment: An Economic Approach." *Journal of Political Economy* (76): 169–217.

5. Cohen, M.A. 1992. "Environmental Crime and Punishment: Legal/Economic Theory and Empirical Evidence on Enforcement of Federal Environmental Statutes." *The Journal of Criminal Law and Criminology* (82): 1054–1108.

6. Macy, J.R. 1991. "Agency Theory and the Criminal Liability of Organizations." *Boston University Law Review* (71): 315–340.

7. Daboub, A.J., A.M.A. Rasheed, R.L. Priem, and D.A. Gray. 1995. "Top Management Team Characteristics and Corporate Illegal Activity." *Academy of Management Review* (Vol. 20, No. 1): 138–170.

8. Simpson, S.S. 1986. "The Decomposition of Antitrust: Testing a Multi-level Longitudinal Model of Profit-Squeeze." *American Sociological Review* (51): 859–875.

9. Baucus, M.S. and J.P. Near. 1991. "Can Illegal Corporate Behavior be Predicted? An Event History Analysis." *Academy of Management Journal* (34): 9–36.

10. Baucus, M.S. 1990. "Pressure, Opportunity, and Predisposition: Broadening the Theory of Illegal Corporate Behavior." Paper presented at the Annual Academy of Management Meeting, San Francisco, CA.

11. DiMaggio, P.J. and W.W. Powell. 1983. "The Iron Cage Revisited: Institutional Isomorphism and Collective Rationality in Organizational Fields." *American Sociological Review* (48): 147–160.

12. Staw, B.M. and E. Szwajkowski. 1975. "The Scarcity-Munificence Component of Organizational Environment and the Commission of Illegal Acts." *Administrative Science Quarterly* (20): 345–354.

13. Baucus, M.S. and J.P. Near. 1991. "Can Illegal Corporate Behavior be Predicted? An Event History Analysis." *Academy of Management Journal* (34): 9–36.

14. Simpson, S.S. 1986. "The Decomposition of Antitrust: Testing a Multi-level Longitudinal Model of Profit-Squeeze." *American Sociological Review* (51): 859–875.

15. Baucus, M.S. and J.P. Near. 1991. "Can Illegal Corporate Behavior be Predicted? An Event History Analysis." *Academy of Management Journal* (34): 9–36.

16. Daboub, A.J., A.M.A. Rasheed, R.L. Priem, and D.A. Gray. 1995. "Top Management Team Characteristics and Corporate Illegal Activity." *Academy of Management Review* (Vol. 20, No. 1): 138–170.

17. Beasley, M.S., J.V. Carcello, and D.R. Hermanson. 1999. Fraudulent Financial Reporting. 1987–1997. An Analysis of U.S. Public Companies. Research Commissioned by the Committee of Sponsoring Organizations of the Treadway Commission. Jersey City, NJ: AICPA.

18. Baucus, M.S. and J.P. Near. 1991. "Can Illegal Corporate Behavior be Predicted? An Event History Analysis." *Academy of Management Journal* (34): 9–36.

19. Beasley, M.S., J.V. Carcello, and D.R. Hermanson. 1999. Fraudulent Financial Reporting. 1987–1997. An Analysis of U.S. Public Companies. Research Commissioned by the Committee of Sponsoring Organizations of the Treadway Commission. Jersey City, NJ: AICPA.

Chapter 5

Taxonomy and Schemes

INTRODUCTION

Management may attempt to use creative accounting techniques to make the company look good financially by engaging in financial statement fraud. Auditors should have a healthy skepticism when auditing financial statements. This chapter presents financial shenanigans including illegitimate earnings management to commit financial statement fraud. Taxonomies of financial statement fraud are also developed to identify common fraud schemes and related red flags. The effectiveness of the red flag approach and a model of the whistle-blowing process in attacking and detecting financial statement fraud is also examined in this chapter.

FINANCIAL SHENANIGANS

Financial shenanigans are defined by Schilit (1993)[1] and recited by Crumbley and Apostolou (2001)[2] as "acts or omission intended to hide or distort the real financial performance or financial condition of an entity." Crumbley and Apostolou (2001) argue that management often uses creative accounting techniques to engage in financial shenanigans and attempts to hide them from users of financial statements. Crumbley and Apostolou (2001, .133) suggest that investors, in assessing the quality, reliability, and integrity of financial information, "must attack financial statement and company information the way the fictional Sherlock Holmes approached murder cases."[3] Schilit (1993) and Crumbley and Apostolou (2001) provide a list of financial shenanigans intended to manage earnings by either boosting current year earnings or shift current year earnings to the future. Examples of these shenanigans are early recognition of revenue, creation of fictitious revenue, nonrecognition of liabilities, and deferral of expenses. These and other earnings management techniques and financial shenanigans are thoroughly discussed later in the chapter. Management often uses accounting gimmicks to manage earnings; auditors should be alert to possible red flags signaling outright financial shenanigans intended to hide or distort the real financial position, financial conditions, and cash flows. Examples of symptoms that may indicate that a company may engage in financial statement fraud are as follows.

Continuous Deterioration of Quality and Quantity of Earnings

One of the most significant contributing factors that increases the likelihood of financial statement fraud is a downward trend in both quantity and quality of earnings. Publicly traded companies are required to disclose earnings for the previous three years in their income statement. Auditors should examine both the quality of the reported past three years' earnings, such as the nature of earnings transactions (e.g., nonrecurring transactions, long-term contracts, bill-and-hold transactions), as well as the quantity of earnings.

Inadequacy of Cash Flow

Management may use several earnings management techniques, which are discussed in this chapter, to boost earnings when cash flows do not adequately support the appearance of increased earnings. Auditors should realize that cash is king and use the cash flow statement to verify the quantity, quality, reliability, and legitimacy of the reported earnings. The likelihood of financial statement fraud exists when there is no balance between reported earnings and cash flows. For example, earnings are moving up, while cash flows are drifting downward.

Overstatement of Inventories

Overstatement of inventories and receivables may indicate symptoms of financial difficulties and the possibility of financial statement fraud. Inventory and accounts receivable frauds are commonly used schemes by management to manage earnings and improve the company's financial position. Inventory fraud is one of the most common contributing factors to financial statement fraud. To effectively prevent and detect inventory fraud, the inventory observation audit team should include experienced, competent, and skeptical personnel who pay special attention to inventories that appear not to have been used for some time or that are stored in unusual locations or manners.

Overly Aggressive Accounting

Another important contributing factor to financial statement fraud is the company's use of aggressive accounting principles, methods, and practices in areas such as revenue recognition, depreciation and amortization, and capitalization and deferral of costs. The use of such accounting practices provides a warning that management may engage in financial statement fraud in an attempt to improve the appearance of operational results, financial position, and cash flows.

TAXONOMY OF FINANCIAL STATEMENT FRAUD

Several studies and reports have developed a taxonomy of financial statement fraud consisting of financial statement schemes perpetrated by publicly traded companies. The COSO Report (1999) lists common financial statement fraud techniques in the following categories:[4]

- Improper Revenue Recognition
- Overstatement of Assets other than Accounts Receivable
- Understatement of Expenses/Liabilities
- Misappropriation of Assets
- Inappropriate Disclosure
- Other Miscellaneous Techniques

The COSO Report (1999) identifies these financial statement fraud schemes through content analysis of 204 cases of fraud presented in the SEC's Accounting Auditing Enforcement Releases (AAERs) from 1987 to 1997. The COSO Report states that the two most common techniques used by companies to engage in fraudulent activities are improper revenue recognition techniques to overstate reported revenues and improper techniques to overstate assets.

Improper Revenue Recognition

The COSO Report (1999) indicates that 50 percent of studied fraud companies overstated revenues by recording revenues prematurely or by creating fictitious revenue transactions. Schemes used to engage in such fraudulent financial activities are sham sales, premature revenues before all the terms of the sale were completed, conditional sales, improper cutoff of sales, improper use of the percentage of completion method, unauthorized shipments, and consignment sales. These fraud schemes are thoroughly examined in the next section.

Overstatement of Assets

The COSO Report (1999) reveals that about 50 percent of the studied fraud companies overstated assets by recording fictitious assets or assets not owned, capitalizing items that should have been expensed, inflating existing asset values through the use of higher market values, and understating receivable allowances. Asset accounts most commonly misstated, in the order of ranking of frequency, are inventory; accounts receivable; property, plant, and equipment; loans/notes receivable; cash; investments; patents; and oil, gas, and mineral reserves.

Other Fraud Schemes

Other fraud schemes identified in the COSO Report (1999) are (1) understatement of expenses and liabilities, which counted for only 18 percent of financial statement fraud; (2) misappropriation of assets, involved in only 12 percent of the studied 204 fraud cases; (3) improper disclosures with no financial statement line item effects, which were found in about 8 percent of fraud cases; and (4) other miscellaneous fraud schemes, which accounted for 20 percent of identified financial statement fraud cases.

Bonner, Palmrose, and Young (1998) developed a comprehensive fraud taxonomy by identifying the fraud schemes presented in the studied companies' financial statements according to their type.[5] Bonner et al. (1998) employed several steps in developing their fraud taxonomy. First, they identified and analyzed the sources that present fraud taxonomies, including academic and practitioner articles, books, and training material of professional organizations such as AICPA and ACFE, as well as professional services firms (e.g., Big Five auditing firms). Second, they created several iterations of fraud taxonomies from the identified sources. Finally, they developed a comprehensive list of fraud taxonomies classified into the following categories of fraud:

1. *Fictitious and/or overstated revenues and related assets.* This category consists of fictitious sales such as invoices to phony companies, phony invoices to legitimate companies, and no supporting invoices. Overstated sales involved shipments made to customers for nonordered or cancelled goods, sales recognized for shipment made to a warehouse, recording customer and contract deposits as completed sales, recognizing refunds from suppliers as revenue, and recognizing the entire proceeds from sale of assets (e.g., properties, plants, and equipments, marketable securities, long-term investments) as income.

2. *Premature Revenue Recognition.* This category involves improper revenue recognition by (1) holding the books open beyond the end of the reporting period to record large or unusual transactions shortly before or after the end of reporting periods (e.g., annual or quarterly); (2) shipping products before a sale is consummated or indications that customers are not obligated to pay for shipments; (3) recording bill-and-hold sales transactions or other indications that sales are recognized in advance of shipment; (4) recognizing conditional sales depending on availability of financing, resale to third parties, final acceptance, performance guarantees, and further customer modifications; (5) overstating percentage-of-completion revenues when there are uncertainties about the bona fides of the underlying contract; (6) improperly recording sales returns and allowances; (7) recording sales of products shipped in advance of the scheduled shipment date without customer's agreement; and (8) recognizing partially completed goods in the process of being assembled and shipped to customer as actual sales.

3. *Misclassified Revenues and Assets.* This type of fraud refers to intentional misclassification of (1) unusual, extraordinary, and nonrecurring gains or losses from income related to continuous operation; (2) misclassification of assets to current and noncurrent assets; (3) combining restricted cash accounts with

unrestricted cash accounts; and (4) classifying long-term investments as short-term marketable securities.

4. *Fictitious Assets and/or Reductions of Expenses/Liabilities.* Recording fictitious assets is commonly involved in overstating inventories. Inventory fraud is viewed as one of the major reasons for financial statement fraud. This type of fraud consists of (1) mislabeling scrap, obsolete, and lower-value materials as real inventory; (2) recording consigned inventory as inventory; and (3) receiving fictitious inventory and other assets.

5. *Overvalued Assets or Undervalued Expenses/Liabilities.* Deliberate overvaluing of assets and undervaluing of expenses and liabilities includes (1) large post-due receivables or large receivables from related parties; (2) insufficient allowance for bad debt expenses; (3) inadequate loan loss reserve; (4) insufficient obsolescence reserves for inventories; (5) not adjusting investment in securities for declines in the market value; (6) undervaluing intangibles; and (7) inadequate writeoffs for impaired assets including goodwill.

6. *Omitted or Undervalued Liabilities.* This category of fraud also affects expenses and/or assets and may consist of underestimating pensions and postretirement liabilities and failing to accrue or underaccruing warranties and commission liability.

7. *Omitted or Improper Disclosure.* Footnote disclosures are important elements of quality financial statements. Improper and omitted disclosure of financial items or changes in accounting principles makes financial statements less transparent.

8. *Equity Frauds.* Equity frauds refer to fraudulent financial activities affecting equity accounts such as (1) recording nonrecurrent and unusual income or expenses in equity; (2) inappropriately valuing assets obtained in exchange for stock; and (3) inappropriately selecting the accounting method for merger and acquisition transactions (e.g., purchase versus pooling of interests method).

9. *Related-Party Transactions.* This type of fraud consists of material related-party transactions or amounts that appear unusual or whose purpose is unclear, including (1) fictitious sales to related parties (e.g., affiliated entities, top executives); (2) loans to or from related parties for less than market-effective interest rates; (3) any other less than arm's-length transaction dealing with related parties (e.g., sales of assets); and (4) improper disclosures of related-party transactions.

10. *Financial Frauds Going the "Wrong Directions."* Management is typically much more prone to overstate revenues and assets and understate expenses and liabilities; however, for various reasons (e.g., tax purposes, fear of unwanted mergers and acquisitions), management may engage in financial statement fraud by deliberately understating revenues and assets and/or overstating expenses and liabilities. Management intention is to portray a less

Exhibit 5.1.   Most Frequently Used Fraud Schemes

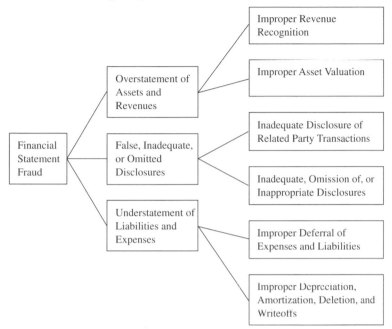

favorable, unattractive, and less impressive financial position, operating results, and cash flows. Examples of this type of fraud are (1) establishing "rainy day reserves" that could be reversed in future years when the company's actual earnings were less favorable; (2) shifting revenues to a subsequent reporting period; (3) recording a fixed asset as an expense; (4) improperly or insufficiently recording capitalized expenditures; (5) overstating liabilities; (6) overstating bad debt expenses; and (7) overestimating depreciation, amortization, and writeoffs of assets.

COMMON FRAUD SCHEMES

Financial statement frauds consist of a wide variety of schemes, ranging from overstatements of revenues and assets to omission of material financial information to understatement of expenses and liabilities. Exhibit 5.1 presents some of the most common financial statement fraud schemes. Examples are:

- *Misclassification of gains.* Often involved in classifying extraordinary or non-operating gains as part of the income from continuing operations.
- *Sham transaction.* Typically associated with co-conspirators for whom the scheme is intended to benefit.

- *Timing of revenue recognition.* Usually consists of early recognition of income intended to overstate sales, which are typically fictitious. Many revenue frauds involve improper cutoffs as of the end of the reporting period.
- *Bill-and-hold sales transaction.* When the customer agrees to buy goods by signing the contract but the seller retains possession until the customer requests shipment. Companies can manage earnings by the early recognition of bill-and-hold sales transactions.
- *Side arrangements.* Often involve sales with conditions set by the purchaser, such as acceptance, installation, and adaptability. Side agreements typically alter the terms of a sale agreement by including unilateral cancellation, termination, or other privileges for the customer to avoid the transaction. Side agreements can result in overstatement of revenue, which is an important contributing factor to the occurrence of financial statement fraud.
- *Illegitimate sales transactions.* Typically relate to recording fictitious sales involving either phantom customers or real customers with false invoices, which are recorded in one reporting period (overstatement) and reversed in the next reporting period.
- *Improper revenue recognition.* Consists of inappropriate use of percentage of completion method of accounting for long-term contracts, where management deliberately misrepresents the percentage of completion when the project is less complete than the amount reflected on the financial statements and often corroborated by fabricated documents.
- *Improper related-party transactions.* Result from the company engaging in less than arm's-length transactions with its top executives or affiliated companies.
- *Improper asset valuations.* Often involved in business combinations of recording fictitious inventory, accounts receivable, or fixed assets as well as improper valuations of these assets.
- *Improper deferral of costs and expenses.* Often involves failure to disclose warranty costs and expenses, inappropriate capitalization of expenses, and omissions of liabilities.
- *Inadequate disclosure or omission of material financial information.* Often associated with deliberate actions by management not to disclose material financial information either within the body of the financial statements, in their related footnotes, or in its Management's Discussion and Analysis (MD&A).
- *Improper cutoff of transactions at end of reporting period.* Often associated with interim quarterly financial statements, which are typically carried on into annual financial statements.

EARNINGS MANAGEMENT

Many recent high-profile financial statement frauds (e.g., Waste Management, Lucent, Sunbeam, Raytheon, Enron) have been attributed to a broad range of earnings management practices, including illegitimate revenue recognition, inappropriate deferral of expenses, fictitious sales, premature sales, reversal, or use of unjustified reserves. These practices have raised serious concerns about the quality of reported earnings and have drawn the attention of the SEC and other regulators and standard-setting bodies (e.g., AICPA, FASB). The tremendous pressure to achieve earnings targets and meet analysts' earnings forecasts can place a heavy burden on the top management teams, in terms of both job security and remuneration. This pressure, coupled with related financial incentives, can encourage management to use aggressive accounting practices and incorrect financial reporting interpretations that may lead to financial statement fraud.

Definitions

Earnings management has been defined differently by academicians, researchers, practitioners, and authoritative bodies. The most commonly accepted definitions of earnings management provided by academicians and researchers in the academic literature are as follows:

1. Schipper (1989, 92): ". . . a purposeful intervention in the external financial reporting process, with the intent of obtaining some private gain."[6]
2. Healy and Wahlen (1999, 368): "Earnings management occurs when managers use judgment in financial reporting and in structuring transactions to alter financial reports to either mislead some stakeholders about the underlying economic performance of the company, or to influence contractual outcomes that depend on reported accounting numbers."[7]
3. Merchant (1987, 168): "Earnings management can be defined as any action on the part of management which affects reported income and which provides no true economic advantage to the organization and may, in fact, in the long-term, be detrimental."[8]

Practitioners in their professional literature often define earnings management in relation to financial statement fraud with special focus on the incentives managers have to manage earnings and the consequences of their actions. Management may attempt to manage earnings through the use of its discretionary choices of accounting policies, accounting judgments, or timing or selection of operating decisions. Managers manage earnings in performing their normal functions. Indeed, most of the earnings management actions are legitimate and consistent with generally accepted accounting principles (GAAP) and within the manager's prerogatives; however, illegitimate earnings management involving deliberate manipulation of earnings in an attempt to meet earnings expectations can be harmful.

Unlike academicians and researchers, practitioners focus on the role of financial information in the decision-making process of investors and creditors as a primary motivation for illegitimate earnings management. The Association of Certified Fraud Examiners (ACFE, formerly National Association of Certified Fraud Examiners, 1993) states that the primary reason for illegitimate earnings management that may constitute financial fraud is "to encourage investment through the sale of stock."[9]

The SEC former chairperson Arthur Levitt, in a September 28, 1998, speech at New York University, refers to earnings management as a game among market participants. Levitt (1998) characterized earnings management as a process of "a game of nods and winks" among corporate managers, analysts, and external auditors. More specifically, Levitt stated that:

> In the zeal to satisfy consensus earnings estimates and project a smooth earnings path, wishful thinking may be winning the day over faithful representation . . . I fear that we are witnessing an erosion in the quality of earnings, and therefore, the quality of financial reporting. Managing may be giving way to manipulation; integrity may be losing out the illusion.[10]

Forms of Earnings Management

The flexibility of GAAP in providing a variety of accepted methods for measuring, recognizing, and reporting financial transactions may be used by management as a tool to manage earnings. The two most commonly used methods of earnings management are "smoothing" and "big bath." The smoothing method can be used by management to smooth the stream of reported earnings by undertaking income-decreasing discretionary accruals (e.g., allowance for bad debt) in good years and income-increasing discretionary accruals (e.g., percentage of completion) in lean years. Contrarily, the "big bath" method of earnings management can be used to undertake income-decreasing discretionary accruals (e.g., write-offs, impairments of assets) in lean years based on the assumption that a poor performance report for one year is not as damaging (e.g., negative market reactions) as several mediocre performance reports. Under "big bath," charges are perpetrated under business combinations or restructuring to avoid future charges related to normal operating costs.

In recent speeches and writings by SEC officials and staff, the main concerns have been illegitimate earnings management that may result in financial statement fraud. Under a category of "Accounting Hocus-Pocus," Levitt discussed the following five major illusions that are threatening the integrity, reliability, and quality of financial reports:[11]

1. *"Big Bath" Charges.* Often involve one-time overstating of restructuring charges by creating "reserves" that can be used to offset future operating costs. The perception is that a one-time loss is discounted by analysts and investors, who will then focus on future earnings.

2. *Creative Acquisition Accounting.* Commonly relates to business combination strategies by using "merger magic" of avoiding future earnings charges through excessive one-time charges for in-process research and development and creation of excessive purchase accounting reserves.

3. *Miscellaneous "Cookie Jar" Reserves.* Usually involve unrealistic assumptions to estimate liabilities for sales returns, loan losses, or warranty costs by establishing reserves in the "good times" and using these to shore up earnings in the "bad times."

4. *Abuse of Materiality Concept.* Often involves deliberate recording errors of intentionally ignoring mistakes in the financial statement under the assumption that their impact on the bottom line (earnings or earnings per share) is not significant enough to change investors' and creditors' investment decisions.

5. *Revenue Recognition.* Commonly involves recording revenue before it is earned, which is before a sale is complete, before the product has been delivered, or while the customer can still void or delay the sale. More than half of the SEC's enforcement cases filed in 1999 and 2000 involved improper revenue recognition, including bill-and-hold sales, conditional sales, fictitious sales, and improper cutoff sales. In these cases, revenues were improperly recognized because (1) sales agreements are not yet accepted by customers; (2) customers unilaterally can terminate or cancel the agreement; (3) delivery of the product or service has not occurred; and (4) the seller has not fully completed all the sale obligations such as installation or training.

COMMON REVENUE FRAUD SCHEMES

Illegitimate earnings management practices of improperly boosting reported earnings by manipulating the recognition of revenue are described by SEC former chairperson Arthur Levitt as "Hocus-Pocus Accounting."[12] The most common methods of illegitimate earnings management are the bill-and-hold transaction and a wide variety of sham transactions involving shipping, billing, and/or related-party transactions.

Bill-And-Hold Schemes

A bill-and-hold scheme is often used by corporations to overstate earnings in an attempt to meet or exceed analysts' expectations, especially for quarterly earnings forecasts. In a bill-and-hold deal, the customer agrees to buy goods by signing the contract, but the seller retains possession until the customer requests shipment. The seller may recognize revenue in compliance with existing GAAP because the transaction meets two conditions of (1) realized or realizable; and (2) earned as required by GAAP. Revenues usually are recognized at the time of sale, which is often delivery of goods or services to customers. While bill-and-hold sales transactions are not necessarily a GAAP violation, they are often used by corporations to manage earnings illegitimately, which may result in financial statement fraud. Thus, auditors should assess the substance of such transactions to make sure they are legitimate and arm's-length transactions.

The SEC has specified in its recent enforcement actions that transactions that meet the following criteria could be recognized as revenues: (1) the company must have a fixed commitment to purchase from the customer, preferably in writing; (2) the risks of ownership must have passed to the buyer; (3) the buyer, not the seller, must have requested the transaction and must have a legitimate business purpose of a bill-and-hold deal; (4) the seller must not retain any significant specific performance obligations, such as an obligation to assist in resale; (5) there must be a fixed delivery date that is reasonable and consistent with the buyer's business purpose; and (6) the goods must be complete and ready for shipment and not subject to being used to bill other orders.[13]

Other Sham Transactions

Sham transactions are typically associated with financial statement fraud and appear to be legitimate sales, but they are not. Examples of sham transactions include (1) sales with a commitment from the seller to repurchase; (2) sales without substance, such as funding the buyer to assure collection; (3) sales with a guarantee by an entity financed by the seller of what would otherwise be considered as an uncollectable receivable; (4) sales for goods merely shipped to another company location (e.g., warehouse); (5) premature revenues before all the terms of the sales were completed by recording sales after the goods were ordered but before they were shipped to the customers or shipping in advance of the scheduled date without the customer's knowledge and instruction.

Improper Cutoff of Sales

Improper cutoff of sales involves keeping the accounting records open beyond the reporting period to record sales of the subsequent reporting period in the current period. This scheme is more effective for manipulation of quarterly revenue than annual revenue by keeping books open so revenue is recorded in that quarter.

Conditional Sales

Conditional sales are transactions recorded as revenues even though the sales associated with transactions involved substantial unresolved contingencies or subsequent agreements that eliminated the customer's obligations to retain the merchandise.

AUTHORITATIVE PRONOUNCEMENTS ON EARNINGS MANAGEMENT

The 1999 COSO Report on Fraudulent Financial Reporting states that more than half of the studied financial statement frauds involved overstating revenues by recording revenues prematurely or fictitiously. The Statement of Financial Accounting Concept (SFAC) No. 6 entitled "Element of Financial Statements" defines revenues as "actual or expected cash flows (or the equivalent) that have occurred or will eventually occur as a result of the enterprise's ongoing major or central operations."[14] Fraudulent revenue is revenue recognized when management deliberately records fictitious revenue that will not eventually occur.

The pervasiveness of financial statement fraud resulting from unacceptable earnings management practices encouraged the SEC to issue two important Staff Accounting Bulletins (SABs) No. 100 and 101.[15] SAB No. 100 addresses restructuring changes, impairments to inventory valuation allowances, and liabilities assumed in connection with business combinations. SAB No. 100 requires registrants to exercise appropriate judgment in applying GAAP to ensure that (1) the balance sheet amounts reflect management's best judgment in the integration process and business combinations; and (2) investors, creditors, and other financial statement users are able to rely on the consistency, comparability, and transparency of financial information disclosed by management. SASB No. 100 further presents the staff's view on how business combination transactions should be measured, recognized, and reported in a consistent and comparable manner.

SAB No. 101 relates to revenue recognition by providing additional guidelines for accountants to follow in complying with GAAP in recording revenue transactions. SAB No. 101 presents the fundamental criteria that must be met before registrants may record revenue: (1) sufficient and competent evidence that an arrangement exists; (2) persuasive evidence that delivery has occurred or that services have been rendered; (3) clear indications that the seller's price to the buyer is fixed or determinable; and (4) collectibility of the price or fee is reasonably assured under purchase agreements.

EARNINGS MANAGEMENT AND FINANCIAL STATEMENT FRAUD

Management often uses its accounting discretion consistent with GAAP to manage earnings in performing its assigned managerial functions. Most earnings management activities, such as using accounting discretions involving judgments and estimates within the GAAP regime, are acceptable even though they may appear aggressive. Deliberate earnings manipulations with the intent to deceive investors and creditors are illegitimate earnings management and constitute financial statement fraud. Exhibit 5.2, adapted from an article by Dechow and Skinner (2000), attempts to make the distinction between fraudulent earnings manipulations and aggressive but acceptable earnings management activities.[16]

Exhibit 5.2.   Distinction between Fraud and Earnings Management

Accounting Choices	"Real" Cash Flow Choices
Within GAAP	
"Conservative" Accounting	
• Overly aggressive recognition of provisions or reserves	• Delaying sales
• Overvaluation of acquired in-process R&D in purchase acquisitions	• Accelerating R&D or advertising expenditures
• Overstatement of restructuring charges and asset writeoffs	
"Neutral" Earnings	• Postponing R&D or advertising expenditures
• Earnings that result from a neutral operation of the process	• Accelerating sales
"Aggressive" Accounting	• Understatement of the provision for bad debts
• Drawing down provisions or reserves in an overly aggressive manner	
Violates GAAP	
"Fraudulent" Accounting	• Recording sales before they are "realizable"
	• Recording fictitious sales
	• Backdating sales invoices
	• Overstating inventory by recording fictitious inventory

Source: Adapted from Dechow, P.M., and P.J. Skinner. 2000. "Earnings Management: Reconciling the Views of Accounting Academics, Practitioners, and Regulators." Accounting Horizons (Vol. 14, No. 2, June): 235–250.

There is a fine line between legitimate earnings management and outright fraudulent earnings management to achieve earnings targets when management is overly interested in the portrayal, rather than the reality, of financial results. The gray area between legitimacy and outright fraud when earnings reports portray the desires of management rather than the reality has recently piqued the interest of the SEC.

Nonfraudulent versus Fraudulent Earnings Management

Earnings management can be classified into two general categories of nonfraudulent and fraudulent earnings management. Nonfraudulent earnings management occurs when companies choose a generally accepted accounting method within the GAAP region that has a direct and favorable impact on the amount and timing of reported income. Flexibility of GAAP gives management latitude to use its professional judgment to choose from a broad range of standards and guidelines those that best suit the needs of its company. For example, the use of some generally accepted accounting methods and policies such as a first-in, first-out (FIFO) inventory valuation method, a straight-line depreciation method for depreciable capital assets, and the flow-through method of accounting for income tax credits produces a higher net income than the use of a last-in, first-out (LIFO) inventory, accelerated depreciation, and the deferral method for the same aforementioned financial items. Thus, the application of a different set of accounting methods could result in different earnings and earnings per share.

The requirement of consistent application of accounting methods from one year to the next somewhat reduces the opportunity of earnings management through the choice of accounting methods. Nevertheless, companies are not required to use the same accounting methods, even in the same industry. Therefore, companies can manage their earnings through the accounting methods they choose. Earnings can also be managed by the flexibility given to management in determining the amount of "soft" accounting estimates, such as allowances for doubtful accounts, warranty reserves, useful life of capital assets, pension expenses, and inventory obsolescence; however, the legitimacy, representational truthfulness, and ethics of nonfraudulent earnings management have been debated in the literature (e.g., Burns and Merchant, 1990; Merchant and Rockness, 1994; MacIntosh, 1995).[17,18,19]

Fraudulent earnings management, however, is not made within the GAAP framework of acceptable accounting methods and, therefore, is an illegal form of earnings management. Examples of fraudulent earnings management schemes are falsification, alteration, and deliberate manipulation of earnings through illegal acts. Financial statement frauds are a set of financial statements that purport to be in accordance with GAAP, but they are not. Furthermore, these fraudulent financial statements are not detected by auditors. Thus, the users of financial statements make decisions based on the false understanding that the statements are fairly presented in accordance with GAAP.

Studies show that profitable firms with favorable financial results can more easily and feasibly raise funds through financing than can poorly performing firms (Brealey et al., 1992).[20] Published financial statements and reported accounting information typically influence the perceptions of potential investors regarding earnings potential and the value of the firm. Thus, management has incentives to exercise income-increasing discretionary accounting alternatives to make the company look good financially by managing earnings. DeAngelo (1986, 405)[21] suggests that management has a strong incentive to hide any deliberate earnings management "since greater payoffs obviously accrue to managers whose accounting manipulations go undetected by the parties that would be adversely affected by them."

Dechow et al. (1996, 4)[22] states that, "Management and existing shareholders benefit from manipulating investors' perceptions of firm value if they can raise additional financing on more favorable terms or see their stock holdings for a higher price." Dechow et al. (1996) found that fraudulent financial reporting is more prevalent when managerial discretion is curtailed and firms have a higher debt-to-equity ratio than nonfraud firms.

Kinney and McDaniel (1989, 74)[23] states that managers "of firms in weak financial condition are more likely to 'window dress' in an attempt to disguise what may be temporary difficulties." Managerial ownership provides incentives for management to increase the value of their ownership interest by fraudulently reporting a better financial performance than otherwise would be reported under GAAP. Loebbecke, Eining, and Willingham (1989)[24] concluded that a high managerial interest in the firm is a red-flag indicator of a potential financial statement fraud. Dechow et al. (1996)[25] found that managers of SEC-investigated firms held a greater percentage of ownership interest than managers of noninvestigated firms. Beasley (1996)[26] also found that firms that engage in financial statement fraud have a higher management ownership than nonfraud firms.

Dechow et al. (1996) investigated firms subject to accounting enforcement actions by the SEC for alleged violations of GAAP to determine the relationship between earnings management and weaknesses in corporate governance structure and the capital market consequences experienced by firms when the alleged earnings manipulations are made available. Dechow et al. (1996) found that an important motivation for illegitimate earnings management is a desire to attract external financing at low cost. They also found that firms engaged in illegitimate earnings management are (1) more likely to have boards of directors dominated by management; (2) more likely to have a chief executive officer (CEO) as chairman of the board of directors; (3) more likely to have a CEO who is also the firm's founder; (4) less likely to have an audit committee; (5) less likely to have an outside blockholder; and (6) more likely to have significantly increased capital costs when violations (illegitimate earnings management) are made public.

SYMPTOMS OF FINANCIAL STATEMENT FRAUD

Several reports and studies have developed a list of symptoms (or better known as red flags) of financial statement fraud. Red flags are important symptoms signaling the likelihood of financial statement fraud. Both internal and external auditors are well qualified and positioned to identify the red flags and develop a risk model to prevent and detect financial statement fraud; however, internal auditors' involvement in the routine activities of the corporation and internal control environment place them in the best position to identify and assess evidence that may signal financial statement fraud.

Qualitative red flags are important pieces of evidence for signaling the likelihood of financial statement fraud. A proper focus on red flags can assist in exploring the underlying factors that cause financial statement fraud. Possible symptoms of financial statement fraud are compiled from several studies and reports, and they are listed in three general categories of (1) organizational structure; (2) financial conditions; and (3) business and industry environments. The list of red flags presented on the following pages is adapted from the Treadway Commission Report (1987); SAS Nos. 53 and 82; Loebbecke et al. (1989)[27]; Albrecht and Romney (1986)[28]; Elliot and Willingham (1986)[29]; Coopers and Lybrand (1977)[30]; and financial statement fraud cases examined and presented in Exhibit 3.1 of Chapter 3.

Red flags in these studies and reports are defined as potential symptoms that may signal the likelihood and risk of financial statement fraud. These studies and reports identify many red flags and examine their relationships with the occurrence or nonoccurrence of financial statement fraud; however, the predictive ability of red flags is limited because no causal relationship exists between red flags and financial statement fraud. In other words, red flag conditions may exist in both fraudulent and nonfraudulent business environments. Elliot and Willingham (1980, p. 8)[31] state that:

> Red flags do not indicate the presence of fraud. They are conditions believed to be commonly present in events of fraud and they, therefore, suggest that concern may be warranted.

Organizational Structure Red Flags

1. A highly domineering top management team
2. Predominantly insider or gray board of directors
3. Ineffective board of directors
4. Compensations for top executives tied to earnings or stock price targets
5. Ineffective, illiterate, and incompetent audit committee
6. Inappropriate "tone at the top"
7. Overly complex organizational structures
8. Frequent organizational changes
9. Frequent turnover of senior management
10. Inexperienced management team
11. Lack of management oversight
12. Irresponsible corporate governance
13. Nonexistent or ineffective audit committee
14. Lack of vigilant board of directors' oversight
15. Management override
16. Autocratic management
17. Excessive or inappropriate performance-based compensation
18. Frequent changes of external auditors
19. Lack of adequate and effective internal control structure
20. Nonexistent or ineffective internal audit function
21. Rapid turnover of key personnel (either quit or fired)

22. Nonexistent corporate code of conduct
23. Ineffective leadership
24. Lack of personnel evaluation
25. Extremely large and decentralized firm
26. Inexperienced and aggressive personnel in key positions
27. No or ineffective communication between the audit committee and external auditors
28. No or infrequent meeting between the audit committee and internal auditors
29. Lack of cooperation and coordination between internal and external auditors
30. Management reluctant to cooperate with external auditors or consider external auditors' suggestions and recommendations
31. Use of several legal counsels
32. Use of several different banks for specified purposes
33. Lack of or ineffective mechanisms for reporting management violations of company policy
34. Conflict of interests within company management
35. Executives with record of malfeasance
36. High percentage of inside and financially interested members on the board of directors
37. Significant management compensation derived from performance-based incentive plan
38. Company holdings as material portion of management's personal wealth
39. Management's job threatened by poor performance
40. Management has lied to regulators and auditors or has been evasive
41. Management's aggressive attitude toward financial reporting
42. Personality anomalies
43. Lax attitude toward internal controls and management policy
44. Lax attitude toward compliance with applicable laws and regulations
45. Poor reputation of management in the business community
46. Frequent disputes between management and external auditors
47. Too much trust in key executives
48. Domination of the company by one or two aggressive individuals
49. Key executives with low moral character
50. Key executives exhibiting strong greed
51. Failure to require top executives to take at least a week's vacation at a time
52. Failure to pay attention to details
53. Wheeler-dealer top executives
54. Struggling to gloss over a temporary bad situation

55. Key executives with a strong desire to beat the system
56. Conflicts of interest within the company
57. Management places undue pressure on auditors
58. Management had engaged in opinion shopping
59. Decentralized organization structure without adequate monitoring
60. Management displays significant disrespect for regulatory bodies
61. Management is overly evasive when responding to audit inquiries

Financial Conditions Red Flags

1. Deterioration of earnings quality as evidenced by a sharp decline in sales volume
2. Unrealistic earnings expectations
3. Unrealistic growth goals
4. Overly complex and unusual business transactions
5. Unusually rapid growth
6. Unusual results or trends
7. Heavy investments or losses
8. Lack of adequate working capital
9. Overemphasis on one or two products, customers, or transactions
10. Excess capacity
11. Severe obsolescence
12. Extremely high debt
13. High rapid expansion through new business or product lines
14. Tight credit, high interest rates, and reduced ability to acquire credit
15. Pressure to finance expansion through current earnings rather than through debt or equity
16. Difficulty in collecting receivables
17. Progressive deterioration in quality and quantity of earnings
18. Significant tax adjustments by the IRS
19. Long-term financial losses
20. Unusually high earnings with a cash shortage
21. Urgent need for favorable earnings to support high price of stock and meet analysts' earnings forecasts
22. Significant litigation, especially between shareholders and management
23. The need for additional collateral to support existing obligations
24. Cash shortage or negative cash flows
25. Difficulties in collecting accounts receivable

26. Continually operating on crisis basis
27. Several losses from major investments
28. Unexpected and sharp decreases in earnings or market share experienced by a company or industry
29. Unrealistic budget pressures
30. Financial pressure to meet or even exceed analysts' forecasts
31. Financial pressure resulting from bonus plans tied to earnings performance
32. Significant off-balance sheet or contingent liability
33. The decision to finance expansion through the use of current earnings rather than through equity or debt
34. Earnings deterioration resulting from significant decreases in revenues or substantial increases in expenses
35. Pressure to meet investors' expectation as determined in analysts' forecasts
36. The need for additional collateral to satisfy debt covenants
37. Highly competitive global markets
38. Inadequate collectibility reserves
39. Substantial doubt about the company's ability to continue as a going concern
40. Significant difficult-to-audit transactions

Business and Industry Environment Red Flags

1. Business conditions that may create unusual pressures
2. Inadequate working capital
3. Major investment in volatile industry
4. Debt restrictions with little flexibility
5. Ongoing or prior investigation by regulators (e.g., SEC, IRS)
6. Aggressive attempts to maintain trends and achieve forecasts
7. Untimely reporting and responses to audit committee inquiries
8. Exposure to rapid technology changes
9. Industry softness or downturns
10. High interest rate and currency exposures
11. Unfavorable economic conditions within the industry
12. Unusually heavy competition
13. Existing loan agreements with little flexibility and tough restrictions
14. Long business cycle
15. Suspension or delisting from stock exchange
16. Fear of a merger
17. Highly computerized operations
18. Unusual and large year-end transactions

19. Many adjusted entries required at the time of audit
20. Provide information to auditors at the last minute
21. Use of liberal accounting practices
22. Inadequate accounting information system
23. Significant related-party transactions
24. Transactions that are difficult to audit
25. Material account balances determined by judgment
26. Introduction of significant new products and services
27. Product or industry in decline
28. Profitability of the company inconsistent with the industry
29. Operating results are inconsistent with macroeconomic industry
30. Aggressively optimistic operating and financial budgets
31. Unusual and significant contractual commitments
32. Pressure to meet investors' high expectations through budgeting process
33. Management doesn't see financial statement fraud as a risk
34. Management ignores irregularities
35. Morale is low, especially among top executives and managerial employees
36. High turnover within the company, especially at top executive level
37. Rapid increase in earnings
38. Aggressive and egotistical top executives
39. Maximizing profits is the corporate mission
40. Salary structure, especially for top executives, is tied to profits
41. Substantial doubt regarding the company's ability to continue as a going concern
42. Adverse legal circumstances
43. Evidence of inside tradings
44. Unjustifiable and high business risks
45. Competition from low-priced imports
46. Excess capacity caused by favorable economic conditions
47. Existence of revocable licenses necessary for continuation of business
48. Numerous acquisitions of speculative ventures in pursuit of diversification
49. Significant inventories and other assets that require special expertise for valuation
50. Long manufacturing cycle and throughput time
51. Little tolerance on debt restrictions
52. Uncertain issues relating to public trading of stock
53. Understated costs and expenses
54. Sizable increases in inventory without comparable increases in sales

Effectiveness of Red Flags

Financial statement fraud standards for external auditors (SAS No. 82) and for internal auditors (SIAS No. 3) require that auditors use the red flag approach in detecting material misstatements due to errors and fraud. Albrecht et al. (2001) reviewed the literature pertaining to the effectiveness of the red flag approach in detecting financial statement fraud.[32] They presented the following potential shortcomings of the red flag approach; (1) difficulties in gathering sufficient evidence regarding committed financial statement fraud primarily because not all committed frauds are detected and not all discovered frauds are reported; (2) lack of consistency and uniformity of financial statement fraud evidence which makes it difficult to draw generalizations about frauds; (3) rare documentation of financial statement frauds detected through the use of red flag approach; and (4) unavailability of sophisticated technologies to analyze large data bases to search for all fraud symptoms (red flags).

Albrecht et al. (2001),[33] conclude that the evidence regarding the effectiveness of red flags in detecting financial statement fraud is neither consistent nor compelling. They suggest the following methods of assessing the effectiveness of the red flag approach in detecting financial statement fraud (1) data mining commercial software such as audit command language (ACL); (2) analytical procedures including horizontal, vertical, ratios and other analysis of financial statements; (3) digital analysis (i.e., Benford's Law) on financial databases, and (4) the empirical fraud-hypothesis approach.

WHISTLE-BLOWING

Definition

Whistle-blowing is defined by Near and Miceli (1988, 5) as the ". . . disclosure by organizational members (former and current) of illegal, immoral, or illegitimate practices under the control of their employers, to persons or organizations that may be able to affect action."[34] According to this definition, whistle-blowing can come from internal parties within the organization or parties outside of the organization. Reporting of sensible issues, including fraud, to internal organization members outside the normal chain of command is viewed as whistle-blowing through internal channels. Reporting of these issues to individuals outside the organization is considered whistle-blowing through external channels.

Whistle-blowing basically means that an individual with knowledge of wrongdoing, including financial statement fraud, informs those with the authority to remedy the wrong of the situation. In the case of financial statement fraud, the appropriate remedial agency could be members of management not involved in the fraud, the board of directors, audit committees, internal auditors, external auditors, or outside regulatory or law enforcement bodies such as the SEC. Gamesmanship, however, is when the person with knowledge of wrongdoing, including financial statement fraud voluntary or *compulsory,* participates with the wrongdoers to cover up or commit the fraud.

Whistle-Blowing as an Internal Control Mechanism

Hooks, Kaplan, and Schultz (1994) argue that whistle-blowing can be used as an effective internal control mechanism by creating an environment that allows individuals to freely provide upstream communication both within and outside the organization to facilitate early detection and possible prevention of financial statement fraud.[35] Ponemon (1994) discusses two aspects of whistle-blowers' decisions to reveal or not reveal a perceived wrongdoing.[36] The first aspect is the underlying motivation of the whistle-blower to divulge sensitive information such as financial statement fraud. The second aspect relates to the full decision-making process of the individual contemplating the whistle-blowing act. The motivation of the whistle-blower is important in reporting wrongdoing, particularly if it is derived for personal gain. Motivated whistle-blowing can damage the quality of the whistle-blowing report and, therefore, the effectiveness and integrity of the company's internal control structure. Exhibit 5.3, adapted from Ponemon (1994, 123)

Exhibit 5.3. Components of the Whistle-blower's Decision-making Process

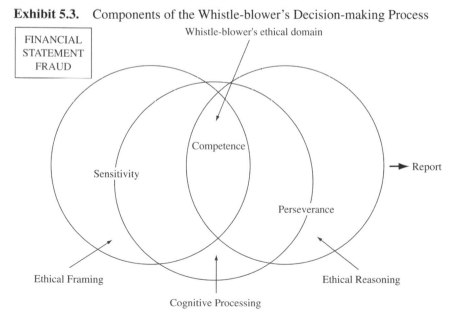

Adapted from Ponemon (1994, 123) Ponemon, L.A. 1994 "Whistle-blowing As An Internal Control Mechanism: Individual and Organizational Considerations." *Auditing: A Journal of Practice and Theory* (Fall): 118–130.

describes an integrated framework for the whistle-blowing decision in the organizational environment. Exhibit 5.3 shows three conditions for carrying out the whistle-blowing decision. The first condition is the ethical sensitivity of the individual to identify the wrongdoing act, signaling financial statement fraud. The second factor is the ethical competence of the individual who identified wrongdoing and the cognitive abilities to develop a strategy for dealing with the problems. The third element is the perseverance to follow through on an ethical course of action given that the wrongdoing was identified and the ethical strategy that was developed for disclosing the whistle-blowing report. These conditions are also influenced by the whistle-blower's ethical reasoning, cognitive process, and ethical framing. The aforementioned three conditions should be met in order to use whistle-blowing as a control mechanism in the organizational environment.

Channels for Communicating Wrongdoing

Ponemon (1994)[37] and Hooks et al. (1994)[38] describe internal and external channels for communicating sensitive issues such as financial statement fraud. The internal channel refers to disclosing wrongdoing to co-workers, top management, the audit committee, and/or the board of directors. External channels can be used to communicate wrongdoing to those outside of the company, such as media, external auditors, and/or a governmental agency. Whistle-blowers typically use internal channels as their first and often only course of action for communicating sensitive issues such as financial statement fraud, primarily because external disclosure may be viewed as a violation of business etiquette, employee loyalty, corporate code of conduct, and/or professional standards. For example, internal auditors are required to refrain from disclosing wrongdoing to individuals outside of their organizations in accordance with the Institute of Internal Auditors (IIA) Statement of Internal Auditors Standards (SIAS) No. 3.[39] Nevertheless, external challenges should be employed as a last resort for communicating wrongdoing when the internal communication fails to resolve the problem.

External auditors are required to use both internal and external channels in communicating sensitive issues such as financial statement fraud. Indeed, Section 301 of the Private Securities Litigation Reform Act of 1995 entitled "Fraud Detection and Disclosure" requires that external auditors design audit procedures to provide a reasonable assurance of detecting illegal acts that would have a direct and material effect on financial statements (e.g., financial statement fraud). The Reform Act also requires external auditors to inform the appropriate level of management and ensure that the audit committee (or the board of directors if there is no audit committee) is informed of financial statement fraud. If, after ensuring that the audit committee or the board of directors is adequately informed, the external auditors determine that financial statement fraud warrants departure from a standard audit report or resignation, the auditors should report the audit conclusion directly to the board of directors. The board of directors, upon receiving such a report, should notify the SEC of the auditors' report no later than one business day thereafter and provide the auditors with a copy of the notice to the SEC. If the board of directors does not act within one business day after the audit report was given to the board, the external auditors should resign, which will cause the registrant to file a Report Form 8-K regarding the resignation or report to the SEC no later than one business day following the failure to receive any notice from the board of directors.

External auditors should not be viewed as whistle-blowers who constantly report discovered errors, irregularities, or fraud to government authorities, however. The perception of external auditors as whistle-blowers is likely to create an adversarial relationship between clients and auditors. The existence of such a relationship would encourage even honest and ethical clients to provide the auditor with less than complete information disclosure and audit evidence out of fear that the auditor will suspect illegal or irregular acts and report them to the enforcement authorities.

A Model of the Whistle-Blowing Process

Hooks et al. (1994) suggest a model of the whistle-blowing process in the context of the internal and external audit functions that is intended to prevent and detect financial statement fraud. This model is presented in Exhibit 5.4 and was initially designed by Graham (1986)[40] and Miceli and Near (1992).[41] This model is developed based on the following assumptions:

- The improved climate for reporting wrongdoing, including financial statement fraud, will attenuate the probability of wrongdoings occurring.
- The potential perpetrator of financial statement fraud is not likely to proceed if prospects of being reported increase.
- The internal control as a mechanism of fraud detection is an important element of the model process that may occur solely within the organization.
- The external audit function as a mechanism for fraud detection is viewed as an important element of the model process that may involve external auditors.
- Many variables affect the likelihood of financial statement fraud, such as management attitude and operating style, existence of corporate codes of conduct, threatened retaliation, cash rewards for reporting, and perpetrator status.
- The presumption that the whistle-blower will progress from left to right in reporting wrongdoings requires a positive decision at each step.

The process of whistle-blowing report starts with an important wrongdoing such as financial statement fraud. The observer of the wrongdoing act may choose to report to a party empowered to at least begin resolution, such as the observer's superior, internal auditors, the audit committee, or external auditors. The observer, after assessing the costs and benefits and other considerations such as the possibility of losing his or her job or perceived lack of loyalty, may decide to report.

Exhibit 5.4. Model of the Whistle-blowing Process

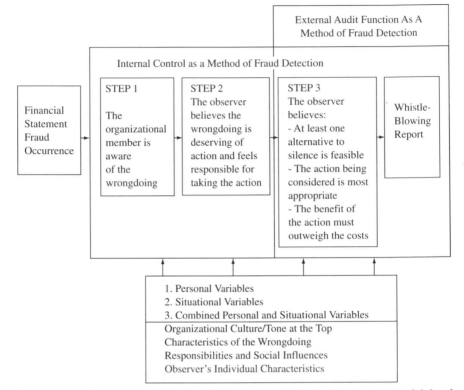

*Adapted from Miceli, M.P., and J.P. Near. 1992. *Blowing The Whistle: The Organizational & Legal Implications for Companies and Employees.* New York: Lexington Books.

Exhibit 5.4 describes this process in three steps of recognition, assessment and assumption of responsibility, and choice of action. The observer first should determine that financial statement fraud has been committed. To become aware of the commission of fraud, the observer should be organizationally placed (e.g., internal auditors, external auditors) to have knowledge of the fraud and be able to objectively verify its occurrence. The observer's position within the company, relative to the perpetrator, is an important contributory factor in obtaining knowledge of the fraud and in recognizing the occurrence.

The second step, as described in Exhibit 5.4, is the assessment of whether the committed and recognized financial statement fraud should be reported. Several factors, such as materiality of recognized fraud, personality characteristics of the observer, observer status, perpetrator status, observer professional stature, and pervasiveness of the evidence, play an important role in assessing whether a recognized fraud should be reported.

The last step in the whistle-blowing decision process is the choice of an action when the observer decides whether to report the recognized financial statement fraud. First, the observer should decide to act by reporting the recognized fraud or remaining silent. If the observer decides to report, then the next decision is to report internally, externally, or both. In making these decisions, the observer should consider the costs and benefits of reporting financial statement fraud. Examples of potential benefits are the feeling that one's action has been effective, increased self-esteem, feeling of doing the right thing, compliance with professional standards and personal ethical values, improved work place, financial awards, and promotions. Examples of the potential costs are possible retaliation by the perpetrator, fear of losing job, perceived lack of loyalty to the organization, violation of corporate codes of conduct or professional standards, the desire or ability to remain anonymous, the perpetrator's power, or the lack of work group support.

Whistle-Blowing Models

Several whistle-blowing models have been suggested to explain and describe the actions taken by whistle-blowers. Rest (1979) developed the following four-component model to explain the complexity of moral decisions:

1. *Recognizing the moral issue.* The observer of the wrongful act must be able to assess possible actions to be taken, their outcomes, and their impact on others.
2. *Making a moral judgment.* The observer must be able to make moral judgments without possible actions and their potential effects on others.
3. *Establishing moral intent.* The observer should have an intention to do what is morally right in the context of applicable moral principles and values.
4. *Engaging in moral behavior.* The observer must be able and willing to follow through with an action to report the wrongdoing act, such as financial statement fraud.[42]

Hooks et al. (1994)[43] suggest a model of whistle-blowing in the context of internal control and external audit functions to prevent and detect fraud. The Hooks et al. (1994) model is built based on an ethical decision process, affected by several factors such as personal values, ethical principles, group norms, codes of conduct, education, organizational stature, and tenure status. Hooks et al. (1994) argue that organizational culture such as the "tone at the top" plays a more important role than characteristics of the wrongdoing, responsibilities and social influences, and the observer's personal characteristics in determining the final action taken in deciding whether to report the committed fraud. The observer should assess action by evaluating each possible alternative in light of the potential costs and benefits.

The Miceli and Near (1992) model implies an ethical decision making process regarding whether to report a wrongdoing. Miceli and Near's model focuses on the impact of personal variables, situational variables, cognitive evaluations of different reactions from management, and other members of the organization on the process of making a whistle-blowing decision.[44]

The Finn (1995) model of whistle-blowing, which is a synthesis of the Rest model and the Miceli and Near model of ethical behavior, shows a whistle-blowing decision process whereby an individual is dealing with a whistle-blowing situation with potentially unethical consequences. This process involves five different stages and, at each stage, the observer assesses previous actions and reactions that are evident in the organizational environment, both from the responses of fellow employees and management.[45] The whistle-blowing model that is most relevant to financial statement fraud and, thus, is used in this book, is Miceli and Near (1992) as portrayed in the article by Hooks et al. (1994). Exhibit 5.4 shows the sequences of the observer's behavior in determining ethical/unethical practices of observing financial statement fraud, evaluating action, and choosing action.

It is expected that top executives' commitments to ethical standards within the company result in a higher level of reporting of unethical behavior and fraudulent activities by employees known as whistle-blowing. A high rate of whistle-blowing may reflect either the honest employee's frustration with the unwillingness of management to exercise adequate control over fraudulent activities or the effectiveness of managerial policies and procedures in enforcing ethical behavior in the company. A low rate of whistle-blowing, however, may indicate either the effectiveness of internal controls to detect fraudulent activities or the employees' fear of the consequences of whistle-blowing or the employees may have trusted the internal controls to prevent and detect fraud.

Fraud Awareness Education

Awareness education can play an important role in reducing instances of financial statement fraud. Characteristics of companies experiencing financial statement fraud have been determined by identifying red flag indicators that suggest financial statement fraud. These red flag indicators are an inadequate and ineffective internal control structure, and the lack of vigilant and effective corporate governance. Empirical studies on financial statement fraud have attempted to identify the red flag indicators that differentiate fraud firms from nonfraud firms. Loebbecke et al. (1989)[46] used a list of red flag indicators that are significantly different between fraud and nonfraud firms. They conclude that although these indicators are significant on a stand-alone basis, they are highly correlated and are not incrementally significant when combined with other factors in a predictive model. By identifying potential red flags, performing the required audit procedures, and documenting the gathered audit evidence, auditors can better defend themselves in the event of litigation after an alleged financial statement fraud.

GENERIC CHARACTERISTICS OF COMPANIES ENGAGED IN FRAUD

Fraud literature has identified and examined the following generic characteristics of fraud companies.

Growth

Prior research (Beasley, 1994)[47] found that a firm's growth may be associated with the likelihood of financial statement fraud. For example, Bell, Szykowny, and Willingham (1991)[48] argue that when the company is in rapid growth pace, management may be motivated to engage in financial statement fraud during a downturn to give the appearance of stable growth. Rapid expansion through mergers and acquisitions can make the internal control structure less effective, which in turn reduces the probability that financial statement fraud can be prevented and detected.

Financial Health

The fraud literature (e.g., Bell et al., 1991; Beasley, 1994)[49,50] indicates that the degree of a company's financial health may be associated with the probability of financial statement fraud. Bell et al. (1991) identify three red flag indicators that suggest an association of financial health and the likelihood of financial statement fraud: (1) inadequate profitability relative to the industry; (2) an undue emphasis being placed on earnings projections; and (3) substantial doubt about an entity's ability to continue as a going concern.

Length of Time Publicly Traded

The corporate governance literature (Beasley, 1994)[51] suggests that the length of time that a company's common stock has traded in capital markets may be associated with the likelihood of financial statement fraud. The Treadway Commission (1987, 29)[52] states that new publicly traded companies may have a proportionately greater risk of financial statement fraud primarily because management may be under greater pressure to manage earnings in order to meet earnings expectations.

Blockholders

The corporate governance literature (Beasley, 1994)[53] suggests that large blockholders (e.g., institutional investors) may serve as a corporate governance mechanism by monitoring management decisions and actions. Thus, large blockholders may reduce the likelihood of financial statement fraud by scrutinizing a firm's operational, investment, financing, and financial reporting activities and holding the board of directors responsible for corporate governance.

Declining Industry

Firms in a declining industry are typically more apt to be engaged in financial statement fraud primarily because they must compete for scarce resources.

Unfavorable Financial Ratios

Fraudulent financial reports reflect financial performance and ratios that are superior to the current industry average performance or better than the company's historical performance or meet analysts' forecasts and targets announced by management previously.

Related-Party Transactions

The primary objective of publicly held corporations is to create and increase shareholder value by generating earnings above and beyond shareholders' desired rate of return on investment. This goal is accomplished when the board of directors and management are working toward protecting the interest of the shareholders. Shareholders' interest is protected when all firms' economic transactions and events are conducted in an arm's-length dealing. This arm's-length dealing may not exist when a firm is engaged in transactions with its board members, management, or affiliates primarily because they have access to proprietary information that may create a conflict of interest. The presence of related-party transactions may cause inappropriate values to be assigned to transactions and financial statement items.

Independent auditors view the existence of related-party transactions as potential conflicts of interest between the firm and its personnel, which may create a potential financial statement fraud (Loebbecke et al., 1989).[54] Firms that engage in numerous related-party transactions may fail to create and/or increase shareholder value, and their legitimacy can be questioned. Sorensen, Grove, and Sorensen (1980)[55] found evidence indicating that firms that engage in fraudulent financial reporting typically have many related-party transactions. Thus, the existence of related-party transactions can be an important red-flag indicator of potential financial statement fraud.

Earnings Management and Persistent Red Flags

Managerial policies, procedures, and accounting practices may also differentiate fraud companies from nonfraud companies. These accounting practices determine whether:

- Both gains and losses on unusual and nonrecurring items are given the same importance or considerations.
- The timing of recognizing transactions is managed and for what purposes they are managed.

- The company's significant estimates and assumptions are reasonable and justifiable and are based on the best information available.
- There is a basis for materiality thresholds being used in measuring, recognizing, and reporting financial transactions and preparing the related financial statements.
- The selected accounting practices appropriately convey the underlying economics of the transactions.
- There have been significant changes in accounting practices and in the management's application of the practices and the use of estimates and judgments.
- The company's disclosures meet the requirements of GAAP.
- Financial presentations and disclosures, including management discussion and analysis (MD&A), tell the whole story.

CONCLUSION

This chapter identified and discussed the taxonomy and schemes of financial statement fraud. The development of fraud taxonomy helps explain common financial statement fraud techniques and management motivations to engage in financial statement fraud. Earnings management, the major contributing factor to the commission of financial statement fraud, was also examined in this chapter. Conditions of pressures on management, the existence of opportunities to perpetrate, and rationalization of either not being detected or the perception of low-cost detection are the primary contributing factors to financial statement fraud. Symptoms of financial statement fraud, consisting of organizational structure red flags, financial conditions red flags, and business and industry environment red flags are thoroughly examined to obtain a better understanding of symptoms signaling the likelihood of financial statement fraud. The use of the whistle-blowing model as an effective internal control mechanism for communicating financial statement fraud was discussed in the last part of this chapter.

ENDNOTES

1. Schilit, H.M. 1993. Financial Shenanigans, New York: McGraw Hill, Inc.
2. Crumbley, D.L. and N. Apostolov. 2001. "Cooking the Books and You Will Go Directly to Jail Without Passing Go." *Journal of Forensic Accounting* Vol. II: 131–138.
3. Ibid.
4. Beasley, M.S., J.V. Carcello, and D.R. Hermanson. 1999. Fraudulent Financial Reporting: 1987–1991: An Analysis of U.S. Public Companies. The COSO Report.
5. Bonner, S.E., Z. Palmrose, and S.M. Young. 1998. "Fraud Type and Auditor Litigation: An Analysis of SEC Accounting and Auditing Enforcement Releases." *The Accounting Review* (Vol. 73, No. 4, October): 503–532.
6. Schipper, R. 1989. "Commentary on Earnings Management." *Accounting Horizons* (December): 91–102.

7. Healy, P.M., and J.M. Wahlen. 1999. "A Review of the Earnings Management Literature and Its Implications for Standard Setting." *Accounting Horizons* 13: 365–383.

8. Merchant, K.A. 1987. *Fraudulent and Questionable Financial Reporting: A Corporate Perspective.* Morristown, NJ: Financial Executives Research Foundation.

9. Association of Certified Fraud Examiners. 1993. *Cooking the Books: What Every Accountant Should Know About Fraud.* New York: NASBA.

10. Levitt, A. 1998. Remarks by Chairperson of the SEC. "The Numbers Game." New York University Center for Law and Business. (September).

11. Ibid.

12. Ibid.

13. Carmichael, D.R. 1999. "Hocus-Pocus Accounting." *Journal of Accountancy* (October): 50–55.

14. Financial Accounting Standards Board (FASB). 1985. Statement of Financial Accounting Concepts. No. 6. Elements of Financial Statements (December): FASB.

15. Securities and Exchange Commission (SEC). 1999. Staff Accounting Bulletin No. 101. Revenue Recognition in Financial Statements (December): SEC.

16. DeChow, P.M., and D.J. Skinner. 2000. "Earnings Management: Reconciling the Views of Accounting Academics, Practitioners, and Regulators." *Accounting Horizons* (Vol. 14, No. 2, June): 235–250.

17. Burns, W. and K. Merchant. 1990. "The Dangerous Morality of Managed Earnings." *Management Accounting* (August): 22–25.

18. Merchant, K., and J. Rockness. 1994. "The Ethics of Managing Earnings: An Empirical Investigation." *Journal of Accounting and Public Policy* (13): 79–94.

19. MacIntosh, N. 1995. "The Ethics of Profit Manipulation: Dialectic of Control Analysis." *Critical Perspectives on Accounting* 6 (August): 289–315.

20. Brealey, R., S. Meyers, G. Sick, and R. Giammario. 1992. *Principles of Corporate Finance.* Toronto: McGraw-Hill Ryerson Limited.

21. DeAngelo, L. 1986. "Accounting Numbers as Market Valuation Substitutes: A Study of Management Buyouts of Public Stockholders." *The Accounting Review* 61(July): 400–420.

22. Dechow, P.M., R.G. Sloan, and A.P. Sweeney. 1996. "Causes and Consequences of Earnings Manipulations: An Analysis of Firms Subject to Enforcement Actions by the SEC." *Contemporary Accounting Research* (Spring): 87–103.

23. Kinney, W., and L. McDaniel. 1989. "Characteristics of Firms Correcting Previously Reported Quarterly Earnings." *Journal of Accountancy and Finance* (11): 71–93.

24. Loebbecke, J., M. Eining, and J. Willingham. 1989. "Auditors' Experience with Material Irregularities: Frequency, Nature, and Detectability." *Auditing: A Journal of Practice & Theory* 9(Fall): 1–8.

25. Dechow, P.M., R.G. Sloan, and A.P. Sweeney. 1996. "Causes and Consequences of Earnings Manipulations: An Analysis of Firms Subject to Enforcement Actions by the SEC." *Contemporary Accounting Research* (Spring): 87–103.

26. Beasley, M. 1996. "An Examination of the Relationship Between the Board of Director Composition and Financial Statement Fraud." *The Accounting Review* 71(October): 443–465.

27. Loebbecke, J. K., and M. M. Eining and J. J. Willingham. 1989. Auditors' Experience with Material Irregularities: Frequency, Nature, and Detectability. *Auditing: A Journal of Practice and Theory* (9): 1–28.

28. Albrecht, W.S., and M.B. Romney. 1986. "Red-Flagging Management Fraud: A Validation." *Advances in Accounting* (Vol. 3): 323–333.

29. Elliot, R.K., and J.J. Willingham. 1980. *Management Fraud: Detection and Deterrence.* New York: Petrocelli Books.

30. Coopers and Lybrand. 1977. "Red Flags for Fraud." *CPA Journal* (August): 76–77.

31. Elliot, R.K., and J.J. Willingham. 1980. *Management Fraud: Detection and Deterrence.* New York: Petrocelli Books.

32. Albrecht, C.C., W.S. Albrecht, and J.G. Dunn. 2001. "Can Auditors Detect Fraud: A Review of the Research Evidence." *Journal of Forensic Accounting* (Vol. II): 1–12.

33. Ibid.

34. Near, J., and M. Miceli. 1988. *The Internal Auditor's Ultimate Responsibility: The Reporting of Sensitive Issues.* Altamonte Springs, FL: Institute of Internal Auditors.

35. Hooks, K., S. Kaplan, and J.S. Chultz, Jr. 1994. "Enhancing Communication to Assist in Fraud Prevention and Detection." *Auditing: A Journal of Practice & Theory* (Fall): 86–117.

36. Ponemon, L.A. 1994. Whistle-Blowing As An Internal Control Mechanism: Individual and Organizational Considerations. Auditing: A Journal of Practice & Theory (Fall): 118–130.

37. Ibid.

38. Hooks, K., S. Kaplan, and J.S. Chultz, Jr. 1994. Enhancing Communication to Assist in Fraud Prevention and Detection. Auditing: A Journal of Practice & Theory (Fall): 86–117.

39. Institute of Internal Auditors (IIA). 1985. Statements of Internal Auditing Standards NO.3: Deterrence, Detection, Investigation and Reporting of Fraud. Altamonte Springs, FL: IIA.

40. Graham, J.W. 1986. *Principled Organizational Dissent: A Theoretical Essay in Research in Organizational Behavior,* Vol. 8, ed. L.L. Cummings and B.M. Staw. Greenwich, CT: JAI Press.

41. Miceli, M.P., and J.P. Near. 1992. *Blowing the Whistle: The Organizational and Legal Implications for Companies and Employees.* New York: Lexington Books.

42. Rest, J.R. 1979. *Development in Judging Moral Issues.* Minneapolis: University of Minnesota Press.

43. Hooks, K., S. Kaplan, and J.S. Chultz, Jr. 1994. Enhancing Communication to Assist in Fraud Prevention and Detection. Auditing: A Journal of Practice & Theory (Fall): 86–117.

44. Miceli, M.P., and J.P. Near. 1992. *Blowing the Whistle: The Organizational and Legal Implications for Companies and Employees.* New York: Lexington Books.

45. Finn, D.W. 1995. "Ethical Decision Making in Organizations: A Management Employee Organization Whistle Blowing Model." *Research on Accounting Ethics* (Vol. 1): 291–313.

46. Loebbecke, J. K., and M. M. Eining and J. J. Willingham. 1989. Auditors' Experience with Material Irregularities: Frequency, Nature, and Detectability. *Auditing: A Journal of Practice and Theory* (9): 1–28.

47. Beasley, M.S. 1994. An Empirical Analysis of the Relationship Between Corporate Governance and Management Fraud. UMI Dissertation Services, Michigan State University.

48. Bell, S., Szykowny, and J.J. Willingham. "Assessing the Likelihood of Fraudulent Financial Reporting: A Cascaded Logit Approach." Working paper (December).

49. Ibid.

50. Beasley, M.S. 1994. An Empirical Analysis of the Relationship Between Corporate Governance and Management Fraud. UMI Dissertation Services, Michigan State University.

51. Ibid.

52. National Commission on Fraudulent Financial Reporting (NCFFR) (The Treadway Commission). 1987. Report on the National Commission on Fraudulent Financial Reporting. New York, NY: AICPA.

53. Beasley, M.S. 1994. An Empirical Analysis of the Relationship Between Corporate Governance and Management Fraud. UMI Dissertation Services, Michigan State University.

54. Loebbecke, J., M. Eining, and J. Willingham. 1989. "Auditors' Experience with Material Irregularities: Frequency, Nature, and Detectability." *Auditing: A Journal of Practice & Theory* 9(Fall): 1–8.

55. Sorenson, J., H. Grove, and T. Sorenson. 1980. "Detecting Management Fraud: The Role of the Independent Auditor." In Gilbert Geis and Ezra Statlend.

Chapter 6

Role of Corporate Governance

INTRODUCTION

During the past two decades, corporate governance has been intensely scrutinized by regulators, authoritative bodies, and others concerned with the public's interests. There has been a great deal of concern about the issue of corporate governance and accountability of publicly traded companies. For example, the report of the Public Oversight Board (POB) of the SEC Practice Section of the American Institute of Certified Public Accountants (AICPA) (1993) states that:

> Corporate governance in the United States is not working the way it should . . . (It) is the failure by too many boards of directors to make the system work the way it should . . . more effective corporate governance depends vitally on strengthening the role of the board of directors.[1]

The corporate governance concept has advanced from the debates on its relevance to how best to protect investor interests and effectively discharge oversight responsibility over the financial reporting process. The recent high-profile alleged financial statement frauds committed by major corporations (Waste Management, Sunbeam, Enron, Lucent, Xerox, MicroStrategy, Cendant, RiteAid, KnowledgeWare) have renewed the interest and increasing sense of urgency regarding a more responsible corporate governance and reliable financial statements. This chapter discusses corporate governance, its participants including, the board of directors, the audit committee, the top management team, internal auditors, external auditors, and governing bodies as well as their role in preventing and detecting financial statement fraud.

DEFINITION OF CORPORATE GOVERNANCE

The concept of corporate governance is poorly defined in the literature through both narrow and broad definitions reflecting special interests of different groups in corporate governance. The Business Roundtable (1997) states:

> Corporate governance is not an abstract goal, but exists to serve corporate purposes by providing a structure within which stockholders, directors, and management can pursue most effectively the objectives of the corporation.[2]

The Organization for Economic Cooperation and Development (OECD) broadly defines corporate governance as:

> The system by which business corporations are directed and controlled. The corporate governance structure specifies the distribution of rights and responsibilities among different participants in the corporation, such as the board, managers, shareholders, and other stakeholders, and spells out the rules and procedures for making decisions on corporate affairs. By doing this, it also provides the structure through which the company objectives are set, and the means of attaining those objectives and monitoring performance.[3]

Cadbury also broadly defines "corporate governance as holding the balance between economic and social goals and between individuals and communal goals."[4]

Narrowly defined corporate governance focuses primarily on the interactions among corporate managers, directors, and shareholders. This definition of corporate governance addresses the concerns of capital providers in assessing the risk associated with their investment, their expectations for rate of return on investment, and continuous monitoring of their capital investments.

Broadly defined corporate governance focuses on the combination of applicable laws, regulations, and listing rules that facilitate, direct, and monitor corporations' affairs in attracting capital, performing effectively and efficiently, increasing shareholder value, and meeting both legal requirements and general societal expectations. Thus, corporate governance is viewed as a mechanism of monitoring the actions, policies, and decisions of corporations in increasing shareholder value.

Corporate governance can be narrowly viewed as the relationships between the company's capital providers (investors and creditors) and the top management team. This narrow definition ignores other constituencies involved in the corporate affairs, such as the board of directors, the audit committee, auditors, governing bodies, suppliers, customers, and other stakeholders. Corporate governance is based on the underlying concept of accountability and responsibility rather than the notion of who has the power and who is in charge. Under effective corporate governance, the top management team is accountable to the board of directors and the board of directors is accountable to the shareholders to create shareholder value. Corporate governance should facilitate the alignment of interests among managers, directors, and investors. The substantial boom in the capital markets and economy during the 1990s has encouraged the creation and maximization of shareholder value as a principle of corporate governance.

Corporate governance, for the purpose of this book, is defined as the mechanism of managing, directing, and monitoring a corporation's business to create shareholder value. Corporate governance participants are the board of directors, the audit committee, the top management team, internal auditors, external auditors, and governing bodies, as depicted in Exhibit 6.1.

Exhibit 6.1. Corporate Governance and Its Functions

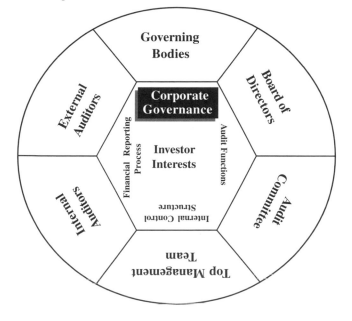

Corporate governance should monitor the interests of investors and creditors by (1) assessing the risk associated with their capital investments in the company resources; (2) evaluating the allocation of their investment for maximum returns; and (3) continuously monitoring the administration of their investments. Corporate governance is a monitoring mechanism for assessing corporate responsibility and accountability through boards of directors, audit committees, management, and auditors to serve and protect investors.

RESPONSIBILITY OF CORPORATE GOVERNANCE

The Blue Ribbon Committee (BRC)[5] revealed the following three conclusions regarding the oversight responsibility of corporate governance, including the audit committee:

1. Quality financial reporting can be achieved only through open and candid communication and close working relationships among the corporation's board of directors, audit committee, management, internal auditors, and external auditors.
2. Strengthening corporate governance, oversight in the financial reporting process of publicly traded companies will reduce instances of financial statement fraud.

3. Integrity, quality, and transparency of financial reports improve investors' confidence in the capital market, whereas incidents of financial statement fraud diminish such confidence.

The role of corporate governance is addressed by the Blue Ribbon Committee (1999, 20) as:

> Good governance promotes relationships of accountability among the primary corporate participants to enhance corporate performance. It holds management accountable to the board and the board accountable to shareholders . . . A key element of board oversight is working with management to achieve corporate legal and ethical compliance. Such oversight includes ensuring that quality accounting policies, internal controls, and independent and objective outside auditors are in place to deter fraud, anticipate financial risks, and promote accurate, high quality, and timely disclosure of financial and other material information to the board, to the public markets, and to the shareholders.[6]

Corporate governance plays a crucial role in improving the efficiency of the capital market through its impact on corporate operating efficiency and effectiveness, earnings growth and employment, and integrity and quality of financial reports.

CORPORATE GOVERNANCE PRINCIPLES

Corporate governance principles and guidelines have been established by several organizations to provide best practices or benchmarks against which to assess the appropriateness of a corporation's corporate governance system. For example, the Toronto Stock Exchange (TSE) established a Committee on Corporate Governance in 1993 to ensure that investors receive sufficient information to assess the effectiveness of the company's corporate governance. The committee issued a report, known as the Dey Report, entitled, "Where Were the Directors? Guidelines for Improved Corporate Governance in Canada" in December 1994.[7] The Dey Report proposed 14 guidelines for corporate governance primarily aimed at the activities of the board of directors. These guidelines are listed in Exhibit 6.1. TSE-listed companies should report on their corporate governance system and on whether their system is in compliance with the guidelines. These guidelines are primarily aimed at the board of directors by (1) specifying the responsibility of the board of directors in the areas of strategic planning, risk management, and internal control; (2) suggesting that the board of directors should be constituted with a majority of unrelated (independent) directors; (3) disclosing whether the majority of board members are unrelated; and (4) discussing orientation and training for new board members, compensation committees, and their functions. The Dey Report does not address the role of internal auditors, external auditors, and governing bodies in the corporate governance process, as discussed in this book. Implementation of the guidelines suggested in the Dey Report would improve the quality of financial reports.

OECD Principles of Corporate Governance

The Organization for Economic Cooperation and Development (OECD) has identified the following five guiding principles of good corporate governance:[8]

1. *Rights of Shareholders.* The basic shareholder rights involve the right to secure methods of ownership registration, cover or transfer shares, obtain relevant and timely corporate information, participate and vote in general shareholder meetings, elect members of the board, and share in company profits.

2. *The Equitable Treatment of Shareholders.* The corporate governance structure should ensure the fair and equitable treatment of all shareholders, including minority and foreign shareholders. This principle recognizes that all shareholders of the same class have the same voting rights and should be treated equally; all shareholders should have the opportunity to obtain effective remedy for any violation of their rights. This principle, while prohibiting insider tradings and abusive self-dealing, requires members of the board of directors and managers to disclose any material interest in transactions or matters affecting the corporation.

3. *Role of Stakeholders.* The corporate governance structure should recognize the rights of stakeholders as established by law and encourage active cooperation between corporations and stakeholders in creating wealth, jobs, and a secure business environment. Stakeholders should also have access to relevant corporate information when they participate in the corporate governance process.

4. *Disclosure and Transparency.* The corporate governance structure should provide timely and accurate disclosure of all material matters regarding the corporation, including the financial situation and operating results, company objectives, major share ownership and voting rights, members of the board and key executives and their remuneration, material foreseeable risk factors, material issues regarding employees and other stakeholders, performance, and governance structures and policies. In addition, financial statements should be audited by an independent auditor, and channels for dissemination of information should be fair, timely, and cost efficient.

5. *Responsibilities of the Board.* The corporate governance structure should ensure the strategic guidance of the company, the effective monitoring of management by the board, and the board's accountability to the company and the shareholders. The board of directors should act on a fully informed basis, in

good faith, and with due diligence and care in performing the assigned functions in the best interest of the company and the shareholders. The board of directors should ensure compliance with applicable laws and regulations and ensure the quality and integrity of the financial reporting process.

These five principles of good corporate governance are centered around the five underlying concepts of accountability, efficiency and effectiveness, integrity and fairness, responsibility, and equality. The corporate governance structure should ensure that those who manage corporate resources (e.g., management) are monitored and held accountable in using these resources efficiently and effectively. Corporate governance constituencies, in fulfilling their responsibilities, should preserve the integrity and fairness of the corporate governance framework. The corporate governance structure should promote shareholder and society confidence and trust in the corporation's affairs by enhancing the transparency of its financial reporting process, which requires audited financial statements to be free from material errors, irregularities, and fraud and not being misleading. Thus, a responsible corporate governance (1) ensures efficient and effective use of corporate resources; (2) ensures compliance with all applicable laws, regulations, and rules governing corporate affairs and the financial reporting process; (3) promotes continuous improvements in corporate performance by allowing best planning for managerial capital acquisition and disbursements; (4) ensures proper accountability by the board of directors and management and effective discharging of their responsibility in achieving the goal of creating shareholder value; and (5) creates trust and confidence in the corporate activities by promoting fair relationships between the company and its shareholders and society at large.

Corporate governance mechanisms are gaining increasing acceptance in all industrial sectors. Recently, government entities including local and state government agencies are placing more importance on the role of organizational governance in continuous improvements of efficiency, effectiveness, and economy of government operations. Organizational governance in public-sector entities consists of the following activities: (1) vigilant audit committees used in overseeing internal control, financial reporting, and accountability; (2) internal audits functions responsible for operational effectiveness and efficiency, evaluating adequacy and effectiveness of internal control, ensuring compliance with applicable laws and regulations, and monitoring financial information; and (3) outsourcing that is usually provided by external auditors to supplement in-house specialized activities, skills, and expertise.[9]

Organizational governance in public-sector entities has made steady progress during the past decade. In the early 1990s, only a small portion (less than 15 percent) of local governments had audit committees or internal audit functions. The most recent studies (e.g., Eckhart et al., 2001)[10] indicate that more than 28 percent of surveyed local governments have audit committees; about one-half (49 percent) have internal audit functions; and more than 22 percent outsource some portion of their audit function to a third-party provider, often external auditors. Great opportunity still exists for improvements in organizational governance in public-sector entities, however, because more than half of governmental entities do not have audit committees, internal audit functions, or use outside services.

ROLE OF CORPORATE GOVERNANCE IN PREVENTING AND DETECTING FINANCIAL STATEMENT FRAUD

Over the past decade, there has been a growing awareness that responsible corporate governance can play an important role in preventing and detecting financial statement fraud. Management ethical behavior and operating style of product innovation, risk taking, proactivity, business venturing, and strategic renewal can have a significant impact on the effectiveness of corporate governance.

Corporate governance simply means the way a corporation is governed through proper accountability for managerial and financial performance. Corporate governance participants used in this book are the board of directors, audit committees, management, internal auditors, external auditors, and governing bodies. The integrity and quality of the capital market primarily depends on the reliability, vigilance, and objectivity of corporate governance, which is thoroughly examined in this book. The 1999 COSO Report on fraudulent financial reporting concludes that (1) "earnings management" in terms of pressures of financial strain or distress may provide incentives for fraudulent activities; (2) top executives (CFOs, CEOs) were associated with 83 percent of the financial statement fraud; (3) active and independent audit committees appear to deter fraudulent financial reporting; and (4) most fraudulent activities were not isolated to a single fiscal period.[11]

Traditionally, the focus has been on the role of external auditors in deterring financial statement fraud. Nevertheless, in recent years, the attention and emphasis are on the entire corporate governance responsibility to ensure the reliability, integrity, and quality of financial reports. The 1999 COSO Report study of alleged financial statement fraud revealed the following:

- Eighty-three percent of the alleged frauds involved the top management team, including the CFO and CEO.
- Other members of the management team, such as controllers, chief operating officers, and senior vice presidents, were also named in several alleged frauds.
- Most alleged frauds were not isolated to a single fiscal period.
- More than half of the alleged financial statement frauds involved overstatement of revenues and assets.
- Committees of the fraud companies typically met only once per year.
- Nearly 25 percent of audit companies did not have an audit committee.

- About 65 percent of audit committee members did not appear to be certified in accounting or to be financially literate.
- Nearly 60 percent of the directors were insider or "gray" directors (e.g., outsiders with special ties to the company or management).
- Forty percent of the boards had not one director who served as an outside or gray director on another company's board.
- Family relationships among directors and/or officers were fairly common.
- The average financial statement fraud was $25 million, and the median was $4.1 million.
- Most financial statement fraud overlapped at least two fiscal periods and often involved both quarterly and annual financial statements.
- Most alleged financial statement frauds (more than 50 percent) involved overstating revenues by recording revenues prematurely or fictitiously.
- Fifty-six percent of alleged sampled fraud companies were audited by a Big Eight/Five professional services firm during the fraud period.
- Most audit reports (55 percent) issued in the last year of the fraud period contained an unqualified opinion.
- Financial statement fraud occasionally implicated the external auditor.
- Some companies changed auditors during the fraud period.
- Consequences of financial statement fraud to the alleged company usually included delisting by national organization stock exchanges, substantial changes in ownership, bankruptcy, and imposed financial penalties.
- In most cases, senior executives were subject to class-action lawsuits and SEC actions that resulted in financial penalties to the executives personally.
- Many individuals were terminated or forced to resign from their executive positions.
- Relatively few of the alleged individuals explicitly admitted guilt or eventually served prison terms.[12]

The National Association of Corporate Best Practices Council identified the following four principles for protecting shareholders against fraud and other illegal acts.[13]

1. *Setting the tone at the top through conduct and communication.* The tone set by the top management team is perhaps the most important factor contributing to preventing and detecting of financial statement fraud. Management's commitment to ethical and lawful behavior should become the cultural core of the company and a model of acceptable and expected conduct by individuals throughout the company.

2. *Director commitment and independence.* The board of directors should be composed of dedicated, knowledgeable, financially literate, and independent

members. Directors should be willing and able to devote the necessary time and energy to fulfill their primary responsibility of creating shareholder value.

3. *Explicit focus on fraud risk.* Prevention and detection of fraud in general, and financial statement fraud in particular should be the main focus of all members of corporate governance from the board of directors to the audit committee, top management team, and auditors.

4. *Effective communication process.* Effective and two-way communication among all members of corporate governance, especially open and continuing communication among the board of directors, the audit committee, management, auditors, and other employees, can substantially reduce the likelihood of financial statement fraud.

Beasley et al. (2000) investigated important corporate governance differences between fraud companies and nonfraud companies in the three most volatile industries of technology, health care, and financial services.[14] They found that (1) fraud companies have weak governance mechanisms comparing to nonfraud industry benchmarks; (2) fraud companies in the technology and financial services industries have fewer audit committees; (3) fraud companies in all three industries have less independent audit committees and less independent boards; (4) fraud companies in all three industries have less internal audit support; and (5) fraud companies in the technology and health care industries have fewer audit committee meetings than nonfraud companies.

CHARACTERISTICS OF CORPORATE GOVERNANCE

The characteristics and attributes of corporate governance most likely to be associated with financial statement fraud are aggressiveness, cohesiveness, loyalty, opportunism, trust, gamesmanship, and control ineffectiveness. Aggressiveness and opportunism can be signified by the company's attitude and motivations toward beating analysts' forecasts about quarterly earnings or annual earnings per share and the attempt to make Wall Street happy by reporting unjustifiable favorable financial performance. Cohesiveness, gamesmanship, and loyalty attributes create an environment that reduces the likelihood of whistle-blowing and increases the probability of coverup attempts. Trust and control ineffectiveness can cause those in an oversight function (e.g., board of directors, audit committee) as well as an assurance function (e.g., internal auditors, external auditors) to be less effective in detecting fraud. Cohesiveness and gamesmanship can cause a sharply defined group boundary of corporate governance that creates high cooperation among corporate governance members to conceal financial statement fraud and impose greater restriction of fraudulent financial information to leak to outsiders. This gamesmanship and cohesiveness can encourage more collusion in the development of financial statement fraud, and if the fraud is discovered by internal or external auditors, push them for coverup. When the members of corporate governance establish trust, it creates less room for suspicion and skepticism, which in turn may reduce the likelihood of auditors detecting financial statement fraud.

CORPORATE GOVERNANCE STRUCTURE

Corporate governance is viewed as interactions among participants in managerial functions (e.g., management), oversight functions (e.g., the board of directors and audit committee), audit functions (e.g., internal auditors and external auditors), monitoring functions (e.g., the SEC, standard setters, regulators), and user functions (e.g., investors, creditors, and other stakeholders) in the governance system of corporations. Corporate governance consists of internal and external mechanisms for managing, directing, and monitoring corporate activities to create and increase shareholder value. Examples of internal mechanisms are the board of directors, the audit committee, management, and internal auditors. Examples of external mechanisms are external auditors, regulators, standard-setting bodies, and capital market participants, including investors, creditors, and other users of corporate reports. Exhibit 6.1 shows interactions among corporate governance participants in ensuring responsible corporate governance, reliable financial reporting process, adequate internal control functions, and effective audit functions.

Board of Directors

The board of directors should perform vigilant and active oversight to be a fiduciary for all stockholders in the corporation. In fulfilling its legal responsibility and requirements, the board of directors should (1) monitor management plans, decisions, and activities; (2) act as an independent leader that takes initiatives to create shareholder value; (3) establish guidelines or operational procedures for its own functioning; (4) meet periodically without management presence to assess company and management performance and strategy; and (5) evaluate its own performance to ensure that the board is independent, professional, and active. The role of the board of directors in corporate governance, particularly in preventing and detecting financial statement fraud, is thoroughly examined in Chapter 7.

A vigilant and effective board of directors can play an important role in preventing, detecting, and reducing financial statement fraud. The board of directors is an important corporate governance mechanism within publicly traded companies that rises out of the separation of decision control of monitoring management activities and residual risk-bearing assumed by shareholders and creditors (Beasley, 1996).[15] Although the board of directors is not usually involved in day-to-day management decisions and actions, it has a unique role of overseeing, monitoring, and controlling management activities. Prior research suggests that the board of directors' composition affects the board's effectiveness as a monitor of management for preventing and detecting financial statement fraud (Beasley, 1996).[16]

Audit Committees

Audit committees are standing committees composed of a nonexecutive and independent board of directors. Audit committees have oversight responsibility over corporate governance and the financial reporting process. The more vigilant the audit committee is in overseeing corporate governance and the financial reporting process, the lower the probability of financial statement fraud. Audit committees may receive information about possible financial statement fraud from employees, internal auditors, or external auditors. Audit committees should investigate this matter thoroughly and report their findings to the board.

The effectiveness of oversight function of the audit committee depends on the attitude, philosophy, and practices of the entire board of directors. The audit committee responsibility is to oversee and monitor the integrity, quality, and reliability of the financial reporting process without stepping into the managerial functions and decisions relating to preparing financial statements.

The audit committee is responsible for overseeing corporate governance, financial reporting, internal control structure, and audit functions. Thus, members of the audit committee must be financially literate, professionally qualified, operationally knowledgeable, and functionally independent to effectively fulfill their vigilant oversight responsibility. The audit committee should meet regularly and as needed with the board of directors, CEO, CFO, treasurer, controller, director of the internal audit function, and external auditors as a group, and in private with each individual to review and assess the quality, integrity, and reliability of financial reports.

Publicly traded companies are required to establish audit committees consisting of nonexecutive and independent directors in order to strengthen their corporate governance; however, in some instances, audit committees are used as window dressing by including gray directors who are not independent of management to serve on audit committees. Prior research (e.g., McMullen, 1996; Beasley, 1996; Dechow et al., 1996)[17–19] suggests that firms that engage in financial statement fraud are more likely to have no audit committee or ineffective audit committees that meet infrequently.

One important mechanism of corporate governance is the vigilant audit committee. The audit committee can minimize the occurrence of financial statement fraud by serving as a conduit for financial information flow to the board of directors and reducing information asymmetries between management and the board of directors. Several studies have found evidence indicating that fraud firms have less active and effective audit committees than non-fraud firms (DeFond and Jiambalvo, 1991).[20]

In recent years, the boards of directors have delegated their responsibility for oversight of the financial reporting process to the audit committee. The audit committee is an integral part of corporate governance to improve the quality of information flow between principal and agent. The audit committee acts as a liaison between management and external auditors, thus reducing the information asymmetries between management and the board of directors. The audit committees were originally recommended as a means of communication between the boards of directors and external auditors in the aftermath of the McKesson and Robbins fraud case in the 1930s. During the mid-1990s, many publicly traded companies have voluntarily established audit committees to improve the reliability of published financial statements.

In 1987, the report of the Treadway Commission indicated that the audit committee can play an important role in preventing and detecting financial statement fraud; however, the effectiveness of an audit committee for monitoring management decisions and actions and for overseeing the financial reporting process has been addressed in many studies and reports.[21] The AICPA's Public Oversight Board (1993) report states that "in too many instances, audit committees do not perform their duties adequately and in many cases do not understand their responsibilities" (p. 50).[22]

The Blue Ribbon Committee on Improving the Effectiveness of Corporate Audit Committees was established in October 1998 by the New York Stock Exchange (NYSE) and the National Association of Securities Dealers (NASD) to address concerns expressed by Securities and Exchange Commission (SEC) former chair Arthur Levitt regarding audit committees' effectiveness.[23] The primary goal of the Blue Ribbon Committee was to study current practices of audit committees and make recommendations to the SEC, corporations, auditors, and self-regulatory organizations about how best to improve audit committees' oversight of corporate governance and the financial reporting process of publicly traded companies.

The Blue Ribbon Committee issued its recommendations in 1999, in the following three general categories: (1) audit committee member independence; (2) qualification and compensation; and (3) audit committees' activities. The NYSE, NASD, American Stock Exchange (AMSE), SEC, AICPA's Auditing Standards Board have established rules implementing the committee's recommendations. These organizations' implementation rules for the committee's recommendations on improving the effectiveness of corporate audit committees are substantially similar and are thoroughly examined in Chapter 8.

Rules implementing the Blue Ribbon Committee's recommendations developed by many organizations (e.g., NYSE, NASD, AMSE, SEC, AICPA) are now in place. These implementation rules substantially affect the structure, composition, functions, and responsibilities of many audit committees, including the requirement of reporting by the audit committee in the annual proxy statement. Audit committees are being called on to consider external auditor independence under Independent Standards Board (ISB) Standard No. 1 and to address it in its charter and annual audit committee report.

The business literature, especially empirical research, cites evidence that proves the potential for audit committee and board governance mechanisms to reduce incidents of financial statement fraud. The lack of vigilant and effective corporate boards of directors and audit committees, especially when controls over top management are weak (e.g., the control environment) can create the opportunity for fraudulent financial reporting. This book focuses on the role of the audit committee and board of governance mechanisms in preventing and detecting financial statement fraud, which has not received its deserved attention in the books already published in the fraud area.

Top Management Team

Management plays an important role in ensuring an effective and responsible corporate governance by managing the business of the corporation to create shareholder value. Management, through the delegated authority from the board of directors, is responsible for developing and executing corporate strategies, safeguarding its financial resources, complying with applicable laws and regulations, achieving operational efficiency and effectiveness, establishing and maintaining an adequate and effective internal control system, and designing and implementing a sound accounting system that provides reliable and high-quality financial reports.

According to the agency theory, a self-interested top management team manipulates financial reporting by engaging in financial statement fraud to its advantage. Thus, the top management team must be monitored and/or have an appropriate incentive structure. The opportunity to engage in financial statement fraud is influenced by the extent of monitoring of the company. The motivation is related to the internal corporate environment and those incentives that affect the interest alignment of the top management team with investors and creditors. Exhibit 6.2 presents both proactive and reactive mechanisms to ensure alignment of top management team interests with those of investors and creditors.

Exhibit 6.2. Monitoring Mechanisms

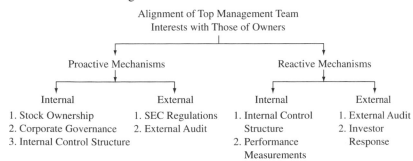

Management should go beyond the minimum compliance with application rules and regulations to satisfy the needs of investors, creditors, and other market participants. The former SEC Chairperson, Arthur Levitt, made the following statement regarding management manipulation of earnings and resulting financial statement fraud: "We are witnessing an erosion in the quality of earnings, and therefore, the quality of financial reporting. Management may be giving way to manipulation; integrity may be losing out to illusion."[24] Mr. Levitt, in his remarks before the Economic Club of New York in October 1999, expressed his concern about the numbers "gamesmanship" that threatens the integrity and quality of the financial reporting process. Levitt stated[25]:

> It's gamesmanship that says it's okay to bend the rules, tweak the numbers, and let small, but obvious and important discrepancies slide; a gamesmanship that tells managers it's fine to cut corners and look the other way to boost the stock price, where companies bend to the desires and pressures of Wall Street analysts rather than to the reality of numbers, and where auditors are pressured not to rock the boat; and a gamesmanship that focuses exclusively on short-term numbers rather than long-term performances.

Excessive pressure on management to meet or even exceed analysts' earnings forecasts creates more incentives for manipulation of earnings and resulting fraudulent financial reporting. The board of directors should set the tone at the top to prevent fraudulent financial reporting. This book focuses on board governance and audit committee mechanisms to counteract this "gamesmanship" movement by examining the importance of (1) open communication by corporate management and financial analysts; (2) vigilant oversight by auditors, audit committees, and an active and independent board of directors; and (3) open communications through greater disclosure among management, the board, and outside directors.

External Auditors

In the corporation form of business, ownership is separated from control; thus, it is necessary to monitor the control to ensure that those who have been entrusted with financial resources are being held accountable for their decisions, plans, and actions. The role of external auditors in corporate governance is to lend credibility to published financial statements by auditing those statements and providing reasonable assurance that investors are receiving relevant, useful, and reliable financial information in making sound business decisions.

The role of external auditors in corporate governance is to provide assurance that management's financial reports conform to the contractual relationship between the principal (investors and creditors) and the agent (top management team) and are free of material misstatements caused by errors and fraud. Thus, in this content, external auditors monitor financial statements issued by management to users of these reports, especially investors and creditors. Potential investors and creditors are also interested in high-quality, accurate, and reliable financial statements in making further investment decisions. The SEC, in its efforts to protect investors' interests, also requires that financial statements of publicly traded companies be audited by independent auditors to ensure compliance with generally accepted accounting principles (GAAP) and to ensure that published financial statements are free from material misstatements. External auditors add value to the published financial statements by detecting material misstatements that increase the likelihood of financial statement fraud.

An independent audit of financial statements lends more credibility, objectivity, and dependability to published financial statements. Published financial statements are perceived to be more credible and legitimate when they are accompanied by an independent audit report; however, no conclusive and supportive evidence indicates that the larger professional services firms (e.g., Big Five) provide a more effective and comprehensive audit in detecting financial statement fraud. For example, McMullen (1996)[26] found a positive relationship between fraudulent financial reporting firms and a non-Big Six auditor, whereas Dechow et al. (1996)[27] detected no significant difference. Auditors have generally exercised more due diligence with a skeptical attitude and a more stringent materiality concern when there was a warning signal of the possibility of financial statement fraud.

The evolution of the auditing profession clearly indicates that the purpose of the audit of financial statements has evolved throughout time. In the early stage of the accounting profession, the detection of fraud, technical and clerical error, and irregularities and errors in principles was the primary purpose of an audit of financial statements. The Industrial Revolution, creation of public corporations, and the SEC Acts of 1933 and 1934 aimed at protecting investors' rights have changed the focus of an audit to provide reasonable assurance regarding "fair presentation" of financial statements in conformity with a specific set of criteria (e.g., GAAP). Recent business failures and occurrences of many fraudulent financial activities have encouraged auditors to give special and well-deserved attention to fraud prevention and detection. Users of audited financial statements typically expect external auditors to detect all financial statement fraud and employees' irregularities, illegal acts, and fraud that affect the quality and integrity of financial reports. External auditors, however, in recognizing the importance of fraudulent financial activities to users of financial statements and in complying with their professional standards, are more concerned with financial statement fraud and material misstatements in the audited financial statements.

External auditors do not certify the accuracy and preciseness of financial statements, nor do they guarantee, that the financial statements are not misstated when they express their opinions on the fair presentation of financial statements in conformity with GAAP. External auditors do not certify a clean bill of financial health for the audited company; instead, they provide only reasonable assurance that the audited financial statements are free from material misstatement. Thus, auditors lend more credibility to the audited financial statements by reducing the information risk that audited financial statements are misleading, false, or fraudulent. Any reduction in the information risk makes the capital markets more efficient and creates more trust and confidence in published financial statements and the related financial reporting process. Therefore, auditors' attestation services are viewed as value-added services that improve the quality and integrity of financial information; however, when auditors occasionally fail to stand up to company management by knowingly or recklessly participating in fraudulent activities or fail to discover financial statement fraud, the market participants ask the logical question of "Where were the auditors?" The published audit failures and fraud situations (e.g., Andersen antifraud case) have raised serious concerns about the efficacy of the audit process and the value of audits in ensuring the reliability and quality of financial information fed to the capital markets.

External auditors are being viewed as, and often accused of, not looking hard enough to detect financial statement fraud. External auditors are being challenged and sued for their association with alleged financial statement fraud by aggrieved investors. External auditors have suffered losses, both monetarily and reputationally, for not properly detecting financial statement fraud. Most recently, on June 19, 2001, the SEC settled enforcement actions against Arthur Andersen, one of the Big Five professional services firms, and four of its current or former partners for their association with the 1992 through 1996 financial statement audits of Waste Management. Arthur Andersen issued unqualified or "clean" opinions on four consecutive years of Waste Management's financial statements, which were misleading because pretax income was overstated by more than $1 billion. The SEC alleged that Arthur Andersen "knowingly and recklessly" issued materially false and misleading audit reports, incorrectly stating that the financial statements were presented fairly, in all material respect, and in conformity with GAAP, and were conducted in accordance with generally accepted auditing standards (GAAS).

Internal Auditors

Society is concerned about the shock of scandals involving defense contractors, savings and loan associations, banks, and the stock market. Thus, strategies and techniques need to be developed to deal with financial statement fraud. Internal auditors are integral parts of corporate governance, and their expertise in internal control is on the front line in preventing and detecting financial statement fraud.

Internal auditors have been viewed as an important contributory factor in achieving operational efficiency and effectiveness in their organizations. The revised definition of internal auditing specifies that internal auditors' activities are extended to evaluating and improving the effectiveness of a company's governance process. Internal auditing is defined by the Institute of Internal Auditors (IIA) as "an independent, objective assurance and consulting activity designed to add value and improve an organization's operations . . . bringing a systematic, disciplined approach to evaluate and improve the effectiveness of risk management, control, and governance processes".[28]

Internal auditing has evolved from a function that was mainly concerned with financial and accounting issues to a function that focuses on a broad range of operating activities and is an integral part of the corporate governance structure. An internal audit function assists all individuals and functions within the company to discharge their responsibilities by providing them with analyses, appraisals, recommendations, counsel, and information to perform their activities.

Internal auditors' activities can be summarized in the following functions of (1) assessing the efficiency and effectiveness of operational performance; (2) ensuring the adequacy and effectiveness of the internal control system in achieving its objectives; (3) reviewing the financial reporting process to ensure its quality and integrity in producing reliable, relevant, useful, and transparent financial information for decision making; (4) ensuring responsible corporate governance; and (5) preventing, detecting, and correcting fraud occurring within the organization, especially financial statement fraud. Internal auditors should continuously monitor the financial reporting process and look for red-flag indicators suggesting the possibility of wrongdoing and illegal acts. Red-flag indicators, such as excessive related-party transactions, must be reviewed to detect any opportunistic behavior by the board and management. The tone set by the board of directors typically influences the behavior of others within the company. Thus, sanctioning of opportunistic behavior by the board may create an environment that will not accept illegal activities as legitimate accounting policies.

Internal auditors often assist management in designing and maintaining adequate and effective internal control structures. Internal auditors are also responsible for assessing the adequacy and effectiveness of such control systems, which provides reasonable assurance with regard to the quality and integrity of the financial reporting process. Internal auditors primarily focus on the assessment of both administrative and accounting internal controls at the division or operations level and less at the corporate level, which involves preparation and dissemination of the financial statements. Thus, although internal auditors may assist the top management team in producing financial statements, the quality, reliability, and integrity of financial statements are management's responsibility.

The internal audit function is an important element of corporate governance, the first-line defense against financial statement fraud, and an often overlooked function in the financial reporting process. The Treadway Commission report (1987)[29] suggested that the SEC require all public companies to maintain an internal audit function that is organizationally independent. The independence of the internal audit function is important to ensure that the internal audit staff can effectively monitor the preparation of financial statements. To achieve independence of internal audit functions, the director of the internal audit function should be appointed by the audit committee and be accountable and report to the audit committee, the CEO, or a superior financial officer who is not directly involved in preparing financial statements. External auditors are increasingly relying on the work of internal auditors in conducting financial statement audits. Thus, the extent of internal auditors' working relationships with external auditors and the effectiveness of internal auditors in preventing and detecting financial statement fraud can considerably improve their enhanced organizational status and professionalism.

Governing Bodies

Concern over highly publicized audit fraud (e.g., Andersen in connection with the audit of Waste Management) has prompted several governing organizations to address the problem of financial statement frauds and auditors' failure to detect them. The governing organizations that may influence public companies' financial reporting process and their corporate governance are the SEC, the AICPA, and organized stock exchanges (NYSE, NASD). The SEC is the agency established by Congress to protect the interests of investors. It has jurisdiction over corporations with a class of securities listed on an national stock exchange or if traded over-the-counter with 500 or more shareholders and $10 million or more total assets. The SEC requires these companies to file financial statements prepared in accordance with GAAP. The auditing profession has been the subject of intense SEC scrutiny. Recently, the SEC has taken the following initiatives to improve the quality of financial reports disclosed by publicly traded companies: (1) strategies to promote high-quality financial reports and punish companies engaged in financial statement fraud; (2) the New Regulation Fair Disclosure (FD) to reduce inside trading of securities in creating a level playing field for all market participants regardless of size and sophistications in trading securities; (3) new rules for audit committees to promote their independence, qualifications, compositions, and effectiveness as an important element of corporate governance; and (4) new rules for auditors' independence to reduce the potential conflicts of interest with their clients and to improve their ability to detect financial statement fraud.

Increasing pressure to reduce financial statement fraud during the past two decades has encouraged the SEC to make financial statement fraud its number one enforcement priority. The SEC is expected to continue its closer scrutiny of corporate financial reporting practices and process to ensure the integrity and quality of corporate financial reports. SEC enforcement director Richard H. Walker stated that, "I anticipate that we will continue to make accounting fraud our No. 1 enforcement priority because it goes to the core of our mission."[30] Former SEC Chairman Arthur Levitt made financial statement fraud the agency's primary enforcement priority, and it is expected that financial fraud will continue to remain the SEC's main focus. Levitt had laid much of the blame for financial statement fraud on corporate top management teams (executives) by deliberately manipulating earnings and other financial results to meet Wall Street analysts' forecasts.

The most common types of financial statement fraud cases filed by the SEC in recent years are the allegations of improper recording of revenue, better known as earnings management. Earnings management occurs when unrealized revenue is recognized or revenue is deferred or allocated to another quarter. In fiscal year 1999, the SEC filed about 90 cases alleging financial statement fraud of companies managing earnings to keep Wall Street happy. Most recently, Learnout &

Houspie Speech Products (L&H) announced that it will restate its financial statements for 1998, 1999, and the first half of 2000 to correct its past accounting "errors and irregularities." This announcement (November 2000) prompted both the NASDAQ stock market and Europe's EUSDAQ market to suspend trading in the company's shares indefinitely. This admission forced its founders to step down as co-chairmen and its CFO to resign from his post. L&H shares sank to an all-time low of $3.30, which is more than 95 percent below their record high of $72.50 in March 2000 on the NASDAQ.

Restatement of earnings to correct faulty prior earnings has caused investors to lose billions of dollars resulting from the sharp decline in market value after earnings corrections and restatements. In addition, SEC civil fraud charges can result in fines against the alleged companies and individuals engaged in financial statement fraud and prohibitions against alleged executives to work for other public companies. In 2000, more than 100 of the SEC's enforcement cases were associated with financial statement fraud and, accordingly, charges were filed against 26 companies, 19 CEOs, and 19 CFOs.

Given the increasing rate of financial statement fraud, the SEC has taken several initiatives to tighten rules to minimize fraud. Arthur Levitt, the former chair of the SEC, made several recommendations on how the SEC can tighten its regulatory oversight to improve the quality of financial reports and called for the entire financial community, including the accounting profession, to work toward improving the value relevance of financial reports. The SEC has tightened the screws on companies that try to cook their books by organizing a financial fraud SWAT team dedicated primarily to pursuing financial statement fraud cases in 2000. The SWAT team consists of four experienced forensic accountants and eight lawyers experienced in fraud investigation.[31] The SEC is also working closely with criminal prosecutors to attack financial statement fraud. These new regulatory initiatives to fight white-collar crimes and prevent financial statement fraud were taken in response to the SEC's concern regarding a series of corporate scandals and fraudulent schemes that threaten the integrity and quality of the financial reporting process. Financial statement fraud committed by Cendant Corporation, Sunbeam Corporation Waste Management and Enron Corporation cost public investors more than $100 billion in market capitalization.

The SEC has filed almost 100 financial enforcement actions per year against publicly traded companies that have engaged in financial statement fraud during the past several years. The SEC SWAT task force has concentrated and will continue to focus on the more complex financial fraud cases involving earnings management. These cases often require a thorough investigation of the alleged companies involving more than 100,000 documents and witnesses.

The accounting profession consists of organizations such as the AICPA, American Accounting Association (AAA), Institute of Management Accountants (IMA), Institute of Internal Auditors (IIA), Financial Executives Institute (FEI), and Association of Government Accountants (AGA). These organizations have formed the Committee of Sponsoring Organizations of the Treadway Commission

(COSO), which has issued several reports addressing the nature and magnitude of financial statement fraud and making recommendations for prevention and detection. Examples of these reports are the 1987 Treadway Commission report of fraudulent financial statements, the 1992 Internal Control Framework, and the 1999 research commissioned by the COSO on fraudulent financial reporting.

The Public Oversight Board (POB), which is an independent, private-sector body that monitors and reports on the self-regulatory programs and activities of the SEC Practice Section (SECPS) of the Division for CPA Firms of the AICPA, has appointed several panels to address the efficacy of the audit process, audit effectiveness, and other issues involving public accounting, the accounting profession, and independent auditors who audit financial statements of publicly traded companies. During the past two decades, the POB has appointed several panels to report and recommend ways to improve audit effectiveness in preventing and detecting financial statement fraud. Examples of these panels are the 1993 Panel on Issues Confronting the Accounting Profession, the 1994 Panel on Strengthening the Professionalism of the Independent Auditor, and the O'Malley Panel on Audit Effectiveness Report and Recommendations (August 31, 2000).

Others

The Role of Corporate Legal Counsel

The function of corporate legal counsel as part of corporate governance has recently received a great deal of attention. Elliot and Willingham (1980)[32] argued that two aspects of lawyers' contributions to corporate governance are their obligation to disclose fraud and their relationships to management and boards of directors.

Codes of Conduct

Corporate codes of conduct can be used to encourage ethical and lawful behavior and to create an environment that discourages business improprieties. The codes, by establishing appropriate ethical policies and procedures, can spell out the types of behavior and actions prohibited.

Institutional Ownership

The presence of a major powerful shareholder encourages a CEO to attempt to be in compliance with all applicable laws, regulations, and rules, including accounting standards. Institutional investors are increasingly becoming powerful players in the corporate governance system. Institutional investors can be classified into long-term institutional owners such as mutual, pension, and retirement funds; and short-term institutional investors such as investment bank and private funds. These institutional investors, through their powerful influence in corporate governance, can positively impact the quality of financial reports and thus, prevent and detect financial statement fraud.

Security Analysts

Wall Street analysts often play an important role in recommending stock and, through market participants' transactions, affecting stock prices. Thus, corporate management may take advantage of this visible role of analysts and treat material information as a commodity to obtain favor with particular analysts. As analysts play the game of obtaining inside information in return for more favorable reports on the company, the pressure to obtain selectively disclosed information and more favorable forecasts has continued to grow.

There may be conflicts of interest or even adversarial relationships between the company's management and its analysts in the sense that analysts attempt to obtain all relevant information about earnings quality, quantity, and growth, whereas top executives are interested in releasing only the good news. Security analysts typically want corporations to be more forthcoming with their financial information by providing voluntary disclosures that portray the economic reality of the business. Management, however, wants to disclose only the required financial information and, occasionally, good news.

CONCLUSION

The financial community and regulators (e.g., the SEC) have recently expressed a great concern about financial statement fraud, including earnings management. Earnings management causes misstatements and erosion in the quality of financial statements. Financial statement fraud can have considerable consequences for public companies and investors' confidence in capital markets. The 1999 COSO report identified about 300 public companies that were involved in alleged instances of financial statement fraud from 1987 to 1997. The COSO report found that in 83 percent of these fraudulent cases, the CEOs and/or CFOs were associated with the financial statement fraud. Other individuals named in the report as involved with fraudulent financial activities were controllers, chief operating officers, board members, other senior vice presidents, and external auditors. A Big Five professional services firm audited 56 percent of the sampled fraud companies during the fraud period.

Publicly traded companies are separate legal entities distinct from owners. Companies are directed and managed in a manner in which one or more individuals [the principals] engage other individual(s) [the agents] to perform some service on the principal's behalf based on a set of defined contractual relationships. These contracts are established to ensure that the agent is functioning in the best interest of the principal and to minimize potential divergences from the principal's interests;

however, these potential divergences exist in reality in corporate America, primarily because contracts are not consistently written and/or enforced.

Corporate governance is designed to provide proper mechanisms to minimize divergences that arise from the separation of ownership and decision control. There are both internal and external corporate governance mechanisms. Internal corporate governance mechanisms are the board of directors, audit committees, internal audit function, and management. External corporate governance mechanisms are external auditors, regulatory bodies, standard setters, corporate law, and capital market competition. A corporate governance structure can help prevent fraudulent reporting from occurring. Companies may structure their boards of directors and audit committees as window dressing to make the governance structure inoperative. The board of directors, audit committee, management, and auditors should become more vigilant.

Corporate governance can be improved as more outsiders are added to the boards of directors and audit committees. The quality of the members of the board and reliability and quality of the information they receive can also influence the effectiveness of corporate governance to discharge its duty. The COSO report (1999) suggests the following ways to improve the effectiveness of corporate governance in preventing and detecting financial statement fraud[33]:

- Employ senior executives who are knowledgeable about financial reporting.
- Require the boards of directors and audit committees to pay special attention to potential pressures on company executives caused by incentives built into executive compensation plans or motivations to meet market analysts' expectations.
- Have the board and audit committee members exercise professional skepticism in evaluating top executives' behavioral actions.
- Pay close attention to the integrity and reputation of top executives.
- Monitor opportunities and motivations for management to override the internal control structure.
- Appoint knowledgeable, experienced, and independent boards of directors and audit committees.

ENDNOTES

1. Public Oversight Board (POB) of the Practice Section, AICPA, 1993. A Special Report on Issues Confronting the Accounting Profession.

2. The Business Roundtable (BRT), 1997. Statement of Corporate Governance. An Association of Chief Executive Officers Committed to Improving Public Policy. (September, p. 2).

3. Organization for Economic Co-operation and Development. 1999. "Corporate Governance" Available: www.oecd.org/defgovernance/Q&A.htm

4. Cadbury, A. 1999. "Corporate Governance: A Framework for Implementation." Washington, D.C.: World Bank Publication.

5. Blue Ribbon Committee (BRC). 1999. Report and Recommendations of the BRC on Improving the Effectiveness of Corporate Audit Committees. The New York Stock Exchange (NYSE) and the National Association of Securities Dealers (NASD).

6. Ibid.

7. Toronto Stock Exchange (TSE). 1994. "Where Were the Directors? Guidelines for Improved Corporate Governance in Canada." *The Dey Report* (December).

8. Organization for Economic Cooperation and Development (OECD). OECD Principles of Corporate Governance. Available: www.oecd.org/daf/governance/principles.htm

9. Eckhart, S., S.K. Widener, and L.E. Johnson. 2001. "Governance and Local Government." *Internal Auditor* (June): 51–55

10. Ibid.

11. Beasley, M.S., J.V. Carcello, and D.R. Hermanson. 1999. Fraudulent Financial Reporting: 1987–1997. An Analysis of U.S. Public Companies. Research Commissioned by the Committee of Sponsoring Organizations of the Treadway Commission. Jersey City, NJ: COSO.

12. Beasley, M.S., J.V. Carcello, and D.R. Hermanson. 1999. Fraudulent Financial Reporting: 1987–1997. An Analysis of U.S. Public Companies. Research Commissioned by the Committee of Sponsoring Organizations of the Treadway Commission. Jersey City, NJ: COSO.

13. National Association of Corporate Directors (NACD). 1999. *1999–2000 Public Company Governance Survey*. Washington, D.C.: NACD.

14. Beasley, M.S., J.V. Carcello, D.R. Hermanson, and P.D. Lapides. 2000. "Fraudulent Financial Reporting: Consideration of Industry Traits and Corporate Governance Mechanisms." *Accounting Horizons* (December): 441–454.

15. Beasley, M.S. 1996. "An Empirical Investigation of the Relation between Board of Director Composition and Financial Statement Fraud." *The Accounting Review* (October): 443–465.

16. Ibid.

17. McMullen, D.A. 1996. "Audit Committee Performance: An Investigation of the Consequences Associated with Audit Committees." *Auditing: A Journal of Practice & Theory* (Spring): 87–103.

18. Beasley, M.S. 1996. "An Empirical Investigation of the Relation between Board of Director Composition and Financial Statement Fraud." *The Accounting Review* (October): 443–465.

19. Dechow, P.M., R.G. Sloan, and A.P. Sweeney. 1996. "Causes and Consequences of Earnings Manipulations: An Analysis of Firms Subject to Enforcement Actions by the SEC." *Contemporary Accounting Research* (Spring): 87–103.

20. DeFond, M.L., and J. Jiambalvo. 1991. "Incidence and Circumstances of Accounting Error." *The Accounting Review* (July): 643–655.

21. National Commission on Fraudulent Financial Reporting (NCFER) (The Treadway Commission). 1987. *Report on the National Commission on Fraudulent Financial Reporting*. New York: AICPA.

22. Public Oversight Board (POB) of the Practice Section. AICPA, 1993. A Special Report on Issues Confronting the Accounting Profession.

23. Blue Ribbon Committee (BRC). 1999. Report and Recommendations of the BRC on Improving the Effectiveness of Corporate Audit Committees. The New York Stock Exchange (NYSE) and the National Association of Securities Dealers (NASD).

24. Levitt, A.1998. Remarks by the Chairperson of Securities and Exchange Commission. "The Numbers Game," at NYU Center for Law and Business, New York, NY. (September 28).

25. Levitt, A. 1999. Remarks by Chairperson of Securities and Exchange Commission before the Economic Club of New York (October).

26. McMullen, D.A. 1996. "Audit Committee Performance: An Investigation of the Consequences Associated with Audit Committees." *Auditing: A Journal of Practice & Theory* (Spring): 87–103.

27. Dechow, P.M., R.G. Sloan, and A.P. Sweeney. 1996. "Causes and Consequences of Earnings Manipulations: An Analysis of Firms Subject to Enforcement Actions by the SEC." *Contemporary Accounting Research* (Spring): 87–103.

28. Institute of Internal Auditors (IIA). "Definition of Internal Auditing: IIA Practices Framework." Available: www.theiia.org

29. National Commission on Fraudulent Financial Reporting (NCFER) (The Treadway Commission). 1987. *Report on the National Commission on Fraudulent Financial Reporting.* New York, NY: AICPA.

30. Roland, N. 2001. "SEC to Stay Focused on Accounting Practices." *Los Angeles Times* (February 28; Business, Part C, Page 8).

31. Sugawaru, S. 2000. "SEC Unit Targets Accounting Tricks: New Team to Focus on Cooked Books." *The Washington Post* (May 26): Financial; F05.

32. Elliot, R.K. and J.J. Willingham. 1980. Management Fraud: Detection and Deterrence. New York: Petrocelli Books.

33. Beasley, M.S., J.V. Carcello, and D.R. Hermanson. 1999. Fraudulent Financial Reporting: 1987–1997. An Analysis of U.S. Public Companies. Research Commissioned by the Committee of Sponsoring Organizations of the Treadway Commission. Jersey City, NJ: COSO.

Chapter 7

Board of Directors' Oversight Responsibility

INTRODUCTION

A vigilant and effective board of directors can play an important role in ensuring the quality, integrity, and reliability of business and financial reports. In overseeing the financial reporting process, the board of directors can prevent and detect financial statement fraud. This chapter examines the role of the board of directors, its composition, functions, attributes, and monitoring role in preventing and detecting financial statement fraud.

THE ROLE OF THE BOARD OF DIRECTORS

The role of the board of directors in corporate America can be best described as a mechanism for preventing the concentration of power in the hands of a small group of top managers and for creating a system of checks and balances in corporations through its given authority by shareholders to hire management and monitor management plans, decisions, and actions. The separation of ownership and control in corporations requires the board of directors to (1) harmonize manager-shareholder (agency) conflicts of interest; (2) safeguard invested capital; (3) approve management decisions; (4) assess managerial performance; and (5) allocate rewards in manners that encourage shareholder value creation. Thus, the effectiveness of the board of directors significantly depends on its independence from the top management team; however, management, through its power to nominate or even select directors, can dominate the board of directors and diminish the effectiveness of the board's responsibility in monitoring management.

The board of directors, as an important internal component of corporate governance, receives its authority from shareholders who use their voting rights to elect board members. The board of directors assumes the responsibility to oversee and monitor managerial decisions and actions. Separation of ownership from the decision-making process, coupled with the risk-diversification strategy of stockholders to invest in securities of numerous firms, causes owners to delegate their authority and decision control to the board of directors. The board of directors delegates its decision-making authority to management, which makes decisions on a day-to-day basis on behalf of shareholders. Furthermore, shareholders, as residual claimants and risk bearing in corporations, are not involved in the day-to-day decision-making process and, accordingly, decision functions are separated from risk-bearing residual claimants. This separation, along with the lack of an adequate incentive and/or costly process for shareholders to be involved in decision control, causes stockholders to elect the board of directors as an internal corporate governance responsible for managerial decision control. Although the board of directors usually delegates its decision functions to management, it retains its decision control and monitoring function by (1) monitoring managerial decision functions; (2) overseeing the adequacy and effectiveness of internal control system; (3) overseeing the effectiveness of audit functions; and (4) overseeing the integrity, reliability, and quality of the financial reporting process, as depicted in Exhibit 7.1.

The board of directors' primary responsibility as the ultimate internal control mechanism is to create shareholder value by minimizing the expropriation of shareholder wealth by management through financial statement fraud. The board of directors is in a unique position and has the ultimate responsibility to monitor management decisions or actions; however, financial statement fraud can occur when management acts self-interestedly and fraudulently to issue materially misleading financial statements and the board of directors fails to monitor manage-

Exhibit 7.1.   Corporate Governance and Its Functions

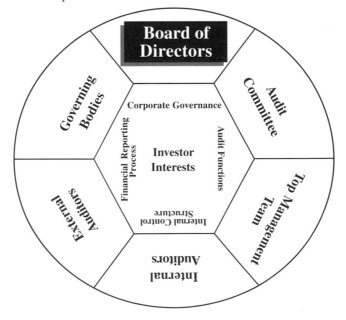

ment actions, oversee the internal controls structure and financial reporting process, and prevent and detect financial statement fraud.

COMPOSITION OF THE BOARD OF DIRECTORS

The board of directors is typically composed of both internal members (e.g., top managers) and external members (e.g., outside, nonemployees). Inside members of the board of directors typically have the ability and experience of using inside information because of their full-time status and inside knowledge that may enhance the quality and quantity of information from internal monitoring systems. Outside members, however, can be more independent in exercising their authority to monitor management decisions and actions. Empirical studies (Fama, 1980; Williamson, 1983),[1, 2] conclude that domination by inside directors, especially top management on the board, can lead to collusion and transfer of shareholder wealth. Thus, it is important to include outside directors on the board to monitor management, reduce agency problems between management and shareholders, and minimize the expropriation of shareholder wealth by management that may arise from financial statement fraud. The 1999 COSO Report found that the boards of directors of 204 studied fraud companies were dominated by insiders and "gray" directors with significant equity ownership and particularly little experience. More than 60 percent of the directors of alleged fraud companies were insiders or "gray" directors who were outsiders but had special ties to company management.[3]

The percentage of outside directors on the board has gradually increased during recent years, primarily because of (1) their perceived independence from top management that improves the monitoring role of the board in minimizing potential management expropriation; (2) shareholders' value of outside directors as reflected in share prices when outside directors are added to the board (e.g., Rosenstein and Wyatt, 1990)[4]; and (3) a trend in practice of an increasing percentage of outside directors on the board. These empirical studies and anecdotal evidence in practice suggest that the higher percentage of outside directors on the board increases its effectiveness in monitoring management decisions and actions and in preventing and detecting financial statement fraud.

The effectiveness of the board of directors as a monitor of management depends on the quality, reputation, and independence of its membership. The presence of outsiders on the board of directors gives the appearance of board independence, but its effectiveness is measured based on the quality of its membership. Fama and Jensen (1983)[5] argue that there is an external market for outside directorships, which provide incentives for outside directors to market them as decision experts who understand and are able to work within decision control systems. This external market for outside directors provides benchmarks for measuring the quality of outside directors' performance.

FUNCTIONS OF THE BOARD OF DIRECTORS

Responsible corporate governance requires that the business of a corporation be conducted under the direction of the board of directors, where the board may delegate to management the authority and responsibility to manage the daily affairs of the corporation. Under an ideal corporate governance structure, the board of directors is able to create shareholder value while oversight functions of the board ensure proper accountability for managerial decisions and activities. The primary functions of the board of directors as stated in the Statement on Corporate Governance of the Business Roundtable are as follows:

- Select, regularly evaluate, and, if necessary, replace the chief executive officer; determine management compensation; and review succession planning.
- Review and, where appropriate, approve the major strategies and financial and other objectives and plans of the corporation.
- Advise management on significant issues facing the corporation.
- Oversee processes for evaluating the adequacy of internal controls, risk management, financial reporting, and compliance, and satisfy itself as to the adequacy of such processes.
- Nominate directors and ensure that the structure and practices of the board provide for sound corporate governance.[6]

RESPONSIBILITIES

The National Association of Corporate Directors (NACD) has recently issued new guidelines to improve the professionalism of board members. The major recommendations of the 1999 NACD guidelines are that directors should meet the following goals:

- Become active participants and decision makers in the boardroom, not merely passive advisors.
- Budget at least four full 40-hour weeks of every board on which to serve.
- Consider a limit on length of service on a board of 10 to 15 years to allow room for new directors with fresh ideas.
- Limit board memberships. Senior executives should sit on no more than three boards, including their own. Retired executives or professional directors should serve on no more than six boards.
- Immerse themselves in both the company's business and its industry, while staying in touch with senior management.
- Be able to read a balance sheet and an income statement and understand the use of financial ratios.

- Own a significant equity position in the company.
- Submit a resignation upon retirement, a change in employer, or a change in professional responsibilities.[7]

Responsibilities of the board of directors vary from one company to another depending on the corporate governance structure, ranging from conducting the business of the company to effective monitoring of management and the achievement of accountability to the company and its shareholders. The Organization for Economic Cooperation and Development (OECD) provided the following guidelines constituting the responsibilities of the board of directors, which have been taken verbatim from the Combined Code of Corporate Governance of the OECD:

1. Board members should act on a fully informed basis, in good faith, with due diligence and care, and in the best interest of the company and the shareholders.
2. Where board decisions may affect different shareholder groups differently, the board should treat all shareholders fairly.
3. The board should ensure compliance with applicable law and take into account the interests of stakeholders.
4. The board should fulfill certain key functions, including:
    - Reviewing and guiding corporate strategy, major plans of action, risk policy, annual budgets and business plans; setting performance objectives; monitoring implementation and corporate performance; and overseeing major capital expenditures, acquisitions and divestitures.
    - Selecting, compensating, monitoring and, when necessary, replacing key executives and overseeing succession planning.
    - Reviewing key executive and board remuneration, and ensuring a formal and transparent board nomination process.
    - Monitoring and managing potential conflicts of interest of management, board members and shareholders, including misuse of corporate assets and abuse in related party transactions.
    - Ensuring the integrity of the corporation's accounting and financial reporting systems, including the independent audit, and that appropriate systems of control are in place, in particular, systems for monitoring risk, financial control, and compliance with the law.
    - Monitoring the effectiveness of the governance practices under which it operates and making changes as needed.
    - Overseeing the process of disclosure and communications.
5. The board should be able to exercise objective judgment on corporate affairs independent, in particular, from management.
    - Boards should consider assigning a sufficient number of non-executive board members capable of exercising independent judgment to tasks

where there is a potential for conflict of interest. Examples of such key responsibilities are financial reporting, nomination and executive and board remuneration.

- Board members should devote sufficient time to their responsibilities.

6. In order to fulfill their responsibilities, board members should have access to accurate, relevant and timely information.[8]

ATTRIBUTES

Stock Ownership

Stock ownership empirical studies (e.g., Feroz, Park, and Pastena, 1991; Shivdasani, 1993),[9, 10] provide evidence indicating that the firm's owners have an incentive to prevent financial statement fraud to protect their investment. These studies conclude that as the percentage of ownership by directors—both outside and inside members—increases, the probability of financial statement fraud decreases. The effective monitoring of management decisions and actions to minimize the probability of financial statement fraud requires adequate time and effort. Thus, financial interest in the company provides incentives for outside directors to more effectively fulfill their responsibility of monitoring managerial decisions. Directors with sizable ownership interest in a firm or control over a large block of votes are more likely to question and challenge management decisions and to monitor management closely to prevent financial statement fraud. A higher percentage of ownership in a firm's outstanding equity should provide individual directors with a strong incentive to promote activities that create shareholder value, which in turn increase the value of the director's investment. Thus, as the extent of ownership interests of outside directors increases, the probability of financial statement fraud should decrease. Beasley (1994) found evidence indicating that outside directors of nonfraud firms hold significantly higher ownership interests than outside directors of fraud firms, and holding financial interests in the firm encourages outside directors to spend the time and effort necessary to effectively monitor management to prevent financial statement fraud.

Empirical research has found that outside directors who hold ownership interest and receive stock-based compensation are typically motivated to monitor the top-level management team including CEOs and become more involved with the company's operation and financial reporting process (Johnson, Hoskisson, and Hitt, 1993).[11] As the stock ownership by outside directors' increases, however, the probability of a firm's CEO and other top management team's attempt to promote control over these outside directors increases. This concern was addressed in Cadbury's (1992) report in the United Kingdom, which prohibits outside directors from holding strong equity positions in their firms.[12] Although this concern in the United States is not currently deemed serious, when companies increase their use of stock ownership as a means of motivating outside directors, the independence, objectivity, and effectiveness of these directors in monitoring management may be compromised.

Leadership of the Board of Directors

The leadership of the board of directors can be unitary or dual. The leadership is dual when the role of the CEO is separated from that of the chair of the board of directors. Unitary leadership exists when one individual holds both the position of the CEO and the chair of the board of directors. Corporate governance can be improved under dual leadership of the board of directors because the individual who chairs the board of directors is expected to exercise significant influence over the board's activities. When unitary leadership exists, it is likely that the interests of shareholders may be compromised. Prior research (e.g., Beasley, 1996; Dechow et al, 1996),[13,14] concludes that companies that engage in financial statement fraud typically have the CEO as the chair of board of directors.

Finkelstein and D'Aveni (1994) reported that 80 percent of the CEOs of large companies serve as chairs of their board of directors.[15] In addition, outside directors are often part of the top management team of other companies and, therefore, have a tendency to grant a CEO great powers (Roe, 1994).[16] Despite all lawsuits brought against directors on the board of not fulfilling their monitoring management responsibility, their accountability remains questionable. Finally, Zarha (1996, 1718), states that:

Directors have increased their coverage of liability and nearly 85 percent of U.S. public manufacturing companies have amended their bylaws to allow them to indemnify outside directors. These factors can include outside directors from the legal consequences of poor decisions.[17]

Monitoring Role of the Board of Directors

The board of directors has an ultimate responsibility for ensuring effective and responsible corporate governance and a reliable financial reporting process. Recently, more institutional pressure has been placed on publicly traded corporations to improve the effectiveness of the board of directors in discharging its responsibility by increasing outside representation on the board and establishing audit committees. Several reports (e.g. Treadway, 1987; COSO 1999; Cadbury 1992)[18–20] suggest that corporate governance is enhanced when activities of management are monitored by individuals who are independent of management and when there is a vigilant oversight by the board of directors. Thus, outside directors on the board can more effectively and objectively oversee management activities and ensure that management interest and goals are congruent with those of shareholders. Corporate governance can be improved as the percentage of outsiders on the board of directors increases.

Fama and Jensen (1983)[21] argued that the board of directors is established by shareholders and board members are elected by shareholders who delegate their authority and responsibility to the board to monitor management because it is costly and impossible for each shareholder to individually monitor day-to-day management decisions and actions. This delegated role of monitoring management makes the board of directors an important component of corporate governance structure. The composition of the board of directors' interests of quality, ownership, degree of outside director representation, competency, and vigilant involvement are relevant factors for board effectiveness in fulfilling its responsibility.

The board of directors is the elected representative of the shareholders responsible for governing the corporation. The board of directors delegates authority to management for functional decision making and the day-to-day conduct of corporate affairs and activities. When the directors are selected by the CEO, they may not be able to exert vigilant oversight responsibility of monitoring management. Several attributes of the board of directors can improve its effective oversight responsibility in monitoring top management's activities. First, boards should not be selected by management in the sense that management should not influence the nominations of the board members. A nominating committee should be composed of nonexecutive directors. Second, most of the board's members should be outside, independent, nonexecutive members who are not part of the management team and financially not dependent on management's discretions. The 1999 COSO Report[22] concludes that, in most fraud companies, boards of directors were dominated by insiders and "gray" directors with considerable equity ownership. The leadership of the board is important in ensuring its responsibility as effective management controls. The chair of the board of directors should not serve as CEO. The third method is to ensure that the board of directors receives adequate information about the company's operations, managerial plans, strategies, decisions, and the financial reporting process.

CHARACTERISTICS IN COMPANIES ENGAGED IN FRAUD

The board of directors, through delegation of its authority to management, is ultimately responsible to shareholders for the business of the corporation, including the integrity and quality of financial reports. Beasley (1998) studied the differences in the characteristics of the board of directors of fraud companies with those of nonfraud companies. Beasley (1998) found that boards of fraud companies differ from boards of nonfraud companies in composition, tenure, and ownership levels of its members, as well as the presence of an inactive audit committee.[23]

Composition of the Board

Several reports (Treadway Commission, 1987; COSO Report, 1999; Blue Ribbon Committee, 1999; POB Report, 2000),[24–27] have addressed the role of the board of directors in preventing and detecting financial statement fraud. These reports recommend changes in the board of director compensation to improve the board's independence by including more outside directors in an attempt to enhance the board's monitoring effectiveness in preventing and detecting fraud. Beasley (1998)[28] found that boards of fraud firms have fewer outside directors and more inside directors (e.g., internal managers) than boards of nonfraud companies (50 percent outside directors for fraud firms compared to 65 percent outside directors for nonfraud firms). Business literature has traditionally classified outside directors as independent directors who have no tie whatsoever to the companies for which they serve as board members; and "gray" directors who hold no internal managerial positions but are affiliated with management through family or business relationships. Gray directors are fundamentally outsiders with special ties to the company or its management. Beasley (1998) found that only 28 percent of the board of directors' members for fraud firms were independent, whereas 43 percent of the board members of nonfraud firms were considered independent. Thus, gray directors of fraud firms represent 44 percent of outside directors compared to 34 percent in nonfraud companies.

Outside Director Tenure

It has been argued that the length of time an outside director serves on the board of directors can influence the director's ability and willingness to challenge managerial decisions, plans, and actions. Beasley (1998)[29] found that an outside director's tenure on the board is longer for nonfraud companies relative to fraud firms. The average tenure for outside directors of nonfraud firms was 6.6 years of service compared to the average tenure of 3.8 years for fraud companies. These results suggest that as length of service on the board increases, the outside director may be less susceptible to peer pressures and more able and willing to scrutinize top management decisions, actions, and plans.

Outside Director Ownership

Business literature finds evidence indicating that a significant equity interest in the company by outside directors can provide more incentives for them to assume more responsibility to monitor top management. Beasley (1998)[30] detected an average cumulative percentage of common stock shares of 12 percent for outside directors of nonfraud firms compared with the average cumulative percentage of ownership of 5.4 percent for outside directors of fraud companies.

Audit Committee Presence and Effectiveness

The vigilant audit committee of the board of directors should oversee the financial reporting process of corporations to ensure its integrity and quality. Beasley (1998)[31] found that only 63 percent of nonfraud companies compared to 41 percent of fraud companies had an audit committee in existence in the year before the fraud. Furthermore, 35 percent of fraud companies with audit committees and 11 percent of nonfraud companies with audit committees never held an audit committee meeting throughout the year. If the number of meetings can be viewed as a measure of audit committees' effectiveness, then it can be concluded that fraud companies had a weaker audit committee relative to nonfraud companies.

In summary, the board of directors' effectiveness in preventing and detecting financial statement fraud can be influenced by the percentage of outside directors on the board, the length of the tenure of board service by outside directors, and the extent of equity interests in the company by outside directors. The review of corporate governance literature indicates that (1) the board of directors is composed of fewer "outside" members for fraud firms than for nonfraud firms; (2) outside members of the board of directors of fraud firms are of lower "quality" than outside directors of nonfraud firms; (3) members of the board of directors of fraud firms hold larger ownership stakes than directors of nonfraud firms; (4) managers (inside members) who serve on the board of directors have higher ownership stakes in fraud firms than managers of nonfraud firms; (5) the chairperson of the board of directors holds a managerial position (e.g., CEO, president) more often for fraud firms than for nonfraud firms; (6) the CEO's tenure on the board of directors for fraud firms is longer than for nonfraud firms; and (7) the average outside director tenure on the board of directors is shorter for fraud firms than for nonfraud firms.

The board of directors can become ineffective in situations when management can override the board of directors' monitoring responsibility by dominating the board of directors; influencing the selection of outside directors; determining or controlling the board of directors meetings and their agenda; and delivering internal and inside information to the selected members. An ineffective board of directors makes financial statement fraud possible. In the wake of Enron's collapse, its board of directors is coming under sharp criticism regarding its independence and role in the crisis. The board of directors' lack of oversight responsibility in allowing the use of private parnerships (Special Purpose Entities) to overstate earnings and understate liabilities has been seriously questioned by injured shareholders and employees. Some directors are subject to potential lawsuits charging that they were engaged in a "massive insider trading."[32]

CONCLUSION

Aligning the interests of managers and shareholders requires vigilant, independent, and effective boards of directors. The effectiveness of the board of directors can be achieved by increasing the representation of outside members on the board. A high ratio of outside directors on the board can improve the board's ability to fulfill its management monitoring responsibility, strengthen corporate governance, enhance objectivity in board deliberations, and improve quality of financial reports. To ensure effectiveness of outside directors, their compensation should be linked to corporate performance and shareholder value creation through stock ownership and stock-based compensation; otherwise, they will be dominated and controlled by inside directors and top management teams. Porter (1992, 71) states that:

> Boards, which have come to be dominated by outside directors with no other links to the company, exert only limited influence on corporate goals. They often lack the time or ability to absorb the vast amounts of information required to understand a company's internal operations. Moreover, most directors have limited stakes in the company they oversee.[33]

Thus, lacking sufficient ownership interest, outside directors may have the same tendency to free-ride as small investors and little incentive to monitor the top management team. Furthermore, the fact that CEOs play an important role in the selection, remuneration, and retention of outside directors limits the outside director's effectiveness.

The board of directors should set the "tone at the top" with clear expectations for and commitment to high-quality financial reports. Each member of the board should be financially literate and knowledgeable of the industry and have the ability to communicate effectively, ask tough questions and evaluate the answers, and be independent from the company, have no material financial interest in the company, and have no material financial and personal relationship with the president, CEO, or CFO. The board of directors should ensure that the audit committee is independent and qualified to effectively perform its oversight responsibility of the quality and integrity of the financial reporting process. A high-quality financial reporting process produces reliable, useful, and relevant financial statements free of material errors, irregularities, and fraud.

Lack of vigilant, continuous, diligent, and proactive participation of the board of directors increases the opportunity for financial statement fraud. The following factors can improve the effectiveness of the board of directors' oversight function: (1) composition of the board in terms of percentage of outside directors and percentage of financially disinterested directors; (2) leadership of the board in the sense that the chair position of the board is separate from the position of CEO; (3) knowledge and understanding of financial statements by individual board members; and (4) operation effectiveness of the board in receiving and thoroughly reviewing relevant information.

ENDNOTES

1. Fama, E. F. 1980. Agency Problem and the Theory of the Firm. *Journal of Political Economy:* 288–308.

2. Williamson, O. E., 1983. Organization Form. Residual Claimants and Corporate Control. *Journal of Law and Economics.* 26:351.

3. Beasley, M. S., J. V. Carcello, and D. R. Hermanson. 1999. Fraudulent Financial Reporting: 1987–1997. An Analysis of U.S. Public Companies. New York, N.Y.: COSO.

4. Rosenstein. S., and J. G. Wyatt. 1990. Outside Directors, Board Independence, and Shareholder Wealth. *Journal of Financial Economics.* 26: 175–191.

5. Fama, M., and C. Jensen. 1983. Separation of Ownership and Control. *Journal of Law and Economics* (June): 301–355.

6. The Business Roundtables (BRT). 1997. "Statement on Corporate Governance." An Association of Chief Executive Officers Committed to Improving Public Policy. (September): 4–5.

7. National Association of Corporate Directors. 1999. The NACD Board Guidelines.

8. Organization for Economic Cooperation and Development (OECD). 1989. OECD Principles of Corporate Governance. Available: www.oecd.org/governance/principles.htm

9. Feroz, E. H., K. Park, and V. S. Pastena. 1991. The Financial and Market Effects of the SEC's Accounting and Auditing Enforcement Releases. *Journal of Accountancy Research* 29: 107–142.

10. Shivdasani, A. 1993. "Board Composition, Ownership Structure, and Hostile Takeovers." *Journal of Accountancy and Economics.* 16: 167–198.

11. Johnson R., R. Hoskisson, and M. Hitt. 1993. Board of Directors Involvement in Restructuring: The Effect Importance of Board Versus Managerial Controls and Characteristics. *Strategic Management Journal* (Vol. 14): 33–51.

12. Cadbury, Sir. A. 1992. Financial Report of the Committee on the Financial Aspects of Corporate Governance. Financial Reporting Council. London Stock Exchange, London (December).

13. Beasley, M. S. 1996. An Empirical Investigation of the Relation Between Board of Director Compensation and Financial Statement Fraud. *The Accounting Review* (October): 443–465.

14. Dechow, P. M., R. G. Sloan, and A. P. Sweeney. 1996. Causes and Consequences of Earnings Manipulations: An Analysis of Firms Subject to Enforcement Actions by the SEC. *Contemporary Accounting Research* (Spring): 1–36.

15. Finkelstein, S., and R. A. D'Aveni. 1994. CEO Quality As Doubled-Edged Sword: How Board of Directors Balance Entrenchment Avoidance and Unity of Command. *Academy of Managerial Journal* (Vol. 37): 1079–1108.

16. Roe, M. J. 1994. *Strong Managers, Weak Owners,* Princeton, NJ: Princeton University Press.

17. Zahra, S. A. 1996. Governance, Ownership, and Corporate Entrepreneurship: The Moderating Impact of Industry Technological Opportunities. *Academy of Management Review* (vol. 39, no. 6): 1713–1735.

18. National Commission on Fraudulent Financial Reporting (NCFFR) (The Treadway Commission). 1987. Report on the National Commission on Fraudulent Financial Reporting. New York, NY: AICPA.

19. Beasley, M. S., J. V. Carcello, and D. R. Hermanson. 1999. Fraudulent Financial Reporting: 1987–1997. An Analysis of U.S. Public Companies. New York, NY: COSO.

20. Cadbury, Sir. A. 1992. Financial Report of the Committee on the Financial Aspects of Corporate Governance. Financial Reporting Council. London Stock Exchange, London (December).

21. Fama, M., and C. Jensen. 1983. Separation of Ownership and Control. *Journal of Law and Economics* (June): 301–355.

22. Beasley, M. S., J. V. Carcello, and D. R. Hermanson. 1999. Fraudulent Financial Reporting: 1987–1997, An Analysis of U.S. Public Companies. New York, N.Y.: COSO.

23. Beasley, M. S. 1998. "Boards of Directors and Fraud." *The CPA Journal* (April): 56–58.

24. National Commission on Fraudulent Financial Reporting (NCFFR) (The Treadway Commission). 1987. Report on the National Commission on Fraudulent Financial Reporting. New York, NY: AICPA.

25. Beasley, M. S., J. V. Carcello, and D. R. Hermanson. 1999. Fraudulent Financial Reporting: 1987–1997, An Analysis of U.S. Public Companies. New York, N.Y.: COSO.

26. Blue Ribbon Committee (BRC) on Improving the Effectiveness of Corporate Audit Committees. 1999. Report and Recommendations of the Blue Ribbon Committee on Improving the Effectiveness of Corporate Audit Committees. New York, NY: NYSE and NASD.

27. O'Malley, S. F. 2000. The Panel on Audit Effectiveness: Report and Recommendations. Public Oversight Board (August). One Station Place, Stanford, CT 06902 .

28. Beasley, Mark S. 1998. "Boards of Directors and Fraud." *The CPA Journal* (April): 56–58.

29. Ibid.

30. Ibid.

31. Ibid.

32. Abelson, R. 2001. Enron Board Comes Under a Storm of Criticism. *The New York Times* (December 16). Available at http://www.nytimes.com.

33. Porter, M. E. 1992. "Capital Disadvantage in America's Failing Capital Investment System." *Harvard Business Review* (70): 65–82.

Chapter 8

Audit Committees and Corporate Governance

INTRODUCTION

The role of audit committees as an integral part of corporate governance has been addressed in several reports (e.g., Treadway Commission, 1987; the Blue Ribbon Committee, 1999).[1, 2] Recent high-profile business failures, financial statement fraud, corporate misconducts, and expanded requirements by the Securities and Exchange Commission (SEC) intended to improve the quality of financial reports necessitate that publicly traded companies revise and expand their audit committees' functions, responsibilities, and charters. Traditionally, many companies have formed audit committees as standing committees of outside directors to oversee the quality of the financial reporting process, internal control structure, and audit functions. Recently, the new rules for audit committees set forth by the SEC, New York Stock Exchange (NYSE), and National Association of Securities Dealers (NASD) empower audit committees to function, on behalf of the board, by playing an important role in the corporate government process intended to protect investors' interests and ensure corporate accountability. In this new capacity, the audit committee oversees the effectiveness of corporate government, integrity of financial reports, adequacy of the internal control structure, and quality of the audit function, as depicted in Exhibit 8.1.

The success of audit committees in fulfilling their oversight responsibility depends on their working relationships with other members of corporate governance, including the board of directors, management, external auditors, internal auditors, legal counsel, and regulatory and standard-setting bodies. Because the audit committee is typically created by a company's board of directors, its functions, responsibilities, and charters should be approved by the board of directors. The audit committee must be independent of management in order to be able to discharge its monitoring responsibilities in overseeing the financial reporting process, internal control structure, and audit functions. Audit committees should establish a close working relationship with both internal and external auditors. Audit committees must have or obtain within a reasonable period the financial literacy necessary to understand applicable laws, regulations, and standards promulgated by regulatory and standard-setting bodies as well as the ability to read and understand four basic financial statements. The emerging interest in corporate governance as evidenced by concerns from investors groups, regulators, and the public regarding

Exhibit 8.1. Corporate Governance and Its Functions

financial statement fraud has underscored the importance of audit committees as a crucial element of corporate governance mechanisms. Former SEC chair Arthur Levitt rightfully stated that:

> Effective oversight of the financial reporting process depends to a very large extent on strong audit committees. Qualified, committed, independent, and tough-minded audit committees represent the most reliable guardians of the public interest—this time for bold action.[3]

EVOLUTION OF AUDIT COMMITTEES

The evolution of audit committees reveals that many companies voluntarily established audit committees in the mid-twentieth century to provide more effective communication between the board of directors and external auditors. Traditionally, audit committees have acted as a liaison between management and external auditors in selecting auditors to preserve auditors' independence, reviewing the company's annual audited financial statements; and interacted with internal auditors in reviewing matters pertaining to internal control structure.

Several reports (Treadway Commission, 1987; COSO, 1992; Section 363.5 of FDIC Improvement Act, 1993; POB, 1993; Kirk Panel, 1994; POB, 1995; Blue Ribbon Committee, 1999; POB, 2000) have addressed the role of the board of directors and its representative audit committee in overseeing corporate governance, the financial reporting process, the internal control structure, and audit functions. These reports and their implications for audit committees are discussed in the following sections. These reports discuss audit committees' structure and organization and suggest guidelines regarding functions, responsibilities, and activities of audit committees without mandating any specific requirements. Boards of directors are recognizing that they need to have greater corporate accountability and fiduciary responsibility, more oversight functions of monitoring management activities, and a broad range of skills, expertise, and financial literacy to effectively fulfill their responsibilities. The board of directors has traditionally looked to the audit committee to ensure responsible corporate governance and a reliable financial reporting process.

The National Commission on Fraudulent Financial Reporting (The Treadway Commission)

The savings and loan association crisis of the 1980s and unprecedented business failure raised concerns about the effectiveness of corporate governance and the quality of financial reports. Thus, the Committee of Sponsoring Organizations (COSO), a private-sector intuitive, jointly funded and sponsored by the American Institute of Certified Public Accountants (AICPA), the American Accounting Association (AAA), the Financial Executives Institute (FEI), the Institute of Internal Auditors (IIA), and the Institute of Management Accountants (IMA) was formed in 1985, to identify factors that lead to fraudulent financial reporting and to recommend strategies and actions that may reduce their occurrence. In October 1987, the COSO issued its first report entitled, "The Report of the National Commission on Fraudulent Financial Reporting," also known as the Treadway Report after the chairman of that commission, former SEC commissioner James C. Treadway.[4] The Treadway Report identified corporate governance principles and made recommendations that would substantially reduce incidents of financial statement fraud.

The Treadway recommendations were aimed for public companies, public accountants, the SEC, and others to improve the regulatory and legal environment and education. The Treadway Report specifically made 11 recommendations regarding the structure and role of the audit committee. These recommendations were the first guidelines about audit committee responsibilities that set standards based on best practices rather than on common practices. Three of the eleven recommendations of the Treadway report pertain to the proper structure of the audit committee. The first recommendation is that the SEC should require all publicly traded companies to establish audit committees composed solely of independent directors. The second recommendation suggests that all public companies establish a written charter for the audit committee specifying its mission, objectives, role, and responsibilities. The third recommendation is that audit committees should have adequate resources and authority to discharge their responsibilities.

The Treadway Report suggests eight recommendations regarding the role, responsibilities, and function of audit committees. These recommendations expand the audit committees' responsibilities to:

- Oversee the quarterly reporting process and approve the financial results of quarterly financial statements.
- Sign a letter for inclusion in the annual reports describing the committee's responsibilities, activities, and accomplishments during the year.
- Review annually the management program to monitor compliance with the code of business conduct in resolving conflict of interests and, accordingly, assist management in preventing and detecting fraud.
- Assume informal, vigilant, and effective oversight of the financial reporting process and the company's internal controls.
- Ensure that the internal auditor's involvement in the audit of the entire financial reporting process is appropriate and properly coordinated with the independent public accountant.
- Review management's evaluation of the factors assisting public accountants in preserving their independence.
- Advise management when it seeks a second opinion on a significant accounting issue such as significant accounting policies or determination of accounting estimates.
- Review management's plans for engaging the company's independent public accountant to perform any attestation function, such as management advisory services and review services.

These recommendations pertain to the audit committee's oversight responsibility in the areas of corporate governance, the financial reporting process, the internal control structure, and audit functions. These oversight responsibilities can play an important role in ensuring the integrity and quality of financial reports and reducing incidents of financial statement fraud.

In summary, the National Commission on Fraudulent Financial Reporting, better known as the Treadway Commission, issued a report in 1987 addressing the role of the audit committee in the areas of corporate governance and the financial reporting process. The Treadway Report focuses more attention on the role of audit committees in overseeing corporate governance activities, the financial reporting process, internal control, and the legal and ethical conduct of company employees and management in preventing and detecting financial statement fraud. Although the Treadway guidelines for audit committees have become the benchmark by which audit committees' performance has been measured, these guidelines are not mandatory, and accordingly, audit committees' functions and responsibilities vary among companies.

COSO Reports

The Treadway Commission called for the COSO groups to (1) develop a common uniform definition for internal control, (2) determine the components of an internal control structure; and (3) provide guidance for assessing the effectiveness of the internal control structure. COSO issued its report entitled "Internal Control— Integrated Framework" in September 1992, which is discussed in Chapter 11;[5] however, the COSO report, while providing a framework for assessing the effectiveness of the internal control structure and its components, emphasizes the important role that the audit committee can play in ensuring management's commitment to an adequate and effective internal control structure. The COSO report underscores the audit committee's role in establishing the tone at the top to promote ethical values and compliance with the established corporate code of conduct.

FDICIA

The U.S. Congress passed the Federal Deposit Insurance Corporation Improvement Act of 1991 (FDICIA) in response to the savings and loan debate.[6] The FDICIA requires that management and the independent auditors of depository institutions report on the effectiveness of internal controls over financial reporting. Section 363.5, 1993 regulations of the FDICIA, requires large financial institutions (more than $3 billion in assets) to establish an independent audit committee of outside, nonexecutive board members. The board of directors of these financial institutions is responsible for determining whether its audit committee is in compliance with the independence requirements of the FDIC rules; and whether members of the audit committee have the necessary experience, financial literacy, and qualifications in banking and related financial management to fulfill their assigned responsibilities. The audit committee is responsible for obtaining and evaluating sufficient information regarding the achievement of the institution's financial, operating, and compliance objectives.

POB Reports

The Public Oversight Board (POB) is an independent, private-sector body that monitors and reports on the self-regulatory activities and programs of the SEC Practice Section (SECPS) of the Division for CPA firms of the AICPA. The POB has appointed several parcels to address a wide variety of issues involving the public accounting and auditing functions. In 1993, the POB issued the Public Interest, a special report that (1) emphasized the importance of reliable audit financial statements in ensuring the efficiency of the capital markets and the well-being of the American economy; (2) recognized the extent and adverse effect of litigation against professional service firms (CPAs); and (3) made recommendations to regain public confidence in published financial statements and the accounting profession.[7] The 1993 POB report encouraged external auditors to assist audit committees in understanding their responsibilities. This report also recommended that direct interface among boards of directors, audit committees, and auditors occur to ensure responsible corporate governance and quality financial reporting.

The second POB report was issued in 1995, entitled "Directors, Management, and Auditors—Allies in Protecting Shareholder Interests."[8] This report emphasized the importance of informed discussions between external audit committees. This report also recommended that the external auditor's engagement letter specify that the client is the audit committee to ensure that the auditor is not beholden to management.

The third report of the POB entitled "The Panel on Audit Effectiveness Report and Recommendations" was issued on August 31, 2000.[9] The 2000 Panel was established in 1998 at the request of the former Chair of the SEC, Arthur Levitt, to examine the current audit model by investigating the way independent audits are performed in light of recent changes in the business environment such as globalization and technological advances. The 2000 report was addressed to several constituents of audited financial statements, including audit committees, professional services firms, the SEC, the standard setters, and the public. The report included in its recommendations the requirement that audit committees preapprove nonaudit services that exceed a threshold amount by identifying and assessing the factors that may affect auditors' independence when performing financial statement audits.

The 2000 panel, while recognizing that audit committees have become an accepted and important element in corporate governance, recommended that the SECPS requires its member CPA firms to report annually to audit committees the total fees received by the audit firm for nonaudit services such as management advisory and other nonalternative services. External auditors should discuss with and confirm to audit committees their independence and disclose all factors and relationships between the auditor and the client's company that may affect auditors' independence.

Institute of Internal Auditors

The Institute of Internal Auditors (IIA) issued a position statement entitled, "The Audit Committee in the Public Sector," in 1991 to underscore the importance of audit committees in the public section.[10] The IIA position states that the audit committee provides a public-sector entity with the following benefits: (1) vigilant oversight of internal control, audit functions, and the financial reporting process; (2) preservation of the independence of the internal audit function; (3) assurance that the proper prompt actions are taken on audit findings; and (4) enhanced communication between management and auditors.

SEC RULES ON AUDIT COMMITTEES

The SEC has traditionally been a long-time advocate of audit committees; however, until recently the SEC has stopped short of making audit committees a requirement for publicly traded companies. In its Accounting Series Release numbers 19 and 123, issued in 1940 and 1972, respectively, the SEC encouraged public companies to establish audit committees. In 1974 and 1978, the SEC adapted rules requiring publicly traded companies under its jurisdiction to disclose in proxy statements whether they have an audit committee. In 1999, the SEC established new rules that eventually require public companies to include reports by their audit committee in their proxy statements and disclose whether their audit committee has a charter and is independent. The new SEC rules underscore the important role audit committees can play in ensuring responsible corporate governance and reliable financial reports that improve the confidence and efficiency of the capital markets and protect investors' interests.

The new SEC rules on audit committees were adopted in December 1999 in response to the Blue Ribbon Committee Report and recommendations and require disclosure about the existence and composition of audit committees as well as their charter and functions. The SEC rules, among other things, require that (1) proxy statements include a report from the audit committee; (2) publicly traded companies disclose in their proxy statements whether their audit committee has a written charter, and file a copy of their charter every three years; and (3) public companies disclose in their proxy statements certain information pertaining to the independence of audit committee members.

A growing number of financial statement frauds committed by major companies has encouraged the SEC and other officials to take action to ensure the integrity and quality of the financial reporting process. In September 1998, the former SEC chairman Arthur Levitt in a keynote speech entitled, "The Numbers Game," raised concerns about the quality of earnings and the integrity of the financial reporting process.[11] Audit committees play an important role in ensuring responsible corporate governance and a reliable financial reporting process. Thus, at the request of the former chairman Levitt, the NYSE and the NASD sponsored the Blue Ribbon Committee on improving the effectiveness of corporate audit committees.[12]

The Blue Ribbon Committee (BRC) issued its report in February 1999 consisting of 10 recommendations to improve the effectiveness of audit committees and five guiding principles for audit committee best practices. In December 1999, both the NYSE and NASD amended their listing standards pertaining to audit committees' members to be financially literate or become financially literate within a reasonable period after their appointment to the audit committee. The recommendations set forth by the BRC and the subsequent rules adopted by the NYSE and NASD and regulations established by the SEC have fundamentally defined the nature, functions, and duties of public audit committees.

The new audit committee rules established by the NYSE and NASD are designed to strengthen the qualifications, effectiveness, and independence of audit committees of publicly traded companies. The new NASD rules on audit committees govern public companies listed on both the American Stock Exchange (AMEX) and companies quoted on the NASDAQ.

AUDIT COMMITTEES AND ORGANIZED STOCK EXCHANGES

Organized stock exchanges in the United States, including the NYSE, the AMEX, and the NASDAQ require that listed companies have audit committees with membership limited primarily to independent directors. These organized stock exchanges have adopted recommendations of the BRC on the formation, compositions, principles, and best practices and accordingly amended their audit committee requirements to strengthen the independence and qualifications of audit committees. The new audit committee rules of the NYSE and NASD, which govern companies listed on both the AMEX and NASDAQ, are presented in the following sections to describe the ways that these rules could improve audit committee effectiveness in preventing and detecting financial statements fraud. A summary of these rules, along with the requirements of FDICIA for audit committees, is presented in Exhibit 8.2.

Listed companies should assess whether their audit committees comply with the new rules as related to (1) independent directors, (2) charter requirements, (3) structure and membership requirements, and (4) compliance.

1. *Independence Rule.* The new rules define independence of audit committee members more rigorously than in the past by specifying the relationships that disqualify a director from being considered independent for purposes of serving on audit committees. A member of an audit committee may not be considered independent if the director:
   - Has been employed by the corporation or its affiliates in the current or past three years,
   - Received any annual material compensation from the corporation or its affiliates (e.g., in excess of 60,000) except for board service, retirement plan benefits, or nondiscretionary compensation.
   - Is an immediate family member who is, or has been in the past three years, employed by the corporation or its affiliates as an executive officer.
   - Has been a partner, controlling shareholder, or an executive office of a major trading partner with the corporation.
   - Has been employed as an executive of another entity where any of the company's executives serve on that entity's compensation committee.

Exhibit 8.2. New Rules on Audit Committees

New York Stock Exchange (NYSE), 1999	National Association of Securities Dealers Automated Quotation Market (NASDAQ), 1999	Federal Deposit Insurance Corporation Improvement Act of 1991 (FDICIA Regulations Section 363-5, 1993)	American Stock Exchange (AMEX), 1999
1. All listed domestic companies are required to have an Audit Committee.	1. All issues are required to have an Audit Committee.	1. Depository institutions insured by the FDIC are required to establish and maintain an Audit Committee.	1. Listed companies of Amex are required to have an audit committee.
2. Audit Committee should be composed solely of independent directors who are financially literate.	2. Audit Committees should consist of at least three members who are financially literate and the majority are independent directors.	2. The established Audit Committee should be composed solely of outside directors who are independent of management.	2. Audit Committees should be composed of at least three members who are financially literate and the majority are independent directors.
3. Domestic listed companies are required to adopt formal written charters for their Audit Committees specifying the committees' responsibilities and practices.	3. All issues are required to adopt formal written charters for their Audit Committees specifying the committees' responsibilities and actions.	3. Members of Audit Committees should have the necessary experience and qualifications in banking and related financial management.	3. Listed companies are required to adopt financial written charters for their Audit Committees specifying the committees' responsibilities and practices.
4. Written affirmation is required of all domestic listed companies regarding the independence and qualifications of audit committee members.	4. All issues regarding the independence and qualifications of audit committee members require written certifications.	4. The Audit Committee should not include only members who are large customers of the financial institution.	4. All listed companies, regarding the independence and qualifications of Audit Committees, require written certifications.

2. *Charter.* Companies are required to adopt a formal written charter that specifies the scope of its responsibilities and functions, including those related to the independence and accountability of independent auditors. The audit committee charter is further discussed later in this chapter.

3. *Structure.* Companies are required to have an audit committee of at least three members and be composed solely of "independent" directors who are financially literate. At least one member of the audit committee must have accounting or financial management skills. Financial literacy is defined as the ability to read and understand fundamental financial statements, including a balance sheet income statement and a cash flow statement. Credentials indicating financial literacy are past employment experience in finance or accounting, professional certifications in accounting (e.g., CPA, CMA, CIA) and past or current position as a chief executive or financial officer or other senior officer with adequate financial oversight responsibilities.

   To meet the requirements of financial literacy under the SEC, NYSE, and NASD, an audit committee member should have a basic understanding of fundamental financial statements and an understanding of the specific company's operations and financial statements. This suggests that only sufficient understanding of managerial business financial skills would satisfy the financial literacy requirement of the rules. It does not necessarily mean that a member should have a thorough understanding of generally accepted accounting principles (GAAP), generally accepted auditing standards (GAAS), or an extensive background as an accounting or financial professional. The audit committee should understand and review revenue recognition practices, deferred costs, accruals, management estimates, and unusual transactions. The audit committee should not only understand the appropriateness and applications of accounting principles, methods, and procedures, but should also be able to challenge management on their application.

4. *Compliance.* To ensure compliance with the SEC, NYSE, and NASD new rules on audit committees, the listed companies should provide a written affirmation (NYSE) or certification (NASD) regarding the independence and qualifications of audit committee members. In addition, listed companies should adopt a formal written audit committee charter and meet the new audit committee structure and membership requirements. Furthermore, new SEC rules require annual proxy statement disclosures regarding audit committee member independence.

BLUE RIBBON COMMITTEE RECOMMENDATIONS

The BRC, in recognizing the important role that audit committees play in corporate governance, the financial reporting process, the internal control structure, and audit functions, made 10 recommendations regarding the independence, structure, and responsibilities of audit committees.[13] These recommendations are made based on two essential principles: (1) Practices and effectiveness of audit committees are the mere reflection of the practices and attitudes of the entire board of directors; and (2) A regulatory, self-regulatory, and legal environment that demands disclosure, transparency, and accountability is necessary. These recommendations are intended to provide guidance for organizations in establishing or redesigning their audit committee charters to ensure more responsible corporate governance and reliable financial reports. The BRC recommendations are summarized in three categories of (1) the independent audit committee; (2) effectiveness of audit committees; and (3) accountability mechanisms of audit committees.

1. *Independence.* The first two BRC recommendations relate to means of strengthening the independence of audit committees. These recommendations are (1) both the NYSE and NASD adopt the independence rule as defined by the BRC for listed companies with a market capitalization above $200 million; and (2) in compliance with the "independence definition" set forth by the BRC, the affected listed companies have an audit committee comprised solely of independent directors. Firms in compliance with the suggestions of several reports (e.g., Treadway Commission, 1987) are increasing the percentage of outside directors on their audit committees to strengthen their corporate governance structure. Kesner (1988) surveyed audit committees of 250 of the Fortune 500 firms and found that firms with audit committees, composed of outside directors having business background and long tenure, appear to be acquiescing to corporate pressures for enhanced governance.[14] Some firms window dress their audit committee with "gray" directors. Gray directors are those individuals who are closely affiliated with and have a strong monetary or historic attachment to the firm, such as its lawyers, major customers and suppliers, and former executives. These gray directors have the appearance of independence, but they cannot be effective vigilantes primarily because of their strong economic and emotional ties to the firm.

2. *Effectiveness.* The BRC made three recommendations aimed at improving the audit committee's effectiveness. These recommendations suggest that the NYSE and the NASD require their listed companies with a market capitalization above $200 million to: (1) have an audit committee comprising a minimum of three financially literate directors; and (2) adopt a formal written charter that is approved by the full board of directors and that specifies the committee's responsibilities, including those related to the independence and accountability of the independent auditors, as well as structure, process, and membership requirements of audit committees. The audit committee charter should be reviewed by the board of directors annually to assess and ensure its adequacy. The third recommendation in this category suggests that the SEC issues rules that require the audit committee for each reporting company to disclose in its proxy statement whether the audit committee has adopted a for-

mal written charter, and if so, whether the audit committee satisfied its responsibilities during the prior year in compliance with its charter. The BRC also recommends that the SEC adopt a "safe harbor" applicable to all disclosures specified in the previous recommendation.

3. *Mechanisms for Accountability.* The final sets of the BRC recommendations are intended to provide mechanisms for accountability among the audit committee, external auditors, and management. The first two recommendations in this category related to external auditors of listed companies of both the NYSE and the NASD. These recommendations suggest that the listing rules for both the NYSE and NASD require that the audit committee charter of listed companies specify that (1) the external auditor is ultimately accountable to the board of directors and audit committee as representative of shareholders; and (2) the audit committee is responsible for receiving a formal written statement from the external auditor specifying all relationships between the auditor and the company consistent with the applicable independence rule of external auditors promulgated by the SEC, AICPA, or other appropriate authorities.

The eighth BRC recommendation suggests that GAAS require that the external auditor discuss with the audit committee the auditors' judgment about the quality, not just the acceptability, of the company's accounting principles as applied in its financial reporting, including discretion used by management in selecting and applying accounting principles, estimates, and disclosures. The ninth recommendation of the BRC suggests that the SEC require all reporting companies under its jurisdiction to include a letter from the audit committee in the company's annual report to shareholders and Form 10-K Annual Report indicating whether management has reviewed the audited financial statements with the audit committee; the external auditors have discussed audit findings with the audit committee; the members of the audit committee have discussed among themselves audit findings; and the audit committee believes that the company's financial statements are fairly presented in all material respects, in conformity with GAAP. Finally, the BRC recommended that the SEC require interim financial statements to be reviewed by external auditors, in accordance with the Auditing Standards Board (ASB) Statement on Auditing Standards (SAS) No. 71 before companies file their Form 10-Q and Form 10-QSB with the SEC.

BLUE RIBBON COMMITTEE GUIDING PRINCIPLES

The BRC recommended five guiding principles for vigilant audit committees to improve their effectiveness in overseeing the accountability of corporate governance, reliability of internal control structure, and appropriateness of audit functions.[15] The proper implementation of these guiding principles can create mechanisms for best practices of audit committees in the corporate governance process and make the relationship between audit committees and other corporate governance participants (e.g., the board of directors, management, auditors, shareholders), as depicted in Exhibit 8.1, more effective. These principles are as follows:

1. The audit committee plays a key role in monitoring the other component parts of the audit process.
2. Independent communication and information should flow between the audit committee and the internal auditor.
3. Independent communication and information should flow between the audit committee and outside auditors.
4. Candid discussions should be held with management, the internal auditor, and outside auditors regarding issues implicating judgment and impacting quality.
5. Audit committee membership must be diligent and knowledgeable.

Implementing these guiding principles can establish certain audit committees' best practices by knowledgeable, diligent, independent, and financially literate directors. The major theme of these guiding principles is that audit committees should be more diligent and knowledgeable in their oversight of corporate governance and the financial reporting process. To effectively fulfill this responsibility, audit committees should work closely with the board of directors, management, internal auditors, and external auditors to ensure responsible corporate governance and reliable, high-quality, and timely financial reports free of material misstatements to the board of directors, shareholders, and investing public.

FUTURE OF AUDIT COMMITTEES

Ernst & Young, one of the Big Five professional service firms, conducted a survey of the audit committee practices at its 60 large public company clients.[16] The purposes of the survey were to identify leading practices of audit committees; develop benchmark practices; and establish a framework to assess the nature and extent of future changes in audit committee practices in response to new SEC rules. The survey results revealed that:

- Almost all of the surveyed companies plan to adopt a high-level audit committee charter rather than a detailed charter that would be published at least once every three years.
- About 84 percent of the companies plan to have regular quarterly communication between external auditors and audit committees, whereas the other 16 percent plan to have such communication on an exception-only basis.
- Very few of the surveyed companies currently include a report of the audit committees in their annual report, proxy statement, or Annual Report on form 10-K,

whereas all publicly traded companies will be required to disclose a report of the audit committee annually in the company's proxy statement.

- Audit committee composition, reporting, and meeting practices are considered highly effective in terms of receiving an adequate information flow continuously to fulfill the assigned oversight responsibilities.
- Most of the audit committees are viewed to perform their meeting activities effectively.
- Audit committee relationships with management, external auditors, and internal auditors are generally viewed as highly effective.
- Surveyed audit committees demonstrated effective leadership attributes measured in terms of setting the tone for teamwork and effective communication, listening emphatically, and having the ability and courage to challenge and act when necessary.

The audit committee's role has evolved over the years, and now with the recommendations of the BRC, the new rules of the SEC, NYSE, AMEX, and NASDAQ and the Auditing Standards Board (ASB), it can be best described as an oversight responsibility in the areas of corporate governance, financial reporting, the internal control structure, and audit functions, as depicted in Exhibit 8.1. Future audit committees are expected to be the ultimate guardians of investors' interests and accountability. Recent developments in audit committee structure, composition, and qualifications will challenge publicly traded companies to improve the oversight functions and practices of their audit committees. This challenge, on one hand, will provide an opportunity to improve corporate governance and the quality of financial reporting, which is in the best interests of investors and the financial community. On the other hand, some of the new requirements, such as financial literacy, inclusion of a report of audit committees annually in the company's proxy statement, and guardian of investor interests, have raised serious concerns that such requirements will increase audit committees' liability. This potential increased liability may ultimately result in either higher compensation for audit committee members or fewer qualified directors willing to serve on audit committees.

Lynn E. Turner, the Chief Accountant of the SEC, describes the proactive oversight responsibility of an active and vigilant audit committee as Three D's of "due diligence and documentation."[17] In fulfilling its proactive oversight of the financial reporting process and the related internal control structure, the audit committee should exercise due diligence by relying on experts such as CFOs, internal auditors, and external auditors to provide the committee with relevant information. The audit committee, with proper counsel from its legal advisors, should also document the processes followed in reaching decisions by means of the committee charter and minutes.

The Pricewaterhouse Coopers study entitled "Audit Committee Effectiveness—What Works Best" (2000), identifies the following forces and trends that will shape the audit committee of the future:[18]

1. *Risk Management and Internal Control.* The board of directors and their representative audit committees should provide more effective oversight over risk management and internal control activities beyond financial reporting to ensure responsible corporate governance.

2. *Faster Communication of Information.* The capital market will continue to demand more reliable, relevant, and timely financial information. Thus, companies will find ways to prepare and disseminate required information both financial and nonfinancial faster to market participants. It is expected that the discounting profession's electronic financial reporting institutions of extensible business reporting language (XBRL) will receive more attention and support from the business community. XBRL-based systems can generate financial information beyond historical financial information to market participants, including information on a company's tangibles, intellectual capital, research and development, and customer base. Thus, audit committees should oversee the reliability and relevance of other information disseminated to market participants.

3. *Reliance on Others.* The new rules on audit committees have expanded audit committee members' responsibilities and functions. The audit committee under the new rules may be viewed as a "watching" committee scrutinizing the corporate governance and financial reporting process. It is expected that future audit committees will seek assistance and advice from internal auditors, external auditors, legal counsel, and others in effectively discharging their extended responsibilities.

4. *Liability.* Audit committee members are faced with more liability than before under the new rules that, if not properly addressed, can cause difficulties in monitoring or recruiting qualified audit committee members.

5. *More Time, More Pay.* The expanded functions of audit committees under the new rules would demand more time commitments of members and need to be compensated adequately to ensure the ability to recruit and retain good-quality directors.

AUDIT COMMITTEE CHARTERS

The BRC recommendations, as well as the new audit committee rules of the SEC, NYSE, and NASD, require that publicly traded companies adopt formal written charters from their audit committee describing their responsibilities. The charter should be approved by the board of directors, periodically reviewed and modified as necessary, and disclosed at least triannually in the annual report to shareholders or proxy statement. A carefully developed charter is the cornerstone for ensuring the proper structure, composition, and qualification of the audit committee. The primary purpose of formally adopting a charter is to effectively establish the audit committee as a functional element of the company's corporate governance. Thus, the audit committee charter will be viewed as a compliance document designed to be an effective mechanism of corporate governance.

The SEC advocates that the audit committee charter contains sufficient details and accountability to discourage financial statement fraud resulting from earnings management and accounting abuses that have deteriorated the quality and integrity of financial reports. The new rules also require that audit committees recommend, based on discussions with management and external auditors, to the board of directors that the financial statements be included in the company's annual report and that the committee believes that financial statements are fairly presented, in all material respects, in conformity with GAAP. This is a tremendous support for this improved oversight responsibility of audit committees; however, it is more likely now that audit committee members will be personally named in litigation for potential negligence regarding alleged financial statement fraud. The SEC argues that existing safe harbors in new rules will protect audit committee members from litigation risk and potential liability under federal and state laws; however, carelessly drafted audit committee charters could provide sophisticated lawyers with an unintended road map of duties to which audit committee members may be held accountable and liable.

To prevent unwanted increased liability for audit committee members under the new rules, companies must seek the advice of legal counsel, including securities litigation specialists, to identify potential weaknesses in the charter that could be exposed in litigation. When establishing or redesigning their charters in conformity with the requirements of the new rules on audit committees, publicly traded companies are strongly advised to consult with experts in corporate governance and audit committees to properly protect audit committee members and the company; however, the improved effectiveness of the audit committees under the new rules is expected to decrease the likelihood of financial statement fraud by providing audit committees with the necessary tools to prevent and detect fraudulent financial activities. Although none of the published charters is being endorsed and publicly traded companies should establish their charters according to their business environment and specifications, their audit committees' attributes, and the requirements of the new rules, Exhibit 8.3 presents a sample of a charter being suggested by one of the Big Five professional service firms.

Exhibit 8.3. Sample Audit Committee Charter

The following is a sample Audit Committee Charter designed to assist boards and their Audit Committees in their consideration of the new rules adopted by the SEC, NYSE, NASDAQ, and AMEX. This sample should be customized to each company's needs. Boards and their audit committees should consult corporate counsel prior to the adoption of an audit committee charter because this sample charter does not render or substitute for legal advice.

Audit Committee Charter

This Audit Committee Charter (Charter) has been adopted by the Board of Directors (the Board) of [name of company] (the Company). The Audit Committee of the Board (the Committee) shall review and reassess this charter annually and recommend any proposed changes to the Board for approval.

Role and Independence: Organization

The Committee assists the Board in fulfilling its responsibility for oversight of the quality and integrity of the accounting, auditing, internal control, and financial reporting practices of the Company. It may also have such other duties as may from time to time be assigned to it by the Board (See *"Additional Functions Frequently Assigned to Audit Committees."* Depending on the circumstances, it may be appropriate to incorporate some of these additional roles and duties in the charter.) The membership of the Committee shall consist of at least three directors who are each free of any relationship that, in the opinion of the Board, may interfere with such member's individual exercise of independent judgment. Each Committee member shall also meet the independence and financial literacy requirements for serving on audit committees, and at least one member shall have accounting or related financial management expertise, all as set forth in the applicable rules of the [select as appropriate: New York Stock Exchange/NASDAQ/American Stock Exchange]. The Committee shall maintain free and open communication with the independent auditors, the internal auditors, and Company management. In discharging its oversight role, the Committee is empowered to investigate any matter relating to the Company's accounting, auditing, internal control, or financial reporting practices brought to its attention, with full access to all Company books, records, facilities, and personnel. The Committee may retain outside counsel, auditors, or other advisors.

One member of the Committee shall be appointed as chair. The chair shall be responsible for leadership of the Committee, including scheduling and presiding over meetings, preparing agendas, and making regular reports to the Board. The chair will also maintain regular liaison with the CEO, CFO, the lead independent audit partner, and the director of internal audit.

The Committee shall meet at least four times a year, or more frequently as the Committee considers necessary. At least once each year the Committee shall have separate private meetings with the independent auditors, management, and the internal auditors.

Exhibit 8.3. *(Continued)*

___

Responsibilities

Although the Committee may wish to consider other duties from time to time, the general recurring activities of the Committee in carrying out its oversight role are described as follows. The Committee shall be responsible for:

- Recommending to the Board the independent auditors to be retained (or nominated for shareholder approval) to audit the financial statements of the Company. Such auditors are ultimately accountable to the Board and the Committee, as representatives of the shareholders.
- Evaluating, together with the Board and management, the performance of the independent auditors and, where appropriate, replacing such auditors.
- Obtaining annually from the independent auditors a formal written statement describing all relationships between the auditors and the Company, consistent with Independence Standards Board Standard Number 1. The Committee shall actively engage in a dialogue with the independent auditors with respect to any relationships that may impact the objectivity and independence of the auditors and shall take, or recommend that the Board take, appropriate actions to oversee and satisfy itself as to the auditors' independence.
- Reviewing the audited financial statements and discussing them with management and the independent auditors. These discussions shall include the matters required to be discussed under Statement of Auditing Standards No. 61 and consideration of the quality of the Company's accounting principles as applied in its financial reporting, including a review of particularly sensitive accounting estimates, reserves and accruals, judgmental areas, audit adjustments (whether or not recorded), and other such inquiries as the Committee or the independent auditors shall deem appropriate. Based on such review, the Committee shall make its recommendation to the Board as to the inclusion of the Company's audited financial statements in the Company's Annual Report on Form 10-K (or 10-KSB [or the Annual Report to Shareholders, if distributed before the filing of the Form 10-K]).
- Annually issuing a report to be included in the Company's proxy statement as required by the rules of the Securities and Exchange Commission.
- Overseeing the relationship with the independent auditors, including discussing with the auditors the nature and rigor of the audit process, receiving and reviewing audit reports, and providing the auditors full access to the Committee (and the Board) to report on any and all appropriate matters.
- Discussing with a representative of management and the independent auditors: (1) the interim financial information contained in the Company's Quarterly Report on Form 10-Q (or 10-QSB) before its filing, (2) the earnings announcement before its release (if practicable), and (3) the results of the review of such information by the independent auditors. (These discussions may be held with the Committee as a whole, with the Committee chair in person, or by telephone.)
- Overseeing internal audit activities, including discussing with management and the internal auditors the internal audit function's organization, objectivity, responsibilities, plans, results, budget, and staffing.

(continues)

Exhibit 8.3.   *(Continued)*

- Discussing with management, the internal auditors, and the independent auditors the quality and adequacy of and compliance with the Company's internal controls.
- Discussing with management and/or the Company's general counsel any legal matters (including the status of pending litigation) that may have a material impact on the Company's financial statements and any material reports or inquiries from regulatory or governmental agencies.

The Committee's job is one of oversight. Management is responsible for preparing the Company's financial statements and the independent auditors are responsible for auditing those financial statements. The Committee and the Board recognize that management (including the internal audit staff) and the independent auditors have more resources and time and more detailed knowledge and information regarding the Company's accounting, auditing, internal control, and financial reporting practices than the Committee does; accordingly, the Committee's oversight role does not provide any expert or special assurance as to the financial statements and other financial information provided by the Company to its shareholders and others.

Additional Functions Often Assigned to Audit Committees

1. Reviewing the annual management letter (with the independent auditors).
2. Reviewing and approving audit fees.
3. Reviewing management "conflict of interest" transactions.
4. Reviewing alleged fraudulent actions or violations of law reported by internal compliance programs or, under the terms of the Private Securities Litigation Reform Act of 1995, by the independent auditors.
5. Reviewing codes of ethics and/or codes of conduct.
6. Reviewing compliance with codes of ethics and/or codes of conduct and the procedures to monitor such compliance.
7. Reviewing the performance of the chief financial officer, chief accounting officer, and director of internal audit.
8. Reviewing financial press releases.
9. Reviewing policies and procedures with respect to expense accounts of senior management.
10. Reviewing and concurring in the appointment, replacement, reassignment, or dismissal of the director of internal audit. Confirming and assuring the objectivity of internal audit.
11. Reviewing the internal audit charter.
12. Self-assessing audit committee performance.

Source: Deloitte & Touche. Available: www.dttus.com/pub/audity2k/audity2k_04.htm

CHARTERS' BENCHMARKS

Based on the BRC recommendations and in compliance with the SEC new rules, the AMEX, NASDAQ, and NYSE have adopted rules that require their listed companies to have formal audit committee charters. Publicly held companies typically differ in their corporate process, openness, strategies, and their audit committees' compositions, structure, and function. Thus, their charter should reflect their corporate environment and uniqueness of their operations. Audit committees' charters should be carefully designed and specify only responsibilities assumed by the audit committee to avoid potential liabilities for directors since they will be now publicly disclosed. Although the nature and extent of the audit committee responsibilities may vary among companies, in general, the charter should include:

- A mission statement or purpose describing the objective of the audit committee in assisting the board of directors in fulfilling its oversight responsibility for corporate governance, the financial reporting process, the internal control structure, and audit functions
- A statement of responsibilities for overseeing corporate governance, including compliance with applicable laws and regulations and code of conduct, the financial reporting problem, internal control structure, and audit functions both internal and external audits
- A statement of authority to conduct or authorize investigations into any matters within its scope of responsibility
- A statement of compositions that the audit committee consists of at least three members who are independent and financially literate as defined by the new rules
- The number of meetings of the audit committee with the board of directors, internal auditors, external auditors, and management and additional meetings as circumstances require
- The scope of the audit committee's responsibilities and how it carries out those responsibilities, including functions, practices, and membership committees' requirements, pressure, and structure
- The independent auditors' ultimate accountability to the board of directors and the audit committee
- The audit committee's responsibility to discuss with the external auditors any factors that may impact on the auditors' objectivity and independence; recommend to the board of directors any action necessary to satisfy the board of auditors' independence; and receive a formal written statement from the independent auditors describing all relationships between the auditors and the company that, in the auditors' judgment, may reasonably be thought of to bear on independence.

Exhibit 8.4 presents the required content of an audit committee charter, as well as suggested content of such a charter as recommended by one of the Big Five professional services firms.

CHAIRPERSON OF AUDIT COMMITTEES

The audit committee chairperson can play an important role in setting a tone and standards for other members to improve their effectiveness. The chairperson of the audit committee should establish a cooperative working relationship with the board of directors, the top management team including the CEO and CFO, the director of the internal audit function, and the lead audit partner by having regular private meetings with them. The new rules have expanded responsibilities and functions, practices, and the frequency and timing of the committee meetings with other constituencies of corporate governance. It is perhaps more practical for the chairperson of the audit committee to discuss the committee oversight functions with the top management team and internal and external auditors before the typical meetings of the full committee with these groups in order to assess the necessary areas of oversight and to establish a definitive timeline for the entire year, including activities pertaining to the internal financial reporting process under the new rules.

AUDIT COMMITTEE REPORT

The BRC recommended and the SEC requires that an audit committee report be disclosed annually in the proxy statement. The audit committee must specify in this report whether the committee has accomplished the following:

- Reviewed and discussed the audited financial statements with management.
- Discussed with the external auditors those matters required to be communicated to the audit committee in accordance with GAAS.
- Received from the external auditors a letter revealing matters that, in the auditors' judgment, may reasonably be thought to bear on the auditors' independence from the company and discussed with them their independence.
- Recommended to the board of directors that the company's audited financial statements be included in the Annual Report on Form 10-K or Form 10-KSB based on discussions with management and external auditors.

The BRC initially recommended that the audit committee express its belief in the fair presentation of financial statements in conformity with GAAP based on a review of the financial statements and discussions with management and external auditors; however, this type of expression of an opinion on the audited financial

Exhibit 8.4. Audit Committee Charter Content

REQUIRED	SUGGESTED
• The scope of the committee's responsibilities and how it carries out those responsibilities, including the structure, processes, and membership requirements. • A statement that the independent auditor is ultimately accountable to the board of directors and the audit committee. • A statement that the audit committee has the authority and responsibility to select, evaluate, and replace the independent auditor. • A statement that the audit committee is responsible for (1) ensuring that the auditor submits a formal written statement regarding relationships and services that may affect objectivity and independence, (2) discussing any relevant matters with the independent auditors, and (3) recommending that the full board take appropriate action to ensure the independence of the auditor.	• Define the committee's authority and specific responsibilities, particularly those relative to: —Arthur Andersen's critical audit committee responsibilities as described previously —Review of compliance with laws and regulations —Monitoring of compliance with the corporate code of conduct and regulatory requirements —Review and assessment of conflicts of interest and related party transactions —Assessment of audit committee performance • Set guidelines for the committee's relationships and meetings. • Define the responsibilities of the audit committee chairperson with: —Other board committees —Management —Internal auditors —External auditors —Others, as appropriate • Set the frequency and general timing of meetings, allowing adequate time for preparation of substantive reporting to the full board. • Define the committee's accountability and reporting requirements to the board and to the shareholders. • Provide the authority for access to internal and external resources as the committee may require. • Set guidelines for committee education and orientation to assure understanding of the business and the environment in which the company operates. • Set guidelines for development of an annual audit committee plan that is responsive to the primary audit committee responsibilities, and for the review and approval of the plan by the full board.

(continues)

Exhibit 8.4. *(Continued)*

REQUIRED	SUGGESTED
	• Communicate committee expectations and the nature, timing, and extent of committee information needs to management, internal and external auditors, and others.
	• Guidelines for the discussion of the quality, not just acceptability, of the company's accounting principles on both an annual and quarterly basis, including:
	—Responsibilities and participation by the audit committee, management (including the Chief Executive Officer, the internal auditors, and legal counsel), and external auditors
	—Timing of the discussions
	• Guidelines for monitoring compliance with SEC Staff Accounting Bulletin No. 99, *Materiality.*
	• Guidelines for preparation of the audit committee report to be included in the company's proxy statements.
	• Guidelines for the review of Stock Exchange certifications and proxy statement disclosures related to the audit committee.

Source: Arthur Andersen. 2000. New Responsibilities and Requirements for Audit Committees (January). Available: http://www.arthurandersen.com

statements is far beyond the assumed oversight functions of audit committees. Thus, the SEC then passed a rule that would have required audit committees to express negative assurance regarding material misstatements or omissions of material disclosures and facts regarding the audited financial statements. Nevertheless, regardless of whether the audit committee report provides positive or negative assurance regarding the fair presentation of financial statements, the report should reflect the assumed responsibilities and oversight functions of audit committees' uniqueness of each company. Audit committees should write their own reports tailored to their responsibilities and oversight activities based on consulting with management, external auditors, and corporate counsel. Exhibit 8.5 presents a sample audit committee report suggested by one of the Big Five professional service firms.

Exhibit 8.5.   Sample Audit Committee Report

Report on audit committee

Date of proxy statement

To the Board of Directors of (company name):

We have reviewed and discussed with management the Company's audited financial statements as of and for the year ended December 31, 2000.

We have discussed with the independent auditors the matters required to be discussed by Statement on Auditing Standards No. 61, *Communication with Audit Committees,* as amended, by the Auditing Standards Board of the American Institute of Certified Public Accountants.

We have received and reviewed the written disclosures and the letter from the independent auditors required by Independence Standard No. 1, *Independence Discussions with Audit Committees,* as amended, by the Independence Standards Board, and have discussed with the auditors the auditors' independence.

Based on the reviews and discussions referred to above, we recommend to the Board of Directors that the financial statements referred to above be included in the Company's Annual Report on Form 10-K (or KSB) for the year ended December 31, 2000.

Name of Audit Committee Chairman

Name of Audit Committee Member

Name of Audit Committee Member

Source: Arthur Andersen. 2000. New Responsibilities and Requirements of Audit Committees (January). Available: www.arthurandersen.com

AUDIT COMMITTEES' RULES FOR PREVENTING AND DETECTING FINANCIAL STATEMENT FRAUD

The role of audit committees as an integral part of corporate governance has been addressed in several reports (e.g., The Treadway Commission, the POB, the NYSE and NASD sponsored in the BRC. The most recent report, the BRC panel on improving the effectiveness of corporate audit committees includes 10 recommendations and five guiding principles aimed at strengthening the directors' independence, qualifications, and compositions to ensure responsible corporate governance and a reliable financial reporting process. Several studies examine the relationships between the existence of audit committees and the absence of financial statement fraud (e.g., Defond and Jiambalvo, 1991; McMullen, 1996; Dechow et al., 1996; Beasley, 1996; Beasley et al., 1999 and 2000).[19-24] These studies found that companies with fraud were less likely to have audit committees composed solely of outside directors. These studies are *extant* in the sense that the association between financial statement fraud and the presence or absence of the audit committee is examined without indicating how the audit committee can prevent or detect financial statement fraud.

Raghunandan et al. (2001) examined the association between audit committee compositions and the committee's interactions with internal auditing and found that audit committees without insider or "gray" directors and with at least one member having an accounting and finance background are more likely to (1) review management interactions with the internal audit function; (2) review the internal auditors' finding and scope; (3) have private access to the chief internal auditor; and (4) have longer meetings with the chief internal auditor.[25] The audit committee of Enron Corporation is coming under sharp criticism for its lack of vigilant oversight function of effective overseeing of Enron financial reporting processess and audit functions. Enron's audit committee members are being questioned for not informing shareholders of Enron's partnership deals and off-balance sheet derivative transactions. Some audit committee members are even accused of "insider trading" for making misleading statements about the company and selling about $1 billion worth of stock during the last three years before the Enron crisis.[26]

The Treadway Commission recognized that audit committees play an important role in preventing and detecting financial statements fraud. The new rules on audit committees by the SEC, NYSE, AMEX, and NASDAQ will improve the effectiveness of audit committee oversight functions pertaining to corporate governance, the financial reporting process, the internal control structure, and audit functions, as depicted in Exhibit 8.1. These improved and expanded audit committee functions and practices enhance the integrity and quality of financial reports and contribute to preventing and detecting financial statement fraud. More specifically, Toby S.F. Bishop, a Fraud and Integrity Partner with Arthur Andersen in Risk Consulting, has suggested the following Top 10 fraud prevention and detection tips for audit committees.

1. Evaluate management's assessment of the significance and likelihood of your company's fraud risks, especially the pressure to meet earnings expectations.
2. Evaluate the internal control best practices that management has implemented to address each fraud risk.
3. Evaluate internal auditors' testing of the effectiveness of each fraud control.
4. Ensure that your company periodically uses a research-based tool to measure the effectiveness of the CEO's efforts to create the right tone at the top to promote ethical behavior and deter wrongdoing.
5. Tell management you have zero tolerance for any cooking the books. Continuously evaluate management's integrity. Even small untruths are telling.
6. Ensure that your internal auditors report directly and candidly to you and have sufficient resources to do a world-class job.
7. Ensure that your internal auditors continually conduct financial statement and other fraud detection tests using the latest computer-assisted methods.
8. Where possible, have your quarterly financial statements tested before release, using the latest financial statement fraud detection tools.
9. For large companies, attach a "fraud sentinel" to your computer system to detect potentially fraudulent transactions on a real-time basis.
10. Have your independent auditors and fraud specialists critically evaluate the results of these items.[27]

CONCLUSION

Recently, in response to the SEC concerns regarding the quality and integrity of the financial reporting process and responsibility of corporate governance, the NYSE sponsored the establishment of the Blue Ribbon Committee (BRC) on Improving the Effectiveness of Corporate Audit Committees. The BRC made recommendations regarding the oversight process of corporate governance and financial reporting to (1) the SEC; (2) the securities markets through the self-regulation organizations (e.g., NASD, NYSE, AMSE); (3) publicly traded companies and their boards of directors, audit committee, and management; and (4) the accounting profession. These recommendations and other initiatives on audit committees have expanded the roles of audit committees in overseeing the achievement of responsible corporate governance and a reliable financial reporting process.

The guidelines for audit committees suggested by the BRC that can be applied to all types of audit committees across all industry sectors are (1) the audit committee's important role and function for overseeing the financial reporting and audit process; (2) objective and independent communication and information flow between the audit committees and internal auditors; (3) continuous and candid discussions with external auditors, internal auditors, and management regarding issues involving judgment and pertaining to corporate governance and the financial reporting process; and (4) knowledgeable, informed, and diligent audit committee membership.

ENDNOTES

1. National Commission on Fraudulent Financial Reporting (NCFFR) (The Treadway Commission). 1987. Report of the National Commission on Fraudulent Financial Reporting. (October). New York: AICPA.

2. Blue Ribbon Committee (BRC) on Improving the Effectiveness of Corporate Audit Committees. 1999. Report and Recommendations of the Blue Ribbon Committee on Improving the Effectiveness of Corporate Audit Committee. New York: NYSE and NASD.

3. Levitt, A. 1999. Chairman, Securities and Exchange Commission. (February 8). Available: www.sec.gov

4. National Commission on Fraudulent Financial Reporting (NCFFR) (The Treadway Commission). 1987. Report of the National Commission on Fraudulent Financial Reporting. (October). New York, NY: AICPA.

5. Committee of Sponsoring Organizations (COSO). 1992. "Internal Control-Integrated Framework." (September, Vol. 1–4). New York: AICPA.

6. The Federal Deposits Insurance Corporation (FDIC). 1993. Regulations of FDIC Improvement Act of 1991. U.S. Congress.

7. Public Oversight Board (POB) of the SEC Practice Section, AICPA. 1993. A Special Report on Issues Confronting the Accounting Profession.

8. Public Oversight Board (POB) of the SEC Practice Section, AICPA. 1995. Directors, Management, and Auditors: Allies in Protecting Stakeholder Interests.

9. Public Oversight Board (POB) of the SEC Practice Section, AICPA. 2000. The Panel on Audit Effectiveness Report and Recommendations.

10. Institute of Internal Auditors (IIA). 1991. *The Audit Committee in the Public Sector.* Altamonte Springs, FL: IIA.

11. Levitt, A. 1998. Remarks by Chairman of Securities and Exchange Commission. "The Numbers Game." NYU Center for Law and Business. New York, NY. (September 28). Available: http://www.sec.gov/news/speech/speecharchive/1998/spch220.txt

12. Blue Ribbon Committee (BRC) on Improving the Effectiveness of Corporate Audit Committees. 1999. Report and Recommendations of the Blue Ribbon Committee on Improving the Effectiveness of Corporate Audit Committee. New York, NY: NYSE and NASD.

13. Ibid.

14. Kesner, I. 1988. "Director's Characteristics and Committee Membership: An Investigation of Type, Occupation, Tenure, and Gender." *Academy of Management Journal* (31 March): 66–84.

15. Blue Ribbon Committee (BRC) on Improving the Effectiveness of Corporate Audit Committees. 1999. Report and Recommendations of the Blue Ribbon Committee on Improving the Effectiveness of Corporate Audit Committee. New York, NY: NYSE and NASD.

16. Ernst & Young. 2000. Survey of Audit Committees. Available: www.ernst&young.com

17. Turner, L.E. 2001. Remarks made by the Chief Accountant of U.S. SEC in the Conference Sponsored by the Washington University School of Law and the Institute for Law and Economic Policy. (March). Available: http://www.sec.gov/news/speech/spch469.htm

18. Pricewaterhouse Coopers and Institute of Internal Auditors. 2000. Audit Committee Effectiveness—What Work Best. Sponsored by the Institute of Internal Auditors Research Foundation.

19. DeFond, M. L., and J. Jiamabalvo. 1991. "Incidence and Circumstances of Accounting Errors." *The Accounting Review* (July): 643–655.

20. McMullen, D.A. 1996. "Audit Committee Performance: An Investigation of the Consequences Associated with Audit Committees." *Auditing: A Journal of Practice and Theory* (Spring): 87–103.

21. Dechow, P.M., R.G. Sloan, and A.P. Sweeney. 1996. "Causes and Consequences of Earnings Manipulations: An Analysis of Firms Subject to Enforcement Actions by the SEC." *Contemporary Accounting Research* (Spring): 1–36.

22. Beasley, M.C. 1996. "An Empirical Investigation of the Relation Between Board of Directors, Composition, and Financial Statement Fraud." *The Accounting Review* (October): 443–465.

23. Beasley, M.S., J.V. Carcello, and D.R. Hermanson. 1999. Fraudulent Financial Reporting: 1987–1997, An Analysis of U.S. Public Companies. New York: COSO.

24. Beasley, M.S., J.V. Carcello, and D.R. Hermanson. 2000. "Fraudulent Financial Reporting: Consideration of Industry Traits and Corporate Governance Mechanisms." *Accounting Horizons* 14.4 (December): 441–454.

25. Raghunandan, K., J. Williams, and D.V. Rama. 2001. "Audit Committee Composition, 'Gray Directors,' and Interaction with Internal Auditing." *Accounting Horizons* 15.2 (June): 105–118.

26. Abelson, R. 2001. Enron Board Comes Under a Storm of Criticism. *The New York Times* (December 16). Availabel at http://www.nytimes.com.

27. Bishop, T.S.F. 2000. Fraud Prevention and Detection Tips For Audit Committee, Available: http://AMRWD5953.arthurandersen.com/website.nsf/content/MarketOfferings AssuranceResourcesFraudPrevention

Chapter 9

Management Responsibility

INTRODUCTION

Management plays an important role in ensuring responsible and effective corporate governance by managing the business of the corporation to create shareholder value. Management, through the delegated authority from the board of directors, is responsible for establishing and executing the corporate strategies, managing the effectiveness and efficient utilization of resources, directing and coordinating operational activities, safeguarding assets, to fulfill its responsibilities, management design and implement sound accounting systems that provide reliable and high-quality financial reports, establish and maintain an adequate and effective internal control system to achieve control objectives, and complying with applicable laws and regulations. Management is an important member of corporate governance, as depicted in Exhibit 9.1 This chapter presents management's responsibility for the financial reporting process, the internal control structure, as well as the prevention, detection, and correction of financial statement fraud.

MANAGEMENT FINANCIAL REPORTING RESPONSIBILITIES

Management is primarily responsible for the quality, integrity, and reliability of the financial reporting process as well as the fair presentation of financial statements in conformity with generally accepted accounting principles (GAAP). Management is also accountable to users of financial statements, particularly investors and creditors, to ensure that published financial statements are not misleading and are free of material errors, irregularities, and fraud. To effectively discharge its financial reporting responsibility, management should (1) identify and assess the circumstances, conditions, and factors that can lead to financial statement fraud; (2) assess and manage the risk of financial statement fraud associated with the identified circumstances, conditions, and factors; and (3) design and implement an adequate and effective internal control process for prevention and detection of financial statement fraud. This chapter presents management's responsibility for the financial reporting process, the internal control structure, as well as the prevention, detection, and correction of financial statement fraud.

Parker and Previts (2000) examined the value drivers of publicly traded companies and managerial plans and actions that created shareholder value. They identified the following value drivers that create shareholder value:

- Quality and execution of strategy
- Quality and credibility of management

Exhibit 9.1.   Corporate Governance and Its Functions

- Market share
- Industry economic outlook
- Effectiveness and efficiency of key processes
- Proper organizational structure to achieve strategy and promote flexibility
- Ability to attract and retain top talent
- Ability to research and innovate
- Ability of corporate culture to adapt to international imperatives
- Ability to develop and utilize intangibles such as networks and human capital.[1]

The newly designed business-reporting model should reflect these value drivers and communicate them on a timely basis directly to all investors and creditors, including institutional investors, investment bankers, and analysts. Such a business reporting model is already developed and recommended by corporations and one of the Big Five professional services firms.

MANAGEMENT'S ROLE IN FINANCIAL STATEMENT FRAUD PREVENTION AND PROTECTION

Authoritative reports place primary responsibility for prevention and detection of financial statement fraud with the company's management (e.g., Treadway, 1987; COSO, 1992).[2,3] The fair presentation of financial statements is the responsibility of management, and, accordingly, management is responsible for the prevention and detection of financial statement fraud. In this regard, management has the responsibility, among other things, to perform the following tasks:

- Establish and maintain a sound accounting information system in compliance with GAAP.
- Design and implement an adequate and effective internal control system over financial reporting.
- Ensure that the company complies with applicable laws and regulations.
- Properly record transactions in accordance with the accounting policies and practices.
- Use appropriate and reasonable accounting estimates.
- Safeguard assets.
- Make all financial records and related financial information available to auditors and fully cooperate with auditors in gathering sufficient and competent audit evidence.
- Provide fair and full disclosure of financial information and relevant nonfinancial information.
- Serve the interests of investors and creditors by creating and increasing the value of their investments.
- Refrain from subordinating judgments to others, under pressure or voluntarily.
- Ensure that published financial statements are free of material misstatements caused by errors or fraud.
- Comply with authoritative reporting standards promulgated by governing bodies, as depicted in Exhibit 9.1.

MANAGEMENT MOTIVES AND INCENTIVES

Publicly traded companies can be motivated by a variety of factors to engage in financial statement fraud. Corporations' rewards and incentive plans focusing on creating shareholder value motivate management to explore profit opportunities by often operating "as closely as possible to the borderline between legality and illegality—the borderline between what is ethical and what is unethical [and] for a variety of reasons, an individual manager or management group may cross over the line."[4] Management is more likely to cross over the line when (1) the line is ill-defined; (2) the perceived probable benefits outweigh the probable costs; (3) there is tremendous internal and external pressure to show more favorable performance and financial results; (4) it has the attitude toward the challenges of living dangerously; and (5) for a broad variety of other personal satisfactions, prestige, or self-image.

Management may be motivated to engage in financial statement fraud because its personal well-being is so closely associated with the well-being of the company through profit sharing, stock-based compensation plans, and other bonuses; and management is willing to take personal risks for corporate benefit (e.g., risk of indictment or personal, civil, and criminal penalties). Investors' investment preferences and ownership interests can influence management's attitude and operating style. For example, management would be less likely to engage in short-term earnings management if investors show preference for long-term return on their investments. Pressure by investors, especially short-term institutional investors, for favorable financial performance can pressure companies to engage in financial statement fraud.

Management is intended to make decisions in the interest of shareholders. Thus, management is under internal and external pressure to maximize shareholder value, as follows:

1. External pressure on financial executives to make "the numbers" each reporting period is the high expectation and desire to not only meet but also exceed the analysts' consensus estimate of earnings.
2. Internal pressure on financial executives can be imposed by other senior management executives to manage earnings. Many executive compensation plans that include stock and earnings-based incentives can increase pressure.

Financial statement fraud can be prevented and detected when companies' financial statements are subject to thorough scrutiny.

Several studies examine motives and opportunities involved in financial statement fraud. Dechow, Sloan, and Sweeney (1996)[5] examined 92 firms that were subject to an enforcement action by the Securities and Exchange Commission (SEC) between 1982 and 1992. They matched fraud firms with a random sample of 92 firms that had not been charged by the SEC based on size, industry, and year of financial statement fraud. Dechow et al. (1996) found two motives associated with fraud firms: (1) a need for external financing as proxied by whether the firm issued securities during the three-year period subsequent to the first year in which financial statement fraud occurred; and (2) closeness to debt covenant constraints as measured by leverage ratio.

Dechow et al. (1996)[6] found no evidence of management attempt to manipulate earnings to improve a profit-based bonus plan or selling personal stock holdings at an inflated price; however, they stated that a weak corporate governance structure provides opportunities for firms to engage in illegal earnings management. Weak corporate governance was evident by the fact that, compared to nonfraud firms, the SEC-investigated firms (1) had more insiders on their boards of directors; (2) were more likely to have the CEO as chair of the board; (3) were more likely to have the founder of the firm as CEO; (4) were less likely to have an audit committee; and (5) were not affected by being audited by a Big Six/Five professional services firms.

Beasley (1996) investigated the importance of corporate governance structures in preventing and detecting financial statement frauds by comparing the attributes of 75 firms that engaged in fraudulent financial reporting during the period 1983 to 1991 with 75 nonfraud firms in the same period, based on their size, industry, and stock exchange.[7] Beasley (1996) found evidence indicating that the likelihood of financial statement fraud (1) decreases when there are nonmanagement directors on the board, the longer the tenure of outside directors on the board, and the larger their ownership interest in the firm; (2) increases as the board increases in size; and (3) remains the same regardless of earnings growth and the existence of an audit committee.[8]

McMullen (1996)[9] investigated the following five types of accounting errors, irregularities, and illegal acts: (1) shareholder lawsuits alleging management fraud; (2) SEC enforcement actions pertaining to financial statement fraud; (3) auditor changes resulting from accounting disagreements; (4) quarterly earnings restatements; and (5) disclosure in the notes to the financial statements of illegal actions during the mid-1980s. McMullen (1986) found that (1) firms with an audit committee were associated with fewer instances of unreliable financial reporting than firms that did not have an audit committee; (2) the litigated firms and the SEC-investigated firms were in a weaker financial position than the non-litigated and non–SEC-investigated firms as measured by earnings growth; and (3) the SEC-investigated firms were less likely to have a Big Eight (now Big Five auditor).[10]

Results of studies on financial statement fraud are inconsistent and controversial, primarily because they do not examine the organizational culture that creates motives and opportunities for financial statement fraud. Loebbecke and Willingham (1988)[11] developed a model suggesting that financial statement fraud is more likely to occur when (1) there is no responsible corporate governance in the sense that individuals within the firm have an attitude or a set of ethical values that predisposes them to engage in fraudulent financial activities; (2) there is a motive to commit a fraud; and (3) opportunities exist and conditions are such that a fraud can be committed. Loebbecke, Eining, and Willingham (1989)[12] tested their model through a survey of 165 KPMG Peat Marwick audit partners who had direct experience with financial statement fraud. The survey shows that financial statement fraud occurs when the firm has a set of ethical values reflected by dishonest management, personality anomalies, lies and evasiveness, an aggressive attitude toward financial reporting, and a history of prior years' irregularities. The survey also reveals that the primary motive of financial statement fraud is a combination of financial and economic pressures signified by poor financial performance, a strong emphasis on earnings, a declining industry, and significant accounting-based contractual agreements. Loebbecke et al. (1989)[13] found that poor corporate governance, evidenced by the existence of material related-party transactions, an inadequate and ineffective internal control structure, and decisions dominated by one individual, provides the opportunity for financial statement fraud. In summary, a set of acceptable accounting alternatives, lack of moral principles and/or ethical values, motive, opportunity, and lack of responsible corporate governance should all be present for firms to engage in financial statement fraud.

Merchant (1987)[14] conducted a panel discussion of 21 academicians and executives to identify the factors contributing to fraudulent and questionable financial reporting practices. The panel considered a poor organizational culture, strong internal and external pressures, and a weak internal control structure as contributing factors to financial statement fraud. A poor organizational culture is characterized by a lack of moral principles, guidance, and leadership; no internal rules, policies, and procedures; and undue emphasis on a corporation's best interests. External pressures are related to environmental uncertainty, whereas internal pressures are associated with profit-based bonus plans and high divisional autonomy. A weak internal control structure exists when there are no adequate control activities, policies, and procedures or control activities are ineffective and are not functioning satisfactorily as intended.

In March 1999, the Committee of Sponsoring Organizations of the Treadway Commission (COSO) issued its report, Fraudulent Financial Reporting: 1987–1997.[15] This study was conducted by three academic researchers who examined approximately 200 cases of alleged fraudulent financial reporting investigated by the SEC. The researchers investigated key characteristics of corporate governance of companies involved in alleged financial statement fraud and made recommendations to improve corporate governance and the financial reporting process. The findings, recommendations of the COSO Report, and their implications for the board of directors, audit committees, management, and external and internal auditors, are addressed throughout the book and should lead to a better understanding of financial statement fraud and ways of reducing its occurrence.

GAMESMANSHIP

The global economy and Internet-based technologies have brought new ideas, inventions, and imperatives that significantly affect the business environment. These contributory factors have affected and will continue to affect the quality and integrity of information provided to investors. The desirability and reality of not only meeting but also exceeding investors' earnings expectations is often a challenge for many managers of publicly traded companies. Creating shareholder value has become the primary goal of corporations. In achieving this goal whenever possible, corporate top executives may try every trick in the book to prevent their company's stock price from falling and to ensure they will receive a bonus or retain their position within the company. Although most U.S. companies are attempting to meet market participants' earnings expectations through continuous improvements in both quality and quantity of earnings, some companies have engaged in unacceptable and illegitimate earnings management practices that eventually undermine investors' confidence in the quality and integrity of the financial reporting process. This unacceptable, unethical, and illegitimate practice of earnings management is viewed by the former SEC Chairperson Arthur Levitt as "a culture of gamesmanship" between companies and security analysts and auditors. The purpose of this game is to "push accounting" guidelines to the limit to create the rosiest profit projections possible to meet analysts' projections and sustain or boost stock prices.[16]

Gamesmanship is defined in the American Heritage Dictionary of the English Language as "the art of practice of using tactical maneuvers to further one's aim to better one's position."[17] Gamesmanship as related to the financial reporting process is defined by Arthur Levitt as the practice that:

> [S]ays it's okay to bend the rules, tweak the numbers, and let small but obvious and important discrepancies slide; a gamesmanship that tells managers it's fine to cut corners and look the other way to boost the stock price; where companies bend to the desires and pressure of Wall Street analysts rather than to the reality of numbers; where auditors are pressured not to rock the boat; and a gamesmanship that focuses exclusively on short-term numbers rather than long-term performance.[18]

This gamesmanship or unacceptable and illegitimate earnings management has not traditionally been considered with such scrutiny. Corporate top management teams are now under more pressure to create shareholder value and, in turn, secure their own positions and compensation. The gamesmanship notion motivates management to use its discretion to choose accounting principles and methods that maximize shareholder value through practices of (1) overstating restructuring charges and creating a buffer with which to meet future Wall Street earnings estimates; (2) using acquisition accounting to overstate future earnings; (3) smoothing earnings by manipulating timing recognition of charges such as loan losses and sales returns; (4) recognizing sales before completion or when the sale is still reversible by customers; (5) overstating revenues and assets; and (6) deferring expenses to portray earnings growth.

Players within the Gamesmanship Practice

The integrity and quality of the financial reporting process in producing useful, reliable, and relevant financial information makes the capital markets efficient and vibrant. When quality information is not present within the capital markets, investors lose their confidence in the financial reporting process, which causes the markets to be no longer efficient. To achieve quality information, many individuals, including management, analysts, auditors, and other market participants, should uphold their traditional duties based on integrity and objectivity. The following hypothetical example illustrates the gamesmanship practice and its players.

The internal audit function of a publicly traded company, in performing a routine review of the system of internal control and in assisting management to prepare quarterly financial statements, discovers a small overstatement of sales that results in a 2 percent increase in earnings. The director of internal auditing brings this overstatement to management's attention. The top management team, including the CEO, finds out that reversing the overstatement would mean the company would miss the consensus analysts' forecasts by a few cents, which would have a significant impact on stock prices. The CEO pressures the company's controller to consider the recorded overstatement of sales as "immaterial" and convinces the controller that other mistakes in reported expenses may offset this overstatement. External auditors, in their review of quarterly financial statements, discover this small overstatement; however, in providing negative assurance on financial statements and under pressure from management, they concur with the controller that the overstatement is "immaterial" and would not warrant modifications to the financial statements to make them conform with GAAP. Thus, no reversal occurs and the company meets the analysts' forecasts.

This hypothetical example clearly describes that materiality threshold leaves room for interpretation by management and auditors to manipulate financial statements and provide misleading financial information to market participants. The example also identifies the players in gamesmanship practice as the top management team, including the CEO and controller, financial analysts, internal auditors, and external auditors.

Gamesmanship has become a great concern because management failed to provide reliable information by either not using acceptable accounting methods or by adhering to the required accounting standards but using them to its advantage to portray a better and rosier picture of financial positions, conditions, and performance. Gamesmanship does not stop at the management level, but extends to analysts, internal auditors, and external auditors who have detected financial statement fraud and failed to report them under pressure from management. Security analysts participate in a gamesmanship process by providing biased reporting on how the companies are doing in estimating earnings forecasts. Analysts may, under pressure, believe they are walking a tight rope of fairly assessing a company's performance without jeopardizing their business relationship with their client. A potential conflict of interest may exist between security analysts and the companies they are reporting on when analysts choose to operate under the famous saying, "If you can't say anything nice, then don't say anything at all." Analysts' optimistic reporting attitudes and practices encourage management to tweak the numbers to meet these high expectations to tailored financial statements more for the benefit of consensus estimates than to reflect the company's financial reality. Many analysts have made a practice to not say anything negative or controversial about their clients because of the fear of losing their client's business or being left out of conference calls. Some analysts even act as a promoter or marketer of their clients rather than independent of their parties. This approach restricts the analysts' ability to provide fair and objective reports on the quality and quantity of their clients' earnings.

Internal auditors should position themselves to stand up to top executives when they engage in financial statement fraud by reporting such incidents to the audit committee. External auditors should observe their professional integrity and objectivity standards by avoiding conflicts of interest with management and not compromising their ethical standards and responsibility to society.

Monitoring Gamesmanship

Monitoring gamesmanship is a challenge for corporate governance primarily because no one is ever certain about the actions someone else is going to take, and not everyone can resist pressure, however, corporate governance should create safeguards to monitor and prevent gamesmanship in order to secure the quality and quantity of financial reports. Some of the safeguards or monitoring methods to combat unhealthy gamesmanship are as follows:

Vigilant Oversight

Management engages in gamesmanship practice by either lowering analysts' and investors' expectations below a level of actual and potential company performance or by tailoring financial reports to match market expectations to prevent any surprises and adverse impacts on stock prices. The board of directors and audit committee should know the company's operations, identify operational and financial risks, and provide safeguards to control their effects on the quality and integrity of financial reports. The vigilant oversight responsibility of both the board of directors and the audit committee is addressed in the report of the Blue Ribbon Committee (BRC).[19] The BRC made 10 recommendations and five guiding principles to improve the effectiveness of oversight functions of the board of directors and the audit committee, which are thoroughly examined in Chapter 8. The BRC's recommendations were entirely, with slight modifications, adopted by the SEC, NYSE, and NASD as rules in determining the qualifications, characteristics, structure, and functions of audit committees of publicly traded companies.

Materiality Threshold

Traditionally, materiality had been viewed as a matter of professional judgment by management, auditors, and others involved with the financial reporting process regarding the importance of information being disclosed in financial statements. The misperception about the materiality concept has been "anything under 5 percent is immaterial, and this would not receive any consideration by management, auditors, and market participants. To clarify this misconception, the SEC issued a staff accounting bulletin in August 1999 to dismiss the popular misconception that "anything under 5 percent is immaterial." The SEC's current position on materiality issues is that "the standard for materiality remains the one provided by the U.S. Supreme Court in 1976: a substantial likelihood that the . . . fact would have been viewed by the reasonable investor as having substantially altered the 'total mix' of information made available.[20] Thus, management and auditors, in using their judgment in assessing materiality, should consider the point of view of investors, creditors, and other users of financial statements.

The SEC has raised concerns that some registrants have misapplied the concept of materiality in the application of GAAP and assessing the effects of errors or noncompliance with GAAP to manage earnings and meet analysts' expectations. It has been improperly interpreted and practiced that even intentional errors and amounts that fall below specified materiality thresholds should not require adjustments. To address the SEC's concerns, the Accounting Standards Board of the AICPA issued SAS No. 89, Audit Adjustments.[21] SAS No. 89 requires the auditor to: (1) address management's responsibility for differences that are discovered during the audit; (2) obtain management's written representation that any unadjusted differences are immaterial; and (3) discuss with the audit committee certain unadjusted audit differences that management has considered are immaterial.

Prevention of Selective Disclosure

Management may attempt to provide security analysts with material nonpublic information in order to favorably affect their earnings forecasts of the company. With analysts being considered as an important source of information for investors, creditors, and other market participants, they can be misled about the company's operating status and performance. Selective disclosure closely resembles ordinary tipping and insider trading in the sense that only a fortunate few gain an information edge from their privileged access to corporate top executives. Tipping and insider trading have been and will continue to be severely punished under the antifraud provisions of the federal securities laws. Until recently, the status of issuer selective disclosure was not adequately addressed by the SEC; however, in August 2000, the SEC approved a new rule, Regulation FD (Fair Disclosure) that will end the practice of selective disclosure, in which officials of publicly traded companies provide material information to Wall Street insiders (e.g., security analysts) before making the information available to the public.[22] Regulation FD requires that when an issuer intentionally discloses material information, it must do so publicly and not selectively.

Regulation FD, one of the three rules issued by the SEC regarding "Selective Disclosure and Insider Trading," defines how publicly traded companies and their senior executives should interact with security analysts and the public in disclosing material financial information. Regulation FD took effect in October 2000 despite considerable efforts by several industry groups to delay its implementation. Regulation FD is intended to reduce the perceived cozy relationship that some analysts shared with top executives of some companies in determining their earnings forecasts. With Regulation FD, the SEC is trying to level the information playing field by refraining companies from releasing market-sensitive information to security analysts and other Wall Street insiders before disclosing such information to the public at large.

The SEC initiatives regarding selective disclosure and the SEC Staff Accounting Bulletin 101 (revenue recognition) address the issues of fair disclosure of financial information. Analysts may have their information channels in gathering certain information that is not readily available to average shareholders. In addition, management has incentives to communicate certain information with analysts before public announcement of information to ensure that analysts have proper earnings expectations. Analysts often make their forecasts based on past earnings quality and quantity as well as earnings growth. Analysts' forecasts can have significant impacts on stock prices primarily because analysts make projections. Companies usually target those projections and often attempt to exceed them or otherwise suffer the consequences.

Regulation FD is intended to create a level playing field for all market participants in terms of their access to corporate material disclosures and information. Regulation FD would bring all market participants, regardless of the size of their holdings, into the information loop. For example, under Regulation FD, if corporate officers wish to inform Wall Street analysts of particular information (e.g., meeting earnings forecasts, new discovery), the same information should be simultaneously disclosed to the public through a press release or other communication means. One danger of Regulation FD is that, in an attempt to protect themselves and fearful of potential liabilities, companies may choose to disseminate fewer disclosures. This potential "chilling effect" of Regulation FD may make the capital markets less informative and efficient.

Regulation FD addresses the potential inappropriate liability and the possible chilling effect of information flow by limiting the implication and application of the rules to only communications with securities professionals and holders of the issuer's securities when it is reasonably foreseeable that the securityholder will trade on the information and restricting the rules to cover only communications by senior issuer officials and those persons who typically communicate with securities analysts or securityholders. These provisions of Regulation FD clearly define that the rules do not cover usual communications with the media or issuer's customers or suppliers in the normal course of business.

Auditor's Independence

External auditors can play an important role in preventing and discouraging gamesmanship behavior. External auditors should detect material misstatements and gamesmanship practices and report them to the board of directors and the audit committee. Auditor independence, in fact and appearance, is important for the effectiveness of the audit process. Recently, several concerns have been raised regarding auditor independence, including (1) limits on types of services external auditors can provide to their clients; (2) the structure of public accounting to assure independence; (3) consequences of public ownership of accounting firms or affiliates; and (4) affiliation of accounting firms with entities that render to audit clients' services that the accounting firms themselves are not permitted to provide.

The SEC, in response to these concerns, among other things, issued Regulation S-X on November 21, 2000.[23] The final rule on independence addresses (1) financial relationships; (2) employment relationships; (3) business relationships; (4) scope of services; (5) contingent fees; (6) quality control standards; and (7) proxy disclosure requirements. The new independence rule, in improving auditors' independence, codifies the existing scope of services restrictions rather than banning an all-inclusive set of nonaudit services. The SEC's new rules on auditors' independence are thoroughly examined in Chapter 11.

Improving the Conduct of an Audit

The Public Oversight Board (POB) Panel on Audit Effectiveness (2000)[24] made several recommendations to improve the effectiveness of financial statement audits and, thus, reduce the incidents of financial statement fraud and gamesmanship practices. High-quality financial audits improve the reliability of financial statements, enhance the quality of financial reports, and contribute to investors' confidence in the accounting profession and the financial reporting process, which, in turn, improves the efficiency of the capital markets. The panel recommended that new accounting standards be developed to assist auditors in detecting any illegal acts that may uncover gamesmanship resulting from fraudulent activities. The panel introduced a "forensic-type audit fieldwork phase" that should be integrated into audit planning in order to enhance the likelihood that auditors will detect material financial statement fraud. Currently, external auditors, in compliance with SAS No. 82, incorporate the risk of financial statement fraud into the audit risk model to determine the nature, timing, and extent of audit procedures without directly aiming audit procedures to detect such fraud; however, the panel recommended that a forensic-type fieldwork phase should become an integral part of the auditing process, and auditors should perform test procedures specifically aimed at detecting gamesmanship practices that may cause financial statement fraud.

MANAGEMENT STOCK OWNERSHIP

The "moral hazard" concept of the agency theory states that whenever the top management team owns less than a 100 percent interest in a corporation, it has incentives to waste, misuse, or divert corporate resources by engaging in fraudulent financial activities. Empirical studies (Jensen and Murphy, 1990; Jensen and Warner, 1988; Beasley, 1994)[25,26,27] show that when managers hold little equity interest in the firm, they have a greater incentive to make managerial decisions to secure their own interest at the expense of stakeholders. Thus, the more financial interest by management in the firm, the stronger incentives to create shareholder value and thus stronger motivation to ensure prevention and detection of financial statement fraud that may adversely affect shareholder wealth. These studies suggest that management ownership in the firm should be viewed as a control mechanism in the sense that managers will be more motivated to create shareholder value and will have less incentive to engage in self-interested activities in an attempt to expropriate stockholder wealth.

Empirical studies find that when managers hold a significant amount of their wealth in the company's stock, they are motivated and better able to maximize the company's value by creating shareholder value. Several proactive and reactive mechanisms can provide reasonable assurance that the interest of the top management team conforms and aligns with that of shareholders. If shareholders are dissatisfied with management performance, they can sell their shares, which would be lower than corporate stock prices. The shareholder actions to sell short and, thus, lowering stock prices, have two monitoring implications for management. First, lower stock prices directly and adversely affect management wealth when management stock ownership is substantial. Second, when stock prices are becoming consistently low, even the worst-managed companies become attractive takeover candidates, which increases the probability of the replacement of the managers of the target company. Thus, the top management team has incentives to manage earnings by disclosing information that increases or creates shareholder value. Thus, shareholders must be convinced that corporate financial reports are reliable and accurate.

The negative correlation is expected to exist between the percentage of management ownership in the firm and the extent of financial statement fraud. When management has a long-term and high-stake ownership in the firm and believes that the probability of detection of financial statement fraud would be high, it would be reluctant to engage in fraud that would have an adverse affect on its stockholdings. Alternately, the probability of financial statement fraud would be higher when management has a low-stake financial interest, a short-term investment horizon, and believes that the probability of detection is low. Thus, management may be engaging in financial statement fraud when the perceived benefits from the fraudulent financial activities, including earnings management, exceed the cost of a decline in the value of its stockholdings when the fraud is detected and disclosed.

MANAGEMENT POWER

Management may attempt to exert power to override the board of directors' ability to effectively exercise its monitoring role, especially when mangement is given the power to control the board of directors. For example, appointment of the chief executive officer (CEO) as the chairperson of the board of directors gives authority to the CEO to determine who is on the board of directors. Outside directors' ties to management and the CEO are usually stronger than the ties to shareholders primarily because of their interest in maintaining board of director seats (Patton and Baker, 1987).[28] In cases when the CEO serves as a chairperson for the board of directors, the CEO determines the board agenda and information provided to the board, which may prevent outside directors from contributing effectively to the monitoring and evaluation of the CEO and other top management (Jensen, 1993).[29]

The function of the chairperson of the board is typically to manage the board and oversee the process of hiring, firing, evaluating, and compensating the CEO. In situations when these two positions are held by one person, a conflict of interest may arise, which makes it difficult for the board to effectively discharge its monitoring role of managerial decisions and actions. Thus, the separation of decision management (e.g., CEO, president) and decision control (e.g., chair of the board of directors) can play an important role in ensuring responsible corporate governance and a reliable financial reporting process. Another factor that can be significant in evaluating the effectiveness of the board of directors' monitoring role is the extent of the CEO's tenure of service on the board of directors. Hermalin and Weisbach (1988)[30] found evidence indicating that an established CEO has relatively more power than a new CEO. Thus, a tenured and experienced CEO can use the seniority status to override monitoring by outside directors and, given the opportunity and motivation, can engage in financial statement fraud.

INTERNAL CONTROL FUNCTION

The sufficiency and effectiveness of the internal control structure play an important role in preventing and detecting financial statement fraud. Public reporting by management on internal controls and external auditors' assurance report could reduce the incidence of financial statement fraud and enhance public confidence in the integrity and reliability of financial reports.

Internal controls are the major components of the company's corporate governance to achieve operational efficiency and effectiveness, preparation of reliable financial reporting, compliance with applicable laws and regulations, and safeguarding assets. Despite the importance of the internal control structure, there are currently no requirements that management include a report on internal controls in its annual reports or auditors provide assurance on such a report; however, recently some companies have voluntarily included a management report on the internal control system and auditors' opinion on the adequacy, effectiveness, and inherent limitations of such a system in their annual reports to shareholders.

The 1992 COSO Report and Statement on Auditing Standards (SAS) No. 78[31,32] define internal control as "a process—affected by an entity's board of directors, management, and other personnel—designed to provide reasonable assurance regarding the achievement of objectives in the following categories: (a) reliability of financial reporting; (b) effectiveness and efficiency of operations; and (c) compliance with applicable laws and regulations." Exhibit 9.2 depicts these three categories of internal control objectives and the five related components. Although management is concerned with achieving objectives in all three

Exhibit 9.2. Internal Control Structure

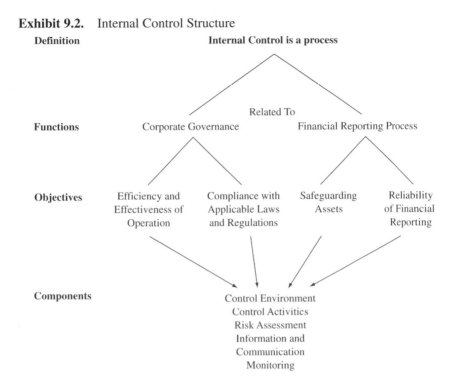

Definition   **Internal Control is a process**

Related To

Functions   Corporate Governance   Financial Reporting Process

Objectives   Efficiency and   Compliance with   Safeguarding   Reliability
                 Effectiveness of   Applicable Laws   Assets   of Financial
                   Operation   and Regulations   Reporting

Components   Control Environment
                                        Control Activities
                                        Risk Assessment
                                        Information and
                                        Communication
                                        Monitoring

categories, independent auditors' main focus is on the company's reliability of financial reporting, including safeguarding assets and compliance with applicable laws and regulations. Internal control is a dynamic process that requires continuous assessment and improvement to achieve the intended objectives. Like any other system, the internal control system cannot be perfect and is subject to inherent limitations of circumvention of controls through collusion, management override of the control system, and inefficiency in implementation. In an environment where these limitations exist, the internal control system cannot prevent and detect all errors, irregularities, and frauds on a timely basis during the normal course of performing business functions. Thus, the internal control system provides only reasonable assurance that the intended control objectives will be achieved. Five components of the internal control structure depicted in Exhibit 9.2 are as follows:

1. *Control environment,* which sets the tone of the organization, provides discipline and structure, and is the foundation for all of the other components of internal controls. Management sets the "tone at the top" through its philosophy, operating style, ethical values, professional attitude, and example. The control environment influences the control consciousness of the company's personnel and includes the following elements: integrity and ethical values, commitment to competence, the board of directors and its representative audit committee, management's philosophy and operating style, assignment of

authority and responsibility, human resources policies and practices, and corporate organizational structure.

2. *Risk assessment* involves identification and analysis of all relative risks, determination of their possible effects on achieving the three categories of control objectives, and management and minimization of the risks to a prudent and manageable level. Risk factors are dynamic and vary in response to changes in the business environment and circumstances. Thus, management should reevaluate and reassess risks in a timely manner to minimize their effects on operations and the financial reporting process. The following circumstances present some of the risks management must consider in its risk assessment, globalization of operations, use of technological advances, changes in operating environment, new personnel, new or revamped information systems, rapid growth, new products or activities, and corporate restructuring.

3. *Control activities* are managerial policies and procedures designed to achieve the three categories of control objectives. Control activities are designed to manage and mitigate the risks assessed by management, and they are related to each category of control objectives.

4. *Information and communication component* is the "central nervous system" of the internal control structure. Management, through this system, communicates its objectives, goals, and related policies and procedures to all individuals within the company and receives feedback from them regarding the assigned responsibilities and the achievement of planned objectives. Management should maintain an effective and efficient information and communication system to ensure proper dissemination of relevant information.

5. *Monitoring component* refers to the periodic and/or continuous assessment of the performance of the internal control structure. Management should monitor the internal control system to ensure its adequacy and effectiveness in achieving the intended objectives. Monitoring should provide feedback to management in a timely manner to determine whether internal control activities are functioning as intended and changes are made as needed.

Management's Responsibility for Internal Controls

Management is primarily responsible for the fair presentation of financial statements. This involves adopting a sound accounting information system that conforms to GAAP in reflecting fair presentation of operating results, financial position, and cash flows; and establishing and maintaining an adequate and effective internal control system to achieve the three categories of control objectives discussed in the previous section, particularly those related to the reliability of financial statements. In following its internal control responsibilities, management sets the "tone at the top" that is ethical, aimed at creating and increasing shareholder value, and promotes reliable financial reports. Risk assessment and risk management of operations and financial reports are also the responsibilities of management. The company's information systems should be properly designed, maintained, and supervised by management. In addition, management is responsible for the timely monitoring of the entire internal control system to ensure that internal control objectives are being achieved and required changes are made as necessary.

Management Report on Internal Controls

Publicly traded companies are not currently required to issue a management report on internal controls; however, many companies include a management report on internal controls in their annual reports to shareholders. The content of such a report varies considerably, but it is centered around the adequacy and effectiveness of the system of internal controls. The Committee of Sponsoring Organizations (COSO) of the National Commission on Fraudulent Financial Reporting issued a report in 1992 entitled "Internal Control—Integrated Framework," which offers guidance on how voluntary management report on internal control should be prepared. The COSO Report[33] suggests that management include a report on internal controls addressing the following issues: (1) financial statement presentation; (2) the nature, objectives, components, and possible limitations of the company's internal controls; (3) the role of the audit committee in overseeing the internal control structure; (4) the role of the internal audit functions in assessing the adequacy and effectiveness of the internal control system; and (5) the role of independent auditors in determining the adequacy and effectiveness of the internal control system in promoting operational efficiency and effectives, producing reliable financial statements, and ensuring adherence to applicable laws and regulations.

Several studies (e.g., Raghunandan and Rama, 1994; Willis and Lightle, 2000)[34,35] examined the content, nature, and structure of the existing voluntary management report on internal control issued by large companies. Exhibit 9.3 provides a sample management report on internal controls. The following issues are commonly addressed in management reports on internal controls:

1. Discussion of fair presentation of financial statements in conformity with GAAP.

2. Description of the nature and purposes of the internal control structure in providing reasonable assurance regarding reliable financial reporting, safeguarding assets, promoting ethical conduct, promoting operational efficiency and effectiveness, encouraging compliance with applicable laws and regulations, including adherence to managerial policies and procedures, and preventing, detecting, and correcting financial statement fraud.

3. Specification of components of the internal control structure, including an internal audit function, the implementation of polices and procedures, the selection and training of competent personnel, and the segregation of duties.

4. Continuous monitoring of the internal control structure, including control activities, internal control environment, and code of business conduct.

Exhibit 9.3.   Management Report on Internal Control

Addressee

Management of NZR Inc. has established and maintains a system of internal control that provides reasonable assurance as to the integrity and reliability of the financial statements, the protection of assets from unauthorized use or disposition, and the prevention and detection of fraudulent financial reporting. The system of internal control provides for appropriate division of responsibility and is documented by written policies and procedures that are communicated to employees with significant roles in the financial reporting process and updated as necessary. Management continually monitors the system of internal control for compliance. The corporation maintains a strong internal auditing program that independently assesses the effectiveness of the internal controls and recommends possible improvements thereto. In addition, as part of its audit of the corporation's financial statements, NZR Inc. completed a study and evaluation of selected internal accounting controls to establish a basis for reliance thereon in determining the nature, timing, and extent of audit tests to be applied. Management has considered the internal auditor's and NZR Inc.'s recommendations concerning the corporation's system of internal control and has taken actions that we believe are cost-effective in the circumstances to respond appropriately to these recommendations. Management believes that, as of December 31, 20xx, the corporation's system of internal control is adequate and effective to accomplish the objectives discussed herein.

Signature

Chief Executive Officer

Signature

Chief Financial Officer

(and/or)

Signature

Controller

Source: This report is extracted from Management's Report on Responsibility for Financial Reporting. Available at http://www.COSO.org/Publications/NCFFR_Part_12.htm.

5. Discussion of the adequacy and effectiveness of the internal control system in providing reasonable assurance in achieving its prescribed objectives, including the inherent limitation of internal controls and cost-benefit considerations.

6. Recognition of the role of the internal audit function in monitoring compliance with established managerial policies and procedures, assessment of their effectiveness, and any recommendations provided by internal auditors to improve controls and correct deficiencies.

7. Reference to the existence of an audit committee consisting of independent members who meet regularly with the independent auditor, the internal audit director, and management. The report also stated functions of the audit committee and that the director of the internal audit function and the independent auditor had full and free access to the audit committee.

8. Reference to the independent audit and the audit report in the annual report. Many of management reports on internal controls made redundant remarks regarding the independent audit report, such as that the audit was conducted in accordance with GAAS and appropriate tests of accounting procedures and records were performed, financial records and minutes were made available to the independent auditor.

9. Most studied management reports on internal controls were signed by the Chief Executive Officer (CEO) and the person directly responsible for financial reporting, such as the Chief Financial Officer (CFO) or Chief Accounting Officer (CAO).

Management reports on internal controls are prepared and published to serve a variety of purposes, including the following:

1. Communicating to investors, creditors, and other users of the report the adequacy and effectiveness of the internal control system in ensuring the achievement of the company's objectives.

2. Discussing the company's efforts to safeguard its resources and reach its strategic goals.

3. Clarifying the role of the audit committee, its functions, responsibilities, and compositions.

4. Emphasizing that the company's internal control system provides reasonable assurance regarding achievement of intended goals and objectives.

5. Describing how the company uses its independent audit services to assist in managing or assessing the internal control system.

6. Discussing that an adequate and effective internal control system can assist in preventing, detecting, and correcting material misstatements in financial reports caused by errors and fraud.

MANAGEMENT ATTITUDE TOWARD FINANCIAL STATEMENT FRAUD

Lawmakers, including the SEC federal regulators, hold Enron Corporation's management and its auditor Andersen responsible for lack of adequate financial disclosures on risks associated with Enron's private partnerships known as Special Purpose Entities (SPEs). Enron has already filed for Chapter 11 bankruptcy reorganization, which was the largest bankruptcy filing in U.S. history, and is planning to restructure its way out of bankruptcy-court protection within a year. Congress criticized Enron's management and Andersen for misleading investors and started an investigation at a joint hearing of two House Financial Services subcommittees. Andersen claimed that it has been misled by Enron's management over these partnerships on the grounds that Enron withheld information from its auditor. Recently, Holmes et al. (2000)[36] examined the relationships between management attitude and specific dimensions of fraud schemes by comparing frauds that were uncovered in organizations where management had implemented and supported internal control systems (SUPPORTIVE) with frauds that occurred in organizations where management was perceived to display a lax attitude towards internal controls (LAX). Holmes et al. (2000) attempted to provide answers to the following three simple but important financial statement fraud–related questions:

1. Does the relationship of the fraud perpetrator to the victim entity differ between SUPPORTIVE organizations and LAX organizations?
2. Does the nature of the fraud schemes used to commit the crime differ between SUPPORTIVE organizations and LAX organizations?
3. Does the method of fraud detection differ between SUPPORTIVE organizations and LAX organizations?[37]

Holmes et al. (2000)[38] found that (1) employees were more likely to be the perpetrator of fraud in organizations where management displayed a lax attitude toward internal controls; (2) a lax attitude by top management toward internal controls encourages unethical behavior on the part of employees, which may result in fraudulent financial activities; (3) more red flags were identified in LAX organizations than SUPPORTIVE organizations before the fraud was detected; (4) perpetrators in organizations with lax attitudes were being prosecuted at the same rate and as severely as in organizations that supported internal controls; and (5) LAX organizations were more likely to fine or transfer perpetrators to discourage the frauds to occur.

CONCLUSION

Management is an important member of the corporate governance structure and is responsible for ensuring effective corporate governance to create shareholder value. Management is also responsible for the quality, integrity, and reliability of the financial reporting process in producing financial statements free of material misstatements caused by errors and fraud. Management may be motivated to engage in financial statement fraud because its personal well-being is so closely associated with the well-being of the company through profit-sharing, stock-based compensation plans, and other bonuses; and management is willing to take personal risks for corporate benefit; however, financial statement fraud can be prevented and detected when a company's financial reporting process is subject to thorough scrutiny by the board of directors, the audit committee, internal auditors, external auditors, and governing bodies, as discussed in this chapter. Nevertheless, the presence of a "gamesmanship" environment enables management to use its discretion to choose accounting practices that portray the rosiest earnings projections to meet analysts' forecasts to sustain or boost stock prices. This chapter provides guidelines in monitoring this perceived gamesmanship and making financial statements free of material misstatements caused by errors and fraud.

ENDNOTES

1. Parker, L.M., and G.J. Previts. 2000. "The Tyranny of the Analysis: Value Driving Information." *Research in Accounting Regulation* 14:265–268.

2. National Commission on Fraudulent Financial Reporting (NCFFR) (The Treadway Commission). 1987. Report of the National Commission on Fraudulent Financial Reporting. New York: AICPA.

3. Committee of Sponsoring Organizations of the Treadway Commission (COSO). 1992. Internal Control-Integrated Framework. New York: COSO.

4. Saunders, D.R. 1978. Psychological Perspectives on Management Fraud. In *Management Fraud: Detection and Deterrence,* co-authored by R.K. Elliot and J.J. Willingham. 1980. New York: Petrocelli Books:108.

5. Dechow, P.M., R.G. Sloan, and A.P. Sweeney. 1996. "Causes and Consequences of Earnings Manipulations: An Analysis of Firms Subject to Enforcement Actions by the SEC." *Contemporary Accounting Research* (Spring): 1–36.

6. Ibid.

7. Beasley, M.S. 1996. "An Empirical Investigation of the Relationship Between Board of Directors Composition and Financial Statement Fraud." *The Accounting Review* (October): 443–465.

8. Ibid.

9. McMullen, D.A. 1996. "Audit Committee Performance: An Investigation of the Consequences Associated with Audit Committee." *Auditing: A Journal of Practice & Theory* (Spring): 87–103.

10. Ibid.

11. Loebbecke, J.K., and J.J. Willingham. 1988. Review of SEC Accounting and Auditing Enforcement Releases. Working paper.

12. Loebbecke, J.K., M.M. Eining, and J.J. Willingham. 1989. "Auditors' Experience with Material Irregularities: Frequency, Nature, and Detectability." *Auditing: A Journal of Practice & Theory* (Fall): 1–18.

13. Ibid.

14. Merchant, K.A. 1987. *Fraudulent and Questionable Financial Reporting: A Corporate Perspective.* Morristown, NJ: Financial Executives Research Foundation.

15. Beasley, M.S., J.V. Carcello, and D.R. Hermanson. 1999. Fraudulent Financial Reporting: 1987–1997, An Analysis of U.S. Public Companies. New York: COSO.

16. Anonymous. 2000. "Fudge Has No Place in Financial Reports." *Investment News* (April 3, V4, p. 16).

17. American Heritage Dictionary of English Language. 1992. New York: Houghton Mifflin Company.

18. Levitt, A. 1999. "Quality Information: The Lifeblood of Our Market." Speech given to The Economic Club of New York by SEC Chairman on October 18. Available: www.sec.gov/news/speeches/spch304.htm

19. Blue Ribbon Committee (BRC) on Improving the Effectiveness of Corporate Audit Committees. 1999. Report and Recommendations of the Blue Ribbon Committee on Improving the Effectiveness of Corporate Audit Committees. New York: NYSE and NASD.

20. Porter, D. 1999. "SEC Ready to Crack Down on Accounting Games." *Crain's Cleveland Business* (September 20): 28.

21. American Institute of Certified Public Accountants. 2000. Statement on Auditing Standards (SAS) No. 89. Auditing Adjustments. AICPA: New York.

22. Securities and Exchange Commission. "Final Rule: Selective Disclosure and Insider Trading." Available: www.sec.gov/rules/fraud/33-7881.htm

23. Securities and Exchange Commission. 2000. Final Rule: Revision of the Commission's Auditor Independence Requirements. Available: www.sec.gov/rules/final/33-7919.htm

24. Public Oversight Board (O'Malley Panel). 2000. The Panel on Audit Effectiveness Report and Recommendations. Stamford, CT (August).

25. Jensen, M.C., and K. Murphy. 1990. "Performance Pay and Top Management Incentives." *Journal of Political Economy.* 98: 225–264.

26. Jensen, M.C., and J.B. Warner. 1988. The Distribution of Power Among Corporate Managers, Shareholders, and Directors. *Journal of Financial Economics.* 20:3–24.

27. Beasley, M.S. 1994. "An Empirical Analysis of the Relation Between Corporate Governance and Management Fraud." UMI Dissertation Services, Michigan State University.

28. Patton, A., and J. Baker. 1987. Why Do Not Directors Rock the Boat? *Harvard Business Review.* 65: 10–12.

29. Jensen, M.C. 1993. "The Modern Industrial Revolution, Exit, and the Failure of Internal Control Systems." *The Journal of Finance* (July): 831–880.

30. Hermalin, B., and M.S. Weisbach. 1988. "The Determinants of Board Composition." *The Rand Journal of Economics* (Winter): 589–606.

31. Committee of Sponsoring Organizations of the Treadway Commission (COSO). 1992. Internal Control-Integrated Framework. New York: COSO.

32. American Institute of Certified Public Accountants (AICPA). 1995. Statement on Auditing Standards (SAS) No. 78. Consideration of Internal Control in a Financial Statement Audit. AICPA New York, NY.

33. Committee of Sponsoring Organizations of the Treadway Commission (COSO). 1992. Internal Control-Integrated Framework. New York: COSO.

34. Raghunandan, R., and D.V. Rama. 1994. Management Reports After COSO: Internal Auditor (August): 54.

35. Willis, D.M., and S.S. Lightle. 2000. "Management Reports on Internal Controls." Journal of Accountancy (October): 57.

36. Holmes, S.A., M. Langford, O.J. Welch, and S.T. Welch. 2000. An Investigation of the Relationship Between Organizational Citizenship and the Characteristics of Fraud. Working paper, Texas A&M University.

37. Ibid.

38. Ibid.

Chapter 10

Role of the Internal Auditor

INTRODUCTION

Internal auditors have made steady progress over the past 50 years and will continue to grow to accommodate an ever-changing business environment. Internal auditors are currently providing audit services for managers at all levels as well as for the board of directors and the audit committee. Internal auditors have become a training ground for top executives including the audit committee members; however, internal auditors' primary responsibility is to assist management at all levels to fulfill their responsibilities by (1) assessing the efficiency, effectiveness, and economy of management performance; (2) making constructive suggestions to continuously improve performance; and (3) monitoring the quality, integrity, and reliability of the financial reporting process. This chapter discusses the role of the internal auditors in corporate governance, the financial reporting process, the internal control structure, and the prevention, detection, and correction of financial statement fraud.

INTERNAL AUDITORS AND CORPORATE GOVERNANCE

Internal auditors' responsibility for preventing and detecting financial statement fraud has been extensively disputed in the accounting literature. Internal auditors are an important part of corporate governance, as depicted in Exhibit 10.1, and are properly positioned to ensure responsible corporate governance and a reliable financial reporting process. Internal auditors' day-to-day involvement with both operational and financial reporting systems and the internal control structure provide them with the opportunity to perform thorough and timely assessment of high-risk aspects of the financial reporting process. Nevertheless, the effectiveness of internal auditors to prevent and detect financial statement fraud depends largely on their organizational status and reporting relationships.

Financial statement fraud is normally perpetrated by the top management team, and internal auditors often find themselves in adversarial relationships when they discover such fraud; however, several Statements on Internal Auditing Standards (SIAS) are issued to provide guidance for internal auditors to protect the integrity, reliability and quality of the financial reporting process. Internal audit standards issued by the Institute of Internal Auditors (IIA) require that internal auditors should be alert to the possibility of intentional wrongdoing, errors, irregularities, fraud, inefficiency, conflicts of interest, waste, and ineffectiveness in the

Exhibit 10.1.   Corporate Governance and Its Functions

normal course of conducting an audit. Internal auditors are also required to inform the appropriate authorities within the organization regarding suspected wrongdoing and follow up to ensure that proper actions are taken to correct the problem.

INTERNAL AUDITORS' RESPONSIBILITIES

Internal auditors must play a proactive role in preventing and detecting financial statement fraud, primarily because of their active involvement in the company's internal control structure and organization status. Unlike external auditors, internal auditors' effectiveness in preventing and detecting financial statement fraud is not constrained by time budgets and the high costs of expanding their examination of managerial policies and procedures and tests of controls. Internal auditors are in the best position to continuously monitor the company's internal control structure by identifying and investigating red flags that could signal the likelihood of financial statement fraud. Internal auditors' appropriate position in the organizational structure, proper training, their knowledge of personnel, familiarity with managerial policies and operating procedures, and understanding of business conditions and the internal control environment enable them to identify and assess red flags signaling the possibility of financial statement fraud.

The role of internal auditors in preventing and detecting financial statement fraud is sufficiently addressed in the authoritative reports and professional standards. The Treadway Commission report (1987)[1] recommends that internal auditors should take an active role in preventing and detecting financial statement fraud. Statement on Internal Auditing Standards (SIAS) No. 3[2] requires internal auditors to take a proactive role in preventing and detecting financial statement fraud by identifying qualitative red flags that signal the possibility of fraud, investigating symptoms of fraud, and reporting their findings to the audit committee or other appropriate level of management.

Financial statement fraud is often perpetrated by top management teams, which are at the level beyond that typically audited by internal auditors. Internal auditors, however, during their normal course of audit may become aware of fraud systems that may affect the quality, integrity, and reliability of financial statements. In these instances, internal auditors should thoroughly investigate the likelihood of financial statement fraud and inform the audit committee regarding the probability of financial statement fraud. Thus, a close working relationship between the audit committee and the internal audit function, particularly private meetings between the chairperson of the audit committee and the chief internal auditor, can improve the quality of financial statements and reduce the likelihood of financial statement fraud.

Internal auditors' working relationship with external auditors can get internal auditors' involvement with the financial reporting process at the highest level of consolidation. Thus, internal auditors are indirectly participating in the final preparation of financial statements through their close coordination and cooperation with external auditors. This situation creates an opportunity for internal auditors to take an active role in ensuring the integrity, quality, and reliability of the financial reporting process; however, new reports (e.g., Blue Ribbon committee, 1999; COSO 1999)[3,4] encourage internal auditors to take an active role in assessing the quality, reliability, and integrity of the financial reporting process.

The following suggestions can enhance the active role of internal auditors in the financial reporting process and thus, their role in preventing and detecting financial statement fraud:

- Schedule meetings between the chief internal auditor and the audit committee regarding the financial reporting process.
- Establish a consolidated financial statement audit function consisting of the audit committee, internal auditors, external auditors, and top management team periodically assessing the quality, reliability and integrity of financial reporting process.
- Organize close cooperation and coordination of the work of external auditors with internal auditors through an integrated audit planning process consisting of the exchange of audit plans, programs, findings, and reports.
- Require that internal auditors report their audit findings related to financial statement preparation, especially when there are symptoms of financial statement fraud, to the audit committee or the board of directors.

- Report to applicable regulatory agencies or even the shareholders upon failure of the audit committee to act on financial statement fraud findings of internal auditors.

- Enhance the status of internal auditors as a part of corporate governance through the higher-level reporting relationship, more access to the audit committee, career development plans for necessary experience, training and knowledge, and sufficient resources to improve internal auditors' role in the financial reporting process and their effectiveness in preventing and detecting financial statement fraud.

- Assess the adequacy and effectiveness of the internal control structure in general, and internal controls over the financial reporting process in particular.

- Evaluate the quality of the financial reporting process, including a review of both annual and quarterly financial statements filed with the SEC and other regulatory agencies.

- Participate with the audit committee and external auditors in reviewing management's discretionary decisions, judgment, selection, and accounting principles and practices as related to the preparation of financial statements.

- Assess the risks and control environment pertaining to the financial reporting process by ensuring that financial reporting risks are identified and related controls are adequate and effective.

- Review risks, policies, and procedures and controls pertaining to the quality, integrity, and reliability of financial reporting.

- Monitor compliance with the company's code of corporate conduct to ensure that compliance with ethical policies and other related procedures promoting ethical behavior is being achieved. The tone set by management encouraging ethical behavior can be the most effective factor in contributing to the integrity and quality of the financial reporting process.

INTERNAL AUDIT FRAUD STANDARDS

Statement on Internal Auditing Standards (SIAS) No. 3 describes the internal auditors' responsibility for fraud deterrence as "examining and evaluating the adequacy and effectiveness of the system of internal control, commensurate with the extent of the potential exposure/risk in the various segments of the organization's operations."[5] According to SIAS No. 3, internal auditors should identify indicators of fraud and, when deemed necessary, conduct an investigation to determine whether a fraud has actually been committed.

SIAS No. 3 provides guidance relating to the internal auditors' responsibility for deterrence, detection, investigation, and reporting of fraud. Thus, standards clearly state that deterrence of fraud is the responsibility of management. Internal auditors, however, should assess the adequacy and effectiveness of actions taken by management in discharging this obligation. Regarding the detection of fraud, SIAS No. 3 is vague about the responsibility of internal auditors. On the one hand, it states that internal auditors should have adequate knowledge of fraud to be able to identify symptoms of fraud and perform audit procedures to detect fraud incidents. On the other hand, it indicates (1) that internal auditors are not expected to have knowledge equivalent to that of a person whose primary responsibility is to detect and investigate fraud; and (2) the routine audit procedures performed by internal auditors are not expected to discover fraud. SIAS No. 3 suggests that fraud investigations be performed by a team consisting of internal auditors, lawyers, investigators, security personnel, and other specialists from inside or outside the organization. Internal auditors' responsibilities regarding fraud investigation are to (1) determine whether adequate and effective internal controls are in place to discover fraud; (2) design audit procedures to discover similar occurrence of similar frauds in the future; and (3) obtain adequate knowledge of investigating similar fraud.

SIAS No. 3 states the following responsibilities of internal auditors for detecting fraud. First internal auditors should obtain sufficient knowledge and understanding of fraud to be able to identify conditions that may indicate existence of red flags that fraud might have occurred. Conditions presented in this article should be useful to internal auditors identifying red flags indicating likelihood of the commission of financial statement fraud. Second, internal auditors should study and evaluate corporate structure to identify opportunities, such as a lack of vigilant and effective corporate governance, and weaknesses in internal control structure that could allow the commission of financial statement fraud given the existence of adequate incentives. Third, internal auditors should evaluate choices made by fraudsters in perpetrating financial statement fraud and decide whether those choices provide further indications (red flags) and what actions should be taken. The 3Cs factors of conditions, corporate structure, and choices discussed in Chapter 4 should assist internal auditors to identify the potential fraudulent red flags and develop a risk model to prevent and detect financial statement fraud. Internal auditors' involvement in the routine activities of their organization and internal control structure place them in the best position to identify and assess indicators (red flags) that may signal financial statement fraud.

Finally, internal auditors should inform the appropriate authorities within the organization regarding the possibility of occurrence of financial statement fraud. There are two different channels, internal and external, for communicating sensitive issues such as financial statement fraud. The internal channel refers to disclosing fraud to appropriate authorities within the organization such as top executives, the audit committee, and the board of directors. External channels can be used to communicate fraud to those outside of the organization including media, external auditors, and authoritative bodies (i.e., SEC). Existing internal auditing standards refrain internal auditors from disclosing any wrongdoing including fraud to a party outside of their organizations.

The internal audit function can protect companies from financial statement fraud when internal auditors are effective in the following three areas: (1) preventing financial statement fraud through adequate and effective internal control systems; (2) detecting financial statement fraud by performing internal audit functions; and (3) reporting detected financial statement fraud to the top management team and the audit committee. Thus, the internal audit function plays a crucial role in preventing and detecting financial statement fraud.

THE EFFICACY OF INTERNAL AUDIT IN FINANCIAL STATEMENT FRAUD PREVENTION AND DETECTION

Internal auditors can be viewed as a first-line defense against fraud because of their knowledge and understanding of their organization's control structure and business environment. Thus, they are well positioned to prevent and detect all types of frauds, including employee fraud and embezzlement and management or financial statement fraud; however, there are several reasons to believe that internal auditors may be reluctant to report negative managerial information such as financial statement fraud, primarily because of the organizational structure and chain-of-command relationships. In most companies, top management teams (e.g., senior management) often make hiring, promotion, performance evaluation, and firing decisions of the chief internal auditors. This may create conflicts of interest in a sense that internal auditors must risk their job and career to report offenses by senior management. The Treadway Report, in recognizing this problem, recommended that the appointment and dismissal of the director of the internal audit department be handled by the audit committee or the board of directors.

Recent studies (e.g., Abbott and Parker, 2000; Raghunandan, Reed, and Rama, 2001; Chadwick, 1995; Kalbers, 1992; McHugh and Raghunandan, 1994)[6–10] reveal that (1) most companies allow senior management to hire and fire the chief internal auditor without involvement from the audit committee; (2) most internal auditors indicate that they would not report any incidents offensive to the top management team, including financial statement fraud, because they would probably be fired and never find an internal audit job; (3) access to the audit committee is often restricted and private meetings with the audit committee are not possible; and (4) senior management usually determines the resources for the internal audit function, including the size of the internal audit staff and budget, which makes the internal auditor reluctant to report problems, especially management fraud, to the audit committee.

Internal auditors, however, are privy to both formal and informal lines of communication in the company and, accordingly, are more likely to have a competitive advantage in financial statement fraud prevention and detection compared to external auditors. External auditors are constrained by the time and budgets determined in a competitive market and by the high cost and, therefore, they cannot be effective in identifying red flags that may signal the existence of financial statement fraud. With adequate training and the proper position in the organizational hierarchy, internal auditors may be in the best situation to identify and assess symptoms that could signal financial statement fraud. More routine involvement of internal auditors with business conditions, the financial reporting process, and the internal control structure could considerably improve their effectiveness as fraud investigators.

External auditors have traditionally been held responsible for detecting financial statement fraud; however, internal auditors are in the best position to discover financial statement fraud. Internal auditors' financial statement fraud deterrence activities consist of actions taken to prevent and discourage financial statement fraud and limit the opportunities for fraud and to assess the company's exposure to fraud. SIAS No. 3 states that the principal mechanism for deterring financial statement fraud by internal auditors is control. Although management is primarily responsible for designing and maintaining an adequate and effective internal control system, internal auditors should assist management in ensuring the effectiveness of such a system in deterring financial statement fraud. Internal auditors should (1) assess the soundness of the company's internal control environment in setting the "tone at the top" in creating an environment for high-quality financial reports; (2) ensure that management expectations regarding financial performance (e.g., earnings projections) are realistic; (3) communicate, implement, and enforce corporate established policies, procedures, and codes of conduct to all affected individuals within the company and monitor their compliance with activities designed to prevent and detect financial statement fraud; (4) improve communications in providing management with adequate and reliable information; and (5) monitor the corporate internal control system and make recommendations to improve its effectiveness in preventing and detecting financial statement fraud.

Internal auditors' responsibilities for detecting, investigating, and reporting financial statement fraud, according to their standards (e.g., SIAS No. 3) are to (1) identify symptoms and red flags that indicate that financial statement fraud may have been perpetrated; (2) identify opportunities (e.g., weak internal control, weak audit committee) that may allow financial statement fraud to occur; (3) assess the identified symptoms and opportunities, investigate the possibility of their occurrences, and determine actions necessary to reduce or minimize their likelihood of occurrences; and (4) notify the appropriate individuals with the company—top executives if they are not involved in fraud or, otherwise, the board of directors and its representative audit committee—for further investigation of the possibility of financial statement fraud.

COOPERATION BETWEEN EXTERNAL AND INTERNAL AUDIT

A company's audit function is conducted by the internal audit department and a professional services firm (CPA), while each has its own responsibilities. The external auditor is responsible for auditing and attesting to the fair presentation of financial statements, whereas the internal auditor is responsible for monitoring the company's operational and financial performance and the internal control structure. The audit committee should ensure that activities of internal and external auditors complement each other, their audit functions are coordinated, and there is open and effective communication between them. To improve the audit effectiveness and efficiency, external auditors should identify the internal audit activities that are relevant to planning the audit of financial statements and, if appropriate, rely on the work of internal auditors in determining the nature, timing, and extent of audit procedures.

The AICPA in realizing the important role that internal auditors can play in preventing and detecting financial statement fraud, issued SAS No. 65: "The auditor's consideration of the internal audit function in an audit of financial statements."[11] SAS No. 65 provides guidance on the extent to which external auditors may rely on the work of the internal auditors in (1) assessing risk; (2) evaluating the strengths of a company's internal control function; and (3) conducting other aspects of the audit. SAS No. 65 focuses primarily on the competence and objectivity of the internal audit department. When evaluation of the internal audit function indicates an adequate level of competence and objectivity, then external auditors may rely on the work of internal auditors. Reliance on the work of well-trained and independently positioned internal auditors should improve external auditors' effectiveness in discovering possible financial statement fraud.

Andersen was both outside and internal auditor of the bankrupt Enron which possibly created conflict of interests that ultimately impaired Andersen's objectivity and integrity. The role of internal auditors is to assist individuals (especially managers) in the organization to fulfill their responsibilities. Internal auditors' responsibilities as related to the financial reporting process and internal control structure are to ensure adequacy and effectiveness of internal controls and integrity of the financial reporting process in producing reliable and useful financial information. The outside auditor's responsibility is to conduct independent audits of financial statements and provide reasonable assurance regarding their fair presentation in conformity with GAAP. Thus, when outside auditors are hired to conduct both external financial audits and internal audits, conflicts of interest can be created that may jeopardize outside auditors independence, integrity, and objectivity as it appears to be the case with Andersen, Enron's auditor. The SEC has addressed this concern in its new independence rule for outside auditors by prohibiting them from doing more than 40 percent of the internal audit function for businesses with more than $200 million in assets effective August 2002. Andersen not only conducted both external financial audits and internal audits for collapsed Enron, but also in a proposal to a Fortune 500 company last year, promoted the idea that conducting both internal auditing and external auditing offers a variety of benefits including "greater knowledge sharing" and "increases team efficiency and overall knowledge about the company."[12]

INTERNAL AUDITS AND THE AUDIT COMMITTEE

The Treadway Commission (1987)[13] recommended that the audit committee get more involved in the internal auditing process by overseeing all internal auditing activities. The Treadway Commission made four recommendations suggesting that the audit committee (1) effectively and vigilantly oversee the company's internal control; (2) review the appropriateness of the corporate code of conduct and compliance with it; (3) review any second opinion sought by management on accounting issues, estimates; and (4) oversee the quarterly reporting process. Internal auditors play a crucial role in the financial reporting process through their involvement with internal controls. Although internal auditors are not primarily responsible for establishing and maintaining the internal control system, they monitor such a system and assess its adequacy and effectiveness. Thus, an internal audit function is a valuable resource to the audit committee in fulfilling its responsibility. To perform their duties most effectively, the audit committee and internal auditor must work closely and should maintain an open line of communication. The chairperson of the audit committee and the director of the internal audit department in particular should have unrestricted access to each other.

The audit committee should perform the following functions:

- Participate in the appointment, promotion, replacement, reassignment, or dismissal of the director of the internal audit function.
- Concur in the establishment of the internal audit function's goals and mission.
- Review activities and the organizational structure of the internal audit department.
- Review the findings and results of the internal audit function and management's responses to the internal auditor's findings and recommendations on internal controls.
- Review the effectiveness of the internal audit department in carrying out its responsibilities.
- Ensure that the internal audit function's involvement in the financial reporting process is appropriate, adequate and effective.
- Ensure that the internal audit department's applied standards and procedures are in compliance with those established by the Institute of Internal Auditors (IIA).
- Review the organizational independence and reporting relationships of the internal audit function.
- Ensure that the internal audit department's staffing and budget are adequate in carrying out the assigned responsibilities.

INTERNAL CONTROL

This section describes the internal control structure as related to the financial reporting process. An adequate and effective internal control structure is perceived to help prevent and detect financial statement fraud. Management is responsible for establishing, maintaining, and monitoring the internal control structure to achieve the organization's objectives and the reliability, integrity, and quality of the financial reporting process.

The Committee of Sponsoring Organizations of the Treadway Commission (COSO) published its report entitled "Internal Controls—Integrated Framework" in September 1992. This report was intended to (1) provide a uniform and comprehensive definition of internal controls that can be used by all interested parties, including management, internal auditors, regulatory bodies, and external auditors; (2) establish components of internal controls; and (3) offer a framework to assess the effectiveness of internal controls for promoting management accountability and transparency in financial reporting.

The COSO Report (1992) defines internal control as:

A process, affected by an entity's board of directors, management, and other personnel, designed to provide reasonable assurance regarding the achievement of objectives in the following three categories:

• Effectiveness and efficiency of operations

• Reliability of financial reporting

• Compliance with applicable laws and regulations[14]

This definition of internal control is viewed by many as the most comprehensive definition, which addresses four major elements of internal control, namely the (1) process, (2) individuals who affect the internal control and are affected by internal control, (3) limitations of internal control by providing only reasonable assurance, and (4) objectives categories. The main critique of this definition came from the General Accounting Office (GAO) and the SEC, stating that the COSO definition does not sufficiently address controls pertaining to safeguarding of assets as required by the Foreign Corrupt Practices Act of 1977. Thus, an addendum to "Reporting to External Parties" of the COSO Report was published in May 1994 addressing the safeguarding of assets objectives of internal control.

Components of Internal Control

COSO 1992 defines the five interrelated components and internal control as:

1. Control environment
2. Risk assessment
3. Control activities
4. Information and communication
5. Monitoring

These internal control components relate to all four objectives of internal control, as depicted in Exhibit 10.2. The control environment consists of integrity, ethical values, organizational structure, management philosophy, operating style, competent personnel, human resource policies and practices, assignment of authority and

Exhibit 10.2. Internal Control Structure

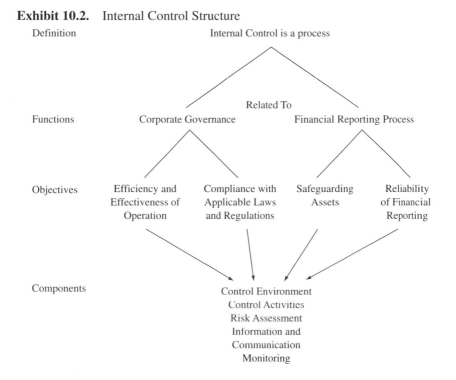

responsibility, and oversight function of the board of directors and its audit committee. The COSO Report emphasizes risk assessment, particularly as it relates to the financial reporting process. Management should assess the information risk that financial statements may be inaccurate, biased, or incomplete, and manage this information risk to a prudent level. Management should perform a risk analysis of both external and internal factors affecting the integrity and quality of the financial reporting process.

Control activities defined by the COSO Report include all managerial policies and procedures designed to ensure that control objectives are achieved. Control activities related to the financial reporting process are intended to prevent, detect, and correct misstatements in the financial statements caused by errors, irregularities, and fraud.

The information and communication component of internal control involves the process of capturing, analyzing, and disseminating relevant information to ensure that personnel receive proper instructions and carry out their assigned responsibilities effectively and efficiently. The monitoring component of internal control requires continuous assessment of the adequacy, effectiveness, and quality of the internal control system. Any discovered errors, irregularities, and frauds should be reported to top management and the audit committee and corrected promptly.

Essential components of an adequate and effective internal control structure that help in preventing, detecting, and correcting financial statement fraud are as follows:

- Commitment from the top management team
- A control environment reflected in the structure, functions, and risks of the company
- Control activities designed to achieve the control objectives of enhancing reliability of financial reporting, improving effectiveness and efficiency of operations, and promoting compliance with applicable laws and regulations
- Continuous and periodic monitoring to ensure the adequacy and effectiveness of the internal control structure
- Communication of the established control activities, policies, and procedures to affected individuals within the corporation
- Proper implementation of control activities and enforcement of control policies and procedures

CONCLUSION

Internal auditors have made steady progress in being viewed as a partner with management in assisting individuals or divisions within the company to achieve the goal of creating and increasing shareholder value. Internal auditors have a demonstrated ability and commitment to add value to their organizations by fostering corporate governance. The role of internal auditors in preventing and detecting financial statement fraud is addressed in the authoritative reports and professional standards (the Treadway Commission 1987 and SIAS No. 3, 1985). These authoritative guidelines require internal auditors to take a proactive role in preventing and detecting financial statement fraud by identifying indicators (red flags) of fraud, assessing their impacts on the quality, integrity, and reliability of financial reports, and reporting the alleged fraud to the appropriate individuals within their organization (i.e., top executives, the audit committee, and the board of directors).

Internal auditors can play an important role in ensuring the adequacy and effectiveness of the internal control system and the integrity and reliability of the financial reporting process. Thus, publicly traded companies should have an independent, effective, competent, and respected internal audit function. The board of directors, audit committee, and top management team should support internal auditors and value their services. External auditors should cooperate and coordinate their audit activities with internal auditors because they know the company, the personnel, the company's business environment and risks, and the internal control structure. Internal auditors should get more involved with the review and audit of financial reporting processes to effectively prevent and detect financial statement fraud. Internal auditors, by not being confounded by time and budget constraints particular to external auditors, should get more involved in fraud prevention and detection in general, and financial statement fraud prevention, detection, and correction in particular.

ENDNOTES

1. National Commission on Fraudulent Financial Reporting (NCFFR) (The Treadway Commission). 1987. Report of the National Commission on Fraudulent Financial Reporting. New York, NY: AICPA.

2. Institute of Internal Auditors (IIA). 1985. Statements of Internal Auditing Standards NO.3: Deterrence, Detection, Investigation and Reporting of Fraud. Altamonte Springs, Fl: IIA.

3. Blue Ribbon Committee (BRC) on Improving the Effectiveness of Corporate Audit Committees. 1999. Report and Recommendations of the Blue Ribbon Committee on Improving the Effectiveness of Corporate Audit Committees. New York, NY: NYSE and NASD.

4. Beasley, M.S., J.V. Carcello, and D.R. Hermanson. 1999. Fraudulent Financial Reporting: 1987–1997, An Analysis of U.S. Public Companies. New York: COSO.

5. Institute of Internal Auditors (IIA). 1985. Statements of Internal Auditing Standards NO.3: Deterrence, Detection, Investigation and Reporting of Fraud. Altamonte Springs, Fl: IIA.

6. Abbott, L.J., and S. Parker. 2000. Auditor Selection and Audit Committee Characteristics. Auditing: A Journal of Practice & Theory (Fall): 47–66.

7. Raghunandan, K., W.J. Reed, and D.V. Rama. 2001. Audit Committee Composition, "Gray Directors," and Interaction with Internal Auditing. Accounting Horizons (June): 105–118.

8. Chadwick, W. 1995. Tough Questions, Tough Answers. Internal Auditor (December): 63–65.

9. Kalbers, L. 1992. Audit Committees and Internal Auditors. Internal Auditor (December): 37–44.

10. McHugh, J. and K. Raghunandan. 1994. Hiring and Firing the Chief Internal Auditor. Internal Auditor (August): 34–39.

11. American Institute of Certified Public Accountants (AICPA). 1988. Statement on Auditing Standards (SAS) No. 65. The Auditor's Consideration of the Internal Audit Function in an Audit of Financial Statements. New York, NY: AICPA.

12. Hilzenrath, D. S. 2001. Enron's Outside Accountants Also Did Inside Audit. *Washington Post* (December 14): E01.

13. National Commission on Fraudulent Financial Reporting (NCFFR) (The Treadway Commission). 1987. Report of the National Commission on Fraudulent Financial Reporting. New York, NY: AICPA.

14. Committee of Sponsoring Organizations of the Treadway Commission (COSO). 1992. Internal Control-Integrated Framework. New York, NY: COSO.

Chapter 11

Role of External Auditors

INTRODUCTION

Users of audited financial statements, particularly investors and creditors, have traditionally held independent auditors responsible for detecting financial statement fraud. Independent auditors, however, in compliance with their professional standards provide only reasonable assurance that financial statements are free of material misstatements whether caused by error or fraud. This chapter presents external auditors, association with published financial statements, the role of independent auditors in detecting financial statement fraud, characteristics of high-quality financial audits, independent auditors report on internal control, and methods of improving audit effectiveness.

INDEPENDENT AUDIT AND FINANCIAL STATEMENTS

External auditors' association with financial reports is through their own report of independent auditor-accompanied published financial statements. Although management is primarily responsible for the fair presentation of financial statements in conformity with the generally accepted accounting principles (GAAP), the auditor's report attests to the fairness of management presentations and/or assertions. The auditor's unqualified report (clean opinion), illustrated for NZR Inc. in Exhibit 11.1, states that the financial statement, including the notes, present fairly, in all material respects, the financial position, the results of operations, and the cash flows for the reported accounting period, in conformity with GAAP. This unqualified report provides reasonable assurance that the published audited financial statements are free of material misstatements caused by errors and fraud; however, some circumstances (e.g., integrity and quality of financial statements are adversely affected by material errors, irregularities, or fraud) warrant audit reports other than an unqualified opinion (e.g., modified unqualified, qualified, disclaimer, adverse).

The presence of financial statement fraud, in particular, warrants external auditors to modify their standard unqualified opinion. Failure of external auditors to detect financial statement fraud either because of negligent auditing or involvement in the fraud to protect their clients at the expense of investors can result in substantial losses to investors and creditors and lawsuits against auditors. The 1999 COSO Report reveals that external auditors were named in more than

Exhibit 11.1.   The Report of Independent Auditor

Board of Directors and Shareholders
of NZR Inc.

We have audited the accompanying consolidated balance sheets of NZR Inc. and subsidiaries as of December 31, 20x1, 20x2, and 20x3, and the related consolidated statements of income, cash flows and shareholders' equity for each of the three years in the period ended December 31, 20xy. These financial statements are the responsibility of the Company's management. Our responsibility is to express an opinion on these financial statements based on our audits.

We conducted our audits in accordance with generally accepted auditing standards. Those standards require that we plan and perform the audit to obtain reasonable assurance about whether the financial statements are free of material misstatement due to error or fraud. An audit includes examining, on a test basis, evidence supporting the amounts and disclosures in the financial statements. An audit also includes assessing the accounting principles used and significant estimates made by management, as well as evaluating the overall financial statement presentation. We believe that our audit provides a reasonable basis for our opinion.

In our opinion, the financial statements referred to above present fairly, in all material respects, the consolidated financial position of Company and subsidiaries as of December 31, 20x1, 20x2, and 20x3, and the consolidated results of their operations and their cash flows for each of the three years in the period ended December 31, 20xy, in conformity with generally accepted accounting principles in the United States of America.

Signature

Date

---

29 percent of the alleged fraud cases, and companies had changed auditors before detection of financial statement fraud in about 25 percent of cases.[1]

INDEPENDENT AUDITOR AND FINANCIAL STATEMENT FRAUD

Financial statement fraud has been and continues to be the focus of the auditing profession. During the early 1990s, external auditors viewed the detection of fraud in general, and financial statement fraud in particular, as the primary purpose of their financial audit. The auditing profession had moved from acceptance of fraud detection as a primary purpose to the expression of an opinion on fair presentation of financial statements during the twentieth century. Recently, the accounting profession has directly addressed the external auditor's responsibility for financial statement fraud detection in its Statement on Auditing Standards (SAS) No. 82 entitled Consideration of Fraud in a Financial Statement Audit.[2] SAS No. 82 requires the independent auditor to consider a broad range of fraud

Exhibit 11.2. Corporate Governance and Its Functions

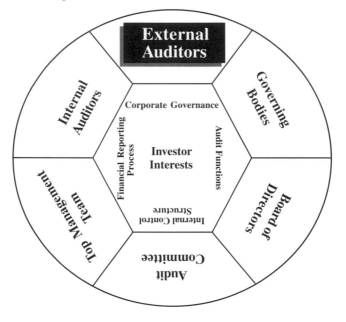

risk factors in assessing the risk of financial statement fraud and to use this assessment in audit planning.

The Auditing Standards Board of the American Institute of Certified Public Accountants (AICPA), by issuing SAS No. 82, attempts to clarify, but not expand, the auditor's responsibility to detect and report financial statement fraud. SAS No. 82 requires auditors to plan and perform the audit to obtain *reasonable assurance* that the financial statements are *free of material misstatement,* whether caused by *fraud or error* (emphasis added). SAS No. 82 makes it clear that the auditor's responsibility for detecting fraud is framed by the concepts of reasonable, but not absolute, assurance and materiality and subject to cost/benefit decisions inherent in the audit process; however, although auditors are not expected to detect all employees' frauds, the general understanding is that a typical financial statement audit should detect material financial statement fraud perpetrated by management to mislead investors and creditors. Independent auditors provide reasonable assurance that financial statements are not materially misstated, meaning that they are free of material errors, irregularities, and fraud. This level of assurance is given in an audit report based on the audit of financial statements.

The external auditor's role in the corporate governance structure, as depicted in Exhibit 11.2, is to provide reasonable assurance regarding the quality, integrity, and reliability of the published, audited financial statements. Thus, it is expected that auditors detect financial statement fraud. In some instances when auditors fail to detect financial statement fraud and it is discovered subsequent to auditors' reports, the effectiveness of financial statement audit is questioned and the usefulness of the audit function is challenged. If audited financial statements are materially misleading and contain material frauds and they are used by investors and creditors for financial decision making, they can lead investors and creditors to allocate their resources uneconomically to unproductive companies. When auditors perform the audit with due diligence by observing generally accepted audit standards (GAAS) and exercising due care, they have fulfilled their professional responsibility.

SAS No. 82 provides guidance on audit procedures to identify and examine related-party transactions, especially when they contain red flags indicating the likelihood of financial statement fraud. For example, when management intentionally fails to disclose material related-party transactions or deliberately records them improperly, there is a higher probability that management also engaged in financial statement fraud. Although red flags do not always indicate financial statement fraud, they are typically a predisposition that is present in many incidents of fraudulent financial reporting activities.

HIGH-QUALITY AUDITS

External auditors lend credibility to the quality and integrity of published financial statements that improves investors' confidence in the financial reporting process and enhances the efficiency of the capital markets. Thus, the effectiveness and quality of financial audits is crucial in producing reliable, relevant, and useful financial statements free of material fraud. In response to the concern regarding the quality of independent auditor's performance, in October 1988, the Public Oversight Board (POB) established the Panel on Audit Effectiveness.[3] For almost two years, the panel studied the way independent audits of financial statements of publicly traded companies are conducted and examined the effects of recent trends (e.g., technological advances, globalization) on the quality of audits. The panel examined a sample of audits of publicly traded companies, gathered empirical data on the quality of auditors' performance, and conducted a survey on audit effectiveness by obtaining insight and input from many who are interested in financial reporting. The panel issued its Exposure Draft in May 2000, had two days of public hearings, and reviewed comments received from individuals who submitted letters of comments or testified during the two days of public hearings. The panel's final report and recommendations was issued on August 31, 2000.

The O'Malley Panel on Audit Effectiveness was established at the request of former chairperson of the SEC, Arthur Levitt, to study the prevailing audit model in 1998.[4] After two years of thorough examination of the way independent audits were performed and assessment of the effects of recent trends in auditing on the public interest, the panel made several recommendations to improve the conduct of audits and governance of the profession. The SEC has expressed its concern for the efficacy of audits because of the increase in financial statement fraud. The O'Malley Panel's investigation was based on the Quasi Peer Review (QPR), including an in-depth review of clients of public accounting firms and surveys of several professional groups. Recommendations of the O'Malley Panel on Audit Effectiveness are summarized into the following five categories of: (1) Conduct of Audit; (2) Leadership and Practices of Audit Firms; (3) Auditor Independence/Nonaudit Services; (4) Governance of the Auditing Profession; and (5) International Perspectives.

Conduct of Audits

The panel concludes that current audit conduct is not ineffective. Although the panel is satisfied that the audit risk model is appropriate, it believes that this risk model should be enhanced, updated, and implemented more consistently. The panel is concerned that the auditing profession has not kept pace with an ever-changing environment and that the profession should address the issue of financial statement fraud resulting mainly from illegitimate earnings management. Thus, the panel made the following recommendations regarding the conduct of audits: (1) audit standards should develop a "forensic-type" fieldwork phase on all audits; (2) auditors should perform some forensic-type audit procedures on every audit to improve the prospects of detecting material financial statement fraud; (3) the Auditing Standards Board (ASB) should make auditing and quality control standards more specific and definitive to promote quality audits; (4) auditing firms should employ comprehensive and rigorous audit methodologies based on the standards to improve the effectiveness of audits and to drive the behavior of their auditors to a higher plane; (5) peer reviews should "close the loop" by reviewing those materials and their implementation on audit engagements, and then reporting their findings to provide assurance to the public that audit performance measures up to high standards and continues to improve; and (6) auditing firms should place more emphasis on the performance of high-quality audits in communications from top management, performance evaluations, training, and compensation and promotion decisions.

Leadership and Practices of Audit Firms

The O'Malley Panel made recommendations to audit firms and calls for actions in four areas of professional leadership, professional development, personnel management, and time pressures on auditors. The panel recommends that (1) audit firms should set "the tone at the top" to reaffirm, within their organizations and to the outside world, the importance of their audit practices and encourage their auditors to maintain objectivity, independence, professional skepticism, and accountability to the public by performing quality audit work; (2) the AICPA should actively and publicly promote the importance of audits; and (3) audit firms should ensure that the performance of high-quality audits is recognized as the highest priority in their professional development activities, performance evaluation, and promotion, retention, and compensation decisions.

Auditor Independence/Nonaudit Services

The O'Malley Panel left the issue of auditor independence and the extent of nonaudit services that can be provided by audit firms to their clients to the SEC and its new audit independence rules; however, the panel recommended that: (1) the Independence Standards Board (ISB) should develop guidance to help auditors, audit committees, and management comply with (a) recent ISB requirements for auditors to disclose independence matters to audit committees, and (b) new SEC disclosure rules for audit committees of public companies; (2) audit firms should identify and assess relevant factors in deciding on whether specific nonaudit services are appropriate for their clients, especially whether the performed nonaudit services facilitate the performance of the audit, improve the client's financial reporting processes, or are otherwise in the public interest; (3) audit committees, in considering appropriate factors, should preapprove significant nonaudit services exceeding threshold levels that they have established; and (4) the SEC and ISB should assess, on a continuous basis, the effectiveness of the disclosures made by public companies under the SEC's new independence rules, and the disclosures made by auditors to audit committees under the ISB's requirements.

Governance of the Auditing Profession

The O'Malley Panel, in recognizing that the auditing profession's system of governance should be unified under a strengthened, independent POB that would oversee the profession's activities with respect to standard setting (other than accounting standards), monitoring, discipline, and special reviews, made the following recommendations pertaining to governance of the auditing profession:

- The POB, AICPA, SECPS, and SEC should cooperate in developing a formal charter for the POB that will strengthen the POB's oversight of the auditing profession and ensure the POB's independence and viability.
- The POB should oversee the ASB, ISB, and the standard-setting activities of the Professional Ethics Executive Committee that relate to audits of public companies.
- Term limits should be implemented for POB members.
- The POB should serve as the body to whom the SEC, state boards of accountancy, the auditing profession, and the public can look for leadership.
- The SECPS should strengthen the peer review process by providing more frequent reviews of the largest firms, increased POB oversight of the reviews, and greater emphasis on the qualitative aspects of the reviews.

- The SEC should mandate a peer review or similar monitoring program subject to the public oversight for all firms that audit SEC registrants, including foreign-based audit firms in their foreign locations.
- The ISB should reconstitute its membership to include four members representing the public and three representing the auditing profession.
- The SEC should respect the POB's authority, as indicated in its new charter, to carry out the profession's self-regulatory activities.
- The SEC should encourage and support the ISB in carrying out its independence mission.

International Perspectives

The panel made several recommendations to the International Federation of Accountants (IFA) pertaining to the global self-regulatory structure of the auditing profession and to audit firms that operate internationally. These recommendations are: (1) the IFA should establish an international self-regulatory system for the international auditing profession that meets certain important criteria, including oversight over standards setting in auditing, quality control, ethics and independence, monitoring, investigation, discipline, and public interest; (2) audit firms should implement uniform audit methodologies worldwide; and (3) a formal collaborative effort should be initiated between the ASB and the International Auditing Practices Committee to harmonize auditing standards and achieve their global acceptance.

In summary, the O'Malley Panel on Audit Effectiveness stated that the most important determinants of audit effectiveness are the personal attributes and skills of the individual auditors that provide structure and definition for their role in society and their involvement in the financial reporting process. The following attributes and skills contribute to a high-quality audit, which, in turn, enhances the prospects of detecting material financial statement fraud: (1) independence in fact and in appearance based on integrity, objectivity, and ethical principles; (2) adherence to ethical and professional standards and a commitment to act objectively and ethically, even in the face of intense pressures; (3) quality professional services to protect the public interest and the investing public; (4) an ability and willingness to use the emerging technological advances; (5) continuous training aimed at providing the auditor with skills necessary to perform high-quality audits; and (6) an ability and willingness to stand up to management or to an audit committee or board of directors if they put pressure on auditors to compromise their professional and ethical standards and their ultimate responsibility to serve the investing public and protect the public interest.

The O'Malley Panel was concerned with the way audits were being performed with respect to the changing environment, including globalization, technological advances, and convergence in industrial sectors. The main recommendation in the area of conduct of audits is the need for auditing standards and methodologies to develop a forensic-type fieldwork phase on all audits to better detect fraud. This phase of the audit should focus on the sheer possibility that dishonest actions by employees or management in overriding of controls, falsification of documents, and alterations of accounts can cause financial statement fraud. Independent auditors should perform surprise substantive testing to expose possible fraudulent activities, examine nonstandard entries that could be a sign of such activities, and investigate opening financial statement balances to determine how certain accounting estimates and judgments were resolved. The panel believes that the performance of forensic-type fieldwork, including surprise substantive audits, should increase the probability of detecting material financial statement fraud and establish implicitly a deterrent to financial statement fraud by posing a greater threat to its successful concealment.

INDEPENDENT AUDIT AND INTERNAL CONTROL

Currently, Statement on Auditing Standards (SAS) No. 78 issued by the Auditing Standards Board (ASB) of the AICPA describes auditors' responsibilities when considering their client organizational internal control structure.[5] SAS No. 78 states that the design and maintenance of an adequate and effective internal control system is the responsibility of management. The auditors' responsibility is to make an assessment of the control risk and its impact on the integrity, reliability, and quality of the audited financial statements. Consideration of the internal control structure is an integrated part of the financial statement audit performed by external auditors. Generally accepted auditing standards (GAAS) state the importance of the internal control structure in the second fieldwork standard:

> A sufficient understanding of the internal control structure is to be obtained to plan the audit and to determine the nature, timing, and extent of tests to be performed (SAS 78, AU319)

Several key elements are included in this audit standard. First, independent auditors are required to obtain only a sufficient understanding of the client's organization internal control structure for a financial statement audit; however, a thorough understanding and assessment of the internal control structure assists external auditors to discover inadequate and ineffective internal control activities that indicate the likelihood of detecting and uncovering financial statement fraud. Thus, to detect financial statement fraud, the auditors' consideration of the internal control structure should go beyond this limited purpose. The second key element is "to plan the audit," which means external auditors should perform a control risk assessment and incorporate into the audit risk model the probability that the internal control structure may fail to prevent and detect financial statement fraud. The third key element is to determine the impact of the internal control risk on the "nature, timing, and extent" of audit test procedures.

Independent auditors' responsibility in a financial audit is to plan and perform the audit to provide reasonable assurance that audited financial statements are free of material misstatements caused by errors or frauds. In effectively fulfilling this responsibility, independent auditors are required to obtain a sufficient understanding of the client's internal control system to properly plan the audit in determining the nature, timing, and extent of audit test procedures. The independent auditor obtains this understanding by studying and reviewing the design and operation of the client's internal control structure. The preliminary review and evaluation of the client's internal control system determines the internal control risk association with management assertions regarding fair presentations of financial statements. If, at this stage, the auditor assesses the control risk at the maximum level, indicating that the prescribed internal control activities are not adequate, no further consideration or test of the client's internal control system is necessary or warranted. If the auditor decides to assess control risk below the maximum level, the tests of controls should be performed to determine the effectiveness of the prescribed control activities. The auditor assesses the internal control risk and its impact on the timing, nature, and extent of substantive tests to gather evidence regarding account balances and classes of transactions.

The only communication requirement of internal controls in conjunction with a financial statement audit is that the independent auditor reports reportable conditions and material weaknesses of internal controls to the company's audit committee or equivalent body. Reportable conditions often represent deficiencies in the design and/or operation of internal controls, which adversely affect the financial reporting process. Material weaknesses in internal controls are reportable conditions that cause the internal control system to fail in preventing, detecting, and correcting material misstatements caused by errors and frauds within a timely period by employees in the normal course of performing their assigned functions. Reports on reportable conditions are restricted to the audit committee, the board of directors, management, and others within the organization. These reports of independent auditors on reportable conditions of the client's internal control system should:

1. Specify that the purpose of the financial statement audit is to express an opinion on fair presentation of financial statements and not to provide assurance on internal controls.
2. Indicate the restriction on distribution of the report for internal managerial purposes.
3. Include the definition of reportable conditions. The reports on reportable conditions may include statements regarding the inherent limitations of internal controls and the nature and extent of auditors' consideration of internal controls.

This type of report on internal controls can be issued only when there are reportable conditions to report. If no reportable conditions are noted by the auditor, then no report on reportable conditions should be issued.

Currently, auditors may review and report on the effectiveness of the client's system of internal controls. The FDICIA requires external auditors to report on management's assertions pertaining to the effectiveness of internal control over financial reporting for banks with $500 million or more in assets.[6] This reporting on the internal control structure is useful and adds value to the integrity and quality of the financial reporting process; however, independent auditors are not required under GAAS to report on the client's internal control system in the course of performing a financial statement audit. Nevertheless, when a company engages an independent auditor to report on its internal control system, the engagement is typically an examination that should meet the following controls:

1. Management accepts full responsibility for the adequacy and effectiveness of its internal control system.
2. Management presents a written assertion about the adequacy and effectiveness of its internal controls.
3. Sufficient evidence exists to support management's evaluation of internal controls.
4. Management's assertion about internal controls is presented in a separate report to accompany the auditor's report.

Examination of internal controls must be performed in accordance with attestation standards included in the Statements on Standards for the Attestation Engagement (SSAE), which require an attestation engagement to be performed only if the management assertion is both capable of evaluation against established or clearly stated criteria. Thus, the company's management must provide auditors with a written assertion because the purpose of the engagement is for the auditor to provide assurance on management's assertion. The independent auditor may issue an unrestricted report on the client's system of internal controls when the related management assertion is clear and it is presented in a specific report by management to accompany the independent auditor's report. Examination of management assertions about the effectiveness of client's internal controls involves:

1. Planning the examination engagement
2. Obtaining sufficient understanding of the internal control system
3. Performing audit procedures on intended internal control activities
4. Assessing the adequacy and effectiveness of internal control activities
5. Expressing an opinion regarding the fair presentation of management's assertion about the effectiveness of internal controls

The audit procedures performed to assess the effectiveness of control activities are inquiries, document examination, observation, and detailed tests of controls. The independent auditor may express unqualified opinions about management's assertion on internal controls when gathered evidence supports management's

Exhibit 11.3.   Independent Accountant's Public Report on Internal Control

---

Addressee

We have examined management's assertion concerning maintenance of effective internal control over financial reporting of NZR Inc. as of December 31, 20x2, included in the accompanying management report. Management is primarily responsible for maintaining effective internal control over financial reporting, based on stated criteria. Our responsibility is to express an opinion on the effectiveness of internal control based on our examination of management assertion.

Our examination was conducted in accordance with attestation standards established by the American Institute of Certified Public Accountants and, accordingly, included obtaining an understanding of internal control over financial reporting, testing, and evaluating the design and operating effectiveness of internal control, and performing such other procedures as we considered necessary in the circumstances. We believe that our examination provides a reasonable basis for our opinion.

Because of inherent limitations in any internal control, misstatements due to error or fraud may occur and not be detected. Also, projections of any evaluation of internal control over financial reporting to future periods are subject to the risk that internal control may become inadequate because of changes in conditions, or that the degree of compliance with the policies or procedures may deteriorate.

In our opinion, management's assertions that NZR Inc. maintained, in all material respects, effective internal control over financial reporting as of December 31, 20xx, based on (identify established criteria) is fairly stated.

Signature

Date

---

assertion. If the auditor finds a material weakness or audit evidence does not support management's assertion, then either a qualified opinion or disclaimer of an opinion may be appropriate. Exhibit 11.3 presents an example of an independent auditor's formal report on internal controls.

In summary, there is currently no requirement that publicly traded companies provide management and auditors' reports on internal controls. The AICPA and the POB have recommended that the SEC require management and auditors of publicly traded companies to report on the company's internal control system to financial reporting; however, the SEC has not yet taken any action based on these recommendations because of the lack of support for such requirements by companies and/or the investing public. The requirement of such a report will probably improve the reporting company's internal control system in presenting, detecting, and correcting financial statement fraud.

External auditors are required to study and evaluate their clients' system of internal controls as part of the audit of financial statements. Existing GAAS require only a limited assessment of the internal control structure necessary to plan the audit included in determining the nature, timing, and extent of substantive test procedures. External auditors, in complying with their professional standards, typically focus on the results of the financial reporting process and place less emphasis on the process itself. Thus, external auditors often do not assess their clients' internal control structure and the financial reporting process that produces financial statements. Nevertheless, an expectation gap exists between the investing public's perceptions of external auditors' involvement with the internal control structure and the extent of auditors' assessment of internal controls in accordance with their professional standards. It appears that market participants place more value on the integrity and quality of the financial reporting process than on the end results of such a process, namely the financial statements. Thus, the adequacy and effectiveness of the internal control structure in preventing, detecting, and correcting errors, irregularities, and fraud are important factors in producing reliable, useful, and relevant financial information. To narrow this perceived expectation gap, external auditors could more thoroughly assess the adequacy and effectiveness of internal controls during the normal audit of financial statements. To achieve this purpose, the AICPA and the auditing profession, especially the Big Five professional services firms, advocate a formal report on internal controls by external auditors.

A former chair of the ASB of the AICPA and a retired partner of Arthur Andersen, LLP, David Landsittel (2000) suggests that external auditors' reports on internal controls should:

1. Make the auditors' role in control evaluation unmistakable to investors. The objectives and extent of auditor involvement would be explicitly defined and disclosed in the auditor's report on internal controls.
2. Add credibility to management reporting on internal controls.
3. Provide more opportunities for auditors to make recommendations and work with management to improve internal controls.
4. Assist audit committees in overseeing the adequacy of internal controls.
5. Facilitate a transition to a new reporting model (i.e., online, real-time accounting system and related continuous electronic auditing).[7]

FRAUD DETECTION AUDIT PROCEDURES

The history of the accounting profession reveals that before the Industrial Revolution and the establishment of the SEC Acts of 1933 and 1934, the primary purpose of financial statement audit was to detect clerical errors, irregularities, and fraud. Thus, traditionally, independent auditors have used fraud detection audit procedures. Since the early 1930s, the primary purpose of financial statement audit has shifted to focus on fair presentation of financial statements. External auditors did not perform much fraud detection audit procedures. Before the issuance of SAS No. 82,[8] external auditors did not perform fraud-detecting procedures as part of normal procedures for every audit unless they were made aware of the possibility of fraudulent financial reporting activities. Ironically, the word *fraud* did not appear in professional audit standards; instead, the words *errors and irregularities* had been used. SAS No. 82, for the first time, addresses independent auditors' consideration of fraud in audit planning but stops short of requiring independent auditors to perform fraud-detecting audit procedures as an integral part of every audit. Most recently, the Panel on Audit Effectiveness suggests integration of a forensic-type fieldwork phase audit into the normal financial statement audit.[9]

A broad variety of audit procedures can be used to detect financial statement fraud. SAS No. 82 provides guidance regarding the auditor's response to the results of risk assessment by making judgments about the risk of material financial statement fraud. This risk assessment affects the audit in the following ways:

Professional Skepticism

Due professional care requires external auditors to exercise professional skepticism, which is an attitude that includes a questioning mind and a critical assessment of auditor evidence. Examples of the application of professional skepticism in assessing the risk of material financial statement fraud are (1) increased sensitivity and due professional care in the selection of the nature, timing, and extent of audit procedures in gathering sufficient and competent audit evidence to substantiate material transactions and account balances; and (2) increased recognition of the need to corroborate management assertions and representations regarding material financial items and matters by performing thorough analytical procedures, examination of documents, and discussion with others within and/or outside the client's company.

Assignment of Personnel

The results of risk assessment may indicate the possibility of financial statement fraud, necessitating assignment of knowledgeable, skilled, and well-trained auditors to ensure detection of fraud. Furthermore, the quality and extent of supervision should recognize the risk of material misstatement caused by financial statement fraud and the qualifications of auditors performing supervision.

Accounting Principles, Policies, and Practices

The possibility of financial statement fraud requires auditors to pay special attention to management's selection and application of significant accounting policies regarding revenue recognition, asset valuation, or capitalization versus expensing major expenditures. The 1999 COSO Report indicates that more than half of the SEC enforcement actions regarding financial statement fraud relate to improper revenue recognition.[10] Thus, auditors should satisfy themselves that the selected accounting principles are appropriate and applied accounting policies are consistent and acceptable.

Internal Controls

When the results of risk assessment indicate the likelihood of financial statement fraud, auditors should ensure that the internal control system is adequate and effective in preventing, detecting, and correcting such fraud. When the internal control risk is considered to be high, indicating the failure of internal controls to prevent and detect risk, auditors should merely rely on their own test procedures to detect financial statement fraud. The degree of internal control risk would determine the extent, timing, and nature of audit procedures performed to discover financial statement fraud.

Effect of Fraud Risk Factors on Audit Procedures

The extent, timing, and nature of audit procedures should be modified when the risk factors indicate the likelihood of financial statement fraud. First, the nature of audit procedures needs to be changed to obtain audit evidence that is more reliable, relevant, and pervasive, and gathered from independent sources outside the company. Second, the timing of audit procedures may need to be changed to be closer to or at year-end. When there are motivations and opportunities for management to engage in financial statement fraud, auditors should perform their audit procedures near or at the end of the reporting period to detect misstatements and assess their impacts on the integrity, quality, and reliability of financial statements. Third, the extent of audit procedures applied should also reflect the assessment of the likelihood of financial statement fraud. Auditors should enlarge the sample size to factor in the additional risk and to ensure that the selected sample will discover suspected financial statement fraud. The audit should be planned with specific attention focused on these areas in which the likelihood of fraud occurrence is higher, particularly in the areas of revenue recognition, accounts receivable, inventories, liabilities, and fixed assets. Thus, auditors should gather persuasive evidence to determine whether material financial statement fraud has occurred or is likely to have occurred, and, if so, its impact on fair presentation of financial statements and the auditors' report should be determined.

Auditors are required to plan and perform an audit to provide reasonable assurance that the financial statements are free of material misstatements caused by errors and frauds. Material misstatements often include overstatements of revenues and assets and understatements of expenses and liabilities. Although management is more prone to overstate revenues and understate expenses to meet analysts' earnings forecasts, auditors should pay attention to both understatements and over-statements of revenues, expenses, assets, and liabilities. Any misstatements of financial transactions or account balances will cause financial statement fraud.

SAS No. 82[11] identifies specific approaches that may be used when it is likely that financial statement fraud has occurred. The suggested audit approaches, among others, include (1) performing certain audit procedures (e.g., analytical procedures, substantive tests); (2) changing audit approach in the current year; (3) counting inventories at a date closer to year-end; (4) investigating the possibility of related-party transactions; (5) performing a thorough review of quarter-end and/or year-end closing entries and further investigation of any unusual closing transaction entries; (6) conducting detailed interviews of personnel involved in areas indicating the likelihood of financial statement fraud; and (7) using the work of specialists when expertise in understanding and detecting the nature and amounts of financial statement fraud is needed.

AUDIT FAILURES

By virtue of expressing an opinion on fair presentations of published financial statements, auditors lend more credibility to financial information and perceivably reduce the information risk that may be associated with financial statements. Information risk is the probability that published financial statements are inaccurate, false, misleading, biased, and incomplete. Any reduction in information risk makes the capital market more efficient, which contributes to more investment and economic growth for the nation. Richard H. Walker, the SEC's Director of Enforcement, in the SEC's "News Item regarding Arthur Andersen consents to Antifraud Injunction" states, "Accountants play a critical role in providing access to our capital markets. We will not shy away form pursuing accountants and accounting firms when they fail to live up to their responsibilities to ensure the integrity of financial reporting process."[12]

Audit failure is defined as independent auditors' lack of due diligence in conducting an audit in accordance with GAAS which has resulted in a faulty performance of not discovering material misstatements in the audited financial statements. The SEC is concerned about the frequency and magnitude of audit failures. Richard Walker, the SEC's director of enforcement, in a speech to the AICPA in Washington in December 1999, stated that "the agency continues to see an unacceptably higher number of busted audits."[13] The SEC continues to bring more enforcement cases against "weak-kneed auditors who (1) do not comply with GAAS in conducting financial audits; (2) do not stand up to pressure from their clients' management by participating in the gamesmanship practice of earnings management; and (3) knowingly and recklessly issue materially false, inappropriate, and misleading audit reports.

The extent and magnitude of audit failures have raised many concerns regarding the effectiveness and efficiency of audits conducted by public accounting firms. The investing community and regulators have often asked the question of "Where were the auditors?" when high-profile companies such as Enron and Sunbeam filed for

Chapter 11 bankruptcy protection resulted from the commission of financial statement fraud. Audit failures have eroded public and investor confidence in integrity and reliability of published audited financial statements. Andersen, one of the Big Five professional service firms, has been associated with the three recent, high-profile alleged financial statement fraud cases of Sunbeam, Waste Management, and Enron Corp. Sunbeam wound up in bankruptcy court and Andersen agreed to pay $110 million to Sunbeam shareholders. Waste Management was sold and Andersen agreed to (1) shoulder part of a $220 million Waste Management settlement; (2) accept, without admitting or denying responsibility, an antifraud injunction from the SEC and a $7 million fine. Enron Corporation filed for Chapter 11 bankruptcy reorganization in December 2001 and Andersen has become the target of a flurry of class action lawsuits and scrutiny by the SEC. The auditing profession, however, asserts that the number of failed audits is insignificant in relation to a great number of diligent audits. Stephen G. Butler, chief executive of KPMG, stated that "I think the fundamental question is: Will you ever get to the point where there are not audit failures? In my view, you won't, just as you won't get to a point where there are no airplane crashes or no automobile crashes, no matter what the safety design or procedures.[14]

IMPROVING AUDIT EFFECTIVENESS

To reduce the cost of audits, auditors may unjustifiably rely on management representatives to document audit procedures when no competent and sufficient evidence is available to validate management's assertions. Unjustifiable reliance on management's assertions increases the likelihood of audit failure to detect material misstatements in the financial statements caused by errors and frauds. Society is holding auditors accountable and responsible for detecting intentional material misstatements of earnings and other fraudulent financial activities. In rendering an opinion on the fairness of financial statements, auditors should be skeptical and alert to conditions, events, and transactions that could indicate errors, irregularities, and fraud; however, auditors provide only reasonable assurance that financial statements are free from material errors, irregularities, and fraud. Nevertheless, investors—both individuals and institutional—often have high expectations regarding the accuracy of audited financial statements.

Investors, creditors, and other users of audited financial statements may lack a full understanding of the inherent limitations of an audit (e.g., the use of sampling, time and cost considerations) under the existing GAAS: Thus, investors, creditors, and other users may presume that an audit will detect all instances of fraud. To narrow this perceived expectation gap, the users of audited financial statements should be further educated regarding the audit objectives and how they are affected by audit methodology because of time constraints and cost limitations. To continuously improve the effectiveness of audits in detecting financial statement fraud, external auditors should consider the recommendations presented in the following sections.

Forensic Field Audit

External auditors are in the best position to detect financial statement fraud and prevent further occurrence of the same fraud. The O'Malley Panel on Audit Effectiveness[15] recommends that external auditors use forensic-type fieldwork audit procedures by using a high level of professional skepticism throughout the audit process and paying special attention to fraud symptoms and red flags that may signal financial statement fraud. Auditors should use forensic-type fieldwork audit procedures and continuous transaction testing in areas particularly susceptible to fraud. In compliance with current GAAS, auditors should employ the audit risk model, which encourages auditors to use judgment in assessing audit risk and in selecting risk-based audit procedures based on the individual client company's nature, condition, and circumstances. This risk-based audit approach of continuous testing of high-risk areas can contribute to efficiency and effectiveness of the audit in detecting financial statement fraud.

To protect investors and creditors and safeguard them from receiving fraudulent and misleading financial information, auditors should ensure that their audit strategy is appropriate in the circumstance; assess and document the client's internal control environment, including management's philosophy and operating style; and conduct appropriate audit procedures in gathering sufficient and competent evidence on the substance rather than the form of the client's policies and procedures. The use of a risk-based audit approach requires auditors to become familiar with their client's business, industry, and operating strategies; however, auditors' close involvement in the daily operation activities and management functions of the client can potentially cause their independence to be questioned or even impaired. For example, the auditor's involvement and direct participation in determining earnings forecasts for the client may create the appearance that the auditor is verifying the accuracy or achievability of the earnings forecast that, in turn, may diminish the auditor's objectivity and independence.

Communication of External Auditors with Audit Committees

Statement on Auditing Standards (SAS) No. 61[16] requires external auditors to inform the audit committee about the scope and results of the independent audit of financial statements. Independent auditors are required to make oral or written communication with the audit committee, or the board of directors in the absence of the audit committee, regarding (1) disagreement with management on significant accounting and auditing matters; (2) significant audit adjustments; (3) accounting estimates; (4) effect of controversial and aggressive accounting policies; (5) accounting for material and unusual transaction; (6) selection or changes in significant accounting policies and their applications; (7) reportable conditions of the internal control system; (8) material misstatements in the financial statements caused by errors or fraud; (9) consultation by management with other accountants; (10) major issues discussed with management before being retained; and (11) difficulties encountered in performing the audit.

The ASB of the AICPA amended SAS No. 61 with two new SAS numbers: 89 and 90.[17,18] SAS No. 89 requires external auditors to communicate to the audit committee suggested by uncorrected misstatements whose effects management believes immaterial. SAS No. 90 requires auditors to discuss with the audit committees their judgment about the quality, not just the acceptability, of the entity's accounting principles and the estimates underlying the financial statements; and certain matters identified in their quarterly review of interim financial information before it is filed with the SEC.

The AICPA (2000)[19] Practice Alert 200-2 requires external auditors to discuss with the audit committee the *quality,* not just the acceptability, of the accounting principles used by the client's entity. This quality discussion with both management and the audit committee should be candid and probing, and should encompass the following: (1) consistency of the company's accounting policies, practices, and their application; (2) consistency, clarity, and completeness of the financial statements and related disclosures; (3) frequency and significance of all transactions with the related parties; (4) financial transactions, events, and items having a significant effect on the representational faithfulness, verifiability, and neutrality of the accounting information; (5) materiality thresholds and whether such thresholds have been consistently applied; (6) audit adjustments identified by auditors, whether or not corrected by management; and (7) consideration of factors affecting revenues and expenses recognition and assets and liabilities valuations.

Auditor's Independence

The performance of substantial attestation services other than financial audit (e.g., nonaudit services) may create a conflict of interest, and users may question the independence of auditors, particularly when the fees for such services significantly exceed the client's audit fees. External auditors must ensure that the availability and performance of nonaudit services does not impair their independence and objectivity for financial statement audits. The SEC has paid a great deal of attention to auditor independence as part of its proactive initiatives to improve the quality of financial reports. The SEC Practice Section of the AICPA, in October 1999, advised member firms to enhance their independence quality control systems by (1) including independence training for all professionals; (2) maintaining a database of clients and other companies from which professionals must be independent; and (3) following due diligence procedures by all professionals before acquiring securities and reporting both apparent rule violations and related corrective action. The SEC has continued monitoring auditors' compliance with independence rules. The ISB[20] commissioned research to gather opinions and insights from several professionals, including CEOs, CFOs, audit committee chairs, auditors, and investment analysts, regarding the issue of how well auditor independence is currently maintained and how best to ensure independence in the firms. The research concludes that overall, auditors currently do not have a problem maintaining independence in fact, but that pressures on objectivity and independence are growing.

ISB Standard No. 1[21] requires the external auditor to discuss with the audit committee relationships between the publicly traded company and the auditor that may reasonably be thought to bear on auditor independence. Auditors should disclose such relationships in writing annually and have a meeting with the audit committee to discuss their impact on auditor independence. This disclosure should foster discussion between the auditor and audit committee and should not be construed by audit committees to imply that auditor independence has already been impaired. An example of the relationship is the extent of a nonaudit service provided to the client's company. Audit committees may question whether the volume of nonaudit services (e.g., technology consulting, internal audit services) provided by the auditor has a bearing on auditor independence.

Efficacy Audit

The SEC expressed concerns about several matters affecting the integrity and quality of financial reporting of publicly traded companies, including aggressive earnings management. Another important issue that has received tremendous attention is auditors' ability to resist overly aggressive earnings management and to discover intentional efforts by management to mislead investors. In October 1998, in response to SEC chair Arthur Levitt's request, the Public Oversight Board, the independent private sector that oversees self-regulatory programs of the SEC Practice Section (SECPS) of the AICPA appointed a Panel on Audit Effectiveness.[22] The panel was charged to examine the way independent audits were performed and to determine the effects on the public interest of recent trends in auditing. For almost two years, the panel examined (1) the adequacy of auditors' professional development; (2) how audits are planned, staffed, and supervised; (3) the appropriateness, competency, and sufficiency of audit documentation; (4) whether firms' quality control systems encompass the necessary elements and related policies and procedures; (5) the overall "tone at the top" and performance measures used by firms in evaluating audit personnel; (6) the need for possible changes in professional standards and the profession's self-regulatory process; (7) users' expectations about auditors' responsibilities and the relationship between audit and nonaudit services; and (8) auditors' responsibilities for detecting financial statement fraud. The panel issued its final report on August 31, 2000, containing its findings and recommendations for professional services firms, the AICPA, SEC, audit committees, management, or other constituencies to improve the quality of financial reporting.

Report on Interim Financial Statements

To enhance the quality and relevancy of the published financial reports and to provide timely and useful financial information to investors and creditors, auditors should report on fair presentation of interim financial statements rather than review of interim financial statements. Reporting on interim financial statements would provide support for the annual financial statements and meet the timely needs of users of financial reports. Effective for quarterly periods ending on or after March 15, 2000, the SEC is requiring timely reviews of interim financial information by independent auditors. Independent auditors should communicate to audit committees matters applicable to interim financial information before filing Form 10-Q or Form 10-QSB.

More Auditors' Involvement

Auditors should get more involved in reviewing and verifying financial information in management discussion and analysis (MD&A) and ensure that MD&A analyses reconcile with financial statements. Auditors should also compare MD&A disclosure to SEC requirements. External auditors' review and report on MD&A is another expanded area of attestation services for external auditors that can improve the quality of financial reports.

Communication with the Board of Directors

Open and candid communication between external auditors and the board of directors and its representative audit committee can improve the quality of financial reports by focusing on the areas that may indicate potential fraudulent financial activities. The audit committee's involvement with the audit process by overseeing the audit strategy can promote the effectiveness of audits. The audit committee should oversee and review the audit plan and scope of audit functions to ensure that the external auditor is independent, competent, and knowledgeable about the client business and industry; however, the extent of the working relationship between the external auditors and the board of directors and the audit committee should not adversely affect the auditors' objectivity and independence. External auditors should avoid any appearance of conflict of interest with their clients and should be careful not to become business partners.

Fraud Auditing

Statement on Auditing Standards (SAS) No. 82, entitled Consideration of Fraud in a Financial Statement Audit, was issued in February 1997 by the Auditing Standards Board (ASB) of the AICPA.[23] Although SAS No. 82 did not increase an independent auditor's responsibility for detecting fraud, it provided guidelines on how the auditor should respond when an assessment indicates a heightened risk of material misstatements of the financial statements because of fraud. SAS No. 82 (1) describes the process of conducting the risk assessment; (2) includes a comprehensive listing of risk factors that an auditor should consider in the risk assessment; (3) provides specific guidance in responding to the results of the risk assessment and documentation of the auditor's risk assessment and response; and (4) offers guidelines in evaluating the results of an audit test and communicating evidence of fraud to management, the audit committee, or others (e.g., SEC, regulatory bodies) as appropriate.

Fraud Risk Factors

SAS No. 82 identifies categories of risk factors (red flags) mostly related to financial statement fraud and two classes of red flags pertaining to misappropriation of assets. Financial statement fraud red flag categories are those associated with (1) management's characteristics and influence over the control environment; (2) industry conditions; and (3) operating characteristics and financial stability. Red flags pertaining to misappropriation of assets are (1) susceptibility of assets to misappropriation; and (2) controls. SAS No. 82 identifies more than 50 risk factors (red flags) related to financial statement fraud and misappropriation of assets. Auditors are required to document the existence of these risk factors and audit considerations and responses to those risk factors either individually or collectively.

SAS No. 82 requires external auditors to consider risk factors as red flags, warning signals, or symptoms that fraud may exist. The following risk factors individually or collectively may be symptoms of possible financial statement fraud: (1) substantial related-party transactions outside the ordinary course of business or with unaudited entities; (2) material, unusual, or highly complex transactions, especially those close to the end of a reporting period; (3) substantial operations or bank accounts in tax havens for which there is no legitimate business justification; and (4) an organizational structure with a huge degree of complexity that is not warranted.

Effective Communication Between Predecessor and Successor Auditors

In compliance with Statement on Auditing Standards (SAS) No. 84,[24] the successor auditor should communicate with the predecessor auditor to obtain information regarding (1) management's attitude toward financial statements; (2) management's operating style and integrity; (3) any disputes or disagreements concerning accounting principles and auditing procedures; (4) the predecessor's communications with the client about internal controls, financial statement fraud, and illegal acts; and (5) reasons for the change of auditors.

CURRENT DEVELOPMENTS IN PUBLIC ACCOUNTING

Professional services firms, including certified public accountants (CPAs), are trusted by society and the business community to provide reasonable assurance regarding the fairness, integrity, and quality of published financial statements. Nevertheless, competitive pressures, conflicts of interest, ineffectiveness in audit functions, many alleged audit failures and frauds, and imperfect self-regulatory disciplines in public accounting firms have raised serious concerns regarding the perceived lack of confidence and trust in the integrity, objectivity, and quality of financial statement audits. In response to these and other concerns, the AICPA and the SEC have taken initiatives to address these issues. These initiatives are taken to (1) improve the effectiveness of audits; (2) enhance the objectivity and integrity of the audit function; and (3) promote forensic-type audit plans to prevent and detect financial statement fraud.

1. The POB of the AICPA in October 1998 at the request of former SEC chairperson Arthur Levitt appointed the Panel on Audit Effectiveness, better known as O'Malley.[25] For almost two years, the O'Malley Panel performed a comprehensive review and assessment of the independent audits and conducted and evaluated the effects of recent trends in auditing on the public interest. The O'Malley Panel made several recommendations to enhance audit effectiveness that in turn should (1) improve the reliability and credibility of financial statements; (2) reduce incidents and probability of financial statement fraud; (3) promote investors' confidence in the accounting profession; and (4) improve the efficiency of the capital market.

2. The SEC, in response to concerns regarding the lack of proper objectivity and integrity of audit functions issued a new rule on auditors' independence. The new rules are intended to (1) reduce the number of audit firm employees and their family members whose investments in audit clients are attributed to the auditor; (2) identify and limit certain nonaudit services that if provided in conjunction with financial statement audits may impair the auditor's independence; (3) require publicly traded companies to disclose in their annual proxy statements, among other things, certain information related to nonaudit services provided by their auditor; and (4) provide investors and capital market participants with greater confidence and trust in the quality, integrity, and objectivity of audited financial statements.

3. Recently, the AICPA has issued two new statements on auditing standards (SASs): No. 89[26] on Audit Adjustment and No. 90[27] on Audit Committee Communications. SAS No. 90 requires that external auditors discuss with the audit committee the quality, not just the acceptability, of the accounting practices, including principles, standards, and methods, used by management in the presentation of financial statements. This quality discussion with both management and their audit committee should address (1) consistency of the company's accounting practices and their application; (2) fairness, clarity, completeness, and consistency of the financial statements and related disclosures; and (3) items having a significant effect on the neutrality, reliability, representational faithfulness, and verifiability of financial information.

4. Professional services firms have undergone substantial changes during the past two decades: (1) In 1999, the top seven professional services firms billed their clients nearly $9.5 billion for audit fees; (2) these top seven CPA firms audited more than 80 percent of all registrants; (3) audit fees of these large accounting firms as a percentage of their total revenue has decreased considerably from 70 percent of total revenues in 1976 to 34 percent of total revenue in 1998; (4) management advisory services of large CPA firms represented

about 15 percent of total revenue in 1981 compared to more than 50 percent of total revenue in 2000; and (5) professional services firms have significantly increased the scope of their attestation, nonattestation, and assurance services ranging from outsourcing almost all managerial functions to quality control certification and asset management. The public accounting profession has moved away from auditing firms to professional services firms providing one-stop shopping for a broad range of financial services. The trend has recently substantially changed as a result of the SEC initiatives and new rules on auditors' independence.

5. Market participants, by virtue of relying on and looking to auditors' reports for obtaining quality financial information, expect that auditors are independent, objective, and impartial with regard to their clients, investing community, and the public. As an independent contractor who audits financial statements and provides reasonable assurance regarding fair presentation of financial statements, the external auditor is expected to be independent, both in fact and appearance, from the management team that prepares financial statements. When auditors bill their clients a substantial amount for nonaudit services, it is then possible that the public may not have the necessary confidence in the role of auditors as independent contractors. The new auditors' independence rule addresses these issues.

6. Professional skepticism is an attitude that presumes the possibility of dishonesty at various levels of management, including gamesmanship, collusion, overriding internal controls, alteration of record, illegitimate earnings management, falsification of documents, and omission of material disclosures. Thus, the proper exercise of professional skepticism by external auditors can play a crucial role in detecting financial statement fraud. The "neutral" concept of professional skepticism is often cited as a significant contributory factor to auditors' failure to detect financial statement fraud (e.g., the COSO Report, 1999).[28] Sufficient professional skepticism should be exercised in every audit engagement and throughout the audit process. The use of the neutral concept of professional skepticism, which indicates that the auditor should neither assume that management is dishonest nor assure unquestioned honesty, does not help auditors detect financial statement fraud.

To successfully detect financial statement fraud, auditors would exercise adequate professional skepticism of presuming the possibility of management dishonesty. This does not imply that auditors distrust management. It simply means auditors should be alert to the possibility of financial statement fraud and should not be satisfied with less than persuasive, competent, and sufficient evidence because of a belief that management is honest. Thus, auditors should ensure that financial statement audits are conducted with an adequate attitude of skepticism of following up on any potential material warning signals, symptoms, and red flags indicating the likelihood of financial statement fraud.

MATERIALITY GUIDANCE

Auditors often have to use their judgment to decide whether an error or misstatement is material enough to influence the decision-making process of investors and creditors. In fact, an auditor's opinion is formed based on the concepts of materiality and audit risk. Auditors, in their audit reports, state whether financial statements fairly present, *in all material respects,* the financial position, results of operations, and cash flows in conformity with GAAP. Thus, sound materiality judgments are important contributory factors in maintaining investor and creditor confidence in the financial reporting process. In making material judgments, auditors consider both qualitative factors (e.g., nature of an item, circumstances) and quantitative factors (e.g., absolute size, relative size, cumulative effects).

Materiality is defined in Statement of Financial Accounting Concept No. 2 as:

> The magnitude of an omission or misstatement of accounting information that, in the light of surrounding circumstances, makes it probable that the judgment of a reasonable person relying on the information would have been changed or influenced by the omission or misstatement.[29]

Audit risk is defined as the risk of issuing an inappropriate audit opinion (e.g., the risk of issuing an unqualified opinion on *materially* misstated financial statements or the risk of issuing an opinion other than unqualified on *materially* stated financial statements). Thus, audit risk is defined in the context of materiality. Auditors use materiality judgments in all stages of an audit process from the planning phase of the audit to the final reporting stage. Auditing standards require auditors to use both qualitative and quantitative factors in assessing materiality. Qualitative factors often used by auditors in making materiality judgments are as follows:

1. Possible impact of misstatement on projected earnings
2. Likelihood of earnings management
3. Existence of restrictive debt covenants
4. Possible impact of misstatement on share price
5. Likelihood of financial statement fraud
6. Potential business combinations (e.g., mergers, acquisitions)
7. Imminent public stock offering
8. Detection of fraud or fraud symptoms in prior periods
9. Risk of litigation
10. Inadequate and ineffective internal control structure
11. Nonexistence of ineffective audit committee
12. Lack of vigilant board of directors

Examples of quantitative factors are absolute size of misstatements, cumulative size, and the amount of misstatements as a percentage of total assets or net income. Auditors, in assessing materiality, should pay special attention to the sensitivity of the capital markets to price-earnings multiples, especially when even a penny-a-share difference between the reported earnings and analysts' forecasted earnings is likely to trigger an investor response that could adversely affect market capitalization by millions of dollars. To assist auditors in making appropriate materiality judgments, the SEC, in its Staff Accounting Bulletin (SAB) No. 99, discusses quantitative factors to consider in assessing materiality and encouraging registrants to record proposed audit adjustments.

RISK FACTORS OF FINANCIAL STATEMENT FRAUD

SAS No. 82[30] states that risk factors that relate to financial statement fraud can be grouped into three categories: (1) management's characteristics and influence over the control environment; (2) industry conditions; and (3) operating characteristics and financial stability.

Risk Factors Pertaining to Management's Characteristics

Risk factors pertaining to management's characteristics and influence over the control environment are aimed at identifying pressure or an incentive to engage in financial statement fraud and perceived opportunity to commit such fraud. The risk factors involving management's motivations to engage in financial statement fraud are the following:

- A considerable portion of management's compensation, represented by bonuses, stock options, or other incentives that pressure management to achieve unduly aggressive targets for operating results, financial position, or cash flow
- Commitments to analysts or creditors of unduly aggressive or unrealistic forecasts
- Undue pressure on management and/or interest by management in maintaining or increasing the company's stock price or earnings trend through the use of unusually aggressive accounting practices (e.g., earnings management)
- The use of inappropriate means to minimize earnings for tax-motivated purposes
- Domination of management by a single person or small group without effective monitoring oversight by the board of directors and/or the audit committe
- Ineffective communication and support of entity values and ethics
- Management failure to correct known reportable conditions
- Management disregard for regulatory authorities
- Management setting unduly aggressive financial targets and expectations for operating personnel
- High turnover of senior management, counsel, or board members

- Management continuing to employ ineffective and incompetent accounting, information technology, or internal audit staff
- Unreasonable demands for auditor completion of the audit or report issuance
- Formal or informal restrictions on auditor access to people or information
- Domineering management behavior or attempts to influence audit scope
- Known history of securities law violations or fraud or allegations of financial statement fraud

Risk Factors Relating to Industry Conditions

Risk factors relating to industry conditions, such as a high degree of competition or market saturation, accompanied by declining margins and unduly aggressive performance measures, can pressure management to improve operating results, financial position, and cash flows. Examples of these risk factors, specified in SAS No. 82, are (1) new accounting, statutory, or regulatory requirements that could impair profitability or financial stability; and (2) extensive market competition or saturation, accompanied by declining margins.

Risk Factors Related to Operating Characteristics and Financial Stability

Factors relating to operating characteristics and financial stability such as unrealistically aggressive sales or profitability incentive programs can pressure management and personnel to engage in fraudulent financial activities. Examples of these factors are (1) an inability to generate operating cash while reporting earnings growth; (2) significant, unusual, or highly complex transactions, especially near year-end, that pose "substance over form" questions; (3) bank accounts or operations in tax-haven locations without clear business purpose; (4) unusually rapid growth or profitability compared to others in the industry; (5) a threat of imminent bankruptcy or hostile takeover; and (6) a poor or worsening financial position when management has personally guaranteed significant entity debt. SAS No. 82 requires a specific fraud risk assessment in every audit engagement, including inquiries of management regarding areas of potential fraud risk and how management is managing these risks or intends to address such risks.

Documentation of Risk Factors

Financial statement fraud is a sensitive issue that requires effective and proper documentation at every stage of the audit process. In planning stages of the audit, auditors should manually or electronically document in the working papers evidence of the performance of the assessment of the risk factors pertaining to financial statement fraud, as well as how fraud risk factors are addressed by auditors and auditors' responses to those risk factors. During the performance of the audit, if the auditor identifies any risk factors or other condition that lead to reassessing fraud risk, the auditor should make the proper documentation describing the auditor's response to those risk factors. SAS No. 82 gives flexibility to auditors in deciding the proper documentation of identified risk factors, auditors' responses to the risk factors, actions taken by auditors, and communication issues related to fraud. Auditors may include the underlying rationale behind the selected risk factors and/or an explanation of the auditor's assessed level of fraud risk and any fraud-related inquiries.

COMMUNICATION OF FRAUD

Once the auditor has discovered a fraud, or a possible fraud, then all evidence regarding the fraud should be reviewed and verified, and the legal counsel should be contacted if it deems necessary; however, the communication should be limited to those who have the need to know. Such communication may involve senior management, the audit committee, the board of directors, and when appropriate, others outside the client's organization. Top-level management is typically involved in financial statement fraud. In this case, the auditor should report the discovered financial statement fraud directly to the audit committee and, in its absence, to the board of directors. If the auditor determines identified fraud risk factors having continuing internal control implications, the auditor should consider these risk factors for inclusion in the required communication of reportable conditions to senior management and the audit committee.

The disclosure of financial statement fraud to parties outside of the client's organization is ordinarily precluded and prevented by the auditor's ethical and legal obligations of conditionality, unless the matter is reflected in the auditor's report; however, the auditor should recognize that, in the case of financial statement fraud, and in the following circumstances, a duty to disclose fraud outside the entity may exist: (1) to comply with certain legal and regulatory requirements; (2) to a successor auditor when the successor auditor makes inquiries in accordance with SAS No. 84, entitled Communications Between Predecessor and Successor Auditors[31]; (3) in response to a subpoena in light of the concept that gathered audit evidence is not privileged and, thus, cannot be withheld from a court of law (e.g., AICPA trial board, SEC lawsuit cases); and (4) to a funding agency or other specified agency in accordance with requirements for the audits of entities that relieve governmental financial assistance.

The Private Securities Litigation Reform Act (PSLRA) of 1995 applies to publicly traded companies covered by the 1934 Securities Act and requires auditors to report discovered financial statement fraud.[32] Section 10a(b) of the act requires auditors to provide the SEC with notification of material illegal acts, including financial statement fraud that has not been responded to on a timely basis by senior management, has been communicated to the audit committee, had been brought to the attention of the board of directors, and has not been reported to the SEC by the board. The PSLRA has effectively created a whistle-blowing obligation for auditors of publicly traded companies. The SEC position has been that illegal acts described in the PSLRA related to financial statement fraud, not to the illegal acts by the client's managers and employees that do not have a direct and material effect on the presentation of financial statements. When the outsider determines that an illegal act has a material effect on the financial statements (e.g., financial statement fraud) but senior management has not taken the appropriate remedial action, either on its own or at the demand of the board of directors, the auditor should communicate that matter to the audit committee and issue a formal report to the board. The board of directors has only one business day to notify the SEC and the auditor of its compliance with notifying the SEC.

Under the PSLRA, auditors are obligated to report to the SEC that they detect financial statement fraud and management will not remedy the situation by restating the financial statements or reporting financial statement fraud to the SEC. The auditor's notification is required even if the auditor decides to resign from the engagement. Failure by the auditor to comply with the required notices may be subject to civil penalties under the 1934 Securities Act.

The provision of SAS No. 82 can be summarized as follows:

1. Describes fraud in general, and financial statement fraud in particular, and its characteristics.
2. Requires specific fraud risk assessment in every audit engagement, particularly when there is an indication of the likelihood of financial statement fraud.
3. Provides guidance when the auditor identifies fraud risk factors.
4. Provides guidance in assessing audit test results.
5. Describes documentation requirements.
6. Provides guidance for internal and, possibly, external communication of fraud.
7. Clarifies, but does not expand, the auditor's responsibility to detect financial statement fraud.
8. Increases documentation requirements.
9. Specifies that an audit conducted in accordance with GAAS is designed to obtain reasonable, rather than absolute, assurance that financial statements are free of material misstatements caused by error or fraud.
10. Reports to the audit committee and the board of directors evidence that financial statement fraud may exist.
11. Represents investors, creditors, and other users of audited financial statements by accepting the ultimate accountability to the board of directors and the audit committee.
12. Reports reportable conditions and material internal control weaknesses to the senior management and the audit committee.

AUDITOR INDEPENDENCE

Auditor's independence is the cornerstone of the auditing profession. Auditors, in compliance with GAAS, conduct their audit by expressing an opinion on fair presentation of operating results, financial position, and cash flows in conformity with GAAP. In rendering an opinion, auditors also provide reasonable assurance that audited financial statements are free of material misstatements caused by fraud and errors. In addition, auditors inform investors, creditors, and other users of audited financial statements that they maintain an independence of mental attitude in conducting the audit and expressing opinion. Thus, investors, creditors, and other users of audited financial statements, look to and rely on auditors' reports regarding the integrity, quality, reliability, usefulness, and relevance of financial information in making investment and other financial decisions; however, several issues detrimental to auditor's independence have resulted in a lack of public confidence in auditors' reports. For example, when auditors collect consulting fees significantly larger than audit fees or when a company recruits and hires an auditor who previously was the company's audit manager or partner for its top executive position, and/or the audit staff has significant financial interest in the client's organization, the investors and public question the potential conflicts of interest and lack of auditor's independence.

The audit fees paid by companies to their independent auditors count only for about one-fourth of total fees charged by auditors to their clients. *U.S. News and World Report* (July 23, 2001) states that "only 27 cents of every dollar companies paid their independent auditors last year had to do with the all-important sign off on corporate financial statements."[33] While there is nothing illegal about external auditors performing other services, such as management and information technology consulting for their clients, the extent of such services has raised concerns regarding "how independent actually are external auditors?"[34]

To address auditors' independence, the SEC issued new rules, after a long process of debates and compromising, which require public companies, for the first time, to disclose fees they paid their external auditors for financial audits and other services. Pricewaterhouse Coopers (PWC) has recently been the target of three ongoing SEC investigations for alleged audit failure to discover financial statement fraud. In May 2001, PWC agreed to pay $55 million to settle a class-action lawsuit by shareholders of MicroStrategy, Inc., which admitted misleading investors about its profitability. In another case, PWC is subject to a pending lawsuit by shareholders of Raytheon Co. who lost millions after the company had to restate its earnings last year. PWC billed Raytheon $51 million last year, from which about 95 percent related to nonaudit services. Exhibit 11.4 shows that Big Five professional services firms receive a substantial portion of their fees (nearly 95 percent) for nonaudit services and only a tiny share of collected fees (about 5 percent) for audit services.

To avoid the appearance of conflicts of interest, which may jeopardize public confidence in auditors' objectivity, integrity, and independence, as well as compliance with the SEC's new rules on auditors' independence, Big Five professional services firms are separating their audit services from their nonaudit services. For example, Ernst & Young sold off its consulting practice in 2000. Andersen's former consulting firm, renamed as Accenture, spun off from Arthur Andersen in 2000. KPMG split off its consulting group in January 2001. PWC is in the process of splitting off its auditing and consulting services. Whether the separation of auditing and consulting services by most of the Big Five and the new rules requiring disclosure

Exhibit 11.4. Partitioning of Fees Collected by Big Five from Selected Clients

Big Five	Client	Fees Collected	Percentage	
			Nonaudit	Audit
Arthur Andersen	Marriott Int.	$31,331,300	96.65	3.35
Deloitte & Touche	GAP	$8,245,000	93.10	6.9
Ernst & Young	Sprint	$66,300,000	96.23	3.77
KPMG	Motorola	$66,200,000	94.11	5.89
Pricewaterhouse Coopers	Raytheon	$51,000,000	94.12	5.88

Source: Securities and Exchange Commission, Available: http://www.sec.gov and also provided in *U.S. News and World Report,* July 23, 2001, page 42.

of fees collected for audit and other services will improve auditors' independence is still an unresolved issue in the financial community that only time will tell.

Definition

Auditor independence is a concept that cannot be easily defined, primarily because it describes an auditor's frame of mind and attitude. The second general standard of GAAS regarding auditor independence states, "In all matters relating to the assignment, an independence in mental attitude is to be maintained by the auditor or auditors." In October 1997, the AICPA issued a white paper defining independence in light of financial information being audited by independent auditors. The White Paper stated that:

> [A]uditor independence is an absence of interests that create an unacceptable risk of bias with respect to the quality or context of information that is the subject of an audit engagement.[35]

Auditors' independence assists auditors to have an objective state of mind by acting with impartiality, integrity, and objectivity; and separating personal interest and obligations from clients' interests. Auditors should maintain independence in both fact and appearance. Independence in fact requires auditors to have an objective state of mind. Appearance of independence requires auditors to avoid any conflict of interest with their clients (e.g., financial or other self-interests) that might jeopardize the public's confidence in auditors' judgment and performance or be perceived as incompatible with the objectivity necessary to fulfill professional responsibilities.

Auditors' independence is governed by several rules and their interpretations established by the AICPA and SEC. In 1997, the SEC and AICPA established the Independence Standard Board (ISB) to address the impact of the rapidly changing and complex business environment on the independence rule-making process and to establish independence standards for auditors. The primary purpose of the ISB has been to establish a principles-based system providing a conceptual framework to assist auditors, management, and audit committees in determining circumstances or factors that may impair auditors' independence.

Most recently, the ISB issued an exposure draft and, subsequently, a new rule of a conceptual framework for auditor independence. The ISB's new rule defines auditor independence as "freedom from those factors that compromise, or can reasonably be expected to compromise, an auditor's ability to make unbiased audit decision."[36] The framework defines two concepts of independence: independence in fact and independence in appearance. Independence in fact refers to the mental attitude of the auditors in the sense that the auditor should have an objective state of mind, being impartial, objective, unbiased with respect to the client and other users of audited financial statements. Independence in appearance, however, is not well defined; it is often described in terms of the perception of investors and other users of financial information toward auditor independence. It means auditors should be perceived to be independent in the minds of investors, creditors, and other users of audited financial statements by avoiding any conflicts of interest that might jeopardize users' confidence in auditors' performance. In the new rule for auditor independence, there is a clear emphasis on the perceptions of the investing public and users of financial information. To mitigate the ambiguity regarding independence in fact and appearance, the framework recommends a three-step process:

1. Identify threats to the auditor's independence and analyze their significance.
2. Evaluate the effectiveness of potential safeguards to address the identified threats, including restrictions.
3. Determine an acceptable level of independent risk that can be tolerated, compromised, and managed.

Based on this new definition of auditors' independence, auditors are not required to be completely free of all the factors that could possibly affect their ability to make objective and unbiased audit decisions, but only free from those that are significantly detrimental to auditors' judgments and rise to the level of compromising the ability to be impartial, objective, and unbiased. Auditors should continuously assess their ability and judgment to have an objective state of mind as well as how activities and relationships with their clients (e.g., the extent of consulting services) would appear to others. Thus, the auditors' consideration of independence should be assessed from two perspectives: (1) how auditors themselves perceive their independence; and (2) how others, particularly the investing public, perceive auditors' independence. In this context, auditors should consider the threats to independence and develop safeguards that support reasonable or perceived independence. The framework identifies five fundamental categories of threats to auditors' independence as self-interest, self-review, advocacy, familiarity, and intimidation.

1. *Self-interest* occurs when auditors act in their own interest (e.g., financial, emotional) rather than serving the interest of the investing public.

2. *Self-review* threats arise when auditors audit their own work or the work of other auditors (e.g., the extent of consulting in accounting system design and information technologies).
3. *Advocacy* occurs when auditors act in the interest of their clients rather than the interest of the investing public by remaining objective and unbiased with regard to all users of audited financial statements.
4. *Familiarity* threat arises when auditors have a close relationship to the client (e.g., being a close relative of the client's top executives).
5. *Intimidation* threat occurs when auditors are directly or indirectly influenced by the client or another third party (e.g., pressure by management to participate in gamesmanship).

The aforementioned threats to auditors' independence can diminish the investing public's confidence in auditors' performance, and, therefore, they should be safeguarded. An important safeguard is the development of procedures to preserve auditor independence, including limits on the extent of consulting services, prohibitions on owning stock of an audit client, and instilling professional values through proper training, firm policies on independence, and enforcement of independence policies throughout the auditing firm. The framework places significant emphasis on relationships that may impair auditors' independence and provides guidance to identify relationships and assess their impact on auditors' independence. The relationships addressed in the framework are as follows:

Financial Relationships

The framework narrowed the circle of individuals within the auditing firm whose investments trigger independence concerns. For example, audit partners who do not even work on audits, along with their family members, are restricted from investments in their audit client's organization. The new rule also eliminates investment opportunities in audit clients for those who work on the audit or are in a position to "influence" the audit.

Employee and Business Relationships

The new rules identify the employment and business positions in which a person can influence the audit client's accounting records or financial statements, which would impair an auditor's independence if held by a "close family member" of the auditor.

Nonaudit Service Relationships

The framework identifies several nonaudit services that may impair auditors' independence, including bookkeeping and other related services, such as information technology design and implementation, approval or valuation services, actuarial services, and internal audit services.

1. *Bookkeeping and Accounting Services.* Auditors are prohibited from maintaining accounting records or preparing financial statements of publicly traded companies, except in emerging circumstances.
2. *Information Technology (IT) Design and Implementation.* Auditors are prohibited to operate or supervise the operation of the clients' IT systems; however, auditors may provide IT consulting services, provided management:
   - Acknowledges to the auditor and audit committee management's responsibility for the IT systems and related internal controls.
   - Identifies a person from within the company to make all management decisions.
   - Makes all the significant decisions for the IT project.
   - Assesses the adequacy and effectiveness of results of the project.
   - Does not rely on the auditor's work as the primary basis for determining the sufficiency of the financial reporting system.

   The client should disclose the total amount of fees for IT services received from the auditor as well as the amounts of audit fees; and state whether the audit committee considered that the provisions of these nonaudit services were compatible with maintaining the auditor's independence.
3. *Appraisal and Valuation Services.* The restriction on appraisal and valuation services only applies where it is reasonably likely that the results of any appraisal or valuation would be material to the financial statements or where the auditor would audit the results.
4. *Actuarial Services.* Actuarial services are limited to the determination of the client's insurance policy reserves and related financial transactions and accounts; however, certain other types of actuarial services are allowed when the client uses its own actuaries or third-party actuaries. Management accepts responsibility for actuarial methods and assumptions, and the auditor does not render actuarial services to an audit client on a continuous basis.
5. *Internal Audit Services.* Internal audit services are limited to 40 percent (measured in terms of hours) of an audit client's internal audit work, with the exception for smaller businesses by excluding companies with less than $200 million in assets. Nevertheless, providing any internal audit services for an audit client is contingent on management taking responsibility for and making all managerial decisions regarding the internal audit function.

In summary, the new guidelines for auditor independence explicitly clarify the relationships and circumstances that may impair auditor independence in fact;

Exhibit 11.5.   Potential Threats to Auditors' Independence and Related Safeguards

Threats	Safeguards
1. Financial or other self-interest	• Monitoring investments
	• Monitoring the extent of nonaudit services provided
	• Policies on independence and compliance with those policies
	• Partner and staff evaluation and compensation methods
2. Self-review of services performed	• Monitoring the extent of nonaudit services provided
	• Separating national consultation function
	• Service line acceptance policies
3. Becoming an advocate for (or against) the client's position	• Client acceptance and retention policies
	• Risk management consultation requirements
	• Peer review
4. Lack of exercising professional skepticism	• Partner rotation
	• Concurring partner reviews
	• Internal inspection/monitoring programs
5. Intimidation or threat by management	• Internal inspection/monitoring programs
	• Internal disciplinary actions
	• Quality control inquiry committee review
	• Monitoring management reputation and attitude

Source: The proposed SEC Rules on Auditor Independence and Consequences. Available: www.aicpa.org/pubs/jofa/oct2000/news.bar.htm

however, the issue of independence in appearance is not completely resolved. Independent auditors should provide reasonable assurance that audited financial statements are free of material misstatements caused by fraudulent error in order to enhance the investing public's ability to make informed investment and business decisions. To effectively fulfill this responsibility, independent auditors should be objective, impartial, and unbiased to the client, investors, creditors, and other users of the audited financial statements. Exhibit 11.5 summarizes the independent threats and related safeguards.

NEW SEC RULES ON AUDITOR INDEPENDENCE

The new auditor independence rules established by the SEC took effect on February 5, 2001. The new rules address the issues affecting an accounting firm's interaction with its SEC audit clients. These issues are (1) financial relationships, (2) employment relationships, (3) business relationships, (4) scope of services, (5) contingent fees, (6) quality control standards, and (7) proxy disclosure requirements. After some alterations, the final rules are more closely aligned with the SEC's common objective of perfecting the public interest.

The SEC has added to the proxy disclosure requirements and taken away from what is considered to be contingent fees. SEC clients must now disclose the fees billed for services rendered by the principal accountant and the audit committee considerations. Instead of adding to the definition of "contingent fee," the SEC decided to eliminate the "value-added" fees from the original definition. The addition of the proxy disclosure requirements and the scaleback of the contingent fee definition illustrates how the SEC did its best to provide well-established auditor independence rules.

The SEC has established four general principles when assessing independence. These principles include whether a particular relationship or nonaudit service (1) creates a mutual or conflicting interest between the accountant and the audit client; (2) places the accountant in a position of auditing his or her own work product; (3) results in the accountant's acting as management or as an employee; or (4) places the accountant in a position of being an advocate for the audit client.

The auditor's independence is perceived to be impaired when investors, creditors, and other users of audited financial statements would conclude that the auditor did not exercise objective, impartial judgment in reaching audit conclusions. The new rules would modernize the requirements for auditor independence in the following areas:

- Investments by auditors or their family members in audit clients
- Employment relationships between auditors or their family members and audit clients
- The scope of services provided by audit firms to their audit clients

The new rules would reduce the number of audit firm employees and their family members whose investment in, or employment with, audit clients would impair an auditor's independence. In particular, they would also identify certain nonaudit services that, if provided to an audit client, would impair an auditor's independence. These rules, however, would not extend to services provided to nonaudit clients. Internal audit services provided by the outside auditor would be limited to 40 percent of total internal audit hours (a restriction that does not apply to operational-type audit work or to companies with less than $200 million in assets). They would provide a limited exception to an accounting firm for inadvertent independence violations if the firm has quality controls in place and the violation is corrected promptly. In circumstances where the outside auditor provides IT consulting services, company management must retain responsibility for managing the project, operating the corporation's computer systems, and monitoring the system of internal control. Companies would also be required to disclose in their annual proxy statements certain information about nonaudit services provided by their auditor during the last fiscal year, such as auditing, information technology, consulting, and other attestation and assurance services.

The new rules have identified nine nonaudit services that impair the independence when auditors offer these services to the audit client: bookkeeping services, financial information systems design and implementation, appraisal or valuation services, actuarial services, internal audit, management functions, human resources, broker-dealer services, and legal services. The rules do not fully ban these services, but restrictions apply when the services are material and do not affect the financial statements. When the audit client had $200 million or less in assets, the independence is impaired if 40 percent of internal audit work related to the internal controls, financial systems, or financial statements are completed by the auditor. In the event that the auditor is not knowledgeable of a violation of independence, the auditor could correct the violation promptly and provide reasonable assurance that the firm and its employees maintained independence. The amendments also call for a proxy statement that includes certain information related to the nonaudit services provided by their auditor. The audit committee must also provide written disclosures of the independence letter from the auditing firm required by the ISB Standard No. 1.

The SEC's Accounting Series Release (ASR) No. 250 required publicly traded companies to disclose in their proxy statements the percentage of fees for nonaudit services in relation to the audit fee and whether these services were approved by the board of directors and its representative audit committee. ASR No. 250 was subsequently withdrawn primarily because of the SEC's concern that the disclosed information was not utilized. Glazan and Millar (1985) examined shareholder reaction to disclosers of ASR No. 250 and found that either independence of the auditors is not important to shareholders or shareholders do not consider nonaudit services as affecting independence of the auditors.[37]

The ISB issued Standard No. 2, Certain Independence Implications of Audits of Mutual Funds and Related Entities, in December 1999. ISB Standard No. 2 addresses auditor investments in mutual funds and other entities that are not audit clients, but are related to mutual fund audit clients. The standard requires the audit firm, audit team, and others to be independent from nonclient sister funds and nonfund entities related to an audit client fund or nonfund entity. In the wake of Enron debacle, lawmakers including the SEC, are investigating its audit work performed by Andersen. Joseph F. Berardino, managing partner and CEO of Andersen, in defending the audit practices of Enron before Congress, stated that "Andersen will have to change...the accounting profession will have to reform itself. Our system of regulation and discipline will have to be improved."[38]

CONCLUSION

Users of financial statements have traditionally relied on independent auditors' judgment, opinion, and assurance that audited financial statements are free of material misstatements caused by errors or fraud. Thus, failure of independent auditors to detect financial statement fraud either knowingly or recklessly can result in substantial losses to investors, creditors, and auditees as well as costly lawsuits against auditors and accounting firms. The SEC has raised concerns about audit failures and is working with criminal prosecutors to attack financial statement fraud and to hold independent auditors more accountable for their audit performance, quality, and effectiveness. This chapter discusses the role of independent auditors in corporate governance and in ensuring the quality, integrity, and reliability of financial reports.

The AICPA, in response to the risk of fraud threatening the quality and integrity of financial information and auditors' responsibility to detect financial statement fraud, issued Statement on Auditing Standards (SAS) No. 82: Consideration of Fraud in a Financial Statement Audit. This statement requires external auditors to explicitly consider the risk that financial statements may be materially misstated because of fraud and perform appropriate audit procedures to detect fraud. SAS No. 82 requires that auditors report to the audit committee financial statement fraud, including fraud involving senior management and fraud that causes a material misstatement of financial statements, regardless of whether perpetrated by senior management or other employees.

ENDNOTES

1. Beasley, M. S., J. V. Carcello and D. R. Hermanson. 1999. Fraudulent Financial Reporting: 1987–1997, An Analysis of U.S. Public Companies. New York: COSO.
2. American Institute of Certified Public Accountants (AICPA). 1997. Consideration of Fraud in a Financial Statement Audit. SAS No. 82. New York: AICPA.
3. Public Oversight Board (POB). 2000. The Panel on Audit Effectiveness Report and Recommendations. (August) Stamford, CT: POB.
4. Ibid.
5. American Institute of Certified Public Accountants (AICPA). 1995. Statement on Auditing Standards (SAS) No., 78. Consideration of Internal Control in a Financial Statement Audit. New York: AICPA.
6. Federal Deposit Insurance Corporation Improvement Act. 1993. Supervisory Guidance on the Implementation of Section 112 of the FDICIA. 1991. (May 11): The Board of Directors of the FDIC.
7. Landsittle, D. L. 2000. "Some Current Challenges". The CPA Journal (October, V70, No. 10): 58.
8. American Institute of Certified Public Accountants (AICPA). 1997. Consideration of Fraud in a Financial Statement Audit. SAS No. 82. New York: AICPA.
9. Public Oversight Board (POB). 2000. The Panel on Audit Effectiveness Report and Recommendations. (August) Stamford, CT: POB.

10. Beasley, M. S., J. V. Carcello and D. R. Hermanson. 1999. Fraudulent Financial Reporting: 1987–1997, An Analysis of U.S. Public Companies. New York: COSO.

11. American Institute of Certified Public Accountants (AICPA). 1997. Consideration of Fraud in a Financial Statement Audit. SAS No. 82. New York: AICPA.

12. Walker, R. H. 2001. The SEC's New Item: Arthur Andersen Consents to Antifraud Injunction. Available: www.sec.gov/newsitem.

13. Walker, R. H. 1999. A Speech to the AICPA in Washington by the SEC's Director of Enforcement (December). Available at /www.sec.gov/news/speech/speecharchive/1999speech.shtml

14. Hilzenrath, D.S. 2001. After Enron, New Doubts about Auditors. Washington Post Staff Writer (December 5): A01.

15. Public Oversight Board (POB). 2000. The Panel on Audit Effectiveness Report and Recommendations. (August) Stamford, CT: POB.

16. American Institute of Certified Public Accountants (AICPA). 1988. Statement on Auditing Standards (SAS) No. 61. Communication with Audit Committees. New York, NY: AICPA.

17. American Institute of Certified Public Accountants (AICPA). 1999. Statement on Auditing Standards (SAS) No. 89. Audit Adjustments. New York, NY: AICPA.

18. American Institute of Certified Public Accountants (AICPA). 2000. Statement on Auditing Standards (SAS) No. 90. Audit Committees Communications. New York, NY: AICPA.

19. American Institute of Certified Public Accountants (AICPA). 2000. Practice Alert 2000-2. Quality of Accounting Principles-Guidance for Discussion with Audit Committee. New York, NY: AICPA.

20. Independence Standards Board (ISB). 1999. ISB Standard No. 1. Independence Discussions with Audit Committees (January): ISB.

21. Ibid.

22. Public Oversight Board (POB). 2000. The Panel on Audit Effectiveness Report and Recommendations. (August) Stamford, CT: POB.

23. American Institute of Certified Public Accountants (AICPA). 1997. Consideration of Fraud in a Financial Statement Audit. SAS No. 82. New York: AICPA.

24. American Institute of Certified Public Accountants (AICPA). 1997. Statement on Auditing Standards (SAS) No. 84. Communications Between Predecessor and Successor Auditors. New York, NY: AICPA.

25. Public Oversight Board (POB). 2000. The Panel on Audit Effectiveness Report and Recommendations. (August) Stamford, CT: POB.

26. American Institute of Certified Public Accountants (AICPA). 1999. Statement on Auditing Standards (SAS) No. 89. Audit Adjustments. New York, NY: AICPA.

27. American Institute of Certified Public Accountants (AICPA). 2000. Statement on Auditing Standards (SAS) No. 90. Audit Committees Communications. New York, NY: AICPA.

28. Beasley, M. S., J. V. Carcello and D. R. Hermanson. 1999. Fraudulent Financial Reporting: 1987–1997, An Analysis of U.S. Public Companies. New York: COSO.

29. Financial Accounting Standards Board (FASB). 1980. Statement of Financial Accounting Concepts No. 2. Quantitative Characteristics of Accounting Information (May): FASB.

30. American Institute of Certified Public Accountants (AICPA). 1997. Consideration of Fraud in a Financial Statement Audit. SAS No. 82. New York: AICPA.

31. American Institute of Certified Public Accountants (AICPA). 1997. Communication Between Predecessor and Successor Auditors. SAS No. 84. New York: AICPA.

32. The Securities and Exchange Commission. 1995. The Private Securities Litigation Reform Act. Available: www.sec.gov.

33. Lavelle, M. 2001. "Auditors Exposed. Cozy Deals Alleged." *U.S. News and World Report* (July 23): 40.

34. Ibid.

35. American Institute of Certified Public Accountants (AICPA). 1997. Serving the Public Interest: A New Conceptual Framework for Auditor Independence. New York: AICPA.

36. American Institute of Certified Public Accountants. 2000. Statement of Independence Concepts: A Conceptual Framework for Auditor Independence, the Independence Standards Board (November). Exposure Draft. New York: AICPA.

37. Glazen, G. W., and J. A. Millar. 1985. "An Empirical Investigation of Stockholder Reaction to Disclosures Required by ASR No. 250". *Journal of Accounting Research* (Autumn): 859–870.

38. Berardino, J.F. 2001. Remarks of Andersen CEO before Congress (December 12). Available at http://www.andersen.com/website.nsf/content/MediaCenterNewsReleaseArchive BerardinoTestimony121201!OpenDocument

Chapter 12

Governing Bodies

INTRODUCTION

Several governing bodies directly or indirectly influence corporate governance and the financial reporting process of publicly traded companies. These governing bodies are classified into two groups of standard-setting bodies and monitoring organizations. Standard-setting organizations consist of the Securities and Exchange Commission (SEC), the Financial Accounting Standards Board (FASB), and the American Institute of Certified Public Accountants (AICPA). The monitoring organizations are the SEC, the AICPA, the SEC Practice Sections (SECPS) of the AICPA, state boards of accountancy, the Independence Standards Board (ISB), and the Public Oversight Board (POB). Other self-regulatory organizations that may influence the financial reporting process are the National Association of Securities Dealers (NASD) and the New York Stock Exchange (NYSE), which recently sponsored the Blue Ribbon Committee (BRC) on Improving the Effectiveness of Corporate Audit Committees (1999).[1] Exhibit 12.1 presents the role of these governing bodies in corporate governance.

Accounting standards used by publicly traded companies to measure, recognize, and disclose economic transactions and events, known as generally accepted accounting principles (GAAP), are currently promulgated by the FASB, the delegated standard-setting body of the SEC. Professional technical standards for auditors are issued by the AICPA's Auditing Standards Board (ASB). The ASB issues generally accepted auditing standards (GAAS) for external auditors to follow in conducting their audits of financial statements. Thus, financial statements are prepared in conformity with GAAP and they are auditing in accordance with GAAS. This chapter presents the role of governing bodies in improving the quality, integrity, and reliability of financial reports.

SECURITIES AND EXCHANGE COMMISSION

The SEC was established in response to the substantial concerns by investors and the public regarding the trustworthiness of securities markets. Congress created the SEC to address, restore, and maintain investor confidence after the 1929 stock market crash. The SEC is an independent federal regulatory agency established through congressional legislation in 1934. The SEC has the authority to prescribe the form and content of financial statements of publicly traded companies. The Security Act of 1933 and the Securities Exchange Act of 1934 were enacted to

Exhibit 12.1.   Corporate Governance and Its Functions

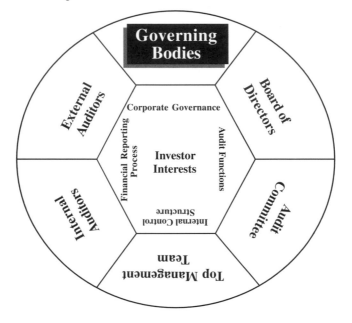

protect investors' interests and to ensure that the capital markets are fair, honest, and efficient. These acts and related rules and regulations issued by the SEC require the disclosures to be made in registration statements and prospectuses used in securities offerings as well as in annual, quarterly, and other public reports filed with the SEC.

The SEC has also been given statutory authority to issue accounting standards for companies under its jurisdiction. The SEC has delegated its standard-setting authority to the private sector (e.g., FASB), while exercising the oversight function of the private sector's standard-setting processes and the right to override, supplement, and/or amend private-sector standards. The SEC also plays an important role in the financial reporting process of registrants through its continuous monitoring of their accounting and reporting practices. The SEC has promoted high-quality financial reports free of material fraud through its continuous oversight functions and following activities. Since its inception in 1934, the SEC has required publicly traded companies to comply with initial and continuing disclosure standards to prevent misleading or incomplete information and to foster informed decisions by investors.

The SEC regulates publicly traded companies in the United States that issue securities to the public and requires the issuance of a prospectus for any new security offering. The SEC was established to protect the interests of investors through its jurisdiction over any corporation with class securities listed on an organized stock exchange (e.g., NYSE, AMSE, NASDAQ) or, if traded over-the-counter, with five or more shareholders and $10 million or more in total assets. The SEC requires public companies under its jurisdiction to submit regular filing of (1) annual reports (10-K); (2) quarterly reports (10-Q); and (3) other reports known as 8-K reports depending on particular circumstances, such as bankruptcy, changes in auditors, and other important events.

Federal securities law prohibits financial statement fraud by publicly traded companies through mandated truthful financial disclosure. Rule 10(b)-5 of the SEC Act of 1934 prohibits disclosure of material untruths and omissions in open-market trades. The SEC Acts of 1933 and 1934 fundamentally constitute security market regulation in the United States. The provisions of these two acts are established to protect investors from fraudulent or misleading information that may cause security price manipulation. In an efficient capital market, security prices reflect the market participants' (e.g., individual investors, analysts, institutional investors) expectations of future cash flows to shareholders. Financial statement fraud, by presenting misleading financial information, can adversely affect the market's expectations and, thus, security prices.

Since 1934, the SEC has been empowered by Congress to make rules and regulations governing registration statements and prospectuses and issued accounting standards for registrants. Publicly traded companies under the SEC jurisdiction that issue misleading financial disclosures are in violation of Rule 10(b)-5 of the SEC Act of 1934. This type of violation constitutes a form of corporate illegal activity (fraudulent activity) subject to SEC legal enforcement procedures that can result in substantial economic losses to the alleged corporation, its top executives, and its stakeholders (e.g., investors, creditors, employees, and customers.)

Statutory Authority of the SEC

The 1934 Act is based on the premise that stock prices are susceptible to misleading financial information, manipulation, and control. The U.S. Congress has authorized the SEC to mandate periodic financial reports by publicly traded companies. These financial reports (annual or quarterly) were required in addition to registration statements, prospectuses, and proxies required by the 1933 and 1934 Acts. These acts (1) prohibit disclosure of false or misleading information and manipulation of fraudulent behavior intended to affect security prices; (2) impose explicit liabilities and penalties on fraudulent financial reporting activities; and (3) disallow the use of nonpublic information by specialists and insiders. Thus, these acts are expected to affect company's management and investor behavior by requiring publication of reliable financial information by management and the use of that information by investors in making capital investment decisions.

Brownlee and Young (1987) argue that empirical studies on the economic consequences of the SEC-mandated disclosure program have focused on two fundamental issues: (1) the impacts of the SEC 1933 Act on new stock issues; and (2) the capital market effects of periodic disclosure requirements (annual or quarterly) under the SEC 1934 Act.[2] Studies (Stigler, 1964; Jarrell, 1981)[3,4] that examined the effects of the 1933 Act on the returns of new stock issues conclude that (1) aggressive investors are typically worse off under the SEC 1933 Act; and (2) risk-averse investors were not necessarily better off under the Act. Empirical studies (Benston, 1973; Ingram and Chewning, 1983)[5,6] on stock market effects of the 1934 Act conclude that (1) there is no significant impact of the 1934 Act on the securities prices; (2) while the 1934 Act may not have affected security returns in the long-term, it may have changed the relative timing of securities prices that constitute the returns.

SEC's Role in Financial Reporting

The SEC Act of 1934 gave the SEC congressional authority to promulgate accounting policies and standards better known as GAAP. The SEC has issued rulings called Accounting Series Releases (ASRs), Financial Reporting Series Releases (FRSRs), and Staff Accounting Bulletins (SABs) to specify acceptable accounting principles for companies under its jurisdiction; however, over the years and for the most part, the SEC has delegated its accounting standard-setting authority to the private sector of the Financial Accounting Standards Board (FASB). The FASB has issued Statements of Financial Accounting Standards (SFASs) and related interpretations through a lengthy deliberation process in establishing GAAP for external financial reporting. During the past three decades, the SEC and FASB have worked closely together in establishing GAAP, with the SEC playing largely an oversight and supportive role.

The SEC has the statutory authority, delegated by Congress, to regulate the securities markets in the United States and establish accounting standards to be used by publicly traded companies under its jurisdiction. Since its establishment about 70 years ago, the SEC has followed a policy, initially set forth in 1938 in Accounting Series Release (ASR) No. 4, of relying primarily on the accounting profession to promulgate accounting standards. This policy was further reaffirmed in ASR No. 150 for accounting standards set forth by the FASB. Statements of Financial Accounting Standards (SFASs) issued by the FASB provide sources of guidelines for corporations in measuring, recognizing, and disclosing financial transactions, items, and reports, and are considered to be GAAP with substantial authoritative support.

In 1938, a few years after its inception, the SEC issued its ASR No. 4, which states that the registrant's financial statements would be accepted if there were "substantial authoritative support" for the accounting practices followed by that registrant. In 1973, shortly after the creation of the FASB as a private accounting standard-setter, in its ARS No. 150, the SEC recognized FASB standards as providing "substantial authoritative support" for accounting practices by registrants. The SEC, in its ARS No. 150, states:

> For purposes of this policy, principles, standards, and practices promulgated by the
> FASB in its Statements and Interpretations will be considered by the Commission as

having substantial authoritative support, and those contrary to such FASB promulgations will be considered to have no such support.[7]

The SEC accounting standard-setting authority is restricted and only applicable to financial statements of publicly traded companies that are under SEC jurisdiction. The FASB standard-setting authority is much broader, and its standards promulgations are applicable to SEC registrants, private companies, small public companies, not-for-profit organizations, and in some cases, to state and local governmental agencies.

The SEC's role in corporate financial reporting accounting to the Report of the SEC Advisory Committee on Corporate Disclosure (1977) is to "assure the public availability in an efficient and reasonable manner and on a timely basis of reliable, firm-oriented information material to informed investment and corporate suffrage decision-making."[8] This overseeing responsibility of the SEC is presumed to assure "the semi-strong capital market efficiency" concept that suggests security prices reflect all available public information, including published financial statements. The SEC regulations of corporate financial disclosure are intended to prevent "market failure." Brownlee and Young (1987)[9] argue that the notion of "market failure" has two fundamental components of the "public good" and "asymmetry" of information. The "public good" nature of corporate financial reports suggests that published corporate financial information is viewed to be public good primarily because (1) the use of such information by one person does not reduce the quantity or quality of the information available to others; (2) nonpurchasers cannot be excluded from consuming it; and (3) financial information passes both the joint consumption and nonexclusivity attributes of public goods. Thus, proper SEC disclosure regulations are necessary to ensure that adequate financial information is produced and disseminated by corporations. In the absence of SEC-mandated financial disclosure, corporations may produce unreliable and insufficient financial information that may lead to suboptimal resource allocation and resulting market failures. The public good concept of corporate financial information deals with the efficiency issue of the capital markets.

The second element of market failure related to the concept of "asymmetry" is the manner in which financial information is distributed among market participants. The asymmetry notion of financial information pertains to the equity issue of publicly available financial information. Asymmetry of financial information suggests that corporate insiders (e.g., management, the board of directors) may know much more about their corporations than do outsiders (investors). This may provide opportunities for insiders to fraudulently take advantage of the possessed monopolistic information to influence stock prices. Thus, SEC regulations prohibit inside tradings that may create inefficiency in the capital market. The SEC's new disclosure regulation (fair disclosure) is intended to create a level playing field for all market participants. Illegal insider trading has received considerable attention by the financial community and generated significant political interest. Thus, the Insiders Trading Sanctions Act of 1984 (Pub L. No. 98-376) extended

SEC enforcement powers regarding insider trading and imposed significant penalties on those found guilty of inside tradings. The severity of the insider problems encouraged Congress to review the SEC's role in the supervision and issuance of accounting standards and the existing structure for establishing disclosure requirements for publicly traded companies.

The SEC has adopted an Integrated Disclosure System since 1980 that requires disclosure of a set of standardized information for both 10-K reporting filed with the commission and the annual report issued to shareholders. This set of integrated disclosure contains the audited financial statements, notes to the financial statements, the auditor's report, a five-year summary of selected financial items (e.g., sales, income), stock market data (e.g., high and low sales prices), and the Management Discussion and Analysis (MD&A) of financial condition and results of operations.

SEC's Regulation Fair Disclosure

The SEC has had great concern over selective disclosure of material information by financial information issuers for several years. Many publicly traded companies disclosed important nonpublic information, such as advance warnings of earnings results and restructuring changes, to securities analysts or selected institutional investors or both before they made full disclosure of the same information to the general public. The investors who had access to the information before others either made a profit or avoided losses. The SEC former chairperson Arthur Levitt states the following regarding the importance of fair disclosure requirements:

> As Wall Street analysts play an increasingly visible role in recommending stocks, some in corporate management treat material information as a commodity—a way to gain and maintain favor with particular analysts. That defies the principles of integrity and fairness and therefore the meritocracy in the U.S. taught to children and practiced through equal opportunity. America's marketplace should be no exception. Instead, it should serve as a beacon. No one should be excluded.[10]

On October 23, 2000, Regulation Fair Disclosure (FD) went into effect and became the law. The regulation would ban the practice of holding conference calls with analysts by invitation only, also known as *selective disclosure.* The SEC proposed such a regulation to provide a more level playing field for those investors who do not have insider or early information on which to base their decisions. The following are reasons for the regulation:

- Certain analysts and individuals had access to information that was not available to the public.
- Assuming the securities markets are efficient, the markets will react to all public and nonpublic information.

- Some companies wanted to appear more profitable than they actually were by using the information to persuade analysts to provide inaccurate positive estimates.
- Technology, such as the Internet, allows information to be distributed much faster.

The SEC has recently adopted a series of new rules, including Regulation FD, Rule 10(b) 5-1, and Rule 10(b) 5-2.[11] These new rules are designed to address the issue of how a publicly traded company's financial records are required to be disclosed, and to whom and when. The need for this new set of regulations and rules came about because of the public demand to address what was seen as a loophole in the laws that prohibit insider trading. While it was (and still is) highly illegal for a private investor to make a stock purchase or sale based on information gathered from a personal contact within the management of a company, many people believed that the practice of allowing the same type of information to be disclosed to a certain group of analysts and to certain large fund managers also violated the intent of the law. Those who are not "in the loop" with these analysts are often left dealing with the consequences of finding that the value of their stock has been driven down because of the actions of these analysts. Or in other cases, the price has been driven too high, and once the news disclosed to the analysts becomes public, the effect on the market becomes one of the analyst being "insulated" from the risk and the average individual investor losing money instead.

Regulation FD requires that, when an issuer or any person acting on behalf of the issuer discloses material nonpublic information to certain enumerated persons (generally, securities market professionals or investors), the issuer must make public disclosure of that same information simultaneously (for intentional disclosures) or promptly (for nonintentional disclosures). Regulation FD concerns issuers or persons acting on their behalf, disclosing nonpublic information to certain persons (usually general securities market professionals and holders of issuers' securities); it must make public disclosure of that information. Timing depends on whether the selective disclosure was intentional or unintentional; for intentional, the issuer's public disclosure must be done simultaneously; for unintentional, public disclosure must be made promptly. The regulation requires that disclosure be made by one or both of these two methods (i.e., by Form 8-K or another method reasonably designed to reach a broad, nonexclusionary distribution of information to the public). Under the regulation, the required public disclosure may be made by filing or furnishing a Form 8-K, or by another method or combination of methods; these methods must be broad and nonexclusionary.

Rule 10(b) 5-1 deals with the issue of insider trading liability arising in conjunction with a trader's "use" or "knowing possession" of material nonpublic information. This rule applies when a person trades "on the basis of" material nonpublic information when the person purchases or sells securities while aware of the information. Also, the rule allows several affirmative defenses (responding to comments), allowing trading under circumstances where it is clearly known that the information was not a factor in the trade decision. Rule 10(b) 5-2 deals with a breach of family or other non-business relationship, giving rise to liability under the misappropriation theory of insider trading. The rule provides three non-exclusive bases for determining that a duty of trust or confidence was owed by a person receiving information, and will provide greater certainty and clarity on this unsettled issue.

Regulation FD will provide several important benefits to investors and the securities markets as a whole. All investors will receive more fair information disclosure, thereby increasing investor confidence in market integrity. Regulation FD, by increasing market confidence, will maintain and enhance extensive investor participation in the market, thus encouraging better market liquidity and efficiency while promoting more effective market capital raising. In addition, benefits from the regulation will likely include unbiased analysis. The access to material information will be on equal footing to all analysts with respect to competition as a result of this regulation. Honest opinions can be expressed by analysts without fear of being denied access to valuable corporate information, as their competitors. As a result of regulation FD, other analysts will not have the competitive edge just because they are able to say better things about issues.

Rule 10(b) 5-2 lists three nonexclusive bases for deciding when a person receiving information is subject to a 'duty of trust or confidence' for purposes of the misappropriation theory of insider trading.[12] The rule will clarify the law on the question of when a family relationship will create a duty of trust or confidence, and it will fill the gap in current law on family members and insider trading.

Many large businesses have already been in full compliance with the regulation even before it was fully approved. Many corporations have used the development of the Internet to offer interested parties to listen to conference calls over the Internet. In addition, firms can directly update their web sites with new disclosures. If the firm updates information with the SEC, the information is put into the EDGAR database, available on the web; however, some people disagree with Regulation FD. Many analysts will have to do other work to get information they usually received by the firms they were researching. Now, they have less access to the changes in earnings information. They have to spend more time collecting information from suppliers and distributors. Many people believe this regulation will decrease the amount of information available for investors to make educated decisions. Many say that Regulation FD will cause a lack of information because the firms will be scared to violate the regulation and will cut all flow of information. Many firms have stated that they will significantly reduce their disclosures with the new regulations. Some corporations will choose to completely stop talking to analysts to remain in compliance with the regulation. Others have criticized Regulation FD in the sense that its implication will cause issuers to release nonpublic information.

Another argument is that provisions on selective disclosure will lead to information overload. There is currently so much information with which investors do nothing. Even if material information is made public, investors may not pay attention to it or use it to their benefit, and the professionals will still have an upper hand. Because it is their jobs, professionals may still have vital information about their companies, the trend of their performance, among other things, just by studying the companies over the years. This will still help them make well-informed trade decisions that investors can never make. Despite this law, analysts and other professionals will continue to get some form of information the public will not have through casual chats with acquaintances they have formed on the job over the years. No amount of regulation can put the average investors on equal footing with securities professionals.

The most important impact Regulation FD will have is its "chilling effect." The "chilling effect" is the likelihood that publicly traded companies will be afraid to disclose some information without violating their role and being accused of selective disclosure. The analysts will also be on the lower end of the stick with the fair disclosure regulation. They will have less accessibility to the changes in company earnings information. The regulation will also require the analysts to spend more time collecting the information they incorporate into the pricing of company stock. There will also be less certainty in the reports analysts provide about the earnings expectations of companies.

Analysts may view the new laws as preventing them from being able to do their jobs in a timely manner because, by the time the analysts get the information and analyze it, that analysis is going to be out of date because the market, upon learning the same news at the same time, is going to react to that information in either a positive or negative manner. But whichever way investors react, that reaction will have an impact on the market and quite possibly change it to the degree that the analysts' reports will become invalid before they can even be issued. Although this may on the surface seem to be the problem of only the analysts, the reality is that while many private investors do their own research, many more rely on the advice of analysts for guidance.

Financial Fraud Detection and Disclosure Act of 1992

This act amended the Securities and Exchange Commission Act of 1934 by adding a new Section 13A to improve fraud detection and disclosure of publicly traded companies. The legislation requires independent auditors to perform adequate audit procedures designed to provide reasonable assurance of detecting illegal acts that would have a direct and material effect on financial statements, identification of material related-party transactions, and assessment of the company's ability to continue as a going concern. This legislation requires that, if external auditors detect a material illegal act that would directly affect financial statements, the auditor should (1) inform the appropriate level of management and the audit committee; (2) if management failed to take timely and appropriate remedial action and management's failure warrants either a departure from a standard auditor's report or a resignation from the audit engagement, then the auditor should report these conclusions directly to the board of directors; (3) the company should inform the SEC within one business day of receipt of the auditor's report; and (4) failure of the company to report to the SEC may force the auditor to resign from the audit engagement or to report the suspected illegalities to the SEC within one business day.

Private Securities Reform Act of 1995

The Private Securities Litigation Reform Act of 1995 (the Reform Act), amended the SEC Act of 1934 by adding Section 10A. Section 10A required that each audit under the SEC Act of 1934 include audit procedures regarding the detection of illegal acts and the identification of related parties. The Private Securities Litigation Reform Act of 1995 became law on December 22, 1995. The U.S. Congress overrode President Clinton's vote in passing this Reform Act. On November 3, 1998, President Clinton signed into law the Securities Litigation Uniform Standards Act of 1998 (Uniform Standards Act).

The three major provisions of the Private Securities Litigation Reform Act of 1995 are (1) the "fair share" proportionate liability rule; (2) the deployment of damage caps; and (3) the requirement for fraud detection and disclosure. King and Schwartz (1997) discuss these three provisions of the act and present suggestions and strategies to address these provisions.[13] They conclude that auditors are required not only to detect illegal acts, including financial statement fraud, but also to determine an appropriate and timely remedial response for management.

The Health Care Paperwork Reduction and Fraud Prevention Act of 2001 was introduced on March 20, 2001, in the 107th Congress as H.R. 1128. The purpose of this act, among other things, is to (1) reduce the amount of paperwork; (2) prevent fraud and abuse through health care provider education; and (3) improve payment policies for health care services.

SEC AND FINANCIAL STATEMENT FRAUD

The SEC Act of 1934 requires financial disclosure to provide investors with adequate information to allow them to make rational economic decisions. The required disclosures were deemed necessary to prevent financial statement fraud; however, Benston (1973)[14] concludes that the required disclosures are neither useful nor timely, and the 1934 Act neither increased investors' confidence in securities nor impacted the fairness of the capital market. Benston (1973) did not find any evidence supporting the underlying assumption that the 1934 Act prevented financial statement fraud.

Feroz, Park, and Pastena (1991)[15] examined the issues pertaining to the financial and market impacts of the SEC's Accounting and Auditing Enforcement Releases (AAERs): (1) the types of accounting and auditing problems that motivate SEC enforcement actions; (2) the consequences of investigations on targets' financial statements, managers, and auditors; and (3) the perceived view of investors and other market participants on the SEC's action. Feroz et al. (1991)[16] found that (1) premature revenue recognition and/or overstatement of current assets, especially receivables and inventories, were the most common cases of AAER-related accounting problems; (2) managers responsible for financial statement fraud usually suffered negative consequences, including job loss and lawsuits; (3) negligent auditors were typically censured or barred from SEC practice; (4) auditors from smaller firms usually received the most severe penalties; (5) the firms that were guilty of financial statement fraud resulting from improper reporting normally experienced a typical two-day around 13 percent negative market return associated with the first disclosure of the alleged reporting violation; and (6) the declines in the market returns were positively associated with the relative income effect of financial statement fraud.

The SEC financial statement fraud activities can be classified in three different groups: (1) SEC fraud prevention activities; (2) SEC fraud detection activities; and (3) SEC fraud enforcement activities. Pincus, Holder, and Mock (1998) conducted a survey of a large sample of management, including officers and directors, attorneys, internal auditors, and external auditors, to determine the effectiveness of the SEC policies and activities in preventing, detecting, and disciplining cases of financial statement fraud. Pincus, Holder, and Mock (1988) conducted a survey to gather answers to two questions: (1) How effective are current SEC policies/activities at preventing, detecting, and disciplining fraud? and (2) What potential changes to current SEC policies/activities would be effective in improving fraud deterrence and detection?[17]Most respondents (63 percent of internal auditors, 56 percent of external auditors, 51 percent of attorneys, and 40 percent of management) replied that financial statement fraud is a problem of moderate to critical proportions.

SEC Fraud Prevention Activities

The respondents generally believed the SEC's policies and activities related to financial statement fraud to be at least somewhat effective. Most respondents stated that the following five fraud prevention activities of the SEC are moderately to very effective: (1) establishment of securities registration requirements; (2) review of registration requirements; (3) establishment of financial reporting requirements; (4) ongoing reviews of quarterly/annual filing; and (5) publicity related to enforcement actions.

There were few significant disagreements among the four groups of respondents regarding the aforementioned SEC fraud prevention activities. Management, internal auditors, and external auditors believed that the SEC's most effective fraud prevention policy and activity is publicity related to enforcement actions, whereas attorneys believed the establishment of financial reporting requirements to be the most effective prevention policy.

SEC Fraud Detection Activities

Pincus et al. (1998)[18] employed the following six SEC fraud detection activities: (1) reviewing any publicly traded company receiving other than an unqualified opinion; (2) reviewing all 8-K reports on auditor changes or unusual events; (3) responding to and considering tips from informants; (4) monitoring registration statements; (5) addressing quarterly annual filings; and (6) monitoring market activity. Although all four groups of respondents ranked the SEC's fraud detection activities as moderately effective, they all agreed that the SEC's most effective fraud detection activity is responding to tips from informants. Although, overall, agreement among the four groups was high, internal auditors rated the effectiveness of monitoring market activities lower than all the other groups; management ranked the effectiveness of monitoring quarterly and annual filings as very high; and attorneys ranked the effectiveness of reviews of other than unqualified opinions higher than all the other groups. The respondents expressed their concern that budget constraints limited the SEC's effectiveness in reviewing quarterly and annual filings.

SEC Fraud Enforcement Activities

Pincus et al. (1998)[19] examined the following seven SEC fraud enforcement activities: (1) referrals of cases to the Justice Department or state prosecutor's office; (2) referral of cases to state ethics boards or state boards of accounting; (3) litigation (e.g., actions brought under Rule 10(b)-5); (4) administrative proceedings against accountants; (5) administrative proceedings against issuers of securities; (6) court injunctions against a company's officers, directors, or employees; and (7) published reports of investigations. Most respondents from all four groups believed that all of the aforementioned SEC fraud enforcement activities are moderately to very effective in preventing and detecting financial statement fraud, except for the referrals to state ethics or accounting boards, which were expressed, at best, as slightly effective enforcement mechanisms.

Suggested Changes to the SEC Current System

The respondents in the Pincus et al. (1998)[20] study were asked to express their views on the effectiveness of 26 possible changes to the current SEC system. The following suggested changes received high rankings by all four groups of respondents: (1) stiffer penalties for those involved in cases of financial statement fraud; (2) requirements for audit committees for all publicly traded companies, and requiring that a majority of the audit committee be outside directors; (3) the requirement that a majority of the board of directors be outside directors; and (4) the development by the SEC of red-flag profiles to help spot cases for investigation. The most current reports (e.g., Blue Ribbon Committee on Audit Committee,

1999[21] and O'Malley Panel on Audit Effectiveness, 2000)[22] have already addressed the aforementioned changes.

SEC Accounting and Auditing Enforcement Releases

Empirical studies of financial statement fraud use the issuance of Accounting and Auditing Enforcement Releases (AAERs) issued by the SEC as a proxy for financial statement fraud. The use of AAERs has several advantages. First, AAERs are an objective means of identifying publicly traded companies with fraudulent financial reporting. Second, AAERs contain most financial statement fraud for companies with auditor litigation. Finally, the nature of financial statement fraud is described in AAERs. The only shortcoming of AAERs is that they limit the SEC enforcement actions, reflecting a specific SEC agenda for publicly traded companies.

ROLE OF THE AMERICAN INSTITUTE OF CERTIFIED PUBLIC ACCOUNTANTS

The American Institute of Certified Public Accountants (AICPA) is a national professional association of more than 330,000 certified public accountants in public practice, industry, government, and academia. Among other things, the AICPA establishes auditing and accounting standards, requires membership in its SEC Practice Section and compliance with the section's membership requirements by firms that audit publicly traded companies under SEC jurisdiction, and mandates peer reviews of all firms with an accounting and auditing practice. These activities are undertaken to protect the public's interest in the quality of financial reporting. The AICPA has issued several publications aimed at providing guidelines for independent auditors to improve their effectiveness in detecting financial statement fraud. Among those publications is Statement on Auditing Standards (SAS) No. 82 to make the auditors more skeptical in looking for errors, irregularities, and fraud in the financial statements. The AICPA has issued Practice Alert No. 98-3 entitled "Revenue Recognition Issues" and posted on its web site (www.aicpa.org) a useful toolkit on revenue recognition and the related audit issues to provide guidelines for auditors in thoroughly examining the legitimacy of other clients' earnings management practices.

Auditing Standard Setters

The Auditing Standards Board (ASB) of the AICPA issues GAAS and their interpretations of Statements on Auditing Standards (SASs) to provide guidance for external auditors in conducting their audits. The ASB also promulgates quality control standards to assess the quality of auditors' performance. The AICPA's Professional Ethics Executive Committee (PEEC) is responsible for changes to and interpretations of the AICPA's Code of Professional Conduct issued to measure personal integrity and professional qualifications of public accountants. The Independent Standards Board was issued in 1997 by the SEC and the AICPA to issue standards on auditor independence regarding the audits of publicly traded companies.

The Professional Ethics Division and the Joint Trial Board of the AICPA establish and enforce technical and ethical standards by investigating and adjudicating disciplinary charges against auditors. The Quality Control Inquiry Committee (QCIC) of the SECPS investigates allegation of an audit failure against a member firm with respect to an audit of an SEC registrant. The Public Oversight Board (POB) is an independent and private sector that was established to monitor and report on self-regulatory programs and activities of the SECPS of the Division for CPA Firms of the AICPA. The POB consists of five members, primarily nonaccountants, with a broad spectrum of business, professional, regulatory, and legislative experience. The POB is responsible for overseeing and reporting on the activities of the SECPS, with the intention to safeguard and act as an advocate of the public interest. The POB was established in 1977 by the AICPA to oversee and report on the Peer Review Program for auditing firms that audit publicly traded companies. The POB's success in the peer review program with increasing public confidence in the accounting profession encouraged the AICPA to continue supporting a POB composed of prominent individuals of high integrity and reputation. Since its inception in 1977, the POB has created several panels (Kirk Panel, 1993; O'Malley Panel, 2000) to address issues challenging the accounting profession.

The O'Malley Panel on Audit Effectiveness (1999)[23] identified the following limitations of the existing governance system for the accounting profession: (1) inadequate public representation on the self-regulatory bodies; (2) lack of unified leadership of several self-regulatory bodies; (3) ineffective communications with the SEC and among different entities in the current system; and (4) lack of consensus of interests and views among members of the AICPA and the AICPA's priorities. These perceived limitations have created an ineffective governance structure and erosion of confidence in the accounting profession. The panel made several recommendations to mitigate the limitations of current governance systems by building on the POB's experience and reputation to establish a unifying oversight body.

The panel suggests that the governance system of the accounting profession be unified under a strengthened, independent POB that oversees the profession's activities, including (1) establishing professional standards; (2) monitoring and measuring performance; (3) ensuring accountability for improper acts and substandard performance through an effective disciplinary system; and (4) identifying and addressing emerging issues and changes in the environment and the profession on a timely basis. The panel's proposed self-regulatory system consists of several governing bodies responsible for different self-regulatory functions. Under the proposed system, (1) the SEC and the POB are responsible for the oversight function; (2) the ASB and ISB and Professional Ethics Executive Committee will perform the standard-setting function; (3) the SECPS Peer Review Committee will perform the monitoring function; (4) the Quality Control Inquiry Committee, the Professional Ethics Executive Committee, and the Joint Trial Board will perform disciplinary functions; and (5) special review panels, convened by the POB with coordination and cooperation of other governing bodies and others, will address major emerging issues, changes, and challenges in the environment and the accounting profession.

Self-regulation or peer regulation related to activities of professional entities outside the firm enhance the quality of the practice. Over the years, CPA firms, including the Big Five, have only been able to stay members of the AICPA if the firm participates in one of the practice-monitoring programs, the SEC Practice Section or Private Companies Practice Service. Objectives of the SEC Practice Section are to:

- Improve the quality of services by CPA firms by establishing practice requirements for member firms.
- Establish and maintain an effective system of self-regulation of member firms by means of mandatory peer review, maintenance of appropriate quality controls, and the imposition of sanctions for failure to meet membership requirements.

In order to remain a member, participants must:

1. Adhere to quality controls standards established by the AICPA.
2. Submit peer reviews of firm's accounting and auditing practice every three years.
   - Conduct reviews in accordance with the review standards established by the section's peer review committee.
3. Ensure that all professionals in the firm reside in the United States and participate in at least 20 hours of continuing professional education every year and in at least 120 every 3 years.
   - Rotate audit partners on SEC engagements periodically.
   - Have an audit partner not involved in the engagement review and concur on audit reports before issuance.
   - Refrain from performing certain management-restricted consulting services.

To improve the quality of financial reporting, the AICPA established the Jenkins Committee to address issues challenging the accounting profession and standard setters. The Jenkins Committee considered users' needs for high-quality financial information, auditors' association with users' needs, alternative ways to meet those needs, and the costs and benefits of the alternatives. The Jenkins Committee made the following recommendations for standard-setting bodies[24]:

• National and international standard setters and regulators should increase their focus on the information needs of users, and users should be encouraged to work with standard setters to increase the level of their involvement in the standard-setting process.
• U.S. standard setters and regulators should continue to work with their non-U.S. counterparts and international standard setters to develop international accounting standards, provided the resulting standards meet users' needs for information.
• Lawmakers, regulators, and standard setters should develop more effective deterrents to unwarranted litigation that discourages companies from disclosing forward-looking information.
• Companies should be encouraged to experiment voluntarily with ways to improve the usefulness of reporting consistent with the committee's model.
• Standard setters and regulators should consider allowing companies that experiment to substitute information specified by the model for information currently required.
• Standard setters should adopt a longer-term focus by developing a vision of the future business environment and users' needs for information in that environment. Standards should be consistent directionally with that long-term vision.
• Regulators should consider whether there are any alternatives to the current requirements that public companies make all disclosures publicly available.
• The AICPA should establish a Coordinating Committee charged to ensure that the recommendations in this report are given adequate consideration by those who can act on them.

Another authority and responsibility delegated to the SEC is monitoring and disciplining external auditors of publicly traded companies. The Division of Enforcement investigates possible violations of the securities laws (SEC Acts of 1933, 1934) and recommends SEC action, either in a federal court or before an administrative law judge, and/or negotiates settlements on behalf of the SEC. Traditionally, the Division of Enforcement of the SEC has used prosecutorial discretion to pursue cases against accountants only if alleged reckless conduct is involved.

The accounting profession, especially CPAs, is recognized worldwide through the AICPA; however, CPA licenses are granted by the state board of accountancy of the individual states. Thus, the state boards of accountancy are the only governmental agencies that register audit firms to practice, handle licensing requirements, and can revoke or suspend them for the violation of ethical conduct or appropriate related standards, laws, and regulations.

AICPA National Conference on SEC Development

Each year, the AICPA sponsors its National Conference on SEC Development to discuss the current accounting and auditing issues facing the accounting profession. The 1999 conference, held in Washington, D.C., was one of the AICPA's largest regular conferences, with almost 2,000 attendees. The main theme of the conference was the need for transparent, high-quality financial reporting, especially in the area of revenue recognition. The SEC concerns regarding financial statement fraud, earnings management, and independence issues were discussed by the speakers, including SEC Commissioner Isaac C. Hunt, SEC Chief Accountant Lynn E. Turner, and Division of Enforcement Director Richard H. Walker.

SEC Commissioner Isaac D. Hunt stated that "Accounting professionals bear a heavy burden in assuring investor confidence, preventing financial fraud, and supporting a fair and efficient marketplace." SEC Chief Accountant Lynn E. Turner stated that "It is the auditor—not the attorney, not the underwriter—to whom the public looks to assure the credibility of financial statements."[25] The Enforcement Division Director Richard Walker warned that fraud is still too common. Deputy Chief Accountant Jan Adams urged registrants to become more personally active, both in the standard-setting process and more significantly in bringing developing matters to the attention of standards setters before they result in significant accounting and reporting diversity.[26]

ROLE OF THE FINANCIAL ACCOUNTING STANDARDS BOARD

The Financial Accounting Standards Board (FASB) has been the designated organization in the private sector for establishing standards of financial accounting and reporting since 1973. The SEC has delegated its accounting standard-setting authority to the FASB to establish authoritative Statements of Financial Accounting Standards (SFAS) to govern the preparation of financial reports. The mission of the FASB is to establish and improve standards of financial accounting and reporting by providing guidance to be used by companies for the measurement, recognition, and reporting of financial transactions and economic events and final preparation of financial statements. To accomplish its mission, the FASB acts to:

1. Improve the usefulness of financial reporting by focusing on the primary characteristics of relevance, reliability, quality, comparability, and consistency;
2. Keep standards current to reflect changes in methods of doing business or changes in the economic environment.
3. Consider promptly any significant areas of deficiency in financial reporting that might be improved through the standard-setting process.
4. Promote the international comparability of accounting standards concurrent with improving the quality of financial reporting.

5. Improve the common understanding of the nature and purposes of information contained in financial reports.[27]

The FASB develops broad accounting concepts and standards for financial reporting. It also provides guidance on implementation of standards. Concepts are useful to guide the board in establishing standards and in providing a frame of reference, or conceptual framework, for resolving accounting issues. The framework will help establish reasonable bounds for judgment in preparing financial information and increase understanding of, and confidence in, financial information on the part of users of financial reports. It also helps the public understand the nature and limitations of information supplied by financial reporting.

The board's work on both concepts and standards is based on research aimed at gaining new insights and ideas. The FASB staff and other entities, including foreign, national, and international accounting standard-setting bodies, conduct research. The board's activities are open to public participation and observation under "due process" mandated by formal Rules of Procedure. The FASB actively solicits the views of its various constituencies on accounting issues. Thus, the FASB's role in corporate governance is to provide the standards and concepts that publicly traded companies must observe in preparing and disseminating financial statements. The FASB's established accounting standards provide uniformity, consistency, and comparability in applying a set of commonly accepted accounting methods and procedures used to produce reliable, useful, and relevant financial information to the investing public for financial decision making.

The FASB deliberation process consists of a chain of events of technical agendas, research procedures, preliminary views, public hearings, exposure drafts, revised exposure drafts, and final statements of financial accounting standards. Accounting standards issued by the FASB are intended to enhance the relevance, usefulness, and reliability of the financial reporting process by providing guidelines for management in making accounting decisions and assisting users of published financial statements in assessing management's decisions.

SEC AND FASB RELATIONSHIP

The SEC, since its inception, has looked to the accounting profession for leadership in promulgating accounting standards to be used by publicly traded companies in measuring, recognizing, and disclosing financial transactions. The FASB has been issuing Statements of Financial Accounting Standards (SFAS) since 1973 that have had "substantial, authoritative support" by the commission. Financial statements that are not prepared in accordance with the SFAS may be considered to have no "substantial authoritative support" and to be misleading. Although the SEC has looked to and relied on the private sector (e.g., FASB) to promulgate GAAP, it may exercise its statutory authority to override, supplement, and/or amend private-sector standards. Since 1978, the SEC has rendered a report to

Congress on its oversight of the accounting profession, including the standard-setting activities of the FASB.

The SEC, since its inception in 1934, has allowed the private sector (e.g. FASB) to establish accounting standards for the external financial reporting process. Although both the SEC and FASB share the common goal of promulgating uniform financial reporting standards to ensure reliability, relevance, and usefulness of financial information for decision making, they may differ on many issues. Armstrong (1974)[28] addressed two of the major controversial issues. First, the SEC distinguishes between average investors and financial analysts as users of financial statements, whereas the FASB advocates general-purpose financial statements. Second, the SEC is more concerned with establishing accounting disclosure, whereas the FASB focuses more on measurement issues.

CONCLUSION

This chapter examines the role of governing bodies (e.g., SEC, AICPA, FASB) in the corporate governance structure. Those governing bodies are primarily responsible for promulgating generally accepted accounting principles (GAAP) to be used by companies in the preparation of financial statements and generally accepted auditing standards (GAAS) to be followed by independent auditors in the audit of financial statements. The SEC has traditionally looked to and relied on the private sector (e.g., FASB) to issue accounting standards, although it may exercise its statutory authority to override, supplement, and/or amend private-sector standards. These governing bodies play an important role in ensuring the quality, integrity, and reliability of the audited financial statements disseminated to the investing public. Vigilant and effective oversight of these governing bodies provides reasonable assurance that published financial statements are free of material misstatements caused by errors and frauds.

ENDNOTES

1. Blue Ribbon Committee (BRC). 1999. Report and Recommendations of the Blue Ribbon Committee on Improving the Effectiveness of Corporate Audit Committee. New York: NASD.

2. Brownlee, E. R., and S. D. Young. 1987. "The SEC and Mandated Disclosure: At the Crossroads." *Accounting Horizons* (September): 17–24.

3. Stigler, G. J. 1964. "Public Regulation of the Securities Market." *Journal of Business* (April): 117–142.

4. Jarrell, G. A. 1981. "The Economic Effects of Federal Regulation of the Market for New Securities Issues." *Journal of Law and Economics* (December): 613–675.

5. Benston, G. J. 1973. "Required Disclosure and the Stock Market: An Evaluation of the Securities and Exchange Act of 1934." *American Economic Review* (March): 132–155.

6. Ingram, R. W. and E. G. Chewning. 1983. "The Effect of Financial Disclosure Regulation on Security Price Behavior." *The Accounting Review* (July): 562–580.

7. Securities and Exchange Commission (SEC). 1973. Accounting Series Releases (ASR) No. 150. Available: www.sec.gov

8. Securities and Exchange Commission (SEC). 1977. The Report of the SEC Advisory Committee on Corporate Disclosure. Available: www.sec.org

9. Brownlee, E. R., and S. D. Young. 1987. "The SEC and Mandated Disclosure: At the Crossroads." *Accounting Horizons* (September): 17–24.

10. Levitt, A. 1999. Opening Statement of Chairman Arthur Levitt. Open Meeting on Regulation Fair Disclosure. Available: www.sec.gov/news/extra/seldisal.htm

11. Securities and Exchange Commission (SEC). 2000. Selective Disclosure and Insider Trading. Available: www.sec.gov/rules/final/33-7881.htm#P14_1382

12. Ibid.

13. King, R. and R. Schwartz. 1997. "The Private Securities Litigation Reform Act of 1995: A Discussion of Three Provisions." *Accounting Horizons* (Vol. 11, Nov. 1): 92–106.

14. Benston, G. J. 1973. "Required Disclosure and the Stock Market: An Evaluation of the Securities Exchange Act of 1934." *American Economic Review* (March): 132–155.

15. Feroz, E, K. Park, and V. S. Pastena. 1991. "The Financial and Market Effects of the SEC's Accounting and Auditing Enforcement Releases." *Journal of Accounting Research* (Vol. 29, Supplement): 107–148.

16. Ibid.

17. Pincus, R. V., W. W. Holder, and J. Mock. 1988. "The SEC and Fraudulent Financial Reporting." *Research in Accounting Regulation* (Vol. 2): 167–185.

18. Ibid.

19. Ibid.

20. Ibid.

21. Blue Ribbon Committee (BRC). 1999. Report and Recommendations of the Blue Ribbon Committee on Improving the Effectiveness of Corporate Audit Committee. New York: NASD.

22. Pubic Oversight Board (POB). 2000. The Panel on Audit Effectiveness Report and Recommendations. (August) Stamford, CT: POB.

23. Ibid.

24. American Institute of Certified Public Accountants. 1994. Improving the Business Reporting-A Customer Focus: Meeting the Information Needs of Investors and Creditors. AICPA Financial Reporting Special Committee. New York: AICPA.

25. The AICPA. 1999. The National Conference on SEC Developments: The 27th Annual Conference, December 7–8, 1999. Washington, D.C.

26. Ibid.

27. Financial Accounting Standards Board (FASB). Available: www.fasb.org

28. Armstrong, M. S. 1974. "Will Washington Listen to the Private Sector?" *Financial Executives* (March): 52–58.

Chapter 13

Fraud in a Digital Environment

INTRODUCTION

During the past decade, the U.S. economy has enjoyed a record-setting growth rate, high employment, and low inflation. The backbone of the new digital economy is emerging communication devices, the Internet, and advanced computing technology. To take full advantage of this emerging digital economy, businesses are employing business-to-business (B2B) and business-to-consumer (B2C) e-commerce by developing (1) a web site with internal resources that integrate long- and short-term organization goals; (2) the scope and scale of e-commerce operations focusing on security, privacy, and other risk management issues. The primary purposes of this chapter are to (1) discuss the emerging digital economy; (2) examine electronic financial reporting; (3) discuss risks associated with electronic business and financial reports; and (4) examine fraudulent financial activities involved in the electronic financial reporting process.

DIGITAL ECONOMY

During the past two years, there has been unprecedented growth in e-commerce. The Internet is revolutionizing the way businesses do business, from the acquisition and serving of customers to receiving payment electronically. Organizations are constantly discovering new ways to deliver products and services electronically. E-commerce is being viewed as an important factor for economic growth in the twenty-first century. The emerging digital economy has received significant attention by regulators and policy makers. Robert J. Shapiro, Under Secretary of commerce for Economic Affairs, states that:

> We all find ourselves in the midst of a technological revolution propelled by digital processing. All around us, in ways and forms we cannot fully appreciate, new digitally-based economic arrangements are changing how people work together and alone, communicate and relate, consume and relax. These changes have been rapid and widespread and often do not fit the established categories for understanding economic developments.[1]

Two facets of the "digital economy" are electronic commerce (which uses the Internet or some other nonproprietary, web-based system) and the information technology advances that enable e-commerce.

The Internet

The Internet was born in 1970, when four university computers and research centers were integrated via a shared network for academic and noncommercial purposes. In the early 1990s, with the introduction of the Mosaic browser (1993) and the Netscape browser (1994), the Internet became accessible to businesses and consumers. The advent of these web browsers significantly increased the use of the Internet for financial transactions at an exponential rate worldwide. Indeed, it took only four years for the Internet to reach 50 million people worldwide, while it took radio 38 years, television 13 years, and personal computers 16 years to achieve the same level of coverage.[2] Initially and continuously, the substantial growth of the Internet has been in consumer transactions (e.g., e-commerce).

The use of e-mail as a means of electronic communication can affect business decisions. Thus, the accuracy and integrity of information communicated through e-mail can be a major contributing factor in determining the reliability of financial information. E-mail messages particularly those without digital signatures can contribute to the occurrence of fraudulent financial activities and misappropriation of assets. For example, Melissa and the Love Bug viruses have caused billions of dollars of damages worldwide. The Emulex e-mail hoax contained misinformation about a company's financial prospects has caused a substantiated drop in the company's stock prices (Smith, 2001).[3] The perpetrators who send viruses and financial misinformation can significantly damage the quality, integrity, and reliability of financial reports. The Emulex hoax was an electronic fraud perpetrated against Emulex that resulted in the significant drop in its stock price and the disappearance of millions in market capitalization within a few hours when a fraudulent and misleading e-mail message was sent to Internet Wire, a news service. A fraudulent news release was sent through e-mail stating that Emulex's CEO was resigning because of the possible enforcement action by the SEC regarding the company's accounting practices. Emulex's stock fell by approximately 61 percent and market capitalization of more than $2 billion was lost. The fraudulent news release was sent by a former employee of Internet Wire for personal financial gain. The perpetrator was eventually caught and sanctioned.

Information Technology

Information technology (IT) has changed and will continue to change every facet of our lives from the way we live, how we work, how companies do business, and how communication and information are being transformed. Almost a decade ago, Robert K. Elliott, (1992, p. 85) stated that:

> IT is creating a wave of change that is crashing over accounting's shoreline. It crashed across the services in the 1980s. And it will crash across accounting in the 1990s.[4]

Technological advances, including the Internet and the use of e-commerce, have drastically changed the way business is done and how decisions are made by management and other users of financial reports. Accounting and financial reporting that provides relevant, useful, and reliable information to support decision making should also change to better serve decision makers. Indeed, Elliott's prediction regarding IT "crashing across accounting" is almost on time. The financial reporting process, during the past decade, has evolved from a manual process of business transactions and hard copy of financial reports to a computerized process and electronic version of financial reports to most recently advanced electronic financial reporting and online, real-time financial reports. The evolution of the financial reporting process indicates a shift away from static financial statements presented once a year to dynamic electronic financial reporting developed online and in real time. Electronic financial reports are intended to be more dynamic, relevant, current, complete, and comprehensible.

ELECTRONIC COMMERCE

E-commerce has already revolutionized the way business is conducted and the way organizations advertise, market, and sell their products and services. E-commerce is broadly defined as conducting business communications and transactions over computer-mediated networks. Exhibit 13.1 describes the types of e-commerce and their related strategies.

E-commerce strategies are as follows:

- Business-to-business (B2B) refers to online exchange of products and services involving transactions between businesses and suppliers (e.g., CISCO).

Exhibit 13.1. Electronic Commerce Strategies

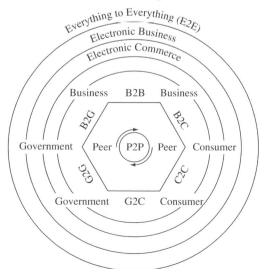

- Business-to-consumer (B2C) is an online strategy of business dealing directly with consumers (e.g., Amazon.com).
- Consumer-to-consumer (C2C) is an online strategy of consumers dealing directly with consumers (e.g., eBay).
- Business-to-government (B2G) deals with electronic transactions between businesses and governmental agencies local, state, and federal.
- Government-to-government (G2G) e-commerce strategy includes all online programs and activities between government agencies (e.g., electronic transfer of funds and direct deposit).
- Government-to-consumer (G2C) refers to online transactions between governmental agencies and consumers (e.g., electronic transfers of state subsidy checks).
- Peer-to-Peer (P2P) relates to sharing of computer capabilities between application platforms.

In the past two years, the number of B2Bs in the marketplace expanded from 400 to more than 1,000, and the amount of B2B transactions is estimated at more than $2.1 trillion for the year 2000.[5] Electronic data interchange (EDI) is a segment of B2B that has transformed the business environment primarily because many companies (e.g., Wal-Mart) require that their suppliers must develop EDI capabilities for online orders, shipments, and inventories. B2C, the online services provided by businesses to their customers, is also growing significantly. These services range from Internet service providers (ISPs) to direct selling of products via company web sites. E-cash and e-banks are two examples of B2C that are drastically changing the way banks operate and provide products and services to their customers. C2C is typically promoted through online auction forums such as eBay.com. These online forums bring potential buyers and sellers together where the negotiated price (among users) determines the selling price. E-commerce strategies and related transactions are presented in Exhibit 13.2.

E-commerce has provided businesses with many opportunities to save costs and continuously improve their performance. Customers can log on to a company's web site to shop for their products and services. Companies are able to accept orders online and payment electronically. Thus, e-commerce facilitates expediting orders, invoices, acknowledgements, and payments. The emerging e-commerce arena is so significant that the White House has appointed an e-commerce senior advisor to focus on the developments, opportunities, challenges, and significance of e-commerce in our society today.[6] Businesses of all sizes and in all industries can benefit significantly from the proper use of e-commerce. Small businesses can benefit from e-commerce to compete with larger companies for the same market or to reach out to the global marketplace. Large businesses need e-commerce to maintain their market share in the global marketplace, promote continuous growth, and reach new markets.

Exhibit 13.2. E-commerce Strategies and Transactions

Type	Description
Business to Business (B2B)	Businesses establish B2B capabilities through vendor-provided services and/or in-house resources.
Business to Consumer (B2C)	B2C offers companies opportunities to (1) improve communication and information management within the organization and with customers; (2) lend innovation and growth; and (3) increase the "bottom line."
Consumer to Consumer (C2C)	C2C refers to an online strategy of consumers dealing directly with consumers such as online auctions, eBay.
Business to Government (B2G)	B2G creates capabilities for companies to conduct online business with a wide variety of governmental agencies through an online auction to ensure competition (e.g., online government contracts with businesses replacing traditional sealed-bid auctions versus the online auctions).
Government to Consumer (G2C)	G2C provides opportunities for governmental agencies to disseminate information online, effectively, and efficiently (e.g., registering voters or cars, electronic transferring of state subsidy checks, and purchasing government-issued licenses online).
Government to Government (G2G)	G2G fosters online intergovernmental and activities between government agencies (e.g., digitized requests between agencies or employees for travel reimbursement).

In summary, e-commerce can provide businesses with unprecedented opportunities of broader market reach, increased efficiency and effectiveness, improved customer service, significant cost savings, instant communication with trading partners and consumers, improved profit margins through supply chain management, and better forecasting of customer demands for products and services.[7] There are fundamentally 10 reasons why a company should be using e-commerce to improve its competitive position in the global electronic marketplace: "(1) getting started is easy; (2) faster and cheaper delivery of information; (3) quick feedback on new products; (4) improved customer service; (5) global audience; (6) leveling the field of competition; (7) a strategic tool; (8) it's cheaper than a phone call; (9) enhanced business-to-business links; and (10) because your competitors are."[8] E-commerce has and will continue to improve the way organizations advertise, market, and sell their products and services.

E-commerce transactions are expected to grow from about 100 billion in 1999 to 7.3 trillion by 2004, which will count for 66 percent of the gross domestic product (GDP) in 2004, according to a recent estimate in the *New York Times*.[9] Organizations currently engaged in e-commerce or actively planning to use e-commerce are expecting rapidly increasing technological expansion and revenues.

CHANGES IN BUSINESS ENVIRONMENT

To understand why current business reports are not value relevant and not useful for financial decision making, it is necessary to analyze and understand the changes that have been taking place in business and how these changes have impacted information needs of users of business reports. The three fundamental changes in the business environment are (1) technological advances; (2) globalization of economy and business; and (3) convergence in the financial and capital market. The following sections examine these three changes in the business environment and their impacts on the financial reporting process.

Information Technology (IT)

Today's business increasingly is driven by information technology. Technology has not only rewritten the rules of business but also has made information preparation and dissemination inexpensive. Technological advances, including the Internet, have taken the form of low-cost, high-speed digital data transmission by using hardware that produces information quickly and easily and using software that reduces and, in many cases, eliminates much of the time, space, and other constraints to information. The progress in information technology, while reducing both transaction costs and asymmetric information problems, has increased economies of scale and scope in all business sectors. New technology, including e-commerce, provides both businesses and customers with a greater degree of information efficiency.

Several recent initiatives by the AICPA and the Canadian Institute of Chartered Accountants (CICA) address the impact of information technology on the accounting and auditing environment. First, in March 1999, a joint study group of the CICA and Accounting Standards Board (ASB) of the AICPA issued a report entitled "Continuous Auditing."[10] This report (1) discusses conditions that must be met for continuous auditing to be successful and viable; (2) examines how a hypothetical continuous audit engagement might be performed within the context of existing Canadian and United States assurance, attestation, and audit standards; and (3) identifies areas where further research is needed to effectively utilize continuous auditing in continuous assurance, attestation, and audit services. Second, in November 1999, a joint task force of the AICPA and CICA issued AICPA/CICA SysTrust®, entitled "Principles and Criteria for Systems Reliability".[11] SysTrust is a service designed to provide assurance about a system's reliability, integrity, security, quality, availability, and maintainability to management, customers, and business partners. SysTrust assurance can improve the reliability and integrity of accounting information systems in producing quality financial information free of material errors, irregularities, and fraud.

Globalization of Economy and Business

Online, real-time, and instantaneous information coupled with efficient and effective methods of transportation have enabled the world to become one giant marketplace. E-commerce enables businesses and consumers to buy products and services through the Internet in the global market as readily as they can from a local business.

The past decade witnessed a strong movement in the United States and other countries toward internationalization and harmonization of accounting standards and practices. Several standard-setting bodies worldwide have worked toward establishing a high-quality global financial reporting framework. The most active standard-setting bodies, among others, are the SEC, FASB, the International Federation of Accountants (IFAC), the International Accounting Standards Committee (IASC), the International Organization of Securities Commission (IOSCO), the International Coordination Committee for the Accountancy Profession (ICCAP), and the International Organization for Standardization (ISO).

In February 2000, the SEC issued a concept release and requested comments on the elements of a high-quality global financial reporting framework and the quality of the International Accounting Standards (IASs). IASs are promulgated by the IASC, which was established in 1973 by professional accounting groups in the United States and eight other industrialized countries as an independent and private standard-setting body to improve and harmonize accounting standards.

The nature and extent of global business, investors' and lenders' high interests in the international capital markets, and the move toward creating a giant global marketplace have encouraged the SEC to increase its involvement in several forums to develop a globally accepted, high-quality financial reporting framework. The SEC has been working with the IASC through the IOSCO to establish a set of accounting standards for cross-border offerings and listings. The globalization of economies, businesses, and capital markets, combined with the free trade agreements of the North American Free Trade Agreement (NAFTA) and General Agreement on Trade and Tariffs (GATT) have provided great impetus for the SEC's extensive involvement in high-quality and globally accepted international accounting standards.

Globalization is the most extensive and profound challenge facing the business community in the United States and abroad. The challenges of globalization compel the business community to better understand why and how major international events and developments affect business practice and conduct. As the business environment becomes more globalized, businesses are forced to face and respond to increasing international challenges and opportunities.

Convergence in the Financial and Capital Market

Convergence within the industry (e.g., the financial services industry among banks, insurance companies, mutual funds, and brokerages) has significantly affected the relationship between the company and its investors. There is now greater demand for timely disclosure of financial information. Convergence across industries has also changed financial reporting and relationships with financial markets and major market players.

The logic of a universal financial service (e.g., one-stop shopping for all financial services and products) offering a variety of financial products and services is compelling. Universal banking (bancassurance) has been practiced in Germany, Canada, and other countries, but, until recently, it has not been permitted in the United States. The Gramm-Leach-Bliley (GLB) Financial Modernization Act of 1999, which officially went into effect in March 2000, permits banks, securities firms, insurance companies, mutual funds, and brokerage firms to freely enter each others' business or consolidate.[12] The GLB Act allows creation of "financial holding companies" that may conduct a broad range of financial services, including insurance, securities underwriting, commercial banking, asset management, merchant banking, and real estate development and investment.

The recent wave of consolidations in the financial services industry has resulted in fewer but larger financial services organizations. The consolidation and convergence in the financial services industry could be the result of natural global market forces driving the industry toward larger organizations to achieve lower costs, higher profitability, and the ability to compete effectively in the global market. Traditionally, the financial services and products of banks, insurance companies, mutual funds, and brokerage firms were distinguishable and their roles separated. Today, the differences among functions of these financial services providers are becoming less noticeable.

The provisions of the GLB Act are summarized as follows:[13]

1. Permits commercial banks to affiliate with investment banks.
2. Allows companies that own commercial banks to offer all types of financial services.
3. Permits subsidiaries of banks to offer a broad range of financial services that are not allowed for banks themselves.
4. Creates "financial holding companies (FHC)" that may conduct a broad range of financial activities including commercial banking, insurance and securities underwriting, and merchant banking, as well as real estate development and investment.
5. Establishes restrictions on the locations of the new or expanded nonbank financial activities within the banking organizations.

6. Permits financial holding companies to conduct activities that are "complementary" to banking.

7. Grandfathers for 10 years the nonfinancial activities of firms predominantly engaged in financial business, with the possibility of a five-year extension.

8. Establishes the Federal Reserve Board as the primary regulator of financial holding companies.

9. Provides for functional regulation of financial activities by state and other federal agencies.

10. Gives the Treasury Department and the Federal Reserve the right to veto each other's decisions on new financial powers.

11. Requires financial institutions to establish privacy policies to prevent disseminating information about customer accounts to third parties. These policies should be disclosed at the start of a customer relationship and once a year thereafter.

12. Affects the implementation of the Community Reinvestment Act of 1977 (CRA), including the requirement that a bank holding company cannot become a financial holding company unless all the company's insured depository institutions have a CRA rating of at least satisfactory.

The passage of the GLB Act has raised some concerns that its implementation may (1) create concentration of economic power in the financial services industry that would make it more difficult for government to oversee the industry's activities and strategies in managing risk; and (2) cause more exposure for improper safeguarding of customer information and consumer financial privacy. To address those concerns, the GLB Act requires the Federal Reserve's "umbrella" supervisory authority over financial holding companies and four privacy provisions for sharing of customer information with others and protecting the privacy of customers' information. Specifically, the GLB Act requires financial services organizations to (1) establish and annually disclose a privacy policy; (2) provide customers the right to opt out of having their information shared with nonaffiliated third parties; (3) not share customer account numbers with nonaffiliated third parties; and (4) abide by regulatory standards to protect the security and integrity of customer information. Internal auditors can take an important proactive role in safeguarding customer information and ensuring consumer financial privacy in compliance with the requirements of the GLB Act.

Privacy is a critical issue under the GLB Act, which allows combined institutions to share customers' personal financial information internally and with affiliated groups. The violation of privacy can be disturbing because financial holding companies start offering one-stop shopping for loans, insurance, and investment services and products. The GLB Act provides customers with new rights to prevent financial service organizations from sharing their data with companies outside the corporate group, such as telemarketers, even though there are no curbs on data sharing among affiliated companies. Internal auditors with experience in the

Committee of Sponsoring Organizations (COSO) internal control provisions and requirements can provide valuable assistance to their organizations in implementing, maintaining, and monitoring the privacy policies and systems they are required to establish under the GLB Act.

ELECTRONIC FINANCIAL REPORTING

Traditionally, computers have been used in accounting for more than 50 years. The use of computers in processing financial transactions dates back to the mid-1930s, when IBM's punch card tabulators were used by big companies and government agencies in accounting. Subsequently, mainframes were used to process transactions electronically by middle-market companies as costs of computers dropped in the late 1960s and early 1970s. Finally, during the 1980s, low-cost personal computers (PCs) brought computers to all-sized businesses.

The currently prepared and disseminated web-based financial reports are exact electronic reproductions of the printed annual reports. Practically, they are electronic duplications of the traditional printed financial reports with no value added except they are readily available. Animated graphics, videos, and sound web-based financial reports, while improving the look and feel of information, add nothing to the usefulness of the information. Use of the Internet in the electronic financial reporting process should go beyond speed and accessibility and the next level of providing navigation through the information and making information readable by several application resources for a wide variety of purposes. The extensible business reporting language (XBRL) format is designed to accomplish this advanced level of using the Internet in the electronic financial reporting process.

Web-based reports offer many advantages to investors, creditors, and other users of financial information. The web is relatively inexpensive and facilitates a quick way to communicate with many users electronically; however, no standard currently exists for reporting information on the Internet, and it is often difficult to find accounting data for particular companies on the web. The evolution of the financial reporting process in the United States indicates a steady but slow move away from the paper-based historical financial reports to online reporting of historical financial reports on web sites, to online reporting of financial reports in Hypertext Markup Language (HTML), which allows for linking one section of the report to other relevant sections and documents, and to more advanced, reactive, online reporting by using extensible markup language (XML) and its financial offspring, extensible business reporting language (XBRL) to make financial information more interactive and consistent.

Businesses are currently using XML to conduct their transactions for placing orders, making reservations, and scheduling shipments. XML format will make the web accessible to agents and other automated processes to obtain computer-interpretable data sheets, including price lists, and then request quotes, place orders, and track shipments. XML enables data to define itself by creating marked-up files consisting of a set of tags that describe the information. XML is promoted by the World Wide Web Consortium (W3C), which is a vendor consortium unlike ISO, which is an international standards body. XML gained W3C recommendation status in February 1998. XML has gained international ground for electronic document exchange. XML is a subset of the ISO standard generalized markup language (SGML).

To foster and promote e-commerce worldwide, a 30-member consortium composed of financial, accounting, government, business, and technology organizations has developed e-commerce financial reporting standards. XBRL, a new freely licensed specification, provides reliable and efficient electronic exchange and extraction of financial information across all technology formats, including the Internet. Information entered in XBRL format can be produced as a printed financial statement for external reporting purposes, EDGAR documents required for SEC disclosure, an HTML document for a web site, or a printed document for specialized reporting.

XBRL is the most technological development that affects the business reporting process since the creation of the Internet. Under the XBRL format, an amount—let's say, 501000 Inventory for the first quarter of 2001—can be entered once and would retain the attributes of where it belongs in a financial statement. It can be transported into spreadsheets, databases, printed reports, web pages, EDGAR, and more without changing its attributes or data reentry. Thus, business reports or any information can be entered once in XBRL format and communicated and transformed to (1) the SEC's EDGAR in a 10K or 10Q report; (2) the IRS on a tax reform; (3) the organization's web site; (4) the entity's financial statement report writer; (5) an independent auditor's database for audit purposes; (5) credit agencies for credit rating; (6) the printed portion of the entity's annual report; and/or (7) other reporting purposes.

SEC Chairman Arthur Levitt in the fall 2000 council of the AICPA, while addressing the members, stated that:

> I would like to see you hone specific, but plain English definitions for the types of information you believe should be included in public disclosure. I would like to see you take your XBRL project a step further, providing account classifications for companies in common industries. In short, I challenge you to turn all of this data into meaningful information for investors.[14]

Subsequent to Levitt's remarks and encouraging words about XBRL, Barry Melancon, President and CEO of the AICPA, responded by saying that:

> The AICPA has been working with XBRL Steering Committee for more than a year to develop XBRL . . . We're encouraged by Chairman Levitt's remarks acknowledging XBRL and recommending its further development. Investors will be significantly helped using XBRL by having access to quicker, meaningful data from financial statements for better investment decisions.[15]

Publication of financial information in the XBRL format can save significant amounts of time and cost in preparing and disseminating financial information as well as in searching and exploring information into other "XML-aware" applications.

The first version of XBRL, "Version 1.0 of the Extensible Business Reporting Language," customized for financial reporting was released on July 31, 2000, which creates a "common taxonomy" (classification) of financial terms for online financial reporting purposes. This taxonomy contains 1,600 standardized tags that allow data to be identified for transport from proprietary systems to browsers or software packages for easy viewing, analysis, a universal exchange, and sharing of data. This version allows preparation of XML-based financial statements using XBRL for the exchange and analysis of financial information.

The first XBRL taxonomy is intended for commercial and industrial companies reporting according to U.S. generally accepted accounting principles (GAAP). An XBRL taxonomy is a classification and directory of financial statement items and definitions that meet the requirements of the overall XBRL specification. This directory describes each data element by a specific type of business entity in the specified industry. The XBRL taxonomies have already been developed for U.S. mutual funds, U.S. federal entities, and commercial and industrial companies that use standards set by the International Accounting Standards Committee (IASC). The use of IASC taxonomy gives a global implication, adoption, and implementation of XBRL.

Further development of XBRL taxonomies for different industrial sectors (i.e., commercial, financial institutions, governmental agencies, and not-for-profit organizations) will promote the use of standardized and electronic financial statement fraud detection approaches and applications. Electronic financial reports published on the Web and the Internet provide an opportunity to identify visible factors (red flags), signaling the likelihood of the occurrence of financial statement fraud.

Benefits of XBRL

XBRL offers many benefits to a variety of users, including investors, analysts, companies, industries, software, vendors, and publishers of financial statements. Much of the demand for XBRL comes from investors, creditors, and other users of financial reports. Under the XBRL format, they are able to extract, analyze, and process electronic financial statements on a more efficient and timely basis. Because XBRL enables a variety of formats, investors, creditors, and other users of financial reports can receive the information they prefer in a specific style of analysis. Furthermore, by making financial information available on corporate web sites via XBRL, investors who have a reasonable understanding of financial reporting can constantly and on a real-time basis obtain the desired financial information.

XBRL lowers the cost of preparing and disseminating financial statements. Currently, publicly traded companies typically prepare three sets of financial statements, including one for external release, one to be filed with the SEC, and one to post on the company web site. Under the XBRL format, financial statements will only need to be prepared one time to be printed, posted on the web, or filed with the SEC. This one-time processing and preparation of financial reports in serving a broad range of purposes should reduce the opportunity for manipulation of financial information and, accordingly, reduce the likelihood of financial statement fraud.

XBR is an open language that offers independent software vendors an incentive to incorporate XBRL into their applications to enhance the usability of this software. Thus, virtually any software product that manages financial information could use XBRL to import and export additional formats. Although XBRL enables users of financial statements to exchange financial information electronically, financial statement publishers and other data aggregators will experience reduced operating costs associated with more efficient data collection and a reduction of errors.

Preparers and users of financial reports can take advantage of the following benefits offered by using the XBRL format for the financial reporting process:

- Can be built into financial and accounting software free of charge, which allows the automatic exchange and reliable extraction of business information across all software formats and technological platforms, including the Internet.
- Makes the preparation, dissemination, and analysis of financial reports more efficient and effective.
- Provides more relevant and reliable information by allowing for technology independence, less human involvement, and more reliable and efficient extraction of financial information.
- Makes financial information more readily available and less expensive by providing faster, more accurate electronic searches for information.
- Creates opportunities for online, real-time accounting systems with a standards-based method of preparing, disseminating, extracting, and analyzing financial information.
- Makes it easier for those with less technological competence to take advantage of powerful tools.
- Enables reporting from multiple locations and departments, which ultimately benefits all users of the financial information supply chain.
- Permits better communication within the financial reporting chain (e.g. shareholders, suppliers, auditors, lenders, employees, governmental agencies).
- Enables plug-and-play systems by creating opportunities to have authentic "roll your own," best-of-breed interoperable systems without having to disclose any additional information beyond what is required under the current accounting standards.
- Empowers internal audit functions with new tool sets for analytical and related risk management issues.

- Creates smooth information flow by (1) reducing the need to enter financial information more than one time; (2) reducing the risk of data entry error; and (3) eliminating the need to manually key information for various formats.
- Applies to all managerial and financial philosophies and concepts, including just-in-time (JIT) inventory planning and controlling, activity-based costing (ABC), balanced scorecard, and value reporting.

Challenges of XBRL

The challenges of XBRL for publicly traded companies are security, scope, continuous assurance, fair disclosure, privacy, membership on an XBRL committee, and implementation of the XBRL-based reporting system.

Security

Electronic financial reporting has created unprecedented security issues that should be addressed to secure the integrity and quality of XBRL-generated information and the trust as well as confidence in electronic transactions. Organizations should ensure that XBRL-prepared and disseminated information is properly safeguarded. The risk of fraud in electronic financial reports is real and can be substantial for businesses. To reduce the risk of fraudulent electronic financial reports, several significant technologies have been developed to validate, authenticate, and secure electronic transactions.

The considerable threat of security breaches encourages software developers such as Microsoft to develop Designing Secure Web-based Applications for Microsoft Windows 2000. It provides a comprehensive insight and pragmatic advice on the process of building secure web-based applications and make recommendations on how to best address security threats.

Information security and related control considerations have always been important organization issues. Electronic financial reports and online e-commerce creates considerable security concerns. Viruses, worms, and hackers put online e-commerce businesses at particular risk. A secure information system is vital to publicly traded companies' operations and the financial reporting process. As security breaches continue to become more prevalent in business environments, companies should consider the appropriate security technologies that help prevent, detect, and correct cyber crime, including electronic financial statement fraud. Security technologies and related safeguarding controls should be designed and implemented. Examples of these security technologies intended to protect information systems and the electronic transfer of information are electronic authorization, electronic authentication, and encryption.

Control considerations for the electronic financial reporting process are security services, antivirus solutions, firewalls, encryption technologies, and intrusion detection. An information security service provides security management, firewall integration, and vulnerability assessments. Security programs, including antivirus software, detect and prevent computer viruses that damage information systems. An effective firewall protects computer systems from hackers on the web. Encryption technologies provide solutions to access controls while intrusion detection alerts companies to hacking and other unauthorized attempts to access their systems. Data integrity and confidentiality are two of the most major elements stressed in security concerns. Data integrity can be enforced through hash totals, while data confidentiality can be enforced through cryptography and encryption. XBRL developers have not yet properly addressed these security measures primarily because XBRL was developed under the premise that data integrity can be improved by taking such measures as supplementary redundant error correction bytes, cryptographic hashing, and signing with a private key.

Security of the XBRL-based financial reporting process is a major challenge for publicly traded companies to ensure that access to electronic data is restricted to authorized personnel and that modifications and destruction of electronic data are restricted to appropriate individuals. Companies should design and implement adequate and effective control activities to safeguard electronically presented financial information from hackers and potential manipulation. Security is an issue that may plague XBRL primarily because many organizations may not be comfortable using a system that transmits their financial information so easily and exposes it to the risk of hackers breaking into their system. Companies can protect the integrity of their XBRL-based financial system and ensure its security by using any of the available Internet security programs such as SysTrust and WebTrust offered by the AICPA.

Scope

The scope of the audit function can be increased by use of the XBRL format. Auditors are no longer limited to sample tests and assessing the sample results as they relate to the transaction population. Highly automated audit procedures should be used to gather sufficient and competent audit evidence. Auditors should perform continuous audit procedures, particularly when the audit process has identified anomalies. Auditors should ensure that their organization's web site, in displaying financial information, is properly indicating when, where, and how the information is hyperlinked to matters outside of financial statements.

Continuous Assurance

The emerging technological frontier (the Internet) has drastically changed the traditional means of preparing and disseminating business information. Currently, many companies publish their business information, including both financial information (e.g., audited financial statements and the independent auditor's report, Forms 10-K and 10-Q) and other information (e.g., management analyses, marketing) electronically. The electronically published business information is highly integrated through hyperlink (e.g., pension accounting policies and practices can be connected with personnel promotion and advancement plans). This makes separation of financial information from other information difficult if not impossible and thus, has raised several concerns for independent auditors. These concerns and questions have been addressed in "Practice Alert 97-1 by the SEC Practice Section Professional Issue Task Force."[16] The appropriate questions raised in the Practice Alert are as follows:

1. What is (are) an independent auditor obligation(s) for other information presented in an electronic site that contains audited financial statements and the related auditor's report? The interpretation to auditing standards pertaining to "other information in electronic sites that contain audited financial statements," addressed this question. The interpretation advises that independent auditors do not have an obligation to read or consider other information included in an electronic site.

2. How may a client ensure the security of information integrity (e.g., hackers) when published on the Internet? The independent auditor should discuss the security and related control activities of electronic sites with the client to ensure integrity of these sites.

3. Can a client who presents audited financial statements and other information on the Internet set it up so that a user knows when they are hyperlinking to matters outside of audited financial statements? Auditors should advise their clients to create distinct boundaries around their audited financial statements and related audit reports and to remind users of this. Alternatively, entities may wish to clearly mark each page of the audited financial statements and related audit report as being a part of the annual report. Entities may also wish to provide a facility to their electronic site that would allow easy and complete access to all parts of audited financial statements and the related audit report in an orderly manner.

The challenge for auditors is to keep assurance on the data up to date, especially when financial information is prepared in online, real-time, XBRL-based format. Continuous auditing can be achieved only by embedding source code into the organization's reporting system that reports abnormalities to auditors for immediate review. Shorter time frames for reporting financial information would result in the need for a high degree of reliable automation in producing information soon after the occurrence of events.

Continuous auditing allows auditors to specify transaction selection criteria to choose the specified transactions and perform both tests of controls and substantive tests throughout the year on an ongoing basis. Thus, auditors should be involved in the design of the XBRL-based accounting system to place the required audit modules in the process and outputs. Continuous auditing gathers audit evidence regarding the following audit questions: (1) how data are electronically gathered; (2) how, where, why, and from what parties the data are originated; (3) what authentication techniques are used; (4) what networks are used to originate and transmit the data; and (5) how the data are processed once they are received by the XBRL system. Auditors also use control agents, which are auditor-defined heuristics applied to a transaction set.[17] The agent, upon finding unusual activities, first searches for similar activities to explain the activity pattern and alerts the auditor regarding unprecedented or unusual activities. Continuous auditing assists auditors in shifting from a reactive to a proactive audit model. XBRL enables auditors to move from a paper-based conventional audit to an electronic-based continuous assurance.

The focus of audit has shifted from manual detection of financial statement fraud to technology-based prevention of financial statement fraud. Although some financial statement fraud may never be prevented, the use of audit software packages can assist auditors to build-in reports and analysis to identify areas of concern when unusual relationships exist. The ability to include internal checks into advance computer systems can enable management and auditors to prevent and detect errors and irregularities that can cause financial statement fraud. The use of technological advances such as computerized audit tools and techniques (CATTs) enable auditors to test almost 100 percent of transactions, which in turn, enable them to more frequently, effectively, and efficiently discover financial statement fraud.

Fair Disclosure

XBRL does not require any further disclosure of financial information beyond what is currently required under the generally accepted accounting principles (GAAP). XBRL is a "GAAP-neutral" tagging structure using a GAAP-specific language to describe financial information by industry sector. XBRL is intended to be used on a global basis by creating tagging data specifications that conform to the various countries' accounting principles and industry practices. XBRL, which enhances the capability of financial reports, enables flexibility to accommodate a company's internal environment, processes, systems, and styles. XBRL enables organizations to comply with the new SEC Regulation FD on "fair disclosure" by electronically and simultaneously disclosing all relevant financial information to all users of financial reports, including analysts and investors. This online and real-time disclosure of financial information creates a level playing field for all users of financial statements, and thereby reduces the likelihood of selective disclosure and inside trading. Thus, XBRL, while not requiring additional disclosure beyond what is currently being presented by organizations, can aid in addressing the new SEC Fair Disclosure regulation with the XBRL format. All parties involved in the business reporting chain will have equal and simultaneous access to publicly available information disseminated by corporations.

Privacy

XBRL is derived from XML, which tags financial information. The tagged information is then accessible to a wide variety of users for different purposes across all programs. As the number of XBRL users worldwide increases, more financial information is captured, stored, and made available electronically worldwide. The power of XBRL enables financial information to be tracked, used, and interpreted without the organization's consent or knowledge. XBRL adds a new direction to the online privacy consideration. The Comptroller of the Currency (OCC) has recently issued a comprehensive handbook that addresses the risks presented by electronic banking, including technology risk management, web privacy policies, cyber-terrorism, consumer compliance, and reporting of computer-related crime.[18]

Section 729 of the GLB Act requires that the OCC and the other federal banking agencies discuss and research banking regulations pertaining to offering online financial services and products, including privacy issues.[19] The privacy issues of providing financial services electronically have been addressed in Title V of the GLB Act, consistent with the current banking regulations of safety and soundness. The OCC's Internet Banking Handbook and other supervisory guidance address the risk presented by electronic banking, including proper safeguarding of customers' identifiable personal information. The GLB Act went into effect in March 2000, and privacy provisions of the act took effect on November 13, 2000. Financial institutions must have established or revised their privacy policies to conform with the privacy provisions of the GLB Act. Furthermore, the passage of the Electronic Signatures in Global and National Commerce Act that gives online electronic documents the same legal status as signed paper documents creates more security and privacy challenges for organizations and poses new security challenges for customers.[20] Inadequate and ineffective privacy policies and systems and lack of proper disclosure of such policies and systems by corporations, especially dot-coms, can alienate customers who are not only concerned about lack of safeguarding of financial information privacy but also are educated and increasingly aware of privacy issues online. Thus, to properly safeguard customers' personal information and to enhance their confidence in this new online universal financial services marketplace, consumers' concerns about privacy must be addressed.

The privacy of information refers to security and confidentiality of personal and financial information obtained by businesses about their customers or trading partners. This privacy of information has not been properly safeguarded and, in many instances, has been violated. Recent examples of e-commerce security lapses are (1) America Online's (AOL) admission in July 2000 that hackers gained access to member accounts through an e-mail virus sent to its employees; (2) lawsuits brought against AOL's Netscape division accusing it of breaking federal privacy laws by tracking customer downloads; and (3) confession by a member of failed consumer-oriented dot-coms regarding selling customers' personal information to the highest bidder.[21] Another example of the privacy-related issue is toysmart.com, which went bankrupt recently and attempted to sell off an extensive customer database as part of its bankruptcy liquidation efforts. The Federal Trade Commission (FTC) ruled that "even failing dot-coms must abide by their promise to protect the privacy rights of their customers" primarily because the company had a posted privacy policy stating that the company would not sell data to third parties.[22]

These incidents of violation and lack of security of customer information have raised several consumer personal and financial privacy issues:

1. Should businesses establish and maintain adequate and effective privacy policies and systems?
2. What information can be gathered and stored by such systems?
3. Should the gathered information be used by the businesses?
4. Can businesses share or sell customers' information without their permission?
5. Can customers verify, change, and/or delete the information?
6. Should there be an independent verification of the established privacy policies and systems?
7. Should the use of cookies be allowed?
8. Is there a need for legislation to protect online consumers' privacy?

The issue of privacy on the Internet is of concern to the business community, consumers, legislators, and society at large. Many private organizations have been forced to address online privacy protection issues of consumers and to proactively advocate for greater privacy security. Several privacy legislations have been passed to secure privacy of information online. The FTC has studied online privacy issues since 1995 and reported periodically to Congress on the state of online privacy and the role and effectiveness of industry self-regulation. The FTC has provided three reports to Congress.[23] In its 1988 "Privacy Online: A Report to Congress," the commission (1) presented the results of its first online privacy survey, which indicated that while almost all (92 percent) surveyed web sites collected identifiable personal information, only 14 percent disclosed their privacy policies and practices; (2) described the fair information practice principles of notice, choice, access, and security; (3) suggested the use of reliable mechanisms (enforcement) to provide sanctions for noncompliance with the four principles; and (4) advocated either governmental or self-regulatory programs to protect privacy online.

In the 1999 Report to Congress entitled "Self-Regulation and Privacy Online," the FTC recommended that self-regulation of privacy issues be given more time while demanding industry efforts to implement fair information practice principles of the 1998 Report.[24] The FTC, in its 2000 Online Privacy Survey, (1) indicated that web sites collect a vast amount of identifiable personal consumer information; (2) found that most of the surveyed sites (97 percent in the random sample and 99 percent in the most popular group) obtain an e-mail address or some other type of individually identifiable information; (3) concluded that there has been continued improvement in the percentage of web sites that post at least one privacy disclosure (88 percent in the random sample and 100 percent in the most popular group); (4) found that only the minority of web sites (20 percent of web sites in the random sample and 42 percent in the most popular group) implement the four "fair information practice principles" of notice, choice, access, and security; (5) suggested that the industry self-regulation initiatives of online privacy seal programs fall far short of broad-based implementation and have not been adequate; and (6) concluded that legislation is necessary to ensure further implementation of fair information practices online.[25]

The House is considering a bill entitled H.R. 4049 to establish a "Commission for the Comprehensive Study of Privacy Protection."[26] This bill includes an AICPA amendment requiring the commission to report on third-party verification as an enforcement mechanism. Since the AICPA has established CPA WebTrust attestation services, CPAs can serve as a third-party verification to examine a business's privacy policy to provide reasonable assurance that its privacy claims are true. When H.R. 4049 becomes law, the commission would also study a broad range of privacy issues, including online privacy, identity theft, privacy in the workplace, and the protection of health, medical, financial, and governmental records. Other congressional bills regarding major privacy issues that were introduced in 1999 and are still pending are the Wireless Privacy Enhancement Act (H.R. 514), Close Pager Authorization Act (S.411), Protection of Children From Online Predators and Exploitation Act (H.R. 1159), Online Privacy Protection Act (S.809), Electronic Rights for the 21st Century Act (E.RIGTS, S.854), Internet Growth and Development Act (H.R. 1685), Electronic Privacy Bill of Rights Act (H.R. 3321), and Secure Online Communication Enforcement Act (S. 2063).

The Internet enables businesses, organizations, and individuals to collect a vast amount of information, which has caused great concern regarding privacy violations. Several privacy groups have been formed worldwide to address the privacy rights and security of individuals browsing through the Internet and web. In June 2000, the World Wide Web Consortium (W3C) introduced the first initiative by the industry regarding web site privacy policies. The consortium developed the Platform for Privacy Preferences Project (P3P) that can translate web site privacy policies into an XML statement viewable in all software programs that can be read automatically by P3P-enabled web browsers.[27] Companies can set their own privacy preferences in their browsers and then use P3P to compare the preferences against the policy at each web site visited. A significant number of web sites already claim P3P compliance, including AOL, AT&T, IBM, Microsoft, and the White House, among others. Internal auditors can ensure that their organization's web site is P3P compliant.

Trust

The use of XBRL can produce and disseminate a significant amount of business information. The accuracy and reliability of distributed information can play an important role in the success of XBRL as a business-reporting vehicle. The accounting profession, especially AICPA by establishing WebTrust standards for practitioners who perform such services for their clients, can provide reasonable assurance on the trustworthiness of XBRL-generated business reports. To obtain customers' confidence regarding the proper stewardship of their personal and financial privacy, many businesses, especially dot-coms, have obtained seals or insignias for their web sites. Many organizations have offered seals for businesses that maintain adequate and effective privacy policies for their web sites.

Effective and efficient privacy seal programs provide reasonable assurance that organizations' (1) privacy policies for the collection, use, and disclosure of identifiable personal information are adequate; (2) privacy practices are in compliance with stated policies; and (3) consumers' complaints are resolved properly and in a timely manner. Several privacy seal programs have been created to (1) protect individually identifiable information; (2) set standards for ethical e-commerce; (3) satisfy guidelines for self-regulation; (4) foster consumer confidence in the way businesses handle personal information online; (5) guarantee that organizations safeguard the collected personal information; (6) promote self-regulation of e-commerce by protecting online privacy; (7) provide a mechanism for consumer-friendly dispute resolution; (8) and require participating organizations to conduct annual assessments of their privacy policies and practices.

The AICPA now offers CPAs the opportunity to develop a new business practice by introducing the WebTrust and SysTrust programs. WebTrust addresses the primary privacy concerns of both the business community and the online customer. WebTrust is the online privacy seal program that indicates that those web sites bearing the CPA WebTrust Seal are trustworthy and reliable with regard to confidential consumer information. CPAs provide reasonable assurance that web sites bearing the WebTrust Seal that offer e-commerce meet standards of consumer information protection, transaction integrity, and sound business practices.

The AICPA/CICA Systems Reliability Task Force has issued an exposure draft entitled "SysTrust™ Principles and Criteria for Systems Reliability."[28] This version 2.0 of SysTrust provides guidelines for the SysTrust assurance service to improve the confidence of management, customers, and business partners of e-commerce systems. Unlike the previous version, this exposure draft would allow practitioners to report on any of the four SysTrust principles of availability, security, integrity, or maintainability. Availability means that the system is available for operation and use. Security indicates that the system is safeguarded against unintended and unauthorized access. Integrity means that the system processing is complete, accurate, timely, and authorized. Maintainability indicates that the system can be updated when necessary. Internal auditors can work with outside auditors to ensure that these four principles of reliability of the system have been achieved.

XBRL Membership

The XBRL steering committee is currently developing industry-specific taxonomies in a wide variety of industries, including commercial, mutual fund reporting, governmental entities, financial services, and not-for-profit organizations. XBRL is gaining global support from the financial community, the accounting profession, software developers, hardware and software vendors, investment companies, and regulators. Exhibit 13.3 shows XBRL committee

Exhibit 13.3. XBRL Steering Committee Members as of February 28, 2001

Accounting Software Developer	Business Firms	Governmental & Not-for-Profit Entities	Hardware and Software Vendors	Investment Companies	Professional Service Firms	Professional Organizations
Advisor Technology Services	ACCPAC International, Inc.	Defense Finance and Accounting Service (DFAS)	Bridge Information Systems	Dow Jones & Company, Inc.	Arthur Andersen, LLP	AICPA
Best Software	ACL Services Ltd.	National Center for Charitable Statistics at the Urban Institute	EKeeper.com	EDGAR Online	BDO Seidman, LLP	Certified General Accountants Association of Canada
Count-net.com	Business Wire	National Information Infrastructure Enterprise Promotion Association	Elemental Interactive	Fidelity Investments	CPA2biz	CICA
e-Numerate Solutions Incorporated	CaseWare International Inc.	PPA GmbH	FinArch	J.P. Morgan & Co. Inc.	Crowe, Chizek and Company, LLP	CPA Australia
ePace Software	Cogniant, Inc.	Practitioners Publishing Company (PPC)	IBM	Moody's Risk Management Services, Inc.	Deloitte & Touche, LLP	Hong Kong Society of Accountants
ePartners, Inc.	Eledger.com, Inc.	SAP AG	Infoteria Corporation	Morgan Stanley Dean Witter	Dresdner Kleinwort Benson	IASB
Epicor Software Corporation	First Light Communications, Inc.	Seattle Pacific University: Center for Professional Development	Innovision Corporation	Standard & Poor's	Ernst & Young, LLP	ICAA

Financial Reporting Solutions (Pty) Ltd.	General Electric Company	Royal NIVRA	Japan Digital Disclosure Inc.	The Woodburn Group	Grant Thornton, LLP	IFAC
Financial Software Group	GlobalFilings, Inc.	Census Bureau	Lawson Software	Thomson Financial	KPMG, LLP	IMA
FRx Software Corporation	HOLT Value Associates		Microsoft Corporation	UsAdvisor, Inc.	KPMG Consulting	Institute of Chartered Accountants in Australia
Gcom2 Solutions	ILumen, Inc.		MIP, Inc.		Pricewaterhouse Coopers, LLP	Institute of Chartered Accountants in England and Wales
Great Plains Software, Inc.	Multex.com, Inc.		Newtec, Inc.		Reuters Group LP	FDIC
Hyperion Solutions Corp.	NavisionDamgaard		Oinke, Inc.			
NetLedger, Inc.	NEC Planning Research Inc. (Japan)		Oracle Corporation			
Sage Software	New River, Inc.		PeopleSoft, Inc.			
Virtual Growth, Inc.	Bowne & Co., Inc.		Syspro			
XBRL Solutions, Inc.						

Source: www.xbrl.org

members according to their specification as of February 28, 2001. XBRL membership structure consists of all Big Five professional services firms, professional organizations, software developers, the international business community, and investment companies. Recently, many publicly traded companies have started to support further development of the XBRL taxonomy, especially when Arthur Levitt, former chair of the SEC, in remarks before the Fall Council meeting on October 24, 2000, suggested the use and further development of XBRL in financial reporting.[29] More specifically, Levitt stated, "I would like to see you [AICPA] take your XBRL project a step further, providing account classifications for companies in common industries."

XBRL Implementation

Corporations should cooperate with software developers and web site designers in further development of software components to establish XBRL-compatible code and to apply XBRL to a variety of software programs. Corporations should effectively and efficiently implement XBRL to take advantage of a broad range of XBRL benefits, including the improved reliability and flexibility of financial reports and possibility of continuous assurance. Proper implementation of XBRL requires (1) development of a taxonomy (specification) that is standardized and uniform among all companies in the same industry; (2) an application that enables the preparation of financial statements "tagged" with the XML-based format adhering to the specification; and (3) style sheets that render information for a specific format or variety of formats.

CONCLUSION

Financial statement fraud attributed to computer crimes in the United States almost doubled to $10 billion in 1999 compared to the previous year and will continue to rise exponentially in part because of the surging popularity of the Internet.[30] Internet-based technologies are (1) transforming major business functions, (2) changing the way companies do business, (3) creating e-business forms of exchanging services and products, and (4) encouraging use of the electronic financial reporting process, especially the newly developed extensible business reporting language (XBRL). Opportunities, complexities, challenges, and changes associated with e-business create risks. Effective management of e-business risks ensures achievement of business objectives and creation of shareholder value. E-business risks that should be effectively managed are (1) security risk, (2) privacy risk, (3) legal and regulatory issues, (4) consumer confidence, and (5) risk of fraudulent electronic financial reports. The Internet-based business transactions shall be safeguarded from theft and fraud.

Organizations using e-business must establish adequate and effective security procedures to ensure the reliability, integrity, and quality of e-business transactions. Organizations must take holistic and proactive approaches to security by building and integrating fail-safes into their e-business systems. Privacy is viewed as a fundamental right, and customers expect organizations conducting e-business to consider privacy measures as their top priority. Privacy protections must be an integral part of the e-business infrastructure. A survey conducted by Pricewaterhouse Coopers reveals that about 90 percent of users are concerned about privacy measures. The legal and regulatory issues and framework of e-business is still in the early stages of development regarding the legitimacy of the content, signatures, and contracts. Management should assess all circumstances that may constitute a contract in an electronic environment. A fundamental issue of e-business is the extent of consumer confidence regarding security, privacy, and disclosure of relevant business practices.

The rapid growth of e-business in general, and dot-com companies in particular has drawn significant attention by the regulatory bodies (e.g., SEC), the accounting profession (e.g., AICPA), and the global business community regarding the legitimacy of their reported earnings and quality of their financial reporting. Users of financial statements especially financial analysts, often focus on revenue growth and gross profit margins of dot-com companies rather than the traditional performance measures of net income and earnings per share. Revenues have often been overstated by incorrectly "grossing up" the effect of transactions when revenues and expenses are reported in offsetting amounts. Gross margins are also overstated by incorrectly classifying costs of sales and marketing expenses. These incorrect accounting practices are being justified in the sense that they do not affect the bottom line.

Many companies are currently preparing and disseminating their business and financial reports electronically. It is expected that unaudited financial information and analyses will also find their way onto electronic bulletin boards and Internet. While this practice satisfies the demand in the marketplace for more timely, readily available, online information, the reliability and credibility of such unaudited financial information have been challenged by many professional organizations (e.g., AICPA, SEC). This is also a little or inadequate formal regulatory process over this online and real-time unaudited financial information that causes a fundamental doubt about its accuracy and consistency. The complexity and challenges associated with e-business create risks and opportunities for virtually all companies, especially dot-coms that do business electronically through the Internet. Audit committees can play an important role in overseeing how the company manages its e-business.

XBRL is intended to provide a more efficient and reliable means of preparing and disseminating business reports. XBRL is just now beginning to take off with its first specification release. Its future holds no limit and will change the way financial information is generated, processed, and used for decision making. The ultimate success of XBRL depends on the extent of the support, cooperation, and effort of a variety of groups. The first group consists of software developers and the accounting profession in developing specifications and applications for XBRL. The second group consists of professional national and international organizations, such as publicly traded companies in supporting and promoting the use of XBRL through their membership. The third group comprises the end users such as CFO, management, controllers, accountants, investors, analysts, and the entire financial information supply chain who use XBRL to prepare, disseminate, and use business reports. XBRL adheres to the existing rules for financial reporting and is expected to have a significant effect on how business information is exchanged in the future. Thus, the integrity, reliability, and quality of the XBRL-based financial information is crucial to the future success of the emerging XBRL project.

ENDNOTES

1. Shapiro, R. J. "The Emerging Digital Economy II." Available. http://www. ecommerce.gov/ede/intro.html.

2. Morgan Stanley U.S. Investment Research: Internet & Retail.

3. Smith, G. S. 2001. "New Age Technology Threats and Vulnerabilities". *Journal of Forensic Accounting* Vol. II: 125–130.

4. Elliott, R. K. 1992. "Commentary on the Third Wave Breaks on the Shores of Accounting." *Accounting Horizons* (July): 61–85.

5. Banham, R. 2000. "The B-To-B Virtual Bazaar." *Journal of Accountancy* (July): 26–30.

6. Coyle, T., and M. Dixon. 1999. "Clinton and Gore Hire New Adviser on E-Commerce Revolution." *America's Community Banker* (November): 8–9.

7. Nikhoo, I. 2000. "There is More to E-commerce than Selling on the Internet." *Los Angeles Business Journal* (March 27): 32.

8. Campbell, A. J. 1998. "Ten Reasons Why Your Business Should Use Electronic Commerce." *Business America* (Vol. 19, No. 5 May): 12–16.

9. *New York Times.* Available: www.nytimes.com.

10. The Study Group. 1999. Research Report: Continuous auditing. The Canadian Institute of Chartered Accountants, American Institute of Certified Public Accountants, Toronto, Ontario: CICA.

11. American Institute of Certified Public Accountants (AICPA). 1999. SysTrust Principles and Criteria for Systems Reliability. Available: www.aicpa.org/assurance/systrust. edannovn.hem

12. American Banker, Inc. 1999. Available: www.americanbanker.com

13. Ibid.

14. Levitt's Address. Available: www.sec.gov/news/speeches/spch410.htm.

15. Hannon, N. 2000. "The Brave New World of XBRL." *Strategic Finance* 6 (December): 73–74.

16. Practice Alert 97-1 The AICPA. *The CPA Letter.* January/February 1997. Available: www.aicpa.org/pubs/cpaltr/Jan 97/suppl/prac.htm.

17. Kogan, A., F. Sudit, and M. Vasarhelyi. "Some Auditing Implications of Internet Technology." Available: www.rutgers.edu/accounting/raw/mikles/tcon3.htm

18. www.occ.treas.gov

19. www.occ.treas.gov

20. Fonseca, B. 2000. "Blanket insecurity? Web security, privacy problems raise confidence issues." *InfoWorld* (July 10, Vol. 22, No. 28): 1.

21. Ibid.

22. Jones, J., and J. Evans. 2000. "Web Privacy Lapse by E-tailer Toysmart Prompts FTC Action." *InfoWorld* (July, Vol. 22, No. 29): 26.

23. www.ftc.gov/piracy/reports

24. www.ftc.gov/os/1999/9907/index

25. www.ftc.gov/reports/privacy 2000

26. www.aicpa.org/pubs/cpaltr/sep2000/aicpa.htm

27. Jackson, W. 2000. "Industry Initiates Web Site Privacy Policy Adoption." *Government Computer News* (August 14, Vol. 19, No. 23): 42.

28. www.aicpa.org/assurance/systrust/edannovn.htm

29. "XBRL Committee Encouraged by SEC Chairman Arthur Levitt's Recommendation That It Be Expanded and Used by Investors and Companies." *Business Wire, Inc.* October 30, 2000.

30. Piller, C. 2000. Cyber-Crime Loss at Firms Doubles to $10 Billion. *Los Angeles Times* (March 22): Business, Part C; Page 1.

Chapter 14

Fraud Examination Practice and Education

INTRODUCTION

Current global economic recessions coupled with international competition, corporate misconduct, and a litigious business environment has made the global economy and business more vulnerable to abuse and fraud. Specifically, during the past decade the revelation of numerous cases of financial statement fraud has caused the business community and the accounting profession to become increasingly concerned about the responsible corporate governance and reliable financial reporting. Society expects accountants to assume more responsibility for providing reasonable assurance regarding the reliability, usefulness, and relevance of financial information. Emerging social, economic, and legal conditions have contributed to an increasing demand for fraud investigation.

Fraud examination applies business, accounting, auditing, and legal concepts to facts or hypothesis under consideration in a legal dispute. Forensic accounting practices include: (1) litigation support consulting; (2) expert witnessing; and (3) fraud examination. Recently, fraud examination has received considerable attention from the business community and the accounting profession. This chapter discusses career and service opportunities in fraud examination for accountants and examines the integration of fraud examination education into the accounting curriculum.

FORENSIC ACCOUNTING PRACTICES

Fraud examination encompasses the field of forensic accounting, defined by Bolonga et al. (1993, 233) as "a discipline that deals with the relationship and application of financial facts to business problems, conducted in a legal setting".[1] Fraud examination is the practice of rigorous data detection and analysis with a built-in suspicion and skepticism that fraud and violation of applicable rules and regulations are always possible. It applies business, accounting, and legal principles, rules, and techniques to financial and legal issues under investigation. Fraud examiners strengthen the financial reporting process by (1) assisting in the deterrence, detection, and reporting of financial statement fraud, and occupational fraud including investment fraud, kickbacks and commercial bribery, bank fraud, credit card fraud, electronic funds transfer fraud, and computer fraud; and (2) conducting fraud vulnerability. Forensic accounting practices include: (1) litigation support consulting; (2) expert witnessing; and (3) fraud investigation (Rezaee et al, 1996).[2]

Litigation Support Consulting

Litigation support consulting activities consist of assisting lawyers to (1) assess the usefulness, reliability, and relevance of financial information; (2) gather financial data; (3) prepare questions for depositions; and (4) conduct interrogations. The field of litigation consulting expanded rapidly during the past decade. Epstein and Spalding (1993) report the following activities on which accounting experts commonly consult: (1) product liability; (2) commercial contract claims; (3) patent, trademark and copyright infringement; (4) mergers and acquisitions; (5) insurance claims; (6) reorganization and bankruptcy; and (7) toxic tort claims.[3] Litigation consultants help lawyers in the areas of financial information detection and analysis. Financial information detection is the process of determining the relevancy, usefulness, and reliability of information presented for a legal action. Financial statement analysis assesses financial information presented to the court and assists attorneys in interpreting the findings. Plaintiff and defense attorneys use financial information detection and analysis in the discovery stage of their own cases in order to prepare for the opposing litigation team's testimony. The forensic accountant's financial knowledge and expertise can be useful to attorneys because they often lack adequate financial knowledge and expertise to effectively represent their clients.

Expert Witnessing

Fraud examiners often serve as expert witnesses. Judges qualify expert witnesses based upon their special knowledge, skill, experience, or training to assist jurors in reaching conclusions of fact in areas beyond their ordinary experience and comprehension. Fraud examiners are often recognized as expert witnesses by judges during judicial proceedings. Accountants serving as expert witnesses must form their opinions objectively and independently and often must use layman's language to simplify technical jargon.

As an expert witness, the accountant can help explain or interpret complex accounting or financial data that otherwise might not be understood. Experts are often utilized in complex financial cases because they are able to explain accounting jargon in lay terms for judges and jury, give an opinion on, and draw conclusions from hypothetical situations on the witness stand. Fraud examiners serving as expert witnesses can assist attorneys in: (1) gathering relevant information; (2) educating them regarding the technical aspects of the case; and (3) providing expert testimony.

Communication skills, presentation style, and self-control are required traits for an expert witness. As an expert witness, the accountant should be aware of the potential dangers of an adversarial environment and attempt to be objective while there is great pressure from the attorney to be partisan. Epstein and Spalding

(1993, 190) point out that "As an expert witness the CPA presents opinions publicly in an objective fashion, but as a consultant the CPA advises and assists the attorney or client in private. In the private role, the CPA provides assistance more like that of an advocate to help the attorney identify case strengths and weaknesses or to develop strategy against the opposition."[4]

Fraud Examination

Fraud examination involves the investigation of financial and other documentation for the criminal activity of fraud. While financial auditing often focuses on detecting material misstatements in financial statements, whether caused by errors or fraud, fraud investigation concentrates on smaller errors, irregularities, or frauds. These small misstatements can indicate potentially large problems with the accounting system. Bologna and Lindquist (1987) state that fraud examiners should determine when (1) transactions seem "odd" as to when they occur, or their frequency, place, amount or the parties they relate to; (2) internal controls are overridden; and (3) chronically low employee motivation and morale occur.[5] Fraud investigators use their knowledge, training, skills, expertise, and intuition to gather evidence that proves beyond a reasonable doubt that fraud has occurred.

Interviewing and interrogating are two essential activities that fraud examiners typically perform. Interviews are usually conducted toward the beginning of the investigative process to obtain relevant information as to the facts and issues regarding the potential fraudulent incident. Interrogation is often reserved for the suspected perpetrators to elicit a voluntary confession from the individual. Fraud investigators should not only ask the right questions but also carefully listen to the responses given and to observe the body language used by the individual under questioning. Fraud investigators should recognize that most fraud cases would eventually end with litigation. Thus, they should be very skeptical and conduct each fraud investigation with the notion that (1) fraud must be proven beyond a reasonable doubt; (2) evidence gathered must be competent, sufficient, persuasive, and convincing; (3) investigation must be conducted in a legal manner; (4) documentation must be adequate; and (5) confession must be voluntary.

Fraud examination is becoming one of the most appealing specialization opportunities to accountants, auditors, and law enforcement professionals. Several reports (i.e., the Treadway Commission, 1987)[6] and studies (i.e., Rezaee et al. 1992; Rezaee and Burton, 1997),[7,8] (1) indicate that the public and business community is becoming more concerned with excessive fraudulent financial activities; (2) suggest that the accounting profession provide guidance on the consideration of fraud in conducting a financial statement audit; and (3) call for the promotion of fraud examination practices and education. To be a successful fraud investigator, the forensic accountant should be an effective examiner, skeptical auditor, and designated professional. The professional designation for fraud examiners is the Certified Fraud Examiner (CFE). The CFE designation is sponsored by the Association of Certified Fraud Examiners (ACFE) and described in the following section.

CERTIFIED FRAUD EXAMINER

The Certified Fraud Examiner (CFE) designation is an excellent credential for the forensic accountant to possess. The CFE is administered by the Association of Certified Fraud Examiners (ACFE; formerly the National Association of Certified Fraud Examiners), which was established in 1988.[9] The membership, as of 2001, is just over 25,000 members who are certified and trained in various aspects of detecting, investigating, and preventing occupational and financial statement fraud as well as white-collar crimes. The members are scattered across 70 countries and have organized local chapters. The association was established (at least in part) to respond to the Treadway Commission Report, which established recommendations to reduce the incidence of fraud, and CFEs have investigated more than 1 million alleged cases of civil and criminal fraud.

The mission of the ACFE is to reduce the occurrence of fraud and white-collar crime by assisting the membership to prevent and detect such occurrences. To fulfill this mission, the ACFE: (1) provide bona fide qualifications for CFEs through a uniform examination; (2) set high standards of admission through demonstrated competence and continuing professional education; (3) require and monitor adherence to a strict code of ethics; (4) serve as an international representative for CFEs to business and government, and (5) promote the public's confidence in the integrity, objectivity, and professionalism of CFEs.[10]

The CFE program is an accrediting process established for individuals who have the specialized skills to detect, investigate, and deter fraud. The CFE designation provides an upper hand to those who wish to practice in the field of fraud investigation. Those who possess the CFE designation will be better prepared to ride the wave of forensic accounting. Specific benefits provided through membership and possession of the designation include: (1) professional recognition within the accounting profession and the business community; (2) career opportunities within the expanding service industry of forensic accounting including fraud investigation; (3) membership in a local chapter that will allow for the communication of ideas and the discussion of issues relevant to the forensic accountant; (4) professional training that will assist the CFE in maintaining current knowledge as well as preparing them for future expertise; (5) publication and periodicals that are designed to keep the CFE informed on current and emerging issues within and related to the profession; and (6) continuing education to keep abreast of current developments in the area of forensic accounting.

Qualifications for receipt of the CFE designation include a baccalaureate degree from a recognized college or university, the equivalent of two years experience in a related field, and the successful completion of the uniform CFE examination. The uniform CFE examination was first administered in 1988. The computerized CFE examination is currently offered only in the U. S. and Canada. A minimum score of 40 points, determined based on any combination of education and experience, is required to sit for the exam. The exam consists of 500 objective and true/false questions in a Windows format in the following four sections (125 questions each): (1) fraudulent financial transactions; (2) legal elements of fraud; (3) fraud investigation; and (4) criminology and ethics. The applicant is allowed three attempts to pass the exam before losing credit for previously completed sections. To successfully pass the exam, a score of 75 percent on each and every part must be achieved.[11]

FRAUD EXAMINATION EDUCATION

Society expects auditors to assume more responsibility for ensuring the integrity, quality, and reliability of audited financial statements. To improve audit effectiveness, the Public Oversight Board (POB, 2000)[12] suggests forensic-type phase to be included in an audit fieldwork. The extent of knowledge required for fraud examiners in conducting fraud investigation, performing litigation services, and giving expert testimony is extensive and should have a prominent position in the accounting curriculum. Rezaee et al. (1996)[13] state that (1) forensic accounting education has traditionally been limited to continuing professional education sessions for practicing accountants, (2) only a few universities teach forensic accounting; and (3) auditing textbooks do not provide sufficient coverage of fraud examination. A survey conducted by Rezaee and Burton (1997)[14] reveals that the majority of responding academicians and practitioners (about 75 percent) indicated that demand for forensic accounting has increased and will continue to increase. Given the demand for fraud examination practice and education, college/university accounting programs should provide forensic accounting education.

Delivery of Fraud Examination Education

Methods of providing fraud examination education consist of offering a separate course in forensic accounting or integrating forensic accounting topics into existing accounting and auditing courses. Peterson and Reider (1999)[15] conducted a survey of a random sample of U. S. universities and found that the majority of respondents (84 percent) integrate forensic accounting and fraud awareness into auditing courses and only about 6 percent offered a specific course on fraud. Examples of the title of courses are fraud auditing, forensic accounting, white collar crime, fraud examination, fraud prevention and detection, auditing of fraud, and Special Topics: Forensic Accounting. These courses were often offered at the graduate level. A survey of both academicians and practitioners conducted by Rezaee and Burton (1997)[16] also reveals that the majority of responding academicians (more than 68 percent) preferred infusing fraud examination topics into existing accounting and auditing courses while the majority of the responding practitioners were more in favor of a separate fraud examination course at either the graduate or undergraduate level. Each approach on its own merit is aimed toward a special class of students and serves its own purpose. The rationale for offering a forensic accounting course at the graduate level is that business students should have a thorough understanding of the various business courses, including accounting, business law, finance, information systems, management, and marketing, covered at the undergraduate level before they are permitted to take a graduate forensic course.

Learning Objectives

Learning objectives of fraud examination education, either through offering a separate course or integration into accounting courses, should be providing knowledge and understanding of fraud examination education and practice and introducing forensic accounting theories, principles, techniques, and tools for performing fraud investigation, litigation consulting engagements, and expert witness services.

Peterson and Rieder (2001)[17] suggest the following objectives of providing knowledge and understanding to students regarding how to:

- Resolve an allegation of fraud (i.e., occupational fraud, misappropriation of assets, financial statement fraud) from inception to disposition;
- Examine documents, gather evidence, and write reports;
- Testify in court as an expert witness;
- Assist lawyers in litigation support services;
- Assess management performance including weaknesses;
- Evaluate internal controls including spotting high risk controls;
- Prevent and deter fraud (i.e., occupational fraud, misappropriation of assets, and financial statement fraud);
- Conduct interviews and interrogations;
- Develop and implement fraud prevention and detection policies.

Content of Fraud Examination Education

To provide fraud examination education to students, accounting programs may group interrelated topics in different modules. Use of a module approach helps accounting programs either offer a 45-hour semester course in forensic accounting or integrate different modules into a variety of accounting and auditing courses. Rezaee and Burton (1997)[18] and Rezaee et al (1996)[19] suggest the following fraud examination modules (1) fraud examination theories, principles, tools, and techniques; (2) fraud examination standards and procedures; (3) financial reporting process; (4) fraud and fraud auditing; (5) investigation and law; (6) evidence-gathering procedures and analysis; (7) litigation consulting; and (8) expert witness. Topics included in these modules as suggested by Rezaee and Burton (1997),[20] Rezaee et al (1996),[21] and Peterson and Reider (2001),[22] in alphabetical order, are:

1. Accounting systems and the detection of fraud
2. Analytical procedures
3. Analyzing financial statements
4. Antitrust
5. Bankruptcy
6. Billing schemes
7. Bribery and corruption investigation
8. Business interruption
9. Business valuations and cost estimates
10. Check tampering
11. Civil and criminal fraud statutes and regulations
12. Common fraud schemes
13. Compliance with applicable laws and regulations
14. Computers and computer fraud
15. Concealing fraud in accounting
16. Concealment investigative methods
17. Conflicts of interest investigating techniques
18. Conversion investigative methods
19. Corporate governance
20. Criminology and white-collar and economic crimes
21. Cyber fraud and computer topics
22. Detecting management and employee fraud
23. Document collection and analysis
24. Elements of fraud, pressure, opportunity, and rationalization
25. Environmental and personal red flags
26. Expert witness and expert testimony techniques
27. Financial statement fraud
28. Financial reporting process
29. Finding assets and people
30. Forensic accounting practices
31. Forensic and general accounting
32. Fraud auditing methodology
33. Fraud perpetrators and their motivations

34. Fraud prevention and fraud policies
35. Fraud schemes
36. Fraud statistics
37. Fraud symptoms and computer-aided fraud auditing techniques
38. Fraud symptoms
39. Fundamentals of fraud
40. Hidden assets
41. Internal control evaluation
42. Interrogation
43. Interview principles and methods to evaluate deception
44. Inventory and asset theft
45. Investigation of financial crimes and legal elements
46. Kiting
47. Knowledge of the legal system
48. Legal elements of fraud
49. Litigation consulting techniques
50. Loss prevention investigation
51. Loss prevention programs
52. Money laundering
53. Occupational fraud
54. Off-book accounting and financial statement fraud
55. On-book accounting and financial fraud
56. Overview of ethics
57. Overview of fraud auditing and fraud investigation
58. Overview of the legal elements of fraud
59. Payroll and expense reimbursement
60. Phases of fraud examination
61. Principles of ethics and corporate code of conduct
62. Professional liability
63. Resolution of allegation of misconduct
64. Rules of evidence
65. Skills required of the forensic accountant
66. Statistical sampling
67. Tax consequences
68. Techniques in locating hidden assets
69. The civil justice system
70. The criminal justice system
71. Theft act investigative methods

72. Theft and skimming
73. Theory of fraud examination and prevention
74. Trial and cross-examination
75. Who commits fraud

These topics can be grouped into appropriate modules and included in fraud examination courses. These fraud examination courses and/ or modules can be taught by using a textbook, such as this book, term papers, projects, cases, guest speakers, and videos. These courses can be conducted as a combination of lecture and seminar. Guest speakers and lecturers specialized in fraud investigation, expert witnessing, and litigation consulting can be invited to present these fraud examination modules.

CONCLUSION

The demand for and interest in fraud examination services such as fraud investigation, litigation support consulting, and expert witnessing has significantly increased during the past several decades. The growing frequency of civil and criminal cases and financial statement fraud perpetrated by large companies (i.e., Waste Management, Lucent, and Sunbeam) has increased the demand for competently trained forensic accountants. This chapter examines forensic accounting practices and education. The emerging area of fraud examination requires that fraud examination education be integrated into the accounting curriculum either through a separate course offering or infusion of the related topics into several accounting and auditing courses.

ENDNOTES

1. Bologna, G.J., R.S. Lindquist, and J.T Wells. 1993. *The Accountant's Handbook of Fraud and Commercial.* New York: John Wiley & Sons.

2. Rezaee, Z., A. Reinstein, and G.H. Lander. 1996. "Integrating Forensic Accounting into the Accounting Curriculum." *Journal of Accounting Education* (Vol.2, No.1): 147–162.

3. Epstein, M.J., and A.D. Spalding. 1993. *The Accountant's Guide to Legal Liability and Ethics.* Homewood, IL: Irwin Publishing Co.

4. Ibid.

5. Bologna, G.J., and R.S. Lindquist. 1987. *Fraud Auditing and Forensic Accounting.* New York: John Wiley & Sons.

6. National Commission on Fraudulent Financial Reporting (NCFFR). 1987. "Report of the National Commission on Fraudulent Financial Reporting" (October), New York, NY.

7. Rezaee, Z., G.H. Lander, and A. Reinstein. 1992. "Forensic Accounting: Challenges and Opportunities." *The Ohio CPA Journal* (August): 20–25.

8. Rezaee, Z., and E.J. Burton. 1997. "Forensic Accounting Education: A Comparison of Academicians and Practitioners Opinions". *Managerial Auditing Journal* (Vol.12, No.3): 479–489.

9. Association of Certified Fraud Examiners (ACFE). About Us. Austin, TX. Available: www.cfenet.com/about/about.asp

10. Ibid.

11. Association of Certified Fraud Examiners (ACFE). Uniform CFE Examination. Austin, TX. Available: www.cfenet.com/membership/uniformcfeexamination.asp

12. POB. 2000. The Panel of Audit Effectiveness Report and Recommendations. (August) Stamford, CT: POB.

13. Rezaee, Z., A. Reinstein, and G.H. Lander. 1996. "Integrating Forensic Accounting into the Auditing Curriculum". *Journal of Accounting Education* (Vol.1, No.2): 147–162.

14. Rezaee, Z., and E.J. Burton. 1997. "Forensic Accounting Education: A Comparison of Academicians and Practitioners Opinions". *Managerial Auditing Journal* (Vol.12, No.3): 479–489.

15. Peterson, B.K., and B.P. Reider. 1999. "Fraud Education of Accounting Students: A Survey of Accounting Educators". *The National Accounting Journal* (Winter). 23–30.

16. Rezaee, Z., and E.J. Burton. 1997. "Forensic Accounting Education: A Comparison of Academicians and Practitioners Opinions". *Managerial Auditing Journal* (Vol.12, No.3): 479–489.

17. Peterson, B.K., and B.P. Reider. 2001. "An Example of Forensic Accounting Courses: Content and Learning Activities". *Journal of Forensic Accounting* (Vol.II): 25–42.

18. Rezaee, Z., and E.J. Burton. 1997. "Forensic Accounting Education: A Comparison of Academicians and Practitioners Opinions". *Managerial Auditing Journal* (Vol.12, No.3): 479–489.

19. Rezaee, Z., A. Reinstein, and G.H. Lander. 1996. "Integrating Forensic Accounting into the Accounting Curriculum". *Journal of Accounting Education* (Vol.2, No.1): 147–162.

20. Rezaee, Z., and E.J. Burton. 1997. "Forensic Accounting Education: A Comparison of Academicians and Practitioners Opinions". *Managerial Auditing Journal* (Vol.12, No.3): 479–489.

21. Rezaee, Z., A. Reinstein, and G.H. Lander. 1996. "Integrating Forensic Accounting into the Accounting Curriculum". *Journal of Accounting Education* (Vol.2, No.1): 147–162.

22. Peterson, B.K., and B.P. Reider. 2001. "An Example of Forensic Accounting Courses: Content and Learning Activities". *Journal of Forensic Accounting* (Vol.II): 25–42.

Index